HIDDEN HISTORIES

GAIL MINAULT

HIDDEN HISTORIES
Religion and Reform in South Asia

edited by
SYED AKBAR HYDER
MANU BHAGAVAN

PRIMUS BOOKS
An imprint of Ratna Sagar P. Ltd.
Virat Bhavan
Mukherjee Nagar Commercial Complex
Delhi 110 009

Offices at
CHENNAI LUCKNOW
AGRA AHMEDABAD BANGALORE COIMBATORE
DEHRADUN GUWAHATI HYDERABAD JAIPUR JALANDHAR
KANPUR KOCHI KOLKATA MADURAI MUMBAI
PATNA RANCHI VARANASI

© Syed Akbar Hyder and Manu Bhagavan for the Introduction and Editorial Selections 2018
© Individual contributors for their respective essays 2018

All rights reserved. No part of this publication may be reproduced, stored in a retrieval system or transmitted, in any form or by any means, without the prior permission in writing of Primus Books, or as expressly permitted by law, by licence, or under terms agreed with the appropriate reproduction rights organization. Enquiries concerning reproduction outside the scope of the above should be sent to Primus Books at the address above.

First published 2018

ISBN: 978-93-86552-84-6 (hardback)
ISBN: 978-93-86552-85-3 (POD)

Published by Primus Books

Laser typeset in Adobe Garamond Pro
by Guru Typograph Technology
Crossings Republic, Ghaziabad 201 009

Printed and bound in India by Replika Press Pvt. Ltd.

This book is meant for educational and learning purposes. The author(s) of the book has/have taken all reasonable care to ensure that the contents of the book do not violate any existing copyright or other intellectual property rights of any person in any manner whatsoever. In the event the author(s) has/have been unable to track any source and if any copyright has been inadvertently infringed, please notify the publisher in writing for corrective action.

for
GAIL MINAULT

Intisāb	Dedication
(Ishrat Afreen)	(Imran Khan)
mērā qad	my stature
mērē bāp sē ūncā niklā	turned out taller than my father
aur mirī māṅ jīt gayī	and my mother won

Contents

List of Editors and Contributors   ix

Acknowledgements   xi

Introduction
MANU BHAGAVAN and SYED AKBAR HYDER   xiii

1. How Maulana Jamal Mian became Pakistani
   FRANCIS ROBINSON   1

2. Belonging and the Beginning of the Past in Pakistan
   AMBER ABBAS   27

3. Timely Disguises: Fantasizing Civility on the Frontier Between India and Europe
   SHAHZAD BASHIR   49

4. Obeying God, Obeying Men: The Feminist Discourse of Dr Farhat Hashmi
   A. AZFAR MOIN   69

5. Syed Ahmad's Problems with Women
   DAVID LELYVELD   91

6. Intimacy and Marriage in Urdu Advice Literature, 1900–1910
   ASIYA ALAM   109

7. Secluded Sovereign: Islam and Women's Empowerment in Nineteenth-Century India
   BARBARA METCALF — 123

8. Raja Bhagvatsinh and Rani Nandkunvarba of Gondal: 'Valiant Champions of Female Emancipation'
   AARTI BHALODIA — 145

9. The Maharaja Grants the Brahman a Boon: The Subordination of History to Myth
   LEAH RENOLD — 159

10. The Case of the 'Holy Dacoit'
    C.M. NAIM — 179

11. From Despair to Divinity: Legacies of Sadat Hasan Manto and Yās Yagānah Changezī
    SYED AKBAR HYDER — 191

12. Learning for the Glory of God v. 'Useful' Knowledge: A Scholarly Muslim Family and Western Schooling in Nineteenth-Century Madras
    SYLVIA VATUK — 223

13. Charismatic Cubs: The Tiger as a Pet
    JULIE E. HUGHES — 259

A Tribute to Gail Minault
ISHRAT AFREEN, MAX BRUCE, IMRAN KHAN — 283

A List of Gail Minault's Publications — 291

Index — 297

Editors and Contributors

SYED AKBAR HYDER is Associate Professor of Asian Studies at the University of Texas at Austin.

MANU BHAGAVAN is Professor of History and Human Rights at Hunter College and the Graduate Center, The City University of New York.

AMBER ABBAS is Assistant Professor of History at Saint Joseph's University, Philadelphia.

ISHRAT AFREEN is an Urdu poet from Pakistan, now living in Houston.

ASIYA ALAM is Assistant Professor of History at the Louisiana State University.

SHAHZAD BASHIR is Aga Khan Professor of Islamic Humanities at Brown University in Providence, Rhode Island.

AARTI BHALODIA is Lecturer in the Center for Asian American Studies at the University of Texas at Austin.

MAX BRUCE is Lecturer of Urdu at the University of California at Berkeley.

JULIE E. HUGHES is an Independent Scholar.

IMRAN KHAN is Lecturer at Austin Community College, Texas.

DAVID LELYVELD is retired Professor of History at William Paterson University, New Jersey.

BARBARA METCALF is Professor Emerita at the University of California at Davis.

A. AZFAR MOIN is Associate Professor of Religious Studies at the University of Texas at Austin.

C.M. NAIM is a Professor Emeritus of South Asian Studies at the University of Chicago.

LEAH RENOLD is Associate Professor of History at Texas State University.

FRANCIS ROBINSON is Professor of History at Royal Holloway, University of London.

SYLVIA VATUK is Professor Emerita of Anthropology at the University of Illinois at Chicago.

Acknowledgements

This book would not have come into being without the generous support of the South Asia Institute, the Hindi Urdu Flagship programme, the Institute of Historical Studies and the Departments of Asian Studies, Religious Studies, and History at the University of Texas at Austin. We are especially indebted to the support of Kamran Ali, Rupert Snell, Martha Selby, Joel Brereton, Patrick Olivelle, Martha Newman, Soheila (Rita) Omrani, Rachel Meyer, Scott Webel, Neha Mohan, Harshvardhan Siddharthan, and Raza Mahboob. David Lelyveld, Michael Meister, Barbara Metcalf, Francis Robinson, and Thomas Metcalf attended the 20 February 2016 celebration of Gail Minault's legacy at the University of Texas at Austin, along with many of her students and colleagues. Professors C.M. Naim and Shahzad Bashir graciously agreed to pay tribute to Professor Minault through their essays. Ishrat Afreen, one of Urdu's towering modern poets, composed verses in honour of Gail Minault's gifts to the worlds of history, gender studies, and literature. Max Bruce and Imran Khan translated these verses into English.

And finally, Gail Minault has meant the world to us at both the personal and the professional level. Her integrity, dedication, and humility, apart from her scholarship, have shaped our lives and careers. *Hidden Histories* is a small token of appreciation for her.

Syed Akbar Hyder
Manu Bhagavan

Introduction

MANU BHAGAVAN and
SYED AKBAR HYDER

WRITING IN 1974 as part of a first wave of releases from her recently completed Ph.D. dissertation, Gail Minault brought into vivid relief the role of Urdu political poetry in South Asia's famed Khilafat Movement.[1] The effort to 'save the Caliph' was part of the subcontinent's response to the breakup of the old Ottoman Empire brought about by the defeat of the Central Powers at the conclusion of the First World War. Minault's essay made a set of foundational contributions to the just-flowering field of South Asian studies. First, it highlighted the efforts of elites to forge unifying identities through the use of religious and cultural symbols, implicitly drawing attention to the cacophonous voices that comprised any community, and warning against taking any particular grouping at face value. Second, in a correlative manner, 'Urdu Political Poetry during the Khilafat Movement', as the piece was titled, drew attention to the masses of everyday people who were the power behind political movements. Urdu poetry was a form long linked to courts and upper-crust parlours, yet, because it was often recited, it was also one that was accessible to those who were illiterate. As a result, the art was uniquely positioned to transverse boundaries and become a form of communication common to all classes. Yet, despite its transgressive potential, or in fact because of it, Urdu poetry was also a distinct component of Indo-Muslim culture, focus on which was the third critical feature of Minault's essay, which unambiguously rejected the idea that one was somehow 'foreign' to the other. Fourth, and finally, 'Urdu Political Poetry' insisted that the study of literature was essential to the study of history, that it was important to open up interdisciplinary conversations to better understand our shared pasts, and thereby our shared presents and futures.

This volume, with contributions from Minault's long-time colleagues and collaborators, as well as many of her students, is meant as a tribute to her and the legacy of her work. The dissertation from which 'Urdu Political Poetry' and her other initial publications were taken was evolved into her landmark 1982 book *The Khilafat Movement: Religious Symbolism and Political Mobilization in India*.[2] Minault's book continued to push boundaries and expand the archive both in terms of conception and utilization, in keeping with the development of social and cultural history in the 1960s in the United States, which informed the writing of her thesis. *The Khilafat Movement* in particular made use of pamphlets and newspapers in both Urdu and English, and unofficial as well as official sources to provide the most comprehensive examination of this critical anti-colonial moment available, an assessment underscored by that fact that this book remains indispensible even thirty years after it was written.

Minault's work emphasized the importance of the Khilafat Movement for mobilizing in new ways outside norms set by the British imperial order. It suggested that there were critical pathways linking nineteenth-century reform movements with twentieth-century political expression. And in revealing these things, both through her use of extraordinary sources and in her focus on Muslims in general, Minault rewrote standard narratives by amplifying the voices of those who had until then been relegated to the margins.

Her dedication to what she terms 'hidden history' led Minault to further focus her attention on the lives of women throughout the subcontinent. She brought out in rapid succession two edited volumes, one on women and political participation in India and Pakistan, and the other, in collaboration with Hanna Papanek, a study of purdah in South Asia. A few years later, she published a translation of Khwaja Altaf Husain Hali's *Majlis un-Nissa* (Assemblies of Women) and *Chup ki Dad* (Homage to the Silent).[3] Hali, like his compatriot Nazir Ahmad, was a renowed reformer who primarily wrote for a male audience, while nonetheless initiating several key conversations regarding women's dignity, rights, and agency.

To better understand this world of male reformers, and to recover women's voices where possible, Minault went back to pamphlets and newspapers, as well as ladies' home journals and to literature broadly geared towards women. In her many excavations, she helped pioneer an innovative methodology that blended both traditional historical techniques with anthropological tools, bringing an ethnohistorical perspective to the study of South Asia. All of this culminated in the publication in 1998 of *Secluded Scholars*, a definitive study of women's education in modern South Asia.[4] Minault fashioned an hermeneutics of age-old texts to reveal the way women transformed the many worlds they inhabited simultaneously: with other women, with institutions that had once held them down, and with male well-wishers. Women summoned print technology to their assistance and teased apart the frameworks of colonial educational and judicial institutions. *Secluded Scholars* highlighted regional as well as transregional family networks and patronage systems to reflect on debates about marriage, divorce, clothing, and ethics.

Through *Secluded Scholars*, as well as her other studies of the Urdu poet Ze Khe Sheen, of the master lexicographer and turn-of-the-century anthropologist Sayyid Ahmad Dehlavi, and of the famed Delhi College, Minault has continued to push the boundaries of scholarship, rejecting hegemonic colonial, nationalist, and patriarchal renderings in favour of the slyly subversive, the transcolonial and international, and the feminist.[5] The 'archive' has proven to be much larger than a repository of government documents and official sources. Minault's key insight has been that people drive politics, societies and culture, not only through movements, but in the everyday, in the mundane, in what is otherwise passed over as unnoteworthy.

The essays in this volume celebrate her contributions and aim to carry Minault's legacy forward with a broad examination of 'hidden histories' related to religion and reform in colonial India. Minault's work, as we have illustrated here, concerns Islam and political mobilization; the centrality of literature and literary aesthetics to historical analysis; an unfailing focus on society's marginalized, especially women; and education as both theory and praxis as means and impediment to upliftment. We have distilled these lines of enquiry into three broad sectional conversations of chapters, though each conversation overlaps with the others as well.

Our first conversation focuses on the way in which Indo-Muslim culture, and a certain kind of 'Muslim-ness' informed political mobilization, giving shape to a variety of identities. Francis Robinson probes the act of becoming an exclusivist citizen of a modern nation-state. Looking at the current of events that forced Jamal Mian, a renowned scion of the religious and cultural Farangi Mahall institution, ultimately to become a Pakistani, this essay compels us to take into account the intertwined economic, religious, and nationalist exigencies that informed the choices of men journeying from one new nation to another, following the events of 1947.

Amber Abbas approaches many of the issues that Robinson tackles, but from the opposite angle. Rather than exploring how a specific individual had to navigate overlapping, contradictory, and imposed frameworks of nationality and citizenship, Abbas examines what kind of role the imaginings of everyday people played in the development and existence of these very frameworks. She asks, when does Pakistani history begin, for whom, and in what way?

Shahzad Bashir sees 1857, rather than Partition, as the critical and creative fissure, because of which social norms and conventions could be upended and rethought. Through a close reading of Nazir Ahmad's *Ibnulvaqt*, regarded as the first Urdu novel, Bashir foregrounds the ways Indians had to navigate the tension between the universalism at the heart of the European civilizing mission and enforced markers of particularity like food and dress. The novel reinforces the idea that contradiction lay at the heart of the late nineteenth-century colonial experiment and thus also at the root of modernity.

Azfar Moin closes this first conversation by discussing the way contemporary Muslim self-identifying feminists in Pakistan, epitomized by Farhat Hashmi, are shaping the ideal Muslim family using both the language of modernity and canonical textual traditions. Reform in this take becomes a method by which everyday people can adapt to various restrictive forces on their lives and selectively accept convoluted and opposing claims to their identity.

Our second conversation picks up from where Moin leaves off to focus broadly on gender reform in the subcontinent. David Lelyveld starts us off by dissecting the very idea of reform through a thorough examination of the nineteenth-century reformer Sir Syed Ahmad Khan and his claim to progressive change. Refracting the contradictions revealed in Bashir's analysis of *Ibnulvakt*, Lelyveld asserts that Sir Syed found the modern road on which he preferred to walk rocky and challenging to traverse, as witnessed by his complex commitment to women's upliftment.

Reformers like Hali and Nazir Ahmad loomed large in late nineteenth- and early twentieth-century conversations on reform, but to the inspiration rather than the neglect of a range of other writers. Asiya Alam reads jointly two such figures, Muhammadi Begum and Sayid Ali Bilgrami, focusing on their texts on women and conjugality. Reform, in her readings, created new restrictions and hierarchies even as it set out distinct pathways to liberation.

Barbara Metcalf looks at elite discourses around reform, aesthetics, gender, and authority, as told through the work of Shah Jahan Begum, the late nineteenth-century ruler of Bhopal. Through the semi-sovereign sphere of the princely state, the Begum was able to lay claim to an Islamic intellectualism rooted in print and literacy, breaking away from a scholarly successionism that had dominated access to knowledge until then. Shah Jahan Begum carved a space and place for herself and for women on her own terms, defying—while remaining circumscribed by—existing patriarchal norms.

Intersecting with Metcalf's focus on princely states and elite women, Aarti Bhalodia ends this thread with an exploration of how reformers in the west Indian state of Gondal conceptualized female emancipation. Bhalodia explores how women surrounding a reformer, in this case the state's ruler Raja Bhagvatsinh, helped articulate progressive policies, particularly regarding education. In fact, radical women surrounded and shaped Bhagvatsinh himself, creating conditions for his trail blazing, globetrotting wife, Nandkunvarba, to thrive. While she too, like Shah Jahan Begum, found herself hemmed in by expectations and social mores, Bhalodia argues that reformers constantly stretched boundaries, and over time, contributed to the eventual expansion and alteration of 'acceptable behavior'.

Our closing conversation is woven around one strand of Bhalodia's chapter: education, broadly defined. Leah Renold turns our attention to the foundation of Banaras Hindu University (BHU)[6] to explore more broadly the ways in which myth and history, oral narratives and memory all interact in South Asia to produce a version of the past that is politically potent in the present. Renold uncovers a popular narrative that the Maharaja of Benares donated land to Pandit Malaviya, a well-known, highly regarded Brahmin, and that this donation became the foundation of the university. Yet the Nizam of Hyderabad too was a generous supporter of BHU. Renold argues that the mythic history she has uncovered functions to reinforce a high-caste majoritarian vision of beneficence, much to the detriment of society as a whole and minorities in particular.

C.M. Naim too interrogates myth and history, but through the prism of the life of Khwaja Hasan Nizami, a colourful, controversial writer and publisher of the early twentieth century who liked to smooth-talk his way into circles of wealth and power. Naim looks at the writings of Zafar Omar, a novelist who skewered Nizami, to dissect the ways in which feuds could play out in the public sphere, even devolve into 'verbal warfare', and yet adhere to a culture of civility.

Sadat Hasan Manto and Yas Yaganah Changezi, as Akbar Hyder argues, challenge such an imaginaire of literary and cultural civility by confronting legacies of sacral importance. Both these Urdu writers briskly propose notions of criticism free of hagiographic trappings. The characters inhabiting the discursive terrains of Manto's prose and Yaganah's poetry provocatively magnify the shortcomings of the existing cultural enterprises grounded in notions of progress, sanity, respectability, and convention.

Sylvia Vatuk refracts some of these institutional and literary issues with an analysis of a particular family of south Indian scholars who raised serious questions about Western education and the utility of the English language. Vatuk sees some faultlines within Muslim elite circles, as temporal and religious authorities disagreed on how best to respond to the demands of the imperial centre. In the process she reveals some surprising strengths and weaknesses that emerged from processes of accommodation and resistance.

Julie Hughes wraps up the conversation, and closes this volume, with a scrutiny of the symbolic evolution of the tiger, often equated with 'Indian-ness', both savage beast and awe-inspiring creature of wisdom and mystery. Hughes' particular interest is in the development of pet-keeping, and the way people were taught to think about tigers and to interact with them, but her story playfully maps onto broader Orientalist tropes concerning the overall transition from the colonial to the postcolonial worlds.

Notes

1. Gail Minault, 'Urdu Political Poetry during the Khilafat Movement', *Modern Asian Studies*, vol. 8, issue 4, 1974, pp. 459–71.
2. Gail Minault, *The Khilafat Movement: Religious Symbolism and Political Mobilization in India*, New York: Columbia University Press, 1982.
3. Gail Minault, ed., *The Extended Family: Women and Political Participation in India and Pakistan*, Columbia, Missouri: South Asia Books, 1981;

Gail Minault and Hanna Papanek, *Separate Worlds: Studies in Purdah in South Asia*, Columbia, Missouri: South Asia Books, 1982; Gail Minault, tr., *Voices of Silence: Khwaja Altaf Husain Hali's Majalis un-Nissa (Assemblies of Women) and Chup ki Dad (Homage to the Silent)*, Delhi: Chanakya Publications, 1986.
4. Gail Minault, *Secluded Scholars: Women's Education and Muslim Social Reform in Colonial India*, Delhi: Oxford University Press, 1998.
5. See for instance, Gail Minault, 'Zahida Khatun Sherwani (Z-Kh-Sh): *Parda-Nashin* Poet of Aligarh', in *Muslim Voices: Traditions and Contexts (festschrift* in honor of Barbara Metcalf), ed. David Gilmartin and Usha Sanyal, New Delhi: Yoda Press, 2012, pp. 218–30; Gail Minault, 'Sayyid Ahmad Dehlavi and the Delhi Renaissance', in *Delhi Through the Ages: Essays in Urban History, Culture, and Society*, ed. Robert Eric Frykenberg, Delhi: Oxford University Press, 1986, pp. 287–98; Minault, 'The Perils of Cultural Mediation: Master Ramchandra and Academic Journalism at Delhi College', in *The Delhi College: Traditional Elites, the Colonial State, and Education Before 1857*, ed. Margrit Pernau, Delhi: Oxford University Press, 2006, pp. 187–200.
6. This is spelt as 'Banaras' here because that is the spelling preferred by the BHU. Where the reference is to the city itself, the spelling 'Benares' has been used throughout.

1

How Maulana Jamal Mian became Pakistani

FRANCIS ROBINSON

JAMAL MIAN DID not plan to become Pakistani, but events between 1947 and 1957 ultimately gave him little choice. His experiences illuminate a process that Wazira Zamindar has described as the 'Long Partition'.[1] We see him slowly coming to terms with the idea that what had been one colonial state was becoming two nation-states. We see him engaging with the technologies of modern statehood as they have been described—permits, passports, visas, no objection certificates—and seeing if he could make them serve the transnational life he wished to lead.[2] At the same time we see him continuing to think, in the manner of his sharif background, in terms of class, background, blood and family, rather than state affiliation. But we also see that in the new world of independent nation-states minor officials might have considerable influence over the outcome of individual lives, however well connected. When it came to the point Jamal Mian either lost faith in the power of the old sharif connections to protect him or, perhaps, no longer thought it appropriate, for whatever reason, that he should use them to do so. All this was set in the context of a decade of great trial for Indian Muslims.

Jamal Mian's Stake in India

Born on 5 December 1919, Jamal Mian was the second son of Maulana Abdul Bari, a leading figure of his day in the Farangi Mahall family of ulama, a noted activist for the interests of Indian Muslims, and a major figure in founding both the Khilafat Movement and the Jamiat ul-Ulama-i Hind. Jamal Mian was deeply conscious of his family's long and distinguished history in India. He knew that his ancestor, Khwaja Jalaluddin, a great grandson of the eleventh-century saint Abdullah Ansari of Herat, came to India for jihad and settled near Delhi in the time of the Sultanate. He knew, too, how Jalaluddin's descendant, Alauddin, brought the family to Awadh in the fourteenth century, settling in Sihali.[3] From Mughal documents in the family archive he could assure himself that since 1559, his family had been supported as scholars by revenue-free grants from the Mughals down to the moment when, in compensation for the murder of his ancestor Mulla Qutbuddin in 1691, his forebears were granted the sequestered property of a European indigo merchant in Lucknow, Farangi Mahall, by the emperor Aurangzeb. In time this became a great muhalla housing many families descended from Mulla Qutbuddin. They were noted for their scholarship, in particular in *ma'qulat*, the Islamic rational sciences, and for pioneering the *Dars-i nizami* madrasa curriculum which came to be taught throughout India. Jamal Mian was closely connected by ties of blood, ties of teaching, and ties of spiritual leadership to many of the notable families of the qasbahs and landed estates around Lucknow, in particular the Qidwais, the Jahangirabads, and the Mahmudabads. He was also strongly attached to four spiritual centres, the '*urs* at which he would always try to attend and from which he acknowledged great spiritual nourishment. There was Bagh Maulana Anwar, where his ancestors were buried in Lucknow; Bansa Sharif, the shrine of Saiyid Shah Abdul Razzaq, whose rise as a Qadri pir in eighteenth-century Awadh had been closely associated with that of the Farangi Mahalli ulama; the shrine of Ahmad Abdul Haqq of Rudauli, founder of the greatest Chishti Sufi centre in Awadh into whose family Jamal Mian married in 1943; and the shrine at Ajmer of Muinuddin Chishti, the founder of the Chishti Sufi order, on whose Dargah Committee Jamal Mian sat. Attendance at the '*urs* celebrations at these shrines, and listening to *qawwali* at those of Chishti affiliation, was a central part of Jamal Mian's devotional life. With this history and these attachments Jamal Mian had powerful reasons for remaining domiciled in India. It was here that most of the things which gave his life meaning existed.[4]

Fighting for Muslim interests was an important part of Jamal Mian's heritage. His great-grandfather, Abdul Razzaq, had played a leading role in the Hanumangarhi jihad to defend the Babri Masjid in 1855. He had donated his turban to be used as a battle standard by the rebels in the Mutiny Uprising; and he was in the forefront in the late 1870s in raising funds to support the Ottomans in their war against the Russians. Because his father, Abdul Bari, was a notable political activist, as a young boy he frequently encountered Muslim, as well as Hindu, activists at home: his relatives and teachers, for instance, Maulanas Inayatullah, Salamatullah and Sibghatullah were well-known organizers and public speakers; his father's disciples, Muhammad and Shaukat Ali, who were the most notable Muslim campaigners of their day; and his grandfather's disciple, Hasrat Mohani, poet, communist, devout Muslim, and ultimately close friend. Jamal Mian had his first exposure to the excitement of grown-up politics when in 1936 Shaukat Ali, on a whim, took him to the Palestine protest conference in Calcutta. He marvelled at the speeches, made his maiden speech, enjoyed ice cream at Magnolia Ice Cream, and made his first trip to the cinema.[5] Later that year he met Jawaharlal Nehru for the first time, when his elder half-brother, Qutb Mian, invited him to Farangi Mahall. Nehru finished the occasion by inviting Jamal Mian to go with him to sit on the platform at the Congress Sessions. He found himself praying alongside Abul Kalam Azad.[6]

Jamal Mian and the Muslim League

Jamal Mian made his formal entry into Muslim politics, when aged seventeen the Raja of Mahmudabad invited him to join the welcoming committee for the Lucknow session of the All-India Muslim League in October 1937.[7] Shaukat Ali was so impressed by Jamal Mian's public speaking on this occasion that he invited the young man to join him on the subsequent Bijnor by-election campaign, during which Jinnah congratulated him on his rhetorical powers.[8] There followed a period of fairly continuous travel to speak for the League in the UP, Bombay, Karachi and through to the North-West Frontier. After the Lahore session in March 1940 he toured Bihar with the Raja of Mahmudabad to promote the Pakistan Resolution.[9]

In 1937 Jinnah had told Jamal Mian that he should not try to make a living out of politics.[10] Then, unbeknown to Jamal Mian, he had asked Mirza Ahmad Ispahani of the great Calcutta business family if he would be able to help him.[11] This meant that when in the early 1940s Jamal Mian turned to the Ispahanis, after failing to raise funds for the

Farangi Mahall madrasa from Adamjee, reputedly the richest Muslim businessman in India, they were waiting for him. From 1942 Jamal Mian was set up as a tea agent for the Ispahanis in the UP. As Jamal Mian's diaries reveal, his work for the League ran alongside the promotion of his business in the UP, although, as Mirza Ahmad would caustically remark, he never had his heart in the business of selling tea.

In April 1943 Jamal Mian was appointed Honorary Joint Secretary of the All-India Muslim League at its Delhi session.[12] This meant that he was no longer just a provincial political figure but a recognized All-India leader. As a result, perhaps, he was asked to give the Eid sermon on the Calcutta Maidan in September 1943. More importantly he played a major role in the 1945–6 election campaign for the provincial and central legislative assemblies, which gave Jinnah a powerful mandate to speak for Indian Muslims. Jamal Mian himself had a personal victory in the Barabanki election which enabled him to enter the UP Legislative Assembly as part of the Muslim League opposition to the Congress.[13] In his campaign speeches he set out what he felt the creation of Pakistan would do for the UP Muslims. Addressing what was described as a 'mammoth gathering of peasants at Sitapur' on 20 October 1945, he declared that those who thought that the establishment of Pakistan would jeopardize the Muslim position in the UP were misguided:

The Lahore Resolution explicitly envisaged the conclusion of a treaty between Hindustan and Pakistan by which the rights of Muslims where they are in a minority will be properly safeguarded. It will not be a mere verbal understanding but will be incorporated in statutes etc. Presuming Hindustan does not abide by this agreement a free Pakistan will exert diplomatic pressure.[14]

Jamal Mian went on to suggest that Pakistan offered a better guarantee of protecting Muslim rights than everyone remaining in a united India and, moreover, it was 'a capitalist-ridden Congress' which had prevented the League from carrying out the agrarian and other reforms the League had envisaged in its 1935 pact with the Congress.[15] As a member of the UP Legislative Assembly Jamal Mian continued some of these themes, seeking to mandate UP members of the Constituent Assembly to support measures to protect minorities,[16] attacking the Congress government of capitalists and mahajans for voting for ministers' substantial emoluments,[17] and attacking government officials in Barabanki for making Congress allegiance the prerequisite for receiving food aid.[18]

The following year Jamal Mian moved to an international level as a promoter of Indian Muslim interests when at Hassan Ispahani's behest he was made the secretary of an Indian Government Trade Delegation to the Middle East (7 March–20 May 1947). The delegation was commissioned by I.I. Chundrigar as Commerce Minister in the interim government. As its membership was entirely Muslim it quickly became, in spite of its ICS support, more a Muslim League than an Indian delegation. Jamal Mian worked hard to promote Jinnah and the Muslim League with business and political leaders across the region, noting with pleasure that the Congress Asia Conference had not been a success as the Arabs had refused to attend on the grounds that there was no Indian Muslim presence.[19]

Jamal Mian's actions, when Pakistan was founded, show that, while he supported the outcome, he remained primarily concerned to support the Indian Muslims as a people. He went with his friends the Raja of Mahmudabad and Dr. Faridi to attend the inauguration of Pakistan in Karachi on 14 August 1947. But the Raja, a devout Shia, never made it. Apparently on a whim, when the train in which the three were travelling reached Rorhi Junction, the Raja decided not to go to Karachi but to travel via Quetta to the Shia shrine city of Mashshad. During a firework party after the inauguration the Prime Minister, Liaquat Ali Khan, asked Jamal Mian if he had enjoyed himself. Jamal Mian replied with a couplet from Hasrat Mohani:

I saw the beauty of your celebrations.
I destroyed my home and saw it go up like fireworks.[20]

After the inauguration Dr. Faridi and Jamal Mian returned immediately to Lucknow.[21] In the dangerous weeks that followed, when many Muslims in India were killed and many UP Muslims migrated, Chaudhuri Khaliquzzaman, whom Jinnah had designated leader of the Indian Muslims, deserted his post. Gandhi had requested Khaliquzzaman to go to Pakistan in October 1947 in order to persuade the Sindhi Hindus not to migrate to India. Khaliquzzaman invited Jamal Mian to join him, but the next that Jamal Mian heard of the mission was that Khaliquzzaman was in Pakistan, had decided to stay there, and had sent a plane to pick up his family.[22]

During his final attendance at the old Muslim League in the context of its Council meeting at Karachi on 14–15 December 1947, Jamal continued to show his concern for Indian Muslims, many of whom had now come to Pakistan. He proposed that the word 'Muslim' whenever it appeared in the main resolution in the phrase 'Pakistan, a Muslim state' should be deleted. His reasoning was, somewhat along the lines of his attack on the emoluments the Congress ministers had awarded themselves in the UP, that the leaders of the League had made themselves comfortable while hundreds of thousands of Indian Muslims, many of them former League workers, were eking out an existence as refugees in Karachi and elsewhere. This was not the behaviour of proper Muslim leaders. Having made himself unpopular, Jamal Mian continued his attack, first with a swipe at Khaliquzzaman for his defection, and then with an assault on Liaquat Ali Khan, who at Partition had not cared to ensure that the Muslim League organization continued to exist in India. In consequence it was withering away; Indian Muslims no longer had appropriate representation.[23]

On the death of Jinnah, Khaliquzzaman became the Chief Convenor of the Pakistan Muslim League. Jamal Mian returned to his life in Lucknow where he focussed on his tea business, on trying to keep his *Hamdam* newspaper going, on his service for the Sunni Waqf Board, on his service for the Ajmer Dargah Committee of Management, and on his service for the Trustees of the Jehangirabad Estate. All of this took place alongside his membership of the Legislative Assembly and his general care for the Farangi Mahall madrasa. He was deeply linked to his Lucknow world.

Things Fall Apart

The years from 1947 to 1950 were arguably the worst that the Indian Muslims had experienced. During the convulsions of Partition their lives were held cheap, as was also the case for Hindus in the lands that were becoming Pakistan. But in the months and years that followed, Indian Muslims were a beleaguered people. They were treated as being personally responsible for the emergence of Pakistan. Many government officials who had opted to stay in India found themselves punished by the loss of their jobs. There were arbitrary arrests as the diaries of Hasrat Mohani, a vigorous worker for his local community, reveal.[24] Muslims were harassed; at Delhi railway station Mohani noticed railway officials and police levying extra sums from Muslim passengers who already had tickets.[25] Muslims and their houses were searched for arms. It did not matter if the Muslims concerned were senior officials or even, as in the case of Syed Mahmud (a spiritual follower of Jamal Mian's father) a member of the Bihar government.[26] In the UP Hindus took advantage of the new Muslim weakness to impose their cultural preferences and deepen their political advantage. In October 1947 the UP government, along with several others, made Hindi the sole language of administration. The banning of cow slaughter soon followed.[27] Muslims continued to migrate. If, in 1947, 200,000 people left Delhi for Karachi, between 1947 and 1950 a further 300,000 plus did.[28] The UP also suffered significant losses. 'The atmosphere was so bad for Muslims', recalled an Aligarh citizen, 'that everybody wanted to migrate from here'.[29]

Muslim misery was compounded by the so-called 'police action' of September 1948 by which India forcibly brought the largest state of the former British India into its union. For at least 150 years Hyderabad had been a source of employment for north Indian Muslims, and more recently it had become an important source of subsidy for Muslim institutions. During the period of the 'police action', between one in ten and one in five of all Muslim males in Hyderabad city were killed, while up to 40,000 Muslims were killed in the state as a whole.[30] As the Government of India sought to rebalance the Hyderabad administration in communal terms, at least 10,000 Muslims lost their jobs in the police, military and bureaucracy.[31] Although Jamal Mian would not have known the scale and detail of these events—Pandit Sunderlal's report on the massacres was, until recently, suppressed by the Government of India[32]—his relatives and spiritual followers in the state would have kept him informed of the nature of events. Jamal Mian, however, would have been acutely aware of one particular outcome of the demise of Hyderabad. Farangi Mahall lost the institutional grant which had long been paid by the Nizam. Jawaharlal Nehru, after some lobbying in late 1948 by Qutb Mian, achieved a stay of execution, but in 1950 the grant was stopped.[33] Things seemed so bad in the autumn of 1948 that Hasrat Mohani planned to give two months of his stipend as a member of the Legislative Assembly, Rs.1,600, to Qutb Mian 'so that his troubles may be lessened'.[34]

Then the fortunes of Jamal Mian's branch of the family began to sink. Jamal Mian found himself being harassed by his branch's old rivals, the Bahr ul-Ulumis. The bad feeling went back to the time when Jamal Mian's ancestor, Alauddin, the son-in-law of Maulana Abdul Ali Bahr ul-Ulum, had succeeded the great scholar as *sajjadanashin* in Madras in the early nineteenth century rather than his son, Abdul Rab. The bad feeling continued into the twentieth century with the Bahr ul-Ulumis taking pro-British positions as against the anti-British stands of Jamal Mian's line.[35] When in 1946 Jamal Mian refounded his father's *Hamdam* newspaper, installing its press in a house adjacent to one owned by the Bahr ul-Ulumis, they went into action. In July 1947 Muhammad Kamil Bahr ul-Ulum's lawyer notified Jamal Mian that they expected to receive damages for the mental and physical stress they endured on account of the press, at the rate of Rs.10 per diem.[36] Jamal Mian won the case. But hostility continued towards him in the muhalla. Stones were thrown into his courtyard from time to time. Such hostilities continued into the 1950s.

Jamal Mian's mood around this time is well-expressed by an elegy he published in *Hamdam* on the dire straits of Lucknow. Entitled *Shahr-e Ashob* after the classical genre mourning lost cities, it consisted of forty stanzas of which the following are typical:

> How can I describe what state Lucknow is in?
> This city which was called the city of gardens,
> Which was considered the centre of fine things,
> Which was the envy of heaven.
> Alas! Fate and the heavens have been unkind to it.
>
> Knowledge is no more, nor wisdom here.
> Goodness gone, beauty lost, love no more!
> Adornment lost, attraction gone, allurement disappeared!
> Festivity gone, spring and freshness no more!
> Each thing is in lament at its helplessness!
>
> Those protectors of peoples' rights are no more.
> Those decent folk, those kind humans are no more.
> Those loyal friends and companions are all gone.
> Those gracious Hindus gone, Muslims disappeared.
> All replaced by vicious wolves and gangsters.[37]

At this low point Jamal Mian was hit by two further serious blows. On 25 November 1948 his elder sister, Sughra, to whom he was deeply attached, as she was to him, died. The one letter from her to him which remains, as well as her poems, are full of love.[38] Sughra had a considerable and varied literary output, most of which she destroyed. As a tribute to her, Jamal Mian published in the month after her death a small collection of her poetry. The following lines from a poem written to the girls of Farangi Mahall and entitled 'Unity' give a sense of the intelligent and sweet person Jamal Mian had lost:

> Learn from the life of the stars O humans.
> How fond they are to each other, and are happy.
> These tiny little stars with their frail beauty
> How they reflect God's taste in beauty!
> They are the punctuation of the author of eternity.[39]

Jamal Mian's children say that whenever Sughra's name came up in conversation, his eyes would fill with tears.

The second blow was the decline of Jamal Mian's tea business, the income from which, as other sources disappeared, had become more important. Among the reasons for the decline were the problems of selling tea branded with the Ispahani name, strongly associated with the movement for Pakistan, in a virulently anti-Muslim atmosphere, and the fact that Jamal Mian had not committed his heart and soul to the business of selling. On 30 December 1948, Mirza Ahmed Ispahani's assessment was brutal:

> With regard to the tea business, there is absolutely no justification for my office here to continue this business in the UP. I was shocked to see that expenses in 1948 have been Rs.16,000 against sales of Rs.35,000. As you have always suggested that this business is of no interest to you, and that for the last 5 or 6 years that you have been handling the business you have not been able to put it on a profitable basis for the Company here it is best that the whole thing is shut down unless you have some arrangement by which you can meet the terms which are being offered to all Indian agents.[40]

A few days later, after Jamal Mian's accounts were thoroughly inspected, Mirza Ahmed declared them 'most unsatisfactory'.[41] These were hard messages to receive from a man who had set him up in business and who had treated him like a son. Matters were not helped when an 'Ansari boy', whom Jamal Mian had recommended, had had to be dismissed for trying to organize the workers.[42]

Battered by these blows Jamal Mian then had to face a crisis for the Muslim League in the UP Legislative Assembly. In the period after Partition, and especially after the assassination of Gandhi, Indian Muslims had been considering how to organize themselves in public life in a way which would not raise suspicions of separatist tendencies. Hasrat

Mohani spent a great deal of energy in 1948 trying to organize Muslim Leaguers, along with socialist and other political elements, into a 'left front' opposition to the Congress.[43] A.K. Azad at meetings in Delhi and Lucknow in April and May 1948 set out to convert the Jamiat ul-Ulama-i Hind into a non-political body, indeed a purely religious body, devoted to the community's interests.[44] Earlier in March 1948 the majority of those present at a Hind Muslim League meeting in Madras, which had been arranged at the Council meeting of the All-India Muslim League in Karachi the previous December, had tried to focus the organization on social and cultural struggle. But they had been opposed by Muhammad Ismail, whom Jinnah had appointed as their convener and chair.[45] Then, after a period of inactivity the old leadership of the provincial Muslim League, with the exception of Khaliquzzaman (now in Pakistan), met at Farangi Mahall. Taking their lead from the majority at the Madras meeting they agreed that the League should refrain from Parliamentary activities and limit itself to the 'struggle for Muslim rights and their protection'. It was resolved that there should be only one organization representing Muslim interests, Z.I. Lari the leader, Nawab Aizaz Rasul the General Secretary, and Jamal Mian, the Secretary. Lari set out to bring all Muslims onto this platform. The Jamiat, in their turn, said that all Muslims should join their organization.[46]

The scene was set for a struggle between the provincial Muslim League and the Jamiat, which came to be conducted as the pettiest of levels. It happened thus, for a long time, the Muslim League had rented offices in Lawrence Mansion in Aminabad, Lucknow, whose owner lived in Karachi. In December 1948 the Parliamentary Secretary to the UP Government asked Aizaz Rasul to allow members of the Jamiat to use a room in the building on a temporary basis. The League, perhaps unwisely, did so. It soon found this civility repaid with hostility. The Jamiat used its influence to persuade the Rent Control and Eviction Officer of Lucknow to allot the building to its secretary, Muhammad Qasim.[47] The Jamiat then removed the Muslim League sign from the building and set out to expand its occupation of it. On 22 February, Jamal Mian made a formal complaint to the District Magistrate on the basis that the Rent Control and Eviction Office had no power to allot the property, and, on the District Magistrate's instructions, sealed the building, taking charge of the key. At the same time he told his League leader that he was determined to throw the Jamiatis out.[48] The matter then went into limbo while the Government decided what to do.[49]

During this period of waiting it would appear that Jamal Mian had an altercation with the Jamiatis which required a formal apology. On 2 April, probably before the District Magistrate, he declared: 'I do hereby solemnly and sincerely apologise to all. I do agree that a curtain should be dropped on [the] past. I most humbly declare "Thy people will be my people and Thy God is my God."'[50]

The episode for which Jamal Mian had to apologize, coming after a year of strain, was in all likelihood a symptom of the nervous breakdown that afflicted him from time to time. Looking back over his life in 1983 he identified this period as the first in which he experienced '"mental imbalance", "nervous breakdown" whatever name one might give it; anxiety of spirit, talking too much, becoming mentally restless in sleep; becoming oversensitive. . . .'[51] On 24 March he was up at 3 a.m. writing a letter of over 4,000 words to G.B. Pant, the Chief Minister, setting out the quarrel with the Jamiat people which he admitted had 'wrecked his peace of mind'.[52] On 18 February he tried to resign from the Legislative Assembly by thrusting a letter into the hands of fellow Muslim Leaguer, Nafisul Hasan, in the debating Chamber. Hasan returned the letter saying that he did not think that Jamal Mian was well and that anyway resignations had to be submitted to the Governor.[53] On 30 March Hasrat Mohani was at Farangi Mahall in the morning:

There Dr Abdul Hamid was attending to Jamal Mian. Jamal Mian has become increasingly oversensitive. I am convinced that this has affected his health. His conversation is disconnected [ukhri ukhri bate]. The attack seems to have disturbed his equilibrium. . . . I was very pained to see this.[54]

Around this time Jamal Mian moved into a period of frenzied activity, typical of his illness involving a wholesale tidying up of his affairs in a mixture of decisiveness and indecisiveness. In late March he told his father-in-law that he was resigning from the UP Legislative Assembly.[55] But then he wavered as he came under pressure from leading Congress figures, Jawaharlal Nehru, G.B. Pant, and Rafi Ahmed Qidwai, to withdraw his resignation.[56] He sent in his formal resignation to the Governor on 26 April and at the same time withdrew his opposition to the allotment of the Muslim League offices to the Jamiat.[57] Around this time he must have resigned as Secretary of the provincial Muslim League as he planned the transfer of all his official papers to Aizaz Rasul, the General Secretary.[58] At the same time he set matters in train to close down his *Hamdam* newspaper. Sadri Ispahani, who in later life he would describe as his closest friend, sent him Rs.2,000 to cover the costs of the closure and medicine and travel, but this was returned immediately with the statement that all expenses were covered.[59] Dr Faridi was to be asked to travel with him to the 'Urs at Rudauli on 14 April and then to on with him to Ranchi.[60] He resigned from the Board of Guardians of the Jehangirabad estate.[61] He even found time to write a letter of apology to the Bahr ul-Ulumis: I from the bottom of my heart beg for forgiveness of my sins and for any pain that I may have caused your household.[62]

With these actions Jamal Mian freed himself to focus on his recovery and on resurrecting his tea business, for which he had been offered new terms by the Ispahanis. Correspondence with Hassan Ispahani, who by this time was Pakistan's ambassador to the USA, makes it clear that Jamal Mian was taking time to recover.[63] In September he was still under doctor's orders and thinking of going to the School of Tropical Medicine in London.[64] After this, concerns about his health seemed to subside. Business worries returned. In August 1949 he admitted to Mirza Ahmed Ispahani that he could not make the business work in Lucknow. Mirza Ahmed responded by inviting him to start again in Calcutta or East Pakistan.[65]

By the end of 1949 news of Jamal Mian's failure to make a living, of the economic threat to Farangi Mahall, and that he might have to work for the Ispahanis in East Pakistan, had begun to spread. Muhammad Ali Zainal Raza, the Bombay businessman with whom he had travelled on the Indian delegation to the Middle East in 1947 was shocked by the thought of the Farangi Mahall madrasa closing. He was even more shocked, moreover, by a misheard rumour that Jamal Mian was working in a jute factory. 'When Muhammad Ali Zainal heard about your illness', Saidur Rahman Qidwai wrote to him, 'he started crying. When he recovered from his weeping he said that "Jamal Mian is a kind of person who only appears rarely. It is a tragedy of the Muslims that a man like him whom I love more than anyone else, should be working in a jute factory"'.[66]

Taking Stock

It was clearly time for Jamal Mian to take stock, to consider how he might be able to earn a living to support his family and help support the madrasa. First, he made a tour of West Pakistan, something he had long discussed with Mirza Ahmed Ispahani.[67] Harpal Singh, the District

Magistrate of Lucknow, with whom he had dealt over the Jamiat dispute and Mahbub Alam, Secretary to the Sunni Waqf Board, helped him to get the all-important No Objection Certificate, which would enable him to return to India. A permit to visit Pakistan was obtained at the High Commission in Delhi. Both these processes indicate how the technologies of modern statehood were beginning to control the movement of people across a region they had once travelled freely. On 27 May Jamal Mian flew to Karachi, where Mirza Ahmed's brother made a car available to him, a Cadillac, and he stayed as usual in the Raja of Mahmudabad's house, 2 Framroze Road. During the social round he quickly discovered many people whom he knew: 'In nearly two days I realised that I had not just arrived in Karachi but also encountered Hyderabad, Bombay, Calcutta, Jaipur, and God knows how many other cities, friends, relatives, connections.'[68] He also noticed differences opening up between India and Pakistan. He marvelled at the fact that the Rupee had a different value in each country. Moreover, he felt that Pakistani Muslims were travelling on a different road from Indian Muslims:

Pakistan has all the roads of worldly progress open to it. But in this success-story there is a danger: that Pakistanis will lose their way in their desire for comfort and pleasure. The Indian Muslims, if they have a fault, it is that they do not have the doors of comfort and pleasure open to them. Only those can live here in India who have the conviction and courage to make a place for themselves and to have the courage to engage in this struggle.[69]

We do not know why Jamal Mian made this tour, which he recorded in a small book-length manuscript for Saidur Rahman Qidwai. In the passage quoted above he seems to be rationalizing a firm decision to stay in India, and perhaps also a decision to earn his living in East Pakistan where he would escape, so he thought, many of the pressures of his old life, pressures, particularly political pressures, which had helped to make him ill. After this, in September 1950 Jamal Mian went on Hajj with his family, Hasrat Mohani, the Raja of Mahmudabad and the Raja of Salempur. Jawaharlal Nehru helped to smooth his passage by making the services of the Indian consulate in Jiddah available to him.[70]

Indian Citizen, Earning a Living in Pakistan

From 1951 Jamal Mian settled down to a new life as a businessman based in Dacca. He was quickly able to make a good living, as indeed were several of his family and their associates, which would have been difficult to achieve in Lucknow. He lived a life which seemed to make light of the divisions between India and Pakistan. He attended the 'Urs celebrations in India that were the centre of his devotional life. His family moved relatively easily between Lucknow and Dacca. He himself continued to mix with the political elite of both countries as if India had never been divided. He found himself vigorously representing the interests of the Ispahanis, now primarily based in Pakistan, in Delhi. As time went on, of course he became subject to the technologies of modern statehood. After much anxiety he did eventually free himself of a case launched under the Evacuee Property Act of 1950. But, having ridden the regime of 'no objection certificates' and by stratagem having got himself an Indian International Passport which had been denied to him, he found himself eventually pinned down when his passport was impounded by the Indian government on the basis of what seems to have been a rumour.

In establishing his business in Dacca in 1951 two men were crucial for Jamal Mian: Mirza Ahmed Ispahani, whom he saw almost every day, and Ghulam Faruque, the Chairman of the Jute Board. Indeed, jute was to be Jamal Mian's prime business. He got himself a jute licence, warehousing and export privileges. Mirza Ahmed introduced him to Narayanganj, the jute trading centre and to the mysteries of jute processing such as 'cutting'. By August 1951 he had a car and a bank account with credit facilities. Mirza Ahmed had made him a commercial agent, his firm was established with Ali Husain Mohani, his friend from madrasa and Lucknow University days, as manager. Because Jamal Mian was not a Pakistani citizen the business was registered as Ansari Ltd. in the name of Habib Mian, the son of Maulana Sibghatullah Farangi Mahalli, a move which would later cause grief.[71]

By this time Jamal Mian felt confident enough of his prospects to ask his wife and family to join him. He rented a property in Agha Sadek Road, identified a plot of land in Magh Bazaar, and started building a house, into which the family moved in early 1953. There was a regular school run, involving Sadri Ispahani. Already by the end of 1951 he was recording significant progress:

This has been a good year. Good health and in terms of general well-being. I have established my business and as far as financial matters are concerned, I have never had so much income. I have moved my family to Dhaka and spent Rs.1,500 in the process. Significantly my relationship with the Ispahani family deepened considerably.[72]

Jamal Mian might have established a business and a home in Pakistan but he was determined that his devotional life in India should not suffer. He maintained a regular attendance at the 'Urs at Ajmer, which was an important social occasion where he might meet his Farangi Mahall relatives, old friends such as Dr. Faridi, and also make new friends such as Pir Sulaiman of Golra in West Pakistan, who was to be an important supporter in later life. Where possible he also attended the 'Urs at Rudauli, where his father-in-law presided, as well as that at Bansa, long central to the spiritual welfare of his family. These took place in the week before the Ajmer celebrations. If his commitments also permitted attendance at the family Bagh in Lucknow, this was so much the better.

There was, however, another dimension of Jamal Mian's life which operated as though the new frontiers did not exist: continued engagement with the political elite of India and Pakistan, most of whom he had known before Partition. At one level he did this at the behest of Mirza Ahmed Ispahani, who wished to make use of his access to Rafi Ahmed Qidwai, Minister of Communications in the Indian Union Cabinet and later Minister of Food and Agriculture. Jamal Mian was sent on errands ranging from rescuing an Orient Airways plane which had been stranded in India to getting Ispahani problems with the Indian tax authorities resolved.[73] In both cases he seems to have been successful. But what is more striking is that Jamal Mian, who might in East Pakistan be meeting Miss Jinnah and be on intimate terms with Khwaja Nazimuddin, Iskander Mirza and his old political boss, Chaudhuri Khaliquzzaman, after he became Governor of East Pakistan, might within days of these encounters be staying in Delhi with Rafi Ahmed Qidwai, meeting Maulana Azad and Feroze Gandhi, and taking tea with Jawaharlal Nehru.[74] Jamal Mian moved amongst his old political friends as if Pakistan had never happened, and the two states were not at daggers drawn. Such behaviour was bound to raise suspicion in the intelligence services, whose personnel usually came from less privileged backgrounds.

It was symptomatic of the betwixt-and-between state in which Jamal Mian found himself that in November 1952 he felt able to give advice to the Pakistan Constituent Assembly. This was the time when Maulana Maududi and his ulama allies were putting pressure on the constitution-making process to take it in an Islamic direction. His unsolicited advice was that the Constitution should be formed on the basis of the final agreement between Britain, the Congress and the Muslim League of 3 June 1947 and the joint statement issued by the leaders of the respective parties on the eve of Partition, and such statement[s] issued by the leaders [as] were instrumental in giving shape to the final agreement . . .'. He was worried by the demand for a religious state; 'this cry of Nizam-e-Islam meaning a constitution based on books of Fiqa [*sic*] and a religious state has brought certain misgivings to my mind . . .'. It meant going back on an agreement 'Movaheda' which was un-Islamic. 'In the case of Pakistan we achieved the State by agreement, and the leaders of the Muslim League before and after Partition declared that Pakistan would be a democratic state giving equal rights to all citizens. Now we cannot set aside this basic principle and it will be un-Islamic on our part [to do so]. . . .' A note in Urdu at the foot of this statement declared: 'I personally handed this to Tamizuddin Khan. Also mentioned this to Shaheed [Suhrawardy]. Also informed Ghulam Mohammad and Nazimuddin on this matter. But no one listened to me. . . .'[75]

At the beginning of 1952 Jamal Mian had been asked by the Lucknow Custodian of Evacuee Property to show cause why he should not be declared an evacuee, and his property in Farangi Mahall evacuee property. The Custodian had been tipped off by Jamal Mian's old antagonist, Muhammad Kamil Bahr ul-Ulumi.[76] Jamal Mian was in danger of the Indian state sequestering property which had been in his family for over 260 years. The threat coincided with the first crisis in his Dacca business and a deteriorating political situation in East Pakistan in which *muhajir*s like himself were becoming the targets of dislike, even hatred.[77] These circumstances set him worrying about whether he should be in Lucknow or Dacca and whether he should become a Pakistani citizen:

I am in great difficulty because I cannot stay in Lucknow because of the growing situation at home. Lucknow brings emotional and spiritual turmoil which I do not feel in Dacca. However, staying on as an Indian in Pakistan with all my Muslim League connections, and doing jute business makes me anxious. Here I worry about politics and jute; there I worry about my financial troubles. I wish I had the true faith and spiritual strength of my ancestors to sustain myself. . . . But as soon as I decide to go to Lucknow I see a whole heap of problems: the situation at home [he refers to the illness of the current sajjadanashin, his half-brother, Qutb Mian]; the unwelcoming environment of the muhalla, the lack of friends and close ones; the intrigues of the antagonists, and on all sides demands for money. That is why I do not like going. But the problem is how long can I live in Pakistan being an Indian national? My wife and children are eager to go back to Lucknow and Rudauli. I am worried that

I have not been able to make a decision on where to be. I have started down this road. Let us see what will happen in future.[78]

In 1954 it appears that Jamal Mian's mind had been made up for him. In April Qutb Mian died. Jamal Mian was needed in Lucknow to oversee the succession to Qutb Mian and to assist in the affairs of the madrasa, which as ever was short of funds. He moved his whole family back to Lucknow. His older children were sent to schools in Lucknow. His eldest daughter remembers a 'fun-filled' period when there were lots of women in the house and guests kept coming from Rudauli and Baragaon.[79] In May and June it seemed as though he was cutting his links with Dacca; he had asked Sadri Ispahani to sell his refrigerator and car for him.[80] Indeed, Sadri felt that Jamal Mian's letters were couched in a way which suggested that he did not intend to return to Dacca.[81] Nevertheless Sadri gave him regular reports on his business which seemed to be doing well in his absence.

More by luck than by judgement, it was a good moment for Jamal Mian to be firmly based in Lucknow. He and Qutb Mian had filed objections to the show-cause notice in the Evacuee Property case on the grounds (1) that Jamal Mian had not migrated to Pakistan, and (2) that five out of six of the properties mentioned in the show-cause notice belonged to Qutb Mian. On 10 December 1953 their objections had been dismissed. They had appealed and their appeal was upheld on 1 June 1954 and a fresh hearing ordered. Jamal Mian's closeness to the Indian political establishment was widely advertised when he led the prayers at the funeral of Rafi Ahmed Qidwai on 24 October 1954. But he still worried about the outcome of the hearing, although this worry was slightly alleviated when on 2 February 1955 he had a dream in which he saw a bearded Jawaharlal Nehru coming to Farangi Mahall and lavishing on him great love and affection.[82] On 22 February Jamal Mian gave evidence in his case at Kanpur. On the 18 June Assistant Custodian A.P. Tripathi decided that Jamal Mian had not migrated to Pakistan with a view to settling there, indeed, his visit (only one was mentioned) was temporary and in connection with his profession as a commission agent. His property (Tripathi did not go into whose property it was) could not be declared evacuee property. On 7 July Jamal Mian was informed of the favourable outcome.[83]

A rough estimate from analysing Jamal Mian's diary suggests that in 1951 he spent thirteen weeks in India, in 1952 seventeen weeks, and in 1953 just four. On this basis he was fortunate that the Custodian's judgement was in his favour. Nevertheless, now the judgement was made, he could consider returning to Dacca and engaging more fully in its social and political life. Further incentives were that the disturbances which had engulfed East Pakistan in 1954, notably the riots at the Adamjee Jute Mill and at the Ispahani-owned Karnaphulli Paper Mill, with their anti-*muhajir* tone, had subsided. Moreover, Jamal Mian had a wife and growing family who clearly missed him when they were apart.[84] In December 1955 the whole family returned to their newly-built house in Eskaton Road, Magh Bazaar, which Jamal Mian had named, somewhat hopefully, Darul Qiam (Place of Stability).

We are not able to track Jamal Mian's movements in the first half of 1956; there is no diary. From most of the second half of the year he was in Dacca, meeting his old friends, Iskander Mirza, Khwaja Nazimuddin and Chaudhuri Muhammad Ali, and mixing with the rest of the Pakistani leadership who were there in force in October. On 30 November he was in Bombay with leading members of the Bohra community, who from time to time he asked to support the Farangi Mahall madrasa, and then he spent much of December in Lucknow, where his mother was very ill. His next visit to India was in March 1957 when, as usual he attended the 'Urs at Ajmer. He then moved on to West Pakistan where he spent most of April, May and June in Karachi. On 19 July he submitted his passport to the Indian High Commission in Dacca so that it could be renewed. On 25 July the Visa Officer telephoned him to say that his passport had been impounded.

From the moment Jamal Mian had begun to work in Dacca he had been worried about his passport. It would appear that initially he was travelling on his old international passport from the time of the Raj. Acquiring an Indian international passport would have been a clear statement of his Indianness so when in 1952 they became available he applied for one. On 15 May he was interviewed in Farangi Mahall by Inspector Babu Lal of the CID, who he later discovered had written a hostile report saying that he was a Pakistani spy.[85] At the same time he had applied for a No Objection Certificate, which was in the gift of the District Magistrate, and this he received on 5 June. Jamal Mian does not mention in his diary actually receiving an Indian passport, despite his anxiety about it. But he clearly did receive one for five years in 1952 as it was part of the evidence he gave at the hearing of the Custodian of Evacuee Property.[86] This may have been just an Indo-Pakistan passport for travel between the two countries. This would explain why in March 1955 he applied with success for an Indian International passport at the Indian Embassy in Baghdad. It was valid up to 15 August 1957, which suggests that it was meant to last no longer than his existing passport. In the post-Partition world this passport had become his badge of Indian citizenship. It was this badge which was impounded. In its place he was given an Emergency Travel Certificate and required to go to India by 31 August 1957 to prove his nationality. He was only permitted to enter India by land and via the Banpur crossing. He was to report on arrival in India any change of address to the local District Magistrate. The certificate was for one, one-way journey. Even though Jamal Mian realized that he was running risks in living, as he had been, between India and Pakistan, the response of the Indian state was unexpected and humiliating.[87]

The immediate reason for the High Commission's actions was a letter from the External Affairs Ministry, 17 May 1957. Indian diplomats had noted that Jamal Mian had been staying with the Raja of Mahmudabad in Karachi for nearly three months and, apparently, he had been overheard making disparaging remarks about India.[88]

Jamal Mian used his connections to try to get the decision revoked. He contacted Ahmed Mohyuddin, an ICS friend in the central government. 'I got your postcard', Mohyuddin replied, 'Very worried. Go as soon as possible to the High Commission and get permission to come to Delhi. Maulana Sahib is very worried. Ajmal [Ajmal Khan, Azad's private secretary] is saying please contact him quickly. If you come Maulana Sahib will talk to Panditji.'[89] 'I am certain that you should now come to Delhi and meet Panditji and Maulana Azad', Mohyuddin declared in a handwritten note a few days later, 'I have not been able to discover where this report has come from, and where it is . . . [this matter] can only be resolved if you come over.'[90] But Jamal Mian was not willing to take the risk that Panditji and the Maulana would be able to resolve his situation. His mother was dying in Lucknow and he needed to go there quickly, but he also needed to be sure that he could return to Dacca, his business, and his family. He immediately got a Pakistani passport, which made him a Pakistani citizen. He then flew to Karachi to get an Indian visa—he preferred to trust C.C. Desai, the Indian High Commissioner there whom he knew rather than take a risk with his opposite number in Dacca—and flew to India. When the Government of India refused to extend this visa, Jawaharlal Nehru arranged for it to be done. Thus Jamal Mian became a Pakistani. His wife did not immediately follow suit. Applying to the Indian High Commission in Dacca for a renewal of her passport in February 1958, she explained that she wanted to maintain her Indian nationality and to keep her children with her.[91] She did not become a Pakistani until 1963.

~

In his *Legacy of a Divided Nation* Mushirul Hasan declared that Jamal Mian left Lucknow for Pakistan 'overnight', leaving Farangi Mahall bereft of his crucial support.[92] It should now be clear that he did no such thing. Jamal Mian went to Pakistan in 1951 because that was the only way in which he could earn a living to support his family and other dependants. He maintained his Indian citizenship, getting both an Indo-Pakistan Passport and an Indian International Passport. Indeed, he maintained his Indian citizenship until, in 1957, he was forced into a corner by the Government of India. This said, in the six years and more that he lived between India and Pakistan he did slowly slide in a Pakistani direction, pushed by the hostility he received in Lucknow and pulled by the relative ease and pleasure of life in Dacca and Karachi.

Through Jamal Mian's experience we can sense the stresses borne by Indian Muslims, particularly if they had been League activists, as they tried to make their way in independent India. They were 'fair game' for those who had backed the nationalists; they also became fair game for rivals in their locality. We have noted how his rivals harassed him through the Evacuee Property Act and equally how Inspector Babu Lal would appear to have prevented him from getting an Indian International Passport, and how a report by diplomats in Karachi led to the impounding of the Indian International Passport that he did get. On the other hand, the Evacuee Property judgement was in his favour, which was most fortunate, and he did seem to receive the No Objection Certificates he needed to travel between India and Pakistan without too much bother. Jamal Mian was able to use his elite connections in India: to further the interests of the Ispahanis, to ease the business of being in Delhi, to smooth the process of Hajj, and to have his visa extended. When it came to the central boon of Indian citizenship, however, this was either a favour he did not feel Nehru was able to grant, or a favour for which he did not wish to beg.[93]

In Jamal Mian's life over the ten years between Partition and the impounding of his passport, we see the machinery of modern statehood—permits, no objection certificates, passports, visas—steadily being imposed to create two separate bodies of citizens where once there had been one. Also, through his eyes, we witness the fashioning of different, if only slightly different, ways of being in real life, from the differing values of the Rupee in India and Pakistan through to the differing roads in life on which the Muslims of the two countries were now travelling. Eventually it became too difficult for Jamal Mian to be domiciled in India and to work in Pakistan. Jamal Mian's 'Long Partition' in terms of citizenship took a whole ten years. But, in fact, the process of Partition in terms of access to the places which gave meaning to his life continued until he died in 2011.

Notes

Gail Minault and I first met in Delhi as we were doing research in December and January 1967–8. At the time I was particularly interested in Maulana Abdul Bari, Jamal Mian's father, as a political figure, and she was interested in him as a leading figure in the Khilafat Movement. Through the kindness of Professor Mohibbul Hasan of the Jamia Millia Islamia we were given an introduction to Abdul Bari's descendants in Farangi Mahall, Lucknow. For six weeks in the early summer of 1968 I stayed with Gail and her then husband, Tom Graham, in Literacy House, Lucknow. We worked together in the Secretariat Archives and in Farangi Mahall. I shall always be grateful to Gail for her hospitality that summer but also for her intellectual generosity in sharing her research with me. I do not recall that Jamal Mian was mentioned in our engagements with the Farangi Mahallis. I was later to discover that, although living in Pakistan, he remained a powerful presence in the lives of the Farangi Mahallis, especially those of Abdul Bari's line.

1. Vazira Fazila-Yacoobali Zamindar, *The Long Partition and the Making of Modern South Asia: Refugees, Boundaries, Histories*, New York: Columbia University Press, 2007.
2. Ibid., pp. 121–226.
3. Typed note by Jamal Mian dated 1951, JMP [Jamal Mian Papers, Karachi]. The psychology of the timing of the writing of this note may be telling; as he set up business in Pakistan he may have felt the need to remind himself of how his family came to be established in the Delhi-Lucknow region.
4. Francis Robinson, *The Ulama of Farangi Mahall and Islamic Culture in South Asia*, New Delhi: Permanent Black, 2001.
5. Jamal Mian, Tape 9, JMP.
6. Jamal Mian, Tape 8, JMP.
7. Raja Amir Ahmad Khan to Jamal Mian, no date, but probably July 1937, Mahmudabad Correspondence, JMP.

8. Jamal Mian, Tape 5A, JMP.
9. Jamal Mian, Biographical note, 1 November 1975 and Raja Amir Ahmad Khan to Jamal Mian, 3 November 1940, Mahmudabad Correspondence, JMP.
10. Jamal Mian, Tape 5A, JMP.
11. Jamal Mian, Tape 4, JMP.
12. Resolution XIV, Thirtieth Session of the All-India Muslim League, Delhi, 24–6 April 1943, Syed Sharifuddin Pirzada, ed., *Foundations of Pakistan: All-India Muslim League Documents: 1906–1947*, vol. II, Karachi: National Publishing House Ltd, 1970, p. 440.
13. The election campaign has been wonderfully described from a boy's-eye view by C.M. Naim, 'The Muslim League in Barabanki: A Suite of Five Sentimental Scenes', Shimla: Indian Institute of Advanced Study, 2010.
14. *Dawn*, 22 October 1945.
15. Ibid.
16. Ibid., 7 July 1946.
17. *United Provinces Legislative Assembly Debates*, 27 April 1946, BL.
18. *Dawn*, 11 July 1946.
19. Jamal Mian's notebooks relating to the Middle East Delegation, 1947, JMP.
20. Jamal Mian, 'Auraq-i Parishan' or Scattered Leaves, mss. no pagination, copied 29 August 1950 by Jamaluddin Abdul Wahab, interestingly on UP Muslim League paper, JMP.
21. Jamal Mian, Note on Dr Faridi, 20 May 1972, JMP.
22. Jamal Mian, Tape 6A, JMP.
23. All-India Muslim League, Council Meeting, Karachi, 14–15 December 1957, Pirzada, *Foundations of Pakistan*, vol. II, pp. 571–2; Jamal Mian, typed essay on Jinnah in English, no date, JMP.
24. Hasrat Mohani, 'Roznama', 14, 17, 19–20 April 1948; 11–12 May 1948, mss. JMP.
25. Ibid., 5 February 1948.
26. Syed Mahmud to S.K. Sinha *c*.1948, V.N. Datta and B. Cleghorn, eds., *A Nationalist Muslim and Indian Politics*, Delhi: The Macmillan Company of India Ltd., 1974, pp. 263–4.
27. Mushirul Hasan, *Legacy of a Divided Nation: India's Muslims since Independence*, Delhi: Oxford University Press, 1997, p. 147.
28. Ibid., p. 173.
29. E.S. Mann, *Boundaries and Identities: Muslims, Work and Status in Aligarh*, Delhi: Sage, 1992, p. 60, quoted in Hasan, *Legacy of a Divided Nation*, p. 176.
30. A.G. Noorani, *The Destruction of Hyderabad*, New Delhi: Tulika Books, 2013, pp. 238–9.
31. Taylor C. Sherman, *Muslim Belonging in Secular India*, Cambridge: Cambridge University Press, 2015, pp. 92–109.
32. Noorani, *Destruction*, p. xxii.

33. Sherman, *Muslim Belonging*, p. 81.
34. Hasrat, 'Roznama', 24 October 1948, JMP.
35. Francis Robinson, *Separatism Among Indian Muslims: the Politics of the United Provinces Muslims 1860–1923*, Cambridge: Cambridge University Press, 1974, pp. 270–2, 293.
36. R.P. Mathur, Vakil, to Muhammad Jamaluddin Abdul Wahab, Proprietor, *Hamdam* Press, Lucknow, 5 July 1947, Personal File, JMP.
37. Jamal Mian wrote under his takhullus, 'Sharir Banbas' 'Mischievous Wanderer', tr. Mahmood Jamal, 'Old Personal Essays and Speeches' File, JMP.
38. Sughra to Jamal Mian, no date but internal evidence suggests 1939, 'Personal File', JMP.
39. Jamaluddin Abdul Wahab, ed., *Nawai Aghaie Kalam-i Sughra*, tr. Mahmood Jamal, 2nd edn., Karachi: Maktaba Khatoon-i Pakistan, 1967.
40. Mirza Ahmed Ispahani to Jamal Mian, 30 December 1948, Ispahani Correspondence, JMP.
41. Mirza Ahmed Ispahani to Jamal Mian, 9 January 1949, Ispahani Correspondence, JMP.
42. Mirza Ahmed Ispahani to Jamal Mian, 2 February 1949; Jamal Mian to Mirza Ahmed Ispahani, 25 February 1949, Ispahani Correspondence, JMP.
43. Hasrat, 'Roznama', 16, 20–1, 24, 27, 29 February and 3–5, 7–8, 20, 22, 25 March 1948, JMP.
44. Hasan, *Legacy*, pp. 211–12.
45. Hasrat, 'Roznama', 10 March 1948, JMP.
46. Jamal Mian to G.B. Pant, Chief Minister UP, 24 February 1949, JMP.
47. Order, 15 February 1949, under the Control of Rent and Eviction Act, JMP.
48. Jamal Mian to Z.I. Lari, 22 February 1949, JMP.
49. Jamal Mian to Harpal Singh, District Magistrate, 9 March 1949, 26 March 1949, on both occasions pressing for a decision, JMP.
50. The quotation is from The Bible, Ruth 1:16. Formal apology drafted on *Hamdam* notepaper, JMP.
51. Jamal Mian, 'Reflections', 25 May 1983, translated from Urdu, JMP.
52. Jamal Mian to G.B. Pant, 24 February 1949, JMP.
53. Nafisul Hasan to Jamal Mian, 19 March 1949, JMP.
54. Hasrat, 'Roznama', 30 March 1949.
55. Jamal Mian to Shah Hayat Ahmed, 26 March 1949, JMP.
56. Jamal Mian to G.B. Pant, 29 March 1949 and Jamal Mian, Note on Nehru, 1963, JMP.
57. Jamal Mian to Harpal Singh, 26 April 1949, JMP.
58. Yardasht, 8 April 1949, JMP
59. Sadri Ispahani to Qutb Mian, 7 April 1949; Jamal Mian To Sadri Ispahani 12 April 1949, Ispahani Correspondence, JMP.
60. Yardasht, 8 April 1949, JMP.
61. Jamal Mian to District Judge, Bara Banki, 8 May 1949, JMP.

62. Jamal Mian to Maulana Muhammad Aslam Bahr ul-Ulumi, 2 Jamadus Sani 1368, 1 April 1949, JMP.
63. Hassan Ispahani to Qutb Mian, 21 April 1949, to Jamal Mian, 4 May 1949, 27 May 1949, 24 June 1949, Ispahani Correspondence, JMP.
64. Sadri to Ispahani to Jamal Mian, 9 September 1949, Ispahani Correspondence, JMP.
65. Mirza Ahmed Ispahani to Jamal Mian, 14 August 1949, Ispahani Correspondence, JMP.
66. Saidur Rahman Qidwai to Jamal Mian, Bombay, 2 January 1950, JMP.
67. Mirza Ahmed Ispahani to Jamal Mian, 15 January 1949, Ispahani Correspondence, JMP.
68. Jamal Mian, Auraq-i Parishan, JMP.
69. Ibid.
70. Jamal Mian, Note on Jawaharlal Nehru, 1963, JMP; K.H. Qadiri, *Hasrat Mohani*, Delhi: Idara-i-Adabiyat-i Delli, 1985, pp. 290–1.
71. Jamal Mian diaries for 1951, JMP.
72. End of year summary, Jamal Mian Diary, 1951, JMP.
73. Jamal to Mirza Razi Sahib 24 December 1949, Personal File, JMP; Jamal Mian Diary, 17–19 April 1951, 8 March and 7, 10 December 1952, JMP.
74. Analysis of Jamal Mian's diary shows that he saw Rafi Ahmed Qidwai on at least ten separate occasions in 1951; for meetings with Pakistan leaders see Jamal Mian diary 27 January 1952, and 2, 6 January and 6 April 1953 (he saw Khaliquzzaman almost every day when he was Governor); and for meetings with Indian leaders, 8 March, 19 May and 22 May 1952.
75. Typed memorandum in English, Dacca, 8 November 1952 JMP. In his submission Jamal Mian also referred to Liaquat Ali Khan's Objectives Resolution (a typing error meant he just wrote 'Objective') to which, as the rest of his submission would suggest, he was profoundly opposed.. His joke about it was that the 'Qarardad-e Muqassid [Objectives Resolution] is the Qarardad-e Mufassid [Disorder Resolution]'. Family tradition reported by Bari Mian, son of Jamal Mian, 27 July 2016.
76. Order in the Court of Sri A.P. Tripathi, Assistant Custodian (Judicial) E.P. Lucknow Circle, Objection Case No. 51 of 54 of Distt. Lucknow, 18 June 1955, JMP.
77. Jamal Mian Diary, 2, 15, 19, 22 January 1952, JMP.
78. Jamal Mian Diary, 24 January 1952, JMP.
79. Farida Jamal, 'Recollections of Ammi Dadi', 2011, JMP.
80. Sadri Ispahani to Jamal Mian, 15 May and 5 June 1954, Ispahani Correspondence, JMP.
81. Sadri Ispahani to Jamal Mian, 20 May 1954, Ispahani Correspondence, JMP.
82. Jamal Mian Diary, 8 January and 2 February 1955, JMP.
83. Order in the Court of Sri A.P. Tripathi, JMP.

84. Jamal Mian Diary, 8 March 1951, and a collection of postcards from Asar, Jamal Mian's wife, to him all undated but all written during the 1950s when they were apart, JMP.
85. Jamal Mian Diary, 16 and 27 May 1952, JMP.
86. Order in the Court of Sri A.P. Tripathi, JMP.
87. Emergency Certificate in the name of Jamaluddin Abdul Wahab alias Jamal Mian, Visa Passport Office, High Commission for India and Pakistan, Dacca, 30 July 1957, Passport File; note on this event by Jamal Mian, stimulated by reading Mushirul Hasan's *Legacy of a Divided Nation*, London, 1997, JMP.
88. Jamal Mian to Chief Visa Officer, Indian High Commission, Dacca, 15 August 1957, Passport File, JMP.
89. Ahmed Mohyuddin to Jamal Mian, 15 September 1957, Passport File, JMP.
90. Ahmed Mohyuddin to Jamal Mian, 20 September 1957, ibid.
91. Mrs Kaniz Fatima Asar to Mr Mahomed Rafique, Chief Visa Officer, Indian High Commission, Dacca, 15 February 1958, Passport File, JMP.
92. Mushirul Hasan, *Legacy*, p. 176.
93. Jamal Mian, Note on Hasan, *Legacy*, and Note on Jawaharlal Nehru, 1963, JMP.

2

Belonging and the Beginning of the Past in Pakistan

AMBER ABBAS

HAYDEN WHITE WARNS historians against 'constructing a specious continuity between the present world and that which preceded it'.[1] With this in mind, what is the task of the historian whose informant is reflecting on his own past world in a manner firmly grounded in his present one? The disruptiveness of Partition cannot be overstated, but is the consideration of the importance of continuity necessarily specious? The consideration of Partition as a process—rather than as an event—allows the incorporation of present narrative reflections on Partition into the narration of it. In oral history narratives I collected in Pakistan in 2005 and 2006, Partition survivors themselves envision their history as continuous even though historians and official narratives have insisted upon the totality of the rupture of Partition.

Gyanendra Pandey, whose 2001 *Remembering Partition* helped establish the importance of memory in defining the historical contours of the event, challenges a historiography that treats Partition violence as a 'problem of origins'.[2] He argues that an overwhelming focus on the sources of tension that led to the creation of the two states obscured the intensity of the trauma. This trauma, after all, disrupted the pre-existing conditions of partition, that is, the context of those very origins.[3] In the narratives I consider here, however, stories about origins serve to frame personal narratives and illuminate meaning. Partition survivors invoked origins to create continuities in the midst of trauma that link them to larger collective identities. As Alessandro Portelli reminds oral historians: 'The first thing that makes oral history different . . . is that it tells us less about *events* than about their meaning.'[4] Oral narratives expose the meaning of events as they persist in the memories of survivors.

Partition disrupted the 'institutional underpinnings of the social order' for Indian Muslims, but it also marked the triumphal creation of Pakistan, and the culmination of a Muslim nationalist movement that had demanded it.[5] The tension between these two outcomes suggests a complexity worth investigating, and yet the experiences of Pakistani Muslims are substantively absent from most partition historiography. To explore the meaning of Pakistan, I asked a dozen or so Pakistani partition survivors the same question, at the conclusion of a longer interview about their own lives and experiences. These narrators fell into two broad categories, some were graduates of the Aligarh Muslim University, an institution designed to serve the sons of the Muslim elite in India that was a hub of pro-Pakistan activism in the 1940s when they were students there. The others were younger and have lived most of their lives in Pakistan, but are scholars and experts on Pakistan's creation and meaning. Their answers reveal the process by which moral meaning is constructed, shared, and linked to powerful collective identities. The question is, when does Pakistan's history begin?

History and Memory

The act of memory is a performative gesture firmly grounded in the present that initiates a process of linking the past to the present and the future.[6] As such, memory constantly redefines the boundaries of those temporal categories. The partition of India has often been treated as a moment in history characterized by horrific violence, but it also brought the independence of two colonial states, the creation of a state based on a claim of nationalism by a religious community, and the beginning of the end—Decolonization lasted 20 years—of the largest empire in the world. It seems impossible to determine the boundaries of such a moment. When can it be said to have begun? Was it with the uprising of 1857 that both Indian and Pakistani nationalists call 'The First War of Independence?' Or was it with the advent of M.K. Gandhi's non-violent movement for Independence? Did Partition begin when the plan was announced on 3 June by the British Viceroy or on 17 August when the border award was made public? And when was it concluded? Was it at sundown on 14 August 1947 or at midnight, by which time India had had its 'tryst with destiny'? Was it when the last Viceroy and first Governor-General of India Louis Mountbatten, left the subcontinent in 1948? Was it when the Indian and Pakistani armies finally came under local control and out from under the command of Supreme Commander Field Marshal Claude Auchinleck? Or when the refugees were finally resettled or the abducted women had been recovered, processes that went on into the 1950s and may never have been successfully completed? Tai Yong Tan and Gyanesh Kudaisya have helpfully suggested that Partition was 'but a trigger for a series of reverberations, the tremors of which can still be felt in the region'.[7] Oral narratives reveal that communities continue to negotiate their own way through those reverberations and tremors by taking solace in memories that give their history stability.

In the memories of survivors, partition's meanings are clear and there is no single moment that can contain the diversity of those meanings. The reflexivity of historical memory draws attention to the meaning of collective identity, itself a shifting category. Michel-Rolph Trouillot, for instance, argues that 'the collective subjects who supposedly remember [the past] did not exist as such at the time of the events they claim to remember. Rather, their constitution as subjects goes hand in hand with the continuous creation of the past'.[8] Using the question of the beginning of Pakistan's history, I examine here how narrators use the starting point of a narrative of history to emplot what follows it, and how that emplotment is constitutive of community itself. The choice of a starting point allows a narrator to identify a moment when the meaning of belonging shifted. Thus the origins claimed mark not just a beginning, but a transition, or re-emplotment of meaning from a pre-existing order to a new one.[9]

One group of narrators educated at the Aligarh Muslim University narrate a history of the Pakistan Movement which centres on the role of Aligarh in the Pakistan Movement and reinforces the centrality of the community cultivated there to show the ways in which university values were mobilized in the demand for statehood. Non-Aligarian narrators, however, locate the starting point of Pakistan's history in miscellaneous other events; that emplotment is related to their conception of self, community, state and citizen.

The collectivity that Aligarh narrators imagine is located at the heart of the Pakistan Movement. It is linked to an intellectual history of Muslim reform movements in northern India in which the Pakistan Movement was the last, and the establishment of the State of Pakistan was the ultimate goal. Pakistan's necessity was justified because people died for it, they sacrificed, they migrated. If it was not necessary then these narrators and others made those sacrifices based on a fallacy, which is not acceptable as a narrative of citizenship, that is, their presence and allegiance to Pakistan as a nation or as an idea was the result of a convoluted accident. The purpose of insisting on the presence of a united Muslim polity is to find a way of giving the Pakistan Movement a meaning. The movement was supposed to represent the downtrodden, alienated Muslims who had been abused first by the British and then by the Hindus, and as such, its motive was the pursuit of justice and freedom for the community. The narrators recall the clarity of Jinnah's vision for Muslims, even if historians cannot.[10]

Other narrators, those not so closely linked with the moral community of the Aligarh Muslim University, also insist on a sense of a united Muslim polity, but defined by a different set of characteristics. It is much more common for these narrators to link the state of Pakistan with the history of Islam in the subcontinent, citing dates as early as 712 CE, the year when Muhammad bin Qasim conquered the province of Sindh. This date is pivotal for the history of Islam in India and marks the arrival of a second 'nation' in the subcontinent. Henceforth, two nations lived alongside one another, but by the 1940s the Muslims realized that Independence would force them into the position of a permanent numerical minority without access to the political power to which they had claim since that date in the eighth century when Arabs invaded Sindh. The imagining of Pakistani history in the context of the long life of Islam in South Asia allows Pakistanis to find their roots not only in the territory that they now occupy, but in terms of a collectivity whose history is older than that of the state. In order to construct and protect this comforting narrative they must enforce covenants of unity on the imagined collectivity. The community must adhere to a founding ideology that both constitutes and supports the narrative of that community. Each narrator imbues a moment with meaning that he applies to a collective identity within Pakistan.

So when—to borrow a question from Trouillot—does the life of a collectivity start?[11] At what point does the narrator locate the coherence of community? What is the beginning of the past?

1857 and The Aligarh Version

While the history of civilization in South Asia begins with the Indus valley (2500 BC), that civilization holds little meaning for the contemporary meaning of belonging in Pakistan. Rather, most historians, and the narrators whose stories are collected here, locate the beginning in 1857, at the end of the upheaval that the British call the Mutiny of 1857, and Indians and Pakistanis call the First War of Independence. As T.R. Metcalf has interpreted it, the uprising of Hindu and Muslim soldiers of the Bengal Army, in service to the British, in 1857 was caused by the fear that the British were trying to 'take away their caste and convert them forcibly to Christianity'.[12] The catalyst for the revolt was a rumour that cartridges for the new Enfield rifle were greased with a combination of beef and pork fat that, if ingested, would strip one of caste. Since the soldier had to pull the cartridge from its case using his teeth, he would certainly ingest the grease and it would pollute, and thus destroy, his caste. Such a stripping of caste would render a man vulnerable to forced conversion to Christianity as he would be alienated permanently from his own community. This controversy erupted at a time of increasing suspicion of the British in the Bengal Army and led to the uprising that soon spread from Meerut across north India.[13] In the end, however, the mutineers, by this time primarily Muslims—who had belatedly installed the ailing Mughal Emperor Bahadur Shah as their leader—were subdued and the British regained control.[14] The Muslims lost their First War of Independence. As a starting point for the history of Pakistan, it was ominous.

This foreboding is reflected in a certain ambivalence in the informants' narratives. One narrator told me that his father's family in north India took 'the wrong side'. The anti-British side. Another insisted that the Hindus who proclaimed that the cartridges were packed in animal fat started the revolt, and that they rallied the Muslim troops to their cause by implying it was pig's fat.[15] These explanations reveal that narrators are not drawn to the *revolutionary* nature of the First War of Independence. In fact, some see the revolting soldiers as traitors to the British, or stooges of the Hindus.

Yet, the events of 1857 provided a powerful moment around which the Muslim community could cohere, and historians and narrators today use the date to signal the beginning of the freedom struggle. It unmistakably marked the end of Muslim rule in the subcontinent and resulted in a restructuring of the British relationship with the Muslim community.

It was in response to the Mutiny of 1857 that W.W. Hunter wrote his *Indian Musalmans: Are they Bound in Conscience to Rebel against the Queen?* in which he purports to determine how deeply rooted the urge to revolt may be in Muslim society. Hunter deploys a host of stereotypes about Muslims to accomplish his goal, and concludes that there are two classes of Muslims: 'Fanatics' [sic] linked to 'seditious masses', and the 'Musalman aristocracy', in whom education could facilitate moderation.[16] Sir Syed Ahmad Khan, a mid-level colonial officer whose family had a long history of government service in the Mughal courts, read Hunter and generally agreed that Muslim culture was in decline. As a response to this, he took it upon himself to invigorate upper class *ashraf* society in northern India. He founded the Mohammedan Anglo-Oriental College in 1875 with the goal of redirecting the path of Muslim civilization in India. In his view, the mighty ruling class that had yielded such formidable Mughal kings as Babur and Akbar, had since descended to a low ebb because of complacency and declining attention to the principles of respectable, or *ashraf* culture. A recultivation of those ideals, along with education would invigorate the Muslims of India and prepare them for leadership when the time came. At this time, despite the recent uprising, neither he nor any other Indian nationalist foresaw independence from the British. Rather, when British power was formalized under the crown, the Muslims were differentiated as a community, marked as a minority, and held largely responsible by the British for the ideological power that drove the uprising.[17]

Although during this period the values of the *ashraf* were reinvigorated—in part due to the efforts of Sir Syed Ahmad Khan and other reformers including Nazir Ahmad and Sheikh Abdullah—narrators remember it as a period of 'relative deprivation' and decline. The Aligarh Muslim University was the shining light in a period of darkness. As Pakistani Major General (Retd) Wajahat Husain told me, after 1857 Sir Syed emphasized that Muslims should be 'getting higher and modern education and coming out of their dark period of ignorance and all that'.[18] Sir Syed also emphasized compromise with the British government, echoing Hunter's advice to the British government to seek compromise and leadership from among the Muslim elite.

That General Wajahat thus placed the beginning of Pakistan's history in 1857 indicates how important he believes this period of decline and reformation was for the coherence of the Muslim community. It was not the actual uprising of 1857 that marked the beginning of the demand for Pakistan. It was not the discontented feelings of the *sepoys* (soldiers) that were continuous with the political discontent of Muslims in the early twentieth century. It was not the impulse to resist that served as a model for later separatists. Rather, it was the impulse to *reform* Muslim culture after the turmoil of 1857 had died down. General Wajahat's emphasis on the reform and its effect on the Muslim polity places the Aligarh Muslim University at the centre of the movement for Muslim solidarity that led to the demand for statehood. The ideal Muslim, in his eyes, was brought up with a strong sense of cultural solidarity and elite values, was highly educated and prepared to be a leader in service of the state. He saw those same values mobilized in the demand for statehood, a reform movement for his time rooted in the values of his own culture.

Similarly, Major General (Retd) Ghulam Umar (of the Pakistan Army) cited Sir Syed's 'politics of educational reform' as the 'basis of trying to awaken the Muslim community'.[19] The Aligarh Muslim University produced some of the most important Muslim reformers, including Mohammad Ali Jauhar, who led the Khilafat Movement in the 1920s.[20] As General Umar described to me why the Khilafat Movement to restore the Turkish caliphate failed, he concluded that, 'one of the characters who emerged politically was M.A. Jinnah'.[21] General Umar created a direct link between Aligarh and Jinnah by placing Mohammad Ali Jauhar and the Khilafat Movement leadership between them. Thus, Jinnah shares the political pedigree of the Muslim reformers of the nineteenth century that fostered the emergence of an apparently unified Muslim community, the same community of which the Muslim League would later seek uncontested leadership in the independence negotiations of the 1940s. However, Jinnah neither attended Aligarh Muslim University nor supported the Khilafat Movement.[22] General Umar easily incorporated him into Aligarh's narrative by identifying him as the heir to the legacy of Muslim reform in the period after 1857. The link was strengthened by Jinnah's commitment to the University and his belief that the young men educated there would go on to be leaders in Pakistan. In General Umar's teleological formulation, the intellectual legacy initiated by Sir Syed led to the rejuvenation of the Muslims and produced leaders who guided the community out of a period of darkness and into freedom in 1947. This intellectual history positions Aligarh to bear the torch of both Sir Syed's and Jinnah's visions for the

Muslim community and independent statehood. It also closely associates the values of the *sharafat* with those of the Aligarh community and advocates for Pakistan.

General Umar further enforced the notion that statehood was achieved in large part due to the development of Aligarh's intellectual legacy. When he spoke of Pakistan's early leadership, he described the disproportionate impact that Aligarh graduates had, once Pakistan was established.

When Pakistan was created, the top hierarchy who actually ran this country, where no infrastructure existed—in India there was infrastructure—there was no central government, there was no capital, there was no this, no that. Even industry was entirely on that side. Who were the people who actually tried to manage this? . . . in fact that was our best period. Who were those people? The Prime Minister was an Aligh[23] the first Pakistan Commander-in-Chief was an Aligh . . . the Chief Minister of Muslim Bengal—East Pakistan—Khwaja Nazimuddin, [and] Sardar Abdur Nishtar.[24]

This narrative centralizes Aligarh Muslim University graduates and emphasizes their role not only in the Muslim nationalist movement, but in fact, in the very establishment of the state. These Aligarh graduates led Pakistan during its 'best period'. After this generation was gone, he said, 'Pakistan went from one trouble into another trouble.'[25] In General Umar's narrative Aligarh men were the most important leaders of Muslims from 1857 to 1951, during which time the community and, later, the state, was led by men of principle according to the values of the *ashraf*.[26] When those values ceased to be embodied in Pakistan's leadership, Pakistan entered a period of decline, similar to that of the post-1857 period. He added that the 'sense of how the Muslim community could come out of that terrible situation where you are just nowhere [grew out of Aligarh]. Now, when I think of the Islamic world, it needs a Sir Sayyid.'[27] General Umar urged a return to the values of his community, a return that must be led by someone who understands the power of the collectivity. If Muslims could cohere today into a unified collectivity, as he believes they did after 1857, then they again could enact reforms that would in turn strengthen that community.

Alternatives to Aligarh

In addition to the 1857 uprising, however, there are other important moments that narrators selected as the 'beginning' of Pakistan's history.

Although non-Aligarian narrators were prepared to acknowledge the importance of the Aligarh Muslim University they certainly did not construct the same uninterrupted narrative with the First War of Independence. In fact, these narrators evoked a different intellectual legacy, one closer to their homes in the Punjab. This narrative focuses more closely on the idea that Muslims and Hindus had always been differentiated into two nations living alongside one another in India. This 'Two Nation Theory' is sometimes attributed to Sir Syed Ahmad Khan.[28] Sir Syed's motives, however, were so closely linked to British loyalism that they are not easily incorporated into non-elite discourses of nation and state formation.

Alternatively, the articulation of the Two Nation Theory can be attributed to Mohammad Iqbal when, as President of the Muslim League, he addressed a meeting at Allahabad in 1930. He spoke of the role of Muslims in the emerging Indian political system, with particular attention to Muslim representation. He settled on the solution that there must be 'self-government within the British Empire or without the British Empire, the formation of a consolidated North-West Indian Muslim state'.[29] Iqbal believed deeply in the unifying force of Islam and referred repeatedly in his speech to the 'ethical ideal' of Islam that had the ability to 'gradually unify scattered individuals and groups and finally transform them into a well-defined people'.[30] This 'well-defined people' had a special role to play in India and had the opportunity to demand a territorial solution to what he called the 'communal problem'. He suggested that Muslims were 'the only Indian people who can fitly be described as a "Nation" in the modern sense of the word' because Hindus lacked a homogenizing force like Islamic philosophy and law.[31] He encouraged unity of thought and action on the part of Muslim League delegates and emphasized that the political voice of Indian Muslims could set an example for future Muslim polities throughout the world. He encouraged Muslims to 'rise above sectional interests and private ambitions'.[32] The defining feature of his philosophy was his call for a permanent 'territorial solution' to the incompatibility of Western democracy with Indian communal demographics.[33] This territorial solution is easily linked to the realization of Pakistan, and as Dr Rafiq Ahmed told me, this solution forms the backbone of the ideology of Pakistan.

Dr Rafiq, as General Secretary of the *Nazaria-i-Pakistan* (Ideology of Pakistan) Trust, believes this ideology to be central to the realization and success of the Pakistani state. Iqbal's vision invokes the powerful history of Islam in the subcontinent that, he said, 'for over five to six hundred years has remained at the forefront; it was a civilization of going ahead'.[34] He traced the origins of the two nations to Islam's arrival in India and stressed essential differences between the two communities to justify the need for Pakistan. The two nations were built on diametrically opposed premises: monotheism and polytheism. Furthermore, he told me, Islam recognizes a principle of equality among people whereas Hindu hierarchy is based on a rigid caste system. These conflicting foundations he said, are 'two basic approaches to life which ultimately became the basis of two nations'.[35] By the twentieth century, conflicts over political power further differentiated the two nations and Muslims were not treated 'on an equal level' by the British, Hindus, or Sikhs.[36] He suggested that India might have remained united had Muslims been treated equally by the ruling power. Here again, the narrative slips into an explanation of Muslim victimhood, not one of reform. In rooting his narrative in the history of Islam in India, Dr Rafiq constructed a continuity in order to show the unique power of Muslim ideology. However, the entrance of politics into his narrative betrays this fragile construction and undermines its stability.

To recover, Dr Rafiq invoked the events of 1857 to demonstrate how British attitudes towards Muslims and Hindus changed when Muslims were 'punished' for 'what [the British] used to call the Mutiny'.[37] He does not attribute responsibility to the Muslims for a revolutionary uprising, but places their involvement within the structure of British power that had the authority to punish dissidents. However, in his view these events led to the practical development of the idea of separateness that Iqbal articulated in 1930. He placed Iqbal's speech within the context of British and Hindu abuse of Muslims, but also argued that the establishment of the Pakistani state was the logical conclusion of the history of Islam in India. As he told me, 'Pakistan is not something which came out of the blue. The realities have been there since the first century in India.'[38] He appealed to a deeply rooted division between Hindus and Muslims, less localized than that of the Aligarh narrators, and with direct reference to the social structure of Islam as Iqbal had done in 1930.

Dr Rafiq suggested that 'the vision of Pakistan, in the light of what [M.A. Jinnah] Quaid-e-Azam believed and what Allama Iqbal believed is to set up a democratic, welfare oriented Islamic country within the programs of life given by Islam.'[39] That the state has not been administered according to this design is not a fault of the vision itself, but of the people, people who do not believe strongly enough in Quaid-e-Azam's vision of unity, and with the leaders who failed to follow Iqbal's guidance and have pursued personal gain in politics rather than the good of the nation. The nation that Iqbal and Dr Rafiq speak of is unified by the 'ethical ideal' that governs the Islamic social structure, not by the cultural values of a certain class of Muslims that the Aligarians recognize in the words of Mohammad Ali Jinnah. Dr Rafiq's narrative more easily incorporates regional and linguistic diversity than does the Aligarh version because the unity of which he speaks is derived from the non-territorial unity of the Muslim faith. However, this vision remains an ideal, as Dr Rafiq said,

The vision of Quaid-e-Azam and Allama Iqbal has not been fully realized—it still remains to be a vision. Visions actually, in no part of the world have been fully achieved. Never. Visions have never been achieved . . . vision is there in Pakistan also. We have this vision.[40]

This 'vision' is the central feature of his understanding of the state of Pakistan and his current work at the *Nazaria-i-Pakistan* (Ideology of Pakistan) Foundation where he trains young people to be productive citizens by teaching the importance of the ideology of Pakistan as it was articulated by Allama Iqbal. This vision has been a powerful one in the public sphere. Today, in Pakistan, Iqbal is frequently featured alongside Jinnah as a founder of the nation.

The ideology that raises Iqbal alongside Jinnah as a founding father draws on two foundational ideas. The first comes from Iqbal's confidence in the unity of Indian Muslims defined by the religious, legal, and social structures of Islam. The second idea is Jinnah's, drawn from Sir Syed's cultural reform movement in the Muslim community. This impulse relies more heavily on political and cultural unity than religious, and places emphasis on common ancestry and history, common values, and common language. Jinnah was dedicated to the idea of a secular state in Pakistan, and 'unhaltingly called for a separation of state and religion'.[41] The invocation of Islamic history leads Dr Rafiq—and increasingly, the public who has been nourished on the idea of the two founders and the two nations—to the conclusion that Pakistan had to become an Islamic state, which it did in 1956, because that was the 'sole purpose of demanding a separate homeland for the Muslims'.[42]

Historian of the Pakistan Movement, Sarfaraz Hussain Mirza, who

I met in his office at the *Nazaria-i-Pakistan* Foundation, suggests that Jinnah's speech of March 1940 should be considered the beginning of the history of Pakistan. It was then, he suggested, that the vision for Pakistan was articulated in the Lahore Resolution (also called the Pakistan Resolution) in which the demand for Muslim autonomy was established. Mirza made passing reference to 1857 to identify the moment after which the Muslim situation in India became less tenable because the main burden of the freedom struggle was 'put on the Muslims'.[43] Mirza implied that the Muslims were selected, perhaps unfairly or erroneously, by the British, to bear the blame for the 1857 uprising. Though he suggested that this early uprising was a foundational event for the Pakistan demand that developed in the 1940s, he too was reluctant to define 1857 as a revolutionary act. He repeated the notion that Muslims were 'framed' to take blame for the activities of many. Still, after 1857, Muslims had to face, 'so many difficulties; they had to face a lot of torture after that time'.[44] Mirza, however, clarified that the movement for Independence really took shape in 1940.

Two different starting points reflect Mirza's two relationships to Pakistan's history. His reference to 1857 was made as a historian of the Pakistan Movement and the Aligarh Muslim University. His personal narrative returned, however, to 1940, the point at which he believes Pakistan's history began. This starting point emphasizes the near miraculous nature of the achievement of statehood.

Have you any example in the world of any country—has any country been created in such a short span? [It could happen] only with a vision, only with a slogan, on the basis of an ideology. This is ideology. The ideology is a requirement. We have geographical boundaries, this is also a requirement, but this is all due to ideological foundations.[45]

He made this argument, however, not with reference to Iqbal or to Sir Syed, but to Jinnah's speech of 22 March 1940. In this speech, Jinnah made clear the differences between the Muslim and Hindu nations when he said that the religious philosophies, customs, and literatures of the two groups were rooted in different civilizations and drew on different sources of history. Jinnah concluded that 'to yoke together two such nations under a single state, one as a numerical minority and the other as a majority, must lead to growing discontent and final destruction of any fabric that may be so built up for the government of such a state'.[46] Sarfaraz Mirza describes this speech as Jinnah's solution for the peaceful coexistence of communities in the subcontinent.

As a child, growing up in the east Punjab cities of Ferozpur and Jalandhar, Mirza's early memories focus on the tensions between Muslims and non-Muslims. In 1947, as violence was tearing communities apart, his family went into hiding and later fled their home seeking safety. At the time that they abandoned their house, however, young Sarfaraz was not there. He recalls:

I was too young, and I was strolling on the road—I don't know where I was, playing in the [cricket] ground or somewhere—meanwhile when I came back I saw that the house was absolutely empty! Everything has been taken away. I saw the Sikhs cutting the throat of the young Muslim children on the road! When I was coming back to my house I saw with my own eyes. They were just, you know, they would cut the head of a child and throw it away and they would just put their sword like that, and do like that [making the motions of impaling the head on the end of the sword and waving it around]. This was the very horrible thing that I saw.[47]

His elder brother later found him and took him to safety with the rest of his family; they all fled to a refugee camp in east Punjab and later to a refugee camp in Pakistan. For Mirza, as a child, escape to Pakistan meant escape from the danger lurking in the streets of Ferozpur, danger that he cannot even put into words here. It meant escape from the physical abuse he endured at the hands of Sikh and Hindu schoolteachers. He is devoted to the idea of Pakistan as a refuge for Indian Muslims and enacts this belief annually with his return, on Independence Day, to the refugee camp near the Lahore Cantonment, where his family stayed on arrival in Pakistan. Each year, he told me, 'On 14 August I hoist the flag of Pakistan over there. That is my Pakistan.'[48] Lahore represented safety for the young Sarfaraz, for the grown man it represents the site of origin of the movement that ultimately provided that safety.

Dr Ahmad Saeed, another Pakistani historian, sets the beginning of Pakistan's history in 1947, at the moment of state formation. Although he has compiled several volumes of documents on the Pakistan Movement, he suggests that history must begin in 1947 for two reasons: the current generations of Pakistanis—born after 1947—know very little of the events of 1947, and furthermore Pakistan cannot afford to remember that the states of Punjab, Sindh, Balochistan and Frontier were resistant to the Muslim League and the idea of Pakistan until the elections of 1946. In those elections, the Muslim League received a majority of seats for the first time in most Muslim majority provinces, and only after intense and focused activity by its activists and students. Prior to those elections, state politics had been determined by parties that represented regional interests, rather than national ones. The reality of this political disunity cannot easily be incorporated into the inclusive narrative of the Pakistan Movement with its claim to represent all of India's Muslims. For Saeed, the League's image of unity must be projected onto the history of Pakistan. The realization of the state proves to him the possibility of unity, and history that challenges that unity cannot be incorporated into the history of the state.

In fact, there was staunch political resistance in several of the Muslim majority provinces—including Punjab, which was dominated by the British loyalist Unionist Party—in the years leading up to Partition. In the face of this resistance Ahmad Saeed suggested that 'Pakistan should have been established in C.P. (Central Provinces), in U.P. (United Provinces) because those people worked for Pakistan. Those people suffered for Pakistan. They could be more loyal than we people living in Punjab, Sindh, N.W.F.P. (North-West Frontier Province) and Balochistan.'[49] Pakistan, he implies, was a reward for those who had fought for Muslim solidarity throughout the movement and the people in the north-west of the subcontinent were undeserving of it. Though practically impossible, he links the territorial definition of Pakistan with the north Indian population that was mobilized by the reform movements of the late nineteenth and early twentieth centuries when he suggests that Pakistan should have been created in UP. In his view, the people in the areas that became territorially defined as Pakistan had demonstrated only an opportunistic loyalty to the Muslim League and supported it only when it presented the best option for retaining power in local arenas.

Deeply unhappy about the domination of Punjabi politics by corrupt landlords, Saeed derided their ingratitude for the political and social opportunity presented by Pakistan. He said they had not upheld the values of Muslim unity that Jinnah and Iqbal described, and the divisive nature of their politics prevented Pakistan from becoming the realization of the founders' dream. However disappointing its reality, Pakistan has provided so much potential for its citizens, so all citizens must be encouraged to support it. It is for this reason that Saeed said that Pakistan's history must begin at the moment that statehood was achieved. It was at this moment that political disunity was necessarily overcome, and for this ideal of unity that people died. Partition martyrs provide the best model of how to prove one's loyalty to the state. All of Pakistan's citizens must be loyal to the vision for Pakistan, and the memory of dissent that challenges the true claim of Muslim unity must be eliminated from Pakistan's history. He echoes Iqbal's suggestion that to be a member of the nation one must be selfless, and he urged loyalty to the territorial integrity of the state. Without it, Muslims had nothing, but in Pakistan, they had all benefited. In order to facilitate an environment in which all citizens can relate to the vision for Pakistan he advocated shortening its historical trajectory, by erasing the memory of difference, to include only the time when the territoriality of Pakistan overwrote political dissent in the interest of unity. This territoriality defined the privilege of citizenship; loyalty meant loyalty to the state as defined within formal national boundaries and in the period after 1947.

The Origin of a Collectivity

These narratives reveal diverse views of Pakistan's history, even among the educated classes. The many different experiences of Pakistani narrators captured here directly impact their understanding of the state and their role as citizens. The historical origin each narrator selected was rooted in his personal experience and reflects some of the diversity that exists among Pakistanis. Even from this small sample, one can see that no single narrative of statehood is capable of incorporating the whole. Each narrative, while making a claim of unity, excludes others.

The production of personal history is a process that is both deeply rooted in past experience and reflective of present circumstances. Lewis A. Coser describes this twofold process in terms of its 'cumulative and presentist aspects'.[50] The refashioning of the past is continuous with it and constructive of it. The many perspectives visible here, and the impact of personal experience on memory formation seem to belie the existence of a collective memory, but in fact, it is the presence of the collectivity that undergirds each of these narratives. At the moment the narrators incorporate themselves and their experiences into a group, they form self-justifying narratives based on that group and begin to use its memories and language to define their outlook.

Each emplotment of Pakistan's history explored above follows a starting point firmly located in a sense of a collectivity. The memories that cohere around that starting point do so not because they are contiguous in time, but because they belong to a narrative common to a group.[51] Each narrator advances the interests of the group when he tells his story. His particular application of facts is guided by his understanding of the meaning of that collectivity and given form by the collectivity itself. In each case, the narrator's starting point is the point at which he recognizes that he belongs to a group. From that point he plots, or sometimes replots his history based on the collectivity's boundaries and forms. Narrators create meaning out of Partition's disruptions by emplotting their own experiences within a social framework that is perceived to be continuous.[52] Does the emplotment of historical memory within the context of the social milieu amount to creating a 'specious' continuity? Do narrators maliciously align themselves with a certain narrative to be allowed to embellish the historical narrative with ideology? The narratives are tendentious, to be sure, and grounded in the present concerns of narrators in relationship to the state, but the imperfections in the narratives alert the historian to the fact that it was not with obscurantist intentions that these narrators constructed their history. In fact, the very inconsistencies in form and style are keys to understanding the very honest nature of these historical stories. Each narrator reveals the contours of the community to which he belongs by giving meaning to events that can be understood in collective terms.

The narrators' identification with a certain collectivity in a certain moment in time reveals the ability of meaning to shift as the idea of the collectivity itself shifts. Aligarh narrators appeared less flexible in their ability to redefine the collectivity once they arrived in Pakistan. They perceived their history as deeply rooted in a set of ideas and values that were embodied in space and voiced by the Pakistan Movement in the demand for statehood. Believing these ideas to be foundational, they could not adapt their own sense of identity after statehood became a reality in a new territory in 1947. Non-Aligarian narrators, however, demonstrate their ability to redefine themselves and the state in terms of a collectivity whose terms shifted once it could be defined by territory. With the transition from the demand for Pakistan to the state of Pakistan it was no longer necessary, their narratives suggest, to define Muslim solidarity in terms of the values of the *ashraf*. In Pakistan, the citizenry must be defined by the ideology of Islam, viewed as the central organizing principle of the Muslim collectivity. The construction of the history of Pakistan, for these narrators, defines and reifies the boundaries of the state and the collectivity at the same time. As Trouillot suggests, in constituting their identities, narrators have created a past for their collectivity, and have also looked back and created a historical collectivity for their past.

In the case of Pakistan, these historical collectivities have been mapped onto the demand for statehood and used to reify contending claims on the loyalties of Pakistan's citizens.

Notes

1. Hayden White, *Tropics of Discourse: Essays in Cultural Criticism*, Baltimore: Johns Hopkins University Press, 1978, p. 50.
2. Gyanendra Pandey, *Remembering Partition: Violence, Nationalism, and History in India*, Cambridge; New York: Cambridge University Press, 2001, p. 49.
3. Ibid., p. 50.
4. Alessandro Portelli, *The Death of Luigi Trastulli and Other Stories: Form and Meaning in Oral History*, Albany: State University of New York Press, 1991, p. 50.
5. Arthur G. Neal, *National Trauma and Collective Memory: Major Events in the American Century*, Armonk, NY: M.E. Sharpe, 1998, p. xi.
6. Mieke Bal, 'Introduction', in *Acts of Memory: Cultural Recall in the Present*, ed. Mieke Bal, Jonathan Crewe, and Leo Spitzer, Hanover, NH: University Press of New England, 1999, p. vii.
7. Tai Yong Tan and Gyanesh Kudaisya, *The Aftermath of Partition in South Asia*, London: Routledge, 2000, p. 8.
8. Michel-Rolph Trouillot, *Silencing the Past: Power and the Production of History*, Boston: Beacon Press, 1995, p. 16.
9. Hayden White, *The Content of the Form: Narrative Discourse and Historical Representation*, Baltimore: Johns Hopkins University Press, 1987, p. 23.
10. For a full investigation of Jinnah's demand see Ayesha Jalal, *The Sole Spokesman: Jinnah, the Muslim League, and the Demand for Pakistan*, Cambridge; New York: Cambridge University Press, 1985.
11. Trouillot, *Silencing the Past*, p. 16.
12. Thomas R. Metcalf, *The Aftermath of Revolt: India, 1857–1870*, Princeton, NJ: Princeton University Press, 1964, p. 47.
13. Ibid., pp. 46–91.
14. Mahmood Farooqui, ed., *Besieged: Voices from Delhi, 1857*, New Delhi: Penguin Books India, 2010.
15. It is true that Muslims in India do not adhere to a rigid 'caste' system as it is perceived in the Hindu tradition, though Muslim social hierarchy is marked by bloodlines that correspond to status. Nonetheless, the anxiety here is about pollution of the body, which would render it impure, and thus 'outcast'. This question of purity was as significant to Muslims with regard to pig fat as it was to Hindus with regard to beef. Javid Iqbal, 'Justice Javid Iqbal: Personal Interview with Amber Abbas June 13, 2006', Lahore, 13 June 2006. Javid Iqbal is the son of Pakistan's Poet Laureate Mohammad Iqbal. He was born

on 5 October 1924 in Sialkot, Pakistan. He was educated in the Government College of the Punjab University in Lahore, where he grew up. He wrote a Ph.D. in Cambridge University and was admitted to the bar. In Pakistan he served in the High Court and retired as Justice of the Supreme Court of Pakistan.
16. W.W. Hunter, *The Indian Musalmans: Are They Bound in Conscience to Rebel against the Queen?*, London: Trubner and Co., 1871, pp. 1–35, 140–206. See also David Lelyveld, *Aligarh's First Generation: Muslim Solidarity in British India*, Princeton: Princeton University Press, 1978, pp. 10–14.
17. Metcalf, *The Aftermath of Revolt*, pp. 289–327.
18. Wajahat Husain, 'Major General Wajahat Husain (Retd): Personal Interview with Amber Abbas June 16, 2005', Lahore, 16 June 2005. Wajahat Husain was originally from Aligarh where he completed all of his education by 1944. At war's end he went for military training at the Indian Military Academy in Dehradun and opted for Pakistan. He first served on the Punjab Boundary Force, then as ADC to the Pakistan Army's Commander-in-Chief before settling down into the Guides Cavalry. He also served Pakistan as an Ambassador to Greece and Australia. He died in February 2013.
19. Ghulam Umar, 'Major General Ghulam Umar (Retd): Personal Interview with Amber Abbas August 8, 2006', Karachi, 8 August 2006. Major General Ghulam Umar completed all of his education in Aligarh before joining the Indian Army in the early 1940s during World War II. He returned to India from Japan after the war and opted for Pakistan. He served in Pakistan's Army during both the 1965 and 1971 Wars, and was Chief of the National Security Council in 1971. He also served as Military Secretary to King Faisal of Saudi Arabia. After retirement he was involved in people-to-people diplomacy with India. He died in January 2009.
20. Gail Minault, *The Khilafat Movement: Religious Symbolism and Political Mobilization in India*, Studies in Oriental Culture, New York: Columbia University Press, 1982.
21. Umar, 'Personal Interview with Amber Abbas August 8, 2006'.
22. Minault, *The Khilafat Movement*, p. 97.
23. A graduate of the Aligarh Muslim University, also called Aligarians.
24. Umar, 'Personal Interview with Amber Abbas August 8, 2006'. General Umar refers here to Prime Minister Liaquat Ali Khan, Commander-in-Chief Ayub Khan, and the first Pakistani Governor of Punjab, Muslim League leader Sardar Abdur Rab Nishtar.
25. Ibid.
26. General Umar neglected to mention that Aligarian Field Marshal Ayub Khan, Pakistan Army's first Pakistani Commander-in-Chief became Chief Martial Law Administrator and later President of Pakistan when he dismissed the government in a bloodless coup in 1958.
27. Umar, 'Personal Interview with Amber Abbas August 8, 2006'.

28. I do not mean to suggest that Sir Syed is the progenitor of the 'Two Nation Theory' or indeed, a 'founder' of Pakistan. Some have suggested this, but others have attributed the theory to Mohammad Iqbal who first suggested a territorial solution, or to V.D. Savarkar, who first discussed it at the 1937 Meeting of the Hindu Mahasabha.
29. Muhammad Iqbal, 'Presidential Address Delivered at the Annual Session of the All-India Muslim League at Allahabad on the 29th December, 1930', in *Iqbal, Jinnah and Pakistan: The Vision and the Reality*, ed. C.M. Naim, Syracuse: Syracuse University Press, 1979, p. 195.
30. Ibid., p. 191.
31. Ibid., p. 205.
32. Ibid., p. 206.
33. Ibid.
34. Rafiq Ahmed, 'Rafiq Ahmed: Personal Interview with Amber Abbas August 5, 2006', Lahore, 5 August 2006. Rafiq Ahmad was born on 3 February 1927 in Lahore. Both sides of his family hail from the old city of Lahore and he spent his childhood there. His father owned the Punjab Stores provisions store in Tollington Market on the Mall. Rafiq Ahmed completed his M.A. in Islamia College in 1948 and a Ph.D. from Oxford University in 1956. He returned to Pakistan and began teaching in Punjab University. Eventually he became Vice Chancellor of Islamia University-Bahawalpur, where he established the campus. He helped to establish the Nazaria-e-Pakistan Foundation in 1999.
35. Ibid.
36. Ibid.
37. Ibid.
38. Ibid.
39. Ibid.
40. Ibid.
41. Ayesha Jalal, 'Conjuring Pakistan: History as Official Imagining', *International Journal of Middle East Studies*, vol. 27, no. 1, February 1995, p. 76.
42. Haji Wali Muhammad Dogar, *Pakistan Studies and Affairs*, Lahore, 1983. Cited in Jalal, 'Conjuring Pakistan', p. 79.
43. Sarfaraz Hussain Mirza, 'Sarfaraz Hussain Mirza: Personal Interview with Amber Abbas July 21, 2006', Lahore, 21 July 2006. Sarfaraz Hussain Mirza was born in Ferozpur, East Punjab in 1942. His father was a policeman and he spent his early years in the civil lines, in the police colony. His family migrated to Pakistan during partition, feeling the threat of violence. He is a scholar of Pakistan history and the editor of several collections of documents. He is a resident scholar at the *Nazaria-i-Pakistan* Foundation.
44. Mirza, 'Personal Interview with Amber Abbas July 21, 2006'.
45. Ibid.
46. Mohammad Ali Jinnah, 'Presidential Address at the All-India Muslim League, Lahore Session, March 1940', in *Some Recent Speeches and Writings of*

Mr Jinnah Vol. I, ed. Jamil-ud-din Ahmad, Lahore: Sh. Muhammad Ashraf, 1952, p. 178.
47. Mirza, 'Personal Interview with Amber Abbas July 21, 2006'.
48. Ibid.
49. Ahmad Saeed, 'Professor Ahmad Saeed: Personal Interview with Amber Abbas July 20, 2006', Lahore, 20 July 2006. Ahmad Saeed was born on 21 July 1942 in Jalandhar, East Punjab, then in India. His family shifted to Lahore in 1947 via military transport. He was educated in the Government College and Punjab University. He taught for many years in Islamia College, Lahore before retiring in 2002. He is now a historian with the *Nazaria-i-Pakistan* Foundation.
50. Lewis A. Coser, 'Introduction to on Collective Memory by Maurice Halbwachs', in *On Collective Memory*, ed. Lewis A. Coser, Chicago and London: University of Chicago Press, 1992, p. 26.
51. Maurice Halbwachs, *On Collective Memory*, ed. Lewis A. Coser, tr. Lewis A. Coser, Heritage of Sociology, Chicago: University of Chicago Press, 1992, p. 52.
52. White, *The Content of the Form*, p. 11.

References

Ahmed, Rafiq, 'Rafiq Ahmed: Personal Interview with Amber Abbas August 5, 2006', Lahore, 5 August 2006.
Bal, Mieke, 'Introduction', in *Acts of Memory: Cultural Recall in the Present*, ed. Mieke Bal, Jonathan Crewe and Leo Spitzer. Hanover, NH: University Press of New England, 1999.
Coser, Lewis A., 'Introduction to on Collective Memory by Maurice Halbwachs', in *On Collective Memory*, ed. Lewis A. Coser, Chicago and London: University of Chicago Press, 1992.
Dogar, Haji Wali Muhammad, *Pakistan Studies and Affairs*, Lahore, 1983.
Farooqui, Mahmood, ed., *Besieged: Voices from Delhi, 1857*, New Delhi: Penguin Books India, 2010.
Halbwachs, Maurice, *On Collective Memory*, ed. and tr, Lewis A. Coser, Heritage of Sociology, Chicago: University of Chicago Press, 1992.
Hunter, W.W., *The Indian Musalmans: Are They Bound in Conscience to Rebel against the Queen?*, London: Trubner and Co., 1871.
Husain, Wajahat, 'Major General Wajahat Husain (Retd): Personal Interview with Amber Abbas, June 16, 2005', Lahore, 16 June 2005.
Iqbal, Javid, 'Justice Javid Iqbal: Personal Interview with Amber Abbas June 13, 2006', Lahore, 13 June 2006.
Iqbal, Muhammad, 'Presidential Address Delivered at the Annual Session of the All-India Muslim League at Allahabad on the 29th December, 1930', in *Iqbal, Jinnah and Pakistan: The Vision and the Reality*, ed. C.M. Naim, Syracuse: Syracuse University Press, 1979, pp. 191–207.

Jalal, Ayesha, 'Conjuring Pakistan: History as Official Imagining', *International Journal of Middle East Studies* 27, no. 1, February 1995, pp. 73–89.

———, *The Sole Spokesman: Jinnah, the Muslim League, and the Demand for Pakistan*, Cambridge; New York: Cambridge University Press, 1985.

Jinnah, Mohammad Ali, 'Presidential Address at the All-India Muslim League, Lahore Session, March 1940', in *Some Recent Speeches and Writings of Mr Jinnah Vol. I*, ed. Jamil-ud-din Ahmad, Lahore: Sh. Muhammad Ashraf, 1952, pp. 159–81.

Lelyveld, David, *Aligarh's First Generation: Muslim Solidarity in British India*, Princeton: Princeton University Press, 1978.

Metcalf, Thomas R., *The Aftermath of Revolt: India, 1857–1870*, Princeton, NJ: Princeton University Press, 1964.

Minault, Gail, *The Khilafat Movement: Religious Symbolism and Political Mobilization in India*, Studies in Oriental Culture, New York: Columbia University Press, 1982.

Mirza, Sarfaraz Hussain, 'Sarfaraz Hussain Mirza: Personal Interview with Amber Abbas, 21 July 2006', Lahore, 21 July 2006.

Neal, Arthur G., *National Trauma and Collective Memory: Major Events in the American Century*, Armonk, NY: M.E. Sharpe, 1998.

Pandey, Gyanendra, *Remembering Partition: Violence, Nationalism, and History in India*, Cambridge; New York: Cambridge University Press, 2001.

Portelli, Alessandro, *The Death of Luigi Trastulli and Other Stories: Form and Meaning in Oral History*, Albany: State University of New York Press, 1991.

Saeed, Ahmad, 'Professor Ahmad Saeed: Personal Interview with Amber Abbas, 20 July 2006', Lahore, 20 July 2006.

Tan, Tai Yong and Gyanesh Kudaisya, *The Aftermath of Partition in South Asia*, London: Routledge, 2000.

Trouillot, Michel-Rolph, *Silencing the Past: Power and the Production of History*, Boston: Beacon Press, 1995.

Umar, Ghulam, 'Major General Ghulam Umar (Ret'd): Personal Interview with Amber Abbas, 8 August 2006', Karachi, 8 August 2006.

White, Hayden, *The Content of the Form: Narrative Discourse and Historical Representation*, Baltimore: Johns Hopkins University Press, 1987.

———, *Tropics of Discourse: Essays in Cultural Criticism*, Baltimore: Johns Hopkins University Press, 1978.

3

Timely Disguises

Fantasizing Civility on the Frontier Between India and Europe

SHAHZAD BASHIR

A person present at the incident when Mr Lawrence was slain said that he was pretending to be a mendicant (*faqir*) when the soldiers killed him. But when the soldiers saw the marks of two bullets on his back, which he was known to have suffered in the battle of Kabul, they recognized him convincingly and he had no answer but silence. The difference between the sources is confounding and one feels flustered, fearing that, tomorrow, another reporter may give a different name for this European (*firangi*).

—'The Death of Mr Lawrence', *Dehli Urdu Akhbar*, 31 May 1857

THE RECOGNIZABILITY OF A human body as a particular person is a concern as crucial as it is fraught with uncertainty. Implicating materiality as well as cognition, it is central to matters as widely divergent as personal identity and the science of forensics. Conceptualized as a process, recognition shows the human body as a layered object, including natal characteristics of skin colour, gender, and distinguishing features, and marks of times and places such

---

*An earlier version of this paper was presented at the workshop 'Civility at the Limits of the Political: India, Europe and the Spirit of the Indian Subject' held at Stanford University in March 2011. I am grateful to Aishwary Kumar and Parna Sengupta for comments leading to revision.

as injury, attire, cultural and social residues, and habitual movement that indicate the ease or otherwise of interacting with other bodies. For all the ways we can parse it, recognition is a profoundly fragile affair, apt to congealment or dissolution in an instant and consequential to the point of death. The question of recognition is also, I believe, critical to the politics of civilization and civility. In this essay, I would like to highlight the place of bodily recognition as a critical mediating point in questions pertaining to civilizational hierarchies, civilizing missions, and the exercise of interpersonal civility. Recognition is central to these issues because it encapsulates the process of going from apprehending the human body as a material object to comprehending its metaphysical significance as well as its place in sociocultural hierarchies. The last two of these procedures determine the recognized body's status as a counterpart to the observing body, seen either as of a higher or equal status and thereby to be treated civilly, or as of lower status, subject to disparagement, exclusion from interaction, or the civilizing mission. I suggest that, in the colonial context, the rhetoric of civilization and the practice of civility functioned necessarily at cross-purposes with each other. Civilization posed a universal scale by which individuals and groups were to be judged. Civility was conditioned first and foremost by the power differential that defined the colonial situation, presumed as the norm between those of European origin and denied to the Indians as unequals. In the final analysis, this led to a cultural situation in which both Indians and Europeans occupied positions that were ambiguous and contradictory rather than rationalizable when it came to civil matters.[1]

The Rebellion of 1857: Fact and Fiction

Broadcast in the feverish atmosphere of Delhi during the great Indian uprising of 1857, the report cited in the epigraph is a poignant case of misrecognition. It concerns Sir Henry Lawrence, a famous veteran of the East India Company's Burmese, Sikh, and Afghan wars who had been appointed Chief Commissioner in Lucknow soon after the annexation of Awadh by the Company in 1856. Lawrence was very much alive and in command of the Company garrison on 31 May, although he did eventually perish on 4 July during the siege of Lucknow.[2] In the report above, the identification of the body conveys more hope than certainty, indexing the sentiment of the Urdu newspaper's anti-British editor.[3] The report also reflects a moment of inversion in India's colonial history, when white rather than brown bodies, and European rather than Indian forms of attire and manners, had become subject to the exercise of power in parts of northern and central India. English men and women trying to survive by pretending to be Indians appear numerous times in reports concerned with the uprising. In later years and decades, this idea would become a trope common to Indian writing on the uprising and British triumphalist fiction penned in the wake of its military failure.[4]

The mutiny of Indians and the vengefulness of the British that followed together constitute perhaps the most thoroughly uncivil episode in Europe's colonial encounter with India. It marks the intensely bloody end of a status quo and the beginning of direct British suzerainty over the subcontinent. The uprising is thus an advantageous chronological fulcrum around which to discuss the issue of civility across Indian-European hyphenations. The uprising caused an eruption of issues long in the making, and it cast an extended shadow on the remaining 90 years of British rule in India. I believe it can be seen as the denouement that exposed the possibilities and contradictions of interaction between the British and their Indian subjects during the colonial period. I am interested in exploring sociohistorical conditions that frame these interactions, particularly those that illuminate political and ethical choices faced by nineteenth-century Indians of a particular social location. Contrary to the viewpoint of most scholarship to date, these choices were concerned more with psychosomatic recognition and rejection rather than simple ideological positioning across the divide separating the colonizer from the colonized. It was, in the end, much easier to adopt ideas of European origin than to rationalize the wearing of European clothes or the eating of European food.

In this paper the argument follows from the observation that, during the nineteenth century, Indians were compelled to address a contradiction regarding Europeans that they could neither accept as rational nor reject as an absurdity. European arguments about their superiority in the colonial context were rooted in an evolutionary paradigm that placed Europeans at the head of the species as *universal* human subjects capable of civilizing others. In direct opposition to this, however, European authority in the colonies was maintained through a highly deliberate cultivation of *particulars* of dress, food, language, and so on, that made the rulers stand apart from the ruled. This placed Indians in an impossible position since European ways of being were, on one hand, defined as civilization, and on the other, unavailable as vehicles for full recognition as equals. Was there any way to resolve this incongruity? What was it about European particularities that endowed them with universality? Could adopting European bodily practices make an Indian civilized in European eyes and be treated with full civility? Was it possible to recover or create Indian particularities that could claim universality and compel civility on the part of Europeans? Buffeted by implications of ideas on one side and the effects of coercive power on the other, Indian navigations aimed at answering these questions symptomize the fact that colonial civility demanded that Indians become 'civilized' while, at the same time, denying them social and political equality concomitant with such civilization.[5]

Nazir Ahmad's *Ibnulvaqt*

In the remainder of this essay, I try to dig further into the fraught nexus between civilization, civility and recognition. My muse for these reflections is a work of historical fiction: Nazir Ahmad's novel *Ibnulvaqt*, which was first published in 1888 and is still in print in both India and Pakistan. Nazir Ahmad is generally regarded as the first novelist in Urdu, writing 'realistic' stories about ordinary life rather than indulging in the fantastical excesses characteristic of earlier prose genres (*dastan* and *qissa*). The novel goes back three decades to the uprising, telling the story of a Delhi Muslim man who adopts English ways after he saves an Englishman from death during the carnage and is rewarded handsomely by the colonial government. The novel is usually read as a didactic tract because of its dry and moralistic tone, although as a whole, it provides no final opinion on whether Indians (particularly Muslims) ought to Europeanize or cultivate a nativist lifestyle. I explore the novel's ambivalence about cultural dilemmas that loomed large in the second half of the nineteenth century. While the language and narrative framing are resolutely anti-fantastic, I suggest that its depiction of unlimited Indian access to the European social and cultural world constitutes a fantasy within the historical context of the late nineteenth century. The fantasy enables a thought experiment aimed at working through the relationships between civilization, civility, and recognition in the colonial context. Over the course of the novel, the idea is dramatized in ever-longer opposing monologues delivered by two protagonists who argue for and against the adoption of European customs. The indecisive and abrupt end affirms the contradictions rather than resolving them.[6]

Nazir Ahmad's novels represent Indian-European encounters in both form and content. Urdu was a new medium for literary expression, rapidly gaining significance in the nineteenth century at the expense of Persian. The author knew English and was self-consciously aware of the European antecedents of the novel as a genre. The story he tells involves close encounters between Indians and Europeans, as seen from the perspectives of such Indians who are acutely conscious of the fact that Europeans occupy a privileged political and cultural position in the world. Consequently, the narrative is not simply a case of Indians and Europeans facing each other. It represents, instead, the predicaments of Indians who were transformed by colonial contact and were trying to make sense of European persons and ideas in the late nineteenth century.

Nazir Ahmad the Novelist

The substantial literature available on Nazir Ahmad (1830–1912) shows that he was quite a character. Honorifics attached to his name connote the spectrum of his affiliations and competencies: 'dipti' for being a deputy collector and a deputy inspector of schools in the colonial administration; 'mawlvi' for coming from a family of Islamic religious professionals and for his specialization in Arabic literature; and 'doctor' for his degrees from Universities. A translator of the Indian penal code from English into Urdu, he was equally known for his fiery oratory at public events, advocating new pathways for Indian Muslims, during the period 1890–1910. While he provided moral and financial support to Sir Syed Ahmad Khan's educational endeavours, he referred to Sir Syed's Quran commentary as a work that attempts to 'knot ears to the buttocks', writing also that it is easier to believe the Quran not to be the word of God than to accept Sir Syed's glosses on the scripture.[7] He boasted to his acquaintances about having arranged his own marriage by charming the daughter of his teacher. A man careful about earning and saving money and charging high interest for informal loans, he nevertheless seems to have bridled at being called a miser. Greatly mindful of the dignity of his attire in public, he is described by a frequent visitor as a sloppy, corpulent old man who lounged around at home draped in a sarong (*tehmad*) unencumbered by any form of knotting at the waist. All in all, then, a competent and energetic man, full of the usual contradictions of human life.[8] Nazir Ahmad's fiction is usually seen to offer solutions for the conflicted cultural situation of the Muslims, this reading being advocated and encouraged in his own non-fictional works, directly as well as by implication. While privileging authorial intention is certainly a fine way to read fiction, I believe the critical assessment of Nazir Ahmad's work to date has not done justice to the internal complexity of his narratives. In this essay, I wish to read Nazir Ahmad's work as a symptom of cultural patterns that are not articulated directly but seem to permeate the form as well as the content of his novels.

Ibnulvaqt gives us a view of Indian and British interaction at a time when separation and intermingling appear to have been seen as both attractive and abhorrent in equal measure. What we see here, I suggest, is an emphatic exemplification of the fact that colonial modernity turned Europeans into self-authenticating universal subjects no matter what their external aspects. This occurred at the same time as Indians became aliens to their pasts, presents, and futures, their identities becoming predicated on European presence or knowledge, irrespective of whether they shunned or assimilated European manners and ideas. The result was civilizational liminality and new, hybrid identities that appeared inauthentic when compared to the pre-colonial past and graceless imitations in front of European manners.

The effects of the new cultural situation are evident in Nazir Ahmad's use of languages in his novels. The Urdu narrative of *Ibnulvaqt* contains interjections in Persian, Arabic, and English. Persian is never translated, suggesting that it is to be taken as wholly readable by the intended audience. Arabic and English are glossed in Urdu, marking their place as universal languages whose status is derived at least in part from their origins outside of India. In other places in his work, Nazir Ahmad advocates the extensive use of Arabic as a counterbalance to the hegemony of English since he sees Muslims' specialness vis-à-vis non-Muslim Indians as being heavily tied to their possession of Arabic.[9] However, in the novel, a major character appears on stage first upon his return from Mecca and has no kind words to say about the Arabs or the Turks. Unlike the situatedness of English in powerful England, the homeland of Arabic is in shambles and the language remains a vehicle for an alternative universality only in theory rather than an achievable reality. The civilizational advantage of Arabic is severely compromised by the fact that those who are deemed its primary possessors seem even worse off than Indian Muslims.

Whatever their internal contradictions, by Nazir Ahmad's time Indian particularities had begun to refashion themselves into universalities in the European image to give rise to competing models of civilization.

In doing so, however, they became beset with the same problems that pertained to European ideas: how was one to claim universality when insisting on maintaining particularities of external forms? If civilization was to be understood as forming a single universal scale, then what was to be done with the corporeal habitus that had compelled civility in the times of one's ancestors?[10]

A Fantasy in Realist Garb

The story provided in *Ibnulvaqt* is straightforward and is usually seen to exemplify the quandary of post-1857 Muslim elites regarding whether to preserve their own heritage (sartorial, linguistic, literary, etc.) or adopt European ways. The novel's central character is named 'Ibnulvaqt', an Arabic term that means 'Son of the Moment'. Initially a hereditary retainer of the Delhi court attached to a royal lady named Ma'shuq Mahal Begum, Ibnulvaqt's life changes drastically when he saves and protects a prominent Englishman, Mr Noble, during the 1857 uprising. Mutual curiosity about political and cultural matters leads Ibnulvaqt and Noble to become involved in lengthy, fully cordial discussions during the latter's three-month refuge with the former. Once British control is re-established, Ibnulvaqt receives a big reward for his loyalty and, under Noble's direction, takes the drastic step of changing his whole mode of life to that of an English gentleman. He is shown to regard his actions as that of a much-needed Indian-Muslim reformer, although this eventually leads to his alienation from his family as well as the English gentry who regard him as an arrogant native upstart. Faced with seemingly insurmountable cultural and financial troubles, Ibnulvaqt is counselled by Hujjatulislam ('Proof of Islam'), the husband of a cousin, who is a deputy collector in the colonial administration but maintains a traditional Indian Muslim lifestyle. He is regarded very well by his European superiors and is able to intercede with them on Ibnulvaqt's behalf in order to lessen his troubles. The sparse plot is fleshed out and propelled forward through the insertion of lengthy descriptive sections and scholastic dialogues on political, epistemological and theological subjects that repeat arguments well known from classical metaphysicians and their modern critics. The novel ends abruptly in the middle of a discussion, without offering a final denouement.[11]

Nazir Ahmad's choice of personal names for his characters was obviously symbolic. For example, Ibnulvaqt's old employer, Ma'shuq (beloved) Mahal Begum, maps to old imperial Delhi and passes away dutifully when the first post-1857 canon shells land in the city. The faithful servant of an Englishman is named Jan Nisar (self-sacrificer). The saved Englishman is named Noble, providing a positive complexion to the fact that he treats Indians as equals and provides Ibnulvaqt access to English society. The man who objects to Ibnulvaqt's adoption of European ways and tries to disenfranchise him is named Mr Sharp. This pattern becomes more complex when we come to the two main characters, Ibnulvaqt and Hujjatulislam, both Islamic religious terms with long histories. Ibnulvaqt is a Sufi concept denoting a person who achieves salvation by escaping the temporal world of generation and corruption and coming to dwell in the eternal present. Hujjatulislam is an honorific applied to religious scholars, most prominently the famous theologian Muhammad al-Ghazzali (d. 1111) among Sunnis, and any number of middle-ranking scholars among Shi'is.[12] Neither of these designations maps to the novel's characters and they are best seen as half-allusions meant to widen their field of associations without direct signification. Aijaz Ahmad offers 'time-server' as an idiomatic translation of Ibnulvaqt into English, although the character is portrayed quite sympathetically and does not seem to fit that distinctly negative connotation.[13] Nazir Ahmad was also accused of caricaturizing Sir Syed Ahmad Khan or his son Syed Mahmud to invent the character of Ibnulvaqt, although he himself denied this explicitly on multiple occasions.[14] To my reading, the most apt translations of the two names seem to be the rather simple 'a man of his time' and 'one who argues for Islam', although Nazir Ahmad can certainly be presumed to have been aware of the baggage the terms carried. Although it has been read nearly universally as a didactic tract, one of the peculiarities of the novel is that it does not offer a single programme for thought or action. Ibnulvaqt and Hujjatulislam are both protagonists, provided with page upon page of justification for and against adopting European dress and habits. They are both entirely sold on European intellect, science and organizational ability, the 'traditional' Hujjatulislam even more so than the Europeanizing Ibnulvaqt. The difference of opinion between the two has to do with attire and mode of living. To reduce the matter to essentials, the ideological impasse at the heart of the novel's plot is thus not whether one should think like the Europeans or believe in what they believe regarding society and politics—they both seem to think well of this prospect—but rather whether one should wear English trousers and eat with cutlery, or wear Indian pants and eat with one's hands.

Nazir Ahmad's fiction is usually described as realist and down to earth, exemplifying the direct and unornamented literary language promoted by institutions such as Delhi College, which Nazir Ahmad attended for a few years before 1857.[15] In the view of many critics, his narratives qualify as novels rather than the old Urdu-Persian genre of *dastan* precisely because they depict realistic human situations rather than fantasy creatures, or humans with superhuman powers performing epic feats.[16] Although all this is certainly true for *Ibnulvaqt*, the story here is quite unrealistic and rather fantastical when seen within its historical context. Its very first two sentences acknowledge that it is an imagined past that, if it ever existed, has long been surpassed: 'If it had been the way things are nowadays no one would have even heard about it. What made Ibnulvaqt so famous was that he chose an English lifestyle at a time when learning English was considered a sign of unbelief and using English goods a form of apostasy.'[17] Moreover, consider the following aspects of the plot: a highly placed colonial official lands at an Indian door in a helpless situation; he happens to speak the vernacular fluently, with full idiomatic control, and is critical of British arrogance and has always had the wish to communicate with a native person regarding the problems faced by Indians; he recognizes his interlocutor as a deeply intelligent and cultured man and urges him to take on the mantle of his community's reformer; he showers his native benefactor with material gifts and utmost moral support on principle, without any consideration of what other Europeans might think; and he sponsors Ibnulvaqt's entrée into British society at a status equal to that of any European. To put it mildly, the likelihood of circumstances arranging themselves in this fashion in post-1857 Delhi were low. The novel is thus best seen as a colonial subject's fantasy of escape from the political and cultural regime facing him. In the novel, the Indian characters have unlimited access to English officials, contrastable with lengthy, somewhat comic scenes in which they are also shown to wait to meet such officials at the expense of their dignity. In one case, Hujjatulislam, who is a deputy collector, explains his general aversion to the society of Englishmen despite his high regard for the English government, by describing the process of going to meet the English collector. While he is a man of considerable status, he must leave his carriage at the gate of the collector's residence to walk a long way to the door, taking care to stop and catch his breath in order not to arrive panting and thus being disqualified from his job on account of not being in good physical shape. Inside the bungalow, there is complete inattention to his presence and he has to be respectful to the servants in order to get news of where the sahib might be. He then remains standing for two hours until given a broken seat, and continues to wait. The sahib is apparently taking a bath, which Hujjatulislam compares to the washing of the corpse on account of how long it seems to go on. He eventually makes it to the sahib's presence but has to stand and wait quietly for him to notice. Some interaction does finally take place between the sahib and a lower functionary, which makes Hujjatulislam wonder about the sahib's capacities given his inability to utter a single sentence of Hindustani correctly after fourteen years of living in India and interacting with locals on a daily basis. The scene ends with Hujjatulislam departing after informing the collector that he had come with no other purpose than to present his regards. In summary, in stark contrast with the novel's fantastic side, barriers of status, language, and race make the breach of the Indian-European divide an abject impossibility. Between the bath, the breakfast, and the inability to learn the language, the Englishman's civilizational imperatives require that he be uncivil to his Indian associates.[18]

The second scene of waiting occurs when Ibnulvaqt goes to meet Mr Noble for the first time after the restoration of British government. Given his part in saving the Englishman's life, he expects to be treated with special consideration. The extent of this turns out to be that he is allowed to wait in an inside room rather than with the multitude of natives milling outside. Noble is delayed while attending to swarms of supplicants at his residence to curry favour or seek redress. Ibnulvaqt is forced to wait a long time while playing around impatiently with the objects and books present in the room.

His interrogations of the native servants do nothing to hurry the process, but when Noble does eventually arrive, he begins, quite against the general custom of the English, with a deep apology for the wait. Noble's eventual civility toward Ibnulvaqt is circumscribed on all sides by the force of colonial circumstances.[19]

The contrast between the way the two waiting scenes end reinforces the nature of the plot. The decent Englishmen within the novel seem to be inordinately full of goodwill toward Indians and regard the trappings of their status as hindrances against a common mission rather than necessary barriers between rulers and ruled.[20] The wishful element implied here is repeated at a later point in the novel as well when Mr Sharp—who turns out to be Ibnulvaqt's nemesis but is well-disposed toward Hujjatulislam and is fluent in the vernacular—immediately admits Hujjatulislam to his presence against his usual habit of not meeting anyone for an hour after his daily evening excursion.[21] Our ability to characterize the novel as a fantasy gradually fades as the narrative progresses. Titillate as it may, access to the English world provides no resolution for the conundrum of whether one should wear English trousers or Indian pants. In a way, the fantasy turns into an interminable purgatory within which the characters remain suspended to the narrative's last word.[22]

The novel's central concern with the multivalent potential of external habitus finds its most salient treatment in the way clothing and food are shown to mediate identity. We read of an Englishman wearing Indian clothes and eating Indian food, and of an Indian doing the opposite. During his period of hiding in Ibnulvaqt's protection, Mr Noble dresses in Indian clothes and is described as being so graceful (*jamah zeb*) that he looks tremendously handsome in them.[23] Similarly, when questioned by people about the culinary arrangements he made for Noble's stay, Ibnulvaqt responds: 'What arrangements were to be made except that the sahib ate what was cooked at home. We did ensure that there were no chilies in his food, and ground salt and black pepper were served in separate containers to him. Among Indian dishes, he particularly relished pulao, kabab, samosa, firni, and other lightly sweet desserts.'[24] The happy times suggested by these comfortable descriptions do not extend to Ibnulvaqt when he decides to undertake the change of habit in reverse. An extended description of his first attempt at eating with utensils at Mr Noble's table shows him unable to aim well towards his mouth, ending up with the following:

Whoever would have seen his face then would have taunted him by saying, 'is that a face or a Diwali cup'. Although he didn't say this, his sudden intakes of breath suggested that he had pricked himself in the lips, gums, or tongue with the fork.... The last foolish and uncouth thing he did was to drink the water in the finger glass.[25]

In later periods, Ibnulvaqt habituates to the new manner of eating, although he claims to refrain from alcohol and keeps wine in his store solely for European guests. The tastelessness of European food is remarked upon a number of times, along with the hint that Ibnulvaqt's palette seems to have craved spices rather more than he was willing to let on.[26]

Along with the food, Ibnulvaqt changes his attire to European clothes of the highest quality and transfers his domicile from inner city Delhi to the more open atmosphere of the English town. The clothes make him uncomfortable and they also make it impossible for him to perform the daily five prayers on account of their stiffness and the amount of time it takes to get in and out of them.[27] Most significantly, no one is fooled by his change of habit to take him as being equal to an Englishman, despite his conscious attempt to promote this idea. In contrast, we recall that Mr Noble's disguise in Indian habit works perfectly, saving his life and going undetected in accord with its intended purpose.

The variant efficacies of the two changes of outer form indicate the way the relationship between the inner and the outer are different for the European and Indian cases. The European subject is shown to be inherently universal on the inside irrespective of what it has on the outside. This manifests itself in the fact that the change of outside circumstances never hints at any possibility that Mr Noble may go native and change permanently. His identity lies many oceans away in England, to which he returns in the long run. Conversely, the lengthy discussions between Ibnulvaqt and Hujjatulislam center on whether Indians must change their outer forms to achieve parity with the English. Whichever way one goes, the external form is essential to Indian identity because it either changes the interior or reflects that which is presumed to be essential about the interior. Indian subjects are thus portrayed as being inherently particular, incapable of occupying the universal position. They have to accept that they are tied to a civilization that is passé, or acquire a new civilization that can never be concordant with their essences.

Towards the very end of the novel, Hujjatulislam is shown to emphasize the particularity of being Muslim by critiquing the likes of Ibnulvaqt in the following words:

They do not understand that when nothing remains to a collectivity of its religion, dress, mode of civilization (*tarz-i tamaddun*), and knowledge, then nothing remains of its group distinction. Whose reform then, and for what these well-wishers? . . . Reform of Muslims will be called reform only when they remain Muslims, meaning they bind themselves to the affect of the religion of their ancestors, and can be recognized as Muslims from afar. It is only after this that their hearts may be tickled toward progress according to the prevailing conditions.[28]

The difference is that Europeans are immune to the pressures faced by Indians. Hujjatulislam's effort to drive a wedge between European culture on one hand and modernity as an impersonal process on the other is a theme quite familiar to us, most prominently in recent years in the vogue for the discourse of multiple modernities.[29] However, it seems to me that the sting remains the same today as in Nazir Ahmad's words published in 1888. The reason for this is not that variant domestications of modernity cannot be documented worldwide. Rather, the difficulty lies in the impossibility of escape from European universality. The real issue then is not simply Ibnulvaqt's effort to refashion his essence by donning European clothes and customs, but that *plus* Mr Noble's ability go undetected as an Indian—and looking damn good at it—while retaining his European essence. The European character has consummate control and can project a stable signified identity as the civilized human subject even when changing outward signifiers at will for purposes of sociopolitical expediency. Indians, in contrast, are either obsolete and frozen in the past (if they cultivate a 'native' aspect) or fakes (if they pretend to be European).

Mr Noble's past, present and future—English as well as Indianized and at whatever point of the narrative we take them—make no difference to the representation of his identity and ideas. Even the grievous harm and consequent immobility he endures during the uprising fail to alter his worldview in the slightest degree. This matter parses quite differently in the cases of Ibnulvaqt and Hujjatulislam. As in all other aspects of the narrative, when it comes to the question of temporality too these two are interlaced characters. The variation between their attires and modes of living in the novel's present time indexes alternate visions of the past, as something that either needs to be overcome, or needs to be perpetuated when looking to the future. The difference is understandable but one wonders about the futility of Nazir Ahmad's investment in the struggle between these characters given that the first sentence of the novel already declares that the battle is over at the time the narrative is being penned. It is here, I think, that Nazir Ahmad's use of the very topic of corporeal affect suggests his appreciation of the fundamental contradictions at work in the context as well as some elements of a politics of subversion.

Civilization and Incivility

Hujjatulislam's insistence that Indian Muslims exemplify their identity through their attire and outward habit is a critical issue that receives no satisfactory justification in the extended dialogues, save the commonsensical claim that not doing so dissolves the boundaries of

Muslims as a collectivity. As presented in Hujjatulislam's words, Ibnulvaqt is deluded in thinking that he can remain a Muslim in essential identity while outwardly behaving like an Englishman. Despite his great regard for the English, he refuses to be seduced by the English claim that Europeans' universal subjectivity is not tied to their outward cultural particularity. In this situation, for him as an Indian, the options are to seek an alternative universality as to be found in Arabic and Islam and resist becoming a native in European garb. By doing so, he insists on different scales for civilization and civility than the one posited as universal by the Europeans. Of the two, resisting assimilation is the more realizable step, one that implies the refusal to meet Europeans on their own grounds, under rules of civility dictated by them. This cannot be done through verbal argument since to enter into a dialogue amounts to acquiescing to a framework that already defeats one's purpose. Subversion seems possible only through an unreasoned, tribalistic insistence on wearing Indian pants rather than English trousers. However, the pants are not a symbol in and of themselves—they become so only because of the steady proliferation of limbs clad in trousers that ones sees around oneself in late nineteenth-century India.

Based on the novel itself as well other evidence from Nazir Ahmad's works, it is fair to say that the author's own sympathies lay with the arguments he presents from Hujjatulislam's mouth. However, the chief reason the novel is a compelling narrative is the fact that Ibnulvaqt's viewpoints are presented with full force of conviction and are not straw figures meant for easy demolition. Hujjatulislam's positions always compel Ibnulvaqt to think further and sharpen his own viewpoint rather than acquiescing with his opponent. Nazir Ahmad's seeming commitment to have both sides represent themselves fully means that an impasse is the only possible conclusion to the novel. The fateful events of 1857 then provide a highly appropriate backdrop to the quandaries of the cultural situation.[30]

The poignant but ultimately indecisive ruminations projected by the novel's characters lead to the seemingly counterintuitive conclusion that, at least under the colonial situation, civilization and civility are processes that strain in opposite directions rather than dovetailing together. If Indian subjects retain or cultivate an Indian form of civilization that varies from European ways, then they are regarded as being on a lower rung of civilization. As in the case of Mr Sharp's treatment of Hujjatulislam, European civility toward the Indian, conforming to the colonial code, is patronizing and directed at one who is regarded as being from an inferior group. But if the Indian subject becomes civilized by adopting European ways, that goes against the colonial arrangement and leads to incivility on the part of Europeans. Mr Sharp's negative attitude toward Ibnulvaqt exemplifies this, and Mr Noble treating Ibnulvaqt civilly is the fantastical exception that proves the rule.

Whether we see it as a set of societal arrangements that has existed over time (European civilization) or as a process applied to an individual or a group (civilization of Europeans), civilization is fundamentally a discriminatory concept. Civilization's ultimate effect is to distinguish between the civilized and the uncivilized, whether in a given moment or over the course of time. Civility, on the other hand, connotes minimalization of distinctions, either momentarily for the sake of orderly social interaction, or in an extended time frame when defining a group's form of general sociability. In Norbert Elias's famous discussion of the evolution of European societies, the two concepts synchronize when civilization is seen as the product of an expansion of incipient forms of civility, in a moment as well as over the course of time. But civilization and civility pull apart in a colonial situation since a power imbalance is the bedrock underneath all interactions between the colonizers and the colonized. Under such circumstances, those who hold power are liable to lose it if they are fully civil to their subordinates and treat them equally. And those whose civilization has come into question are in an impossible position: they can neither assert themselves as civilizationally equal, nor adopt the dominant habitus, which defines civilization, because of structural limitation. The final result in such a situation is a stillborn civilizing process, one whose form is there to be seen but one that cannot be animated into real existence.

Nazir Ahmad's description of the events of 1857 in *Ibnulvaqt* is comprised of two sharply contrasting scenes. On one side he presents the terrible violence, first by the rebels when they take over Delhi and dispose off the British, and then by the British who exercise revenge on the city's population while drawing minimal distinction between rebel and citizen bystander. To be recognized as a punishable enemy in these circumstances is a matter of simplest outward signs of belonging to one side or the other. While mayhem rages outside, Mr Noble sits in Ibnulvaqt's house, protected and cared for by him at considerable risk and in extended debate regarding matters of civilization and progress. In my reading, it is a detail of the greatest significance that the mutual recognition as equals and consequent exemplary civility between Ibnulvaqt and Noble are enacted when both are wearing Indian clothes and eating Indian food. The dramatic inversions of 1857 force the Englishman into Indian refuge, creating circumstances that last only as long as Indians outside the house are able to maintain the upper hand. When European violence returns in the form of revenge as well as the structural conditions of colonialism, Ibnulvaqt and Noble try to recreate their civility, this time in the English town and while dressing and eating like Europeans. This proves to be futile since Ibnulvaqt fails in the effort to be regarded as an equal by Europeans despite his change of habits. But the novel does not show him reverting to his Indian Muslim ways. Suspended between negated pasts and unattainable futures, his character signifies cultural conditions prevalent in the late nineteenth century.

By the time he published *Ibnulvaqt*, Nazir Ahmad was thirty years removed from the severe violence he had witnessed as a young man. These three decades were the most successful period of his life and included climbs up multiple bureaucratic ladders and achievement of considerable renown as a man of letters. These successes indicate a man of his time, well able to manoeuvre expediently in the circumstances that surrounded him. His astuteness as a cultural observer is reflected in the creation of the Indian as well as English characters in *Ibnulvaqt*. Taken together, they bring forth a sociopolitical scene in which the demand for civilization goes hand in hand with the withholding of civility. The novel's equivocal didacticism suggests that, as a realist, Nazir Ahmad well understood this as a fact of the colonial situation. But as a writer of fiction, memory of violent inversions of 1857 seem to have goaded him to fantasize a world in which civilization and civility could be brought into a tandem. Indians changing themselves to match European habits were inconsequential for the possibility of such a world. And this was occurring unaided rapidly in any case, as acknowledged in the novel's first sentence. What was needed were circumstances, such as those that came to exist briefly in 1857, when Europeans were required to seek Indian protection and don Indian clothes.

Notes

1. Margrit Pernau's recent work is also focused on civility, but from a somewhat different perspective than what I am attempting in this essay. Writing in the vein of 'conceptual history' with an impressive empirical range, she maps

out the multiple intellectual and social landscapes occupied by Muslims in Delhi over the course of the nineteenth century. For details, see her *Ashraf into Middle Classes: Muslims in Nineteenth-Century Delhi*, New Delhi: Oxford University Press, 2011.

2. For the circumstances of Sir Henry Lawrence's death see Harold Lee, *Brothers in the Raj: The Lives of John and Henry Lawrence*, Karachi: Oxford University Press, 2002, pp. 333–52. The place of rumour as an essential ingredient in the 1857 uprising is treated in Kim Wagner, *The Great Fear of 1857: Rumours, Conspiracies and the Making of the Indian Uprising*, Oxford: Peter Lang, 2010.

3. For the background and functioning of this periodical see Margrit Pernau, 'The *Dehli Urdu Akhbar* Between Persian Akhbarat and English Newspapers', *The Annual of Urdu Studies* 18, 2003, pp. 105–31. An extensive catalog of Urdu material concerned with the mutiny is available in 'Atiq Siddiqi, *1857: Akhbar awr dastavizen*, Delhi: Maktaba Shahrah, 1966.

4. The use of this trope by a prominent Indian author is the main point of discussion in this essay. For its use in English literature see Gautum Chakravarty, *The Indian Mutiny and the British Imagination*, Cambridge: Cambridge University Press, 2005.

5. The general theme of Europeans and their colonized subjects constructing their identities against each other is the subject of a huge scholarly literature by now. While my discussion in this essay certainly relates to this topic, this is for me a stepping stone to get to the further issue of the connection between recognition and civility as a foundation for thinking about cultural and political subjectivity in the colonial context.

6. *Ibnulvaqt* is available in a good English translation, see Nazir Ahmad, *Son of the Moment*, tr. Mohammed Zakir, New Delhi: Orient Longman, 2002. For Nazir Ahmad's place as a novelist in the history of Urdu literature see C.M. Naim, 'Prize-Winning Adab: A Study of Five Books Written in Response to the Allahabad Government Gazette Notification', in *Moral Conduct and Authority: The Place of Adab in South Asian Islam*, ed. Barbara D. Metcalf, Berkeley: University of California Press, 1984, pp. 290–314; Christina Oesterheld, 'Nazir Ahmad and the Early Urdu Novel: Some Observations', *Annual of Urdu Studies* 16, 2001, pp. 27–42. The most extensive overall study of Nazir Ahmad's life and work is Iftikhar Ahmad Siddiqi, *Mawlvi Nazir Ahmad Dihlavi: Ahval va asar*, Lahore: Majlis-i Taraqqi-yi Adab, 1971.

7. Nazir Ahmad, *Maw'aza-yi hasana*, Lahore: Majlis-i Taraqqi-yi Adab, 1963, pp. 199–200.

8. For the details of Nazir Ahmad's life see Siddiqi, *Mawlvi Nazir Ahmad*. Particularly vivid images of his personal life are provided in Mirza Farhatullah Beg Dihlavi, *Daktar Nazir Ahmad ki kahani, kuchh meri awr kuchh un ki zabani*, ed. Rashid Hasan Khan, New Delhi: Anjuman-i Taraqqi-yi Urdu, 1992, and the collection of letters to his son published under the title *Maw'aza-yi hasana*.

9. Cf. Ahmad, *Maw'aza-yi hasana*, pp. 39–44, 210–14.

10. A full discussion of the question of changing modes of civility among Indian Muslims in the modern period would require engaging the complex of ideas and practices referred to as *adab* in Islamic religio-cultural terminology. Adab's purview ranges between etiquette, rules for proper companionship, and literary genres as well as the social setting for the production of literature. Although adab and civility do have significant overlapping connotations, the concepts' overall semantic ranges cover rather different terrains. I have bracketed the question of adab in the present discussion in order to remain focused on the nexus between the English terms civilization and civility.
11. One interesting aspect of the novel is the absence of a female character of any lasting significance. This is all the more striking because a number of Nazir Ahmad's other novels are focused singularly on Indian Muslim women's education and social roles, see Siddiqi, *Mawlvi Nazir Ahmad*, pp. 312–60.
12. For an early Islamic articulation of 'son of the moment' see Michael Sells, *Early Islamic Mysticism*, Mahwah, New Jersey: Paulist Press, pp. 98–102. For the theological background to the notion of 'proof' and its application to scholars see the article 'Hudjdja' in *Encyclopedia of Islam*, 2nd edn., vol. 3, p. 543.
13. Aijaz Ahmad, *In Theory: Classes, Nations, Literatures*, London: Verso, 1992, p. 116.
14. Siddiqi, *Mawlvi Nazir Ahmad*, pp. 412–13.
15. See Christina Oesterheld, 'Deputy Nazir Ahmad and the Delhi College', in *The Delhi College: Traditional Elites, the Colonial State, and Education before 1857*, ed. Margrit Pernau, New Delhi: Oxford University Press, 2006, pp. 299–324. For the process through which Urdu rose as a colonial language in India, see C.A. Bayly, *Empire and Information: Intelligence Gathering and Social Communication in India, 1780–1870*, Cambridge: Cambridge University Press, 2000, pp. 192–6.
16. See Ralph Russell, 'The Development of the Modern Novel in Urdu', in *The Novel in India: Its Birth and Development*, ed. T.W. Clark, Berkeley: University of California Press, 1970, pp. 117–22.
17. Nazir Ahmad, *Ibnulvaqt*, Lucknow: Uttar Pradesh Urdu Akadami, 1983, p. 1.
18. Ibid., pp. 41–8.
19. Ibid., pp. 30–3.
20. This novel is, of course, a narrative connected to the 1857 uprising as well. Its characterizations contrast interestingly with those of English literature spun from tales of the Mutiny in which the breach between the Indian and European spheres is a problem rather than a positively valued fantasy (see Chakravarty, *Indian Mutiny and the British Imagination*).
21. Ahmad, *Ibnulvaqt*, p. 170.
22. The novel's plot is related to the report that Nazir Ahmad's in-laws saved the life of an Englishwoman during 1857. Ironically, the reward they received

from the British for this loyalty ended up causing dissension in the family itself, see Siddiqi, *Mawlvi Nazir Ahmad*, pp. 14–16.
23. Ahmad, *Ibnulvaqt*, p. 22.
24. Ibid., p. 29.
25. Ibid., pp. 34–5.
26. Ibid., pp. 121, 162.
27. Ibid., pp. 106–9.
28. Ibid., pp. 217–18.
29. For a diverse set of articles on this issue see Shmuel Eisenstadt, *Multiple Modernities*, New Brunscwick, New Jersey: Transaction, 2002.
30. Although Nazir Ahmad's other novels are less ambiguous with respect to their didactic impulse, his instinct as a storyteller seems always to have worked to endow multidimensionality to both positive and negative characters. For example, his *Tawbat al-nusuh* (1874) dramatizes a thoroughgoing condemnation of a culture marred by poetry that had come to be seen as decadent. The dandified young man who is the ultimate embodiment of the intended condemnation is also the novel's most complex character and is made to argue his objections to his moralizing father with great vigour. For a detailed discussion of the cultural issues at stake in this novel see Frances Pritchett, *Nets of Awareness: Urdu Poetry and Its Critics*, Berkeley: University of California Press, 1994.

4

Obeying God, Obeying Men

The Feminist Discourse of Dr Farhat Hashmi

A. AZFAR MOIN

'Mumph, mumph, mumph, mumph . . .', she goes on and on and on, her words and breath echoing and rebounding against her own fully clad frontal, making her sound like Darth Vader's fast talking baby sister. May the force be with her. . . . And the joke is on us.

– Instep Comment, *The News International*

THIS SATIRICAL COMMENT, published anonymously in January 2004 in the Sunday entertainment section of a leading English newspaper in Pakistan, was about Farhat Hashmi's new television show. A self-styled religious leader and educator of Muslim women, Hashmi had become a regular presence on a private Urdu-language channel broadcast via satellite from Dubai into Pakistan. The reviewer's biting sarcasm revealed the deep despair felt in certain Pakistani circles at the popularity of Hashmi's religious message among affluent Pakistani women. She had started an organization, Al-Huda International, in 1994 after returning from the University of Glasgow with a doctorate in Islamic studies. Al-Huda ran popular courses for women to learn the Quran, Quranic Arabic and various other religious disciplines. It also organized a growing network of formal and informal lecture meetings (*dars*) arranged at expensive hotels and members' houses in the affluent suburbs of Islamabad, Lahore and Karachi. In addition, Hashmi had a daily one-hour slot on one of the few FM radio channels in urban Pakistan.[1] By 2003, Al-Huda had become a noticeable enough social phenomenon to merit a BBC online article,[2] 'Pakistan Women Socialites Embrace Islam', which highlighted the class affiliation of Hashmi's primary audience and emphasized Al-Huda's popularity. 'About 1,200 women signed up for Dr Hashmi's year-long course on Koranic translation in Karachi last year. . . . Such was the scholar's renown that the last session, open to the public, drew almost 10,000 women from all over the city.' My interviews with booksellers in Islamabad and Rawalpindi at the time also suggested that sales of religious books for women went up in the urban areas where Al-Huda was active.[3]

This essay examines the 'feminist' discourse of Farhat Hashmi in historical and contemporary contexts. First, I summarize contents of a recorded audio lecture, given in Urdu in 2003 by Hashmi, entitled 'The Key to a Successful Family Life', in which she declares herself a feminist. Then I consider how 'Islam' functions as a component of identity for middle and upper-class Pakistani women and how it gets deployed at the interconnection of state and society, that is, of law and custom. Finally, I provide a comparative analysis of Hashmi's message regarding the cultural position of women with other discourses available to her primary Pakistani audience, ranging from feminist versions of Islamic modernism to the secular liberalism propagated by women active in the public sphere since Pakistan's creation in 1947.

Most of Farhat Hashmi's lectures in 2003 and 2004 are structured as commentaries or explications of certain Quranic verses and so begin with the Arabic recitation and literal Urdu translation of these verses. This is followed by one to three hours of commentary, analysis, moralizing, and polemic. Her tone is mostly balanced and comforting but at times alternates between being patronizing, imploring, and mildly aggressive. Based on her comments and the few instances of audience participation during the lectures, it is likely that these are live recordings of Hashmi addressing a female audience.

Summary of Hashmi's Lecture: 'The Key to a Successful Family Life'

In 2004 there were sixty-one Urdu lectures available from Al-Huda's public website in downloadable form.[4] The lecture studied in this paper, 'The Key to a Successful Family Life'[5] (*azdavaji zindagi main kamyabi ka raz*) consists of commentary on a set of Quranic verses that have been the centre of much debate. These verses relate to the status of woman in the home with respect to the husband and outline rules of conduct for men and women in family relations. Defining women as wives, this lecture makes a larger statement on the role of women in society.

In the rest of this section, I translate and paraphrase Hashmi's lecture. I provide the Urdu text (using a simplified Arabic transliteration scheme) where appropriate and put Hashmi's use of English words in quotes. Hashmi begins by reciting the following Quranic verse and its translation:[6]

Men are the protectors and the maintainers of women, because Allah has made one of them to excel the other, and because they spend (to support them) from their means. Therefore the righteous women are devoutly obedient (to Allah and to their husbands), and guard in the husband's absence what Allah orders them to guard (e.g., their chastity and their husband's property). As to those women on whose part you see ill-conduct, admonish them (first), (next) refuse to share their beds (and last) beat them (lightly, if it is useful); but if they return to obedience, seek not against them means (of annoyance). Surely, Allah is Ever Most High, Most Great.[7]

[Hashmi:] This particular verse often makes women angry (*naraz*) because it implies that their status is not equal to that of men. However, instead of being angry, women should realize that by making men protectors and maintainers of women, God has delivered (*nijat*) women from the responsibility of providing for their families. Instead, the duty of protecting and maintaining the world of the home (*ghar ki dunya*) which is akin to a mini-state has been put on the shoulders of men. This should not be a reason for anger, but rather for joy and thankfulness.

God has made woman the queen of the home (*ghar ki malika*) so she does not have the double duty of earning and producing children. He has not made both men and women equally responsible for maintaining the family for that would be unjust (*zulm*): one country cannot have two prime-ministers; a bus cannot have two drivers; a boat cannot have two navigators. Men have this duty because they have an advantage (*mard ki fazilat*) over women in terms of mental and physical abilities. Women are at a natural disadvantage with respect to men because of bodily differences. They have to deal with the burden of menstruation, pregnancy, and other female bodily functions which prevent them from being equal to men in performing the duty of maintaining the family.

Whenever people have tried to go against this natural organization, it has resulted in women being more suppressed. Even the West is now beginning to realize its errors in trying to equalize the roles of women and men in society. In this regard, an Urdu newspaper, *Nawa-i-Waqt*, on 12 June 1998, reported on a Protestant organization in the United States of America that has more than fifteen million members, including Bill Clinton.[8] This organization had announced its support for separate roles for men and women in the family with an unambiguous acceptance of the dominance (*fawqiyyat*) of men. Among other things the organization stated that a woman should accept her husband's leadership (*sarbarahi*) just like the Church bows down before Christ. Another American journal, *Span*, in July 1989 revealed that women's status in America is not equal that of men; women get paid less than men; women cannot become president; and they must turn to the state in order to obtain protection (*tahaffuz*). One American female commentator has observed that now the state must provide protection to the Western woman because she has rejected man as her maintainer and protector (*qawwam*). Furthermore, in a recent book entitled *What's a Smart Woman like You Doing at Home?* Linda Burton makes a similar argument about the separation of roles for women and men in maintaining and caring for the family which is essentially: 'Man, the bread earner; woman, the character builder'. She relates her own experience of trying to raise two children while having a career and how she came to the conclusion that her appropriate role was to be at home with her children to be their mother.[9]

God has been so kind (*mehrban*) that he has given us [women] rights. The husband has a determined role in the family and it is his responsibility to care for the wife. When women are told to be 'confident, independent and *aham* (important)', it is a deception (*jhansa*). This is due to the absence of piety (*taqwa ki 'adam mawjudgi*) in society. A husband is your servant (*khadim*). A people's leader is also their servant. Satan had said that he would strive to change nature (*fitrat main tabdili payda karun ga*) so that people are never content with their condition. Trying to change the natural role of men and women is such a case. Have the man sit at home and you go out into the world and earn and see what will happen.

A man goes out into the world and suffers hardship to earn a living and feed his family. He makes a sacrifice. In return it is expected that his wife will be obedient to him and see to his needs. One such need is his sexual satisfaction. He is entitled to it even if the wife is not in the 'mood'. If a wife obliges her husband's wishes in this matter against her mood (mood *ke khilaf ja kar*) then she will not only be obeying him but she will also be obeying God (*allah ki ita'at*). There is a tradition of the prophet which states that if a man calls his wife to bed and she does not go to him then angels curse (*la'nat*) her until morning. This is related in al-Bokhari's *Kitab al-Nikah* (Book of Marriage). Another prophetic tradition, associated with Abu Hurayrah, states that if a woman's husband is present then she cannot keep an optional fast (*nafali roza*) without his permission.[10] Obedience to one's husband is 'cooperation' which a woman should happily adhere to. If a man is 'satisfied' then he will do his work diligently.

The concept of 'equality' has caused a lot of damage to homes. Man is man and woman is woman. They are different. The construction (*sakht*) of their 'tissues' and 'cells' is different. How can they be equals? A woman's role requires submissiveness. She must obey her husband. A man's role as a husband requires that he gives 'moral coaching' to his wife. If the wife does not obey him he must first try to convince her softly (*narmi kare*). If that does not work, he should display his displeasure by ignoring her (*be rukhi dikhae*). But if soft measures do not work then he has to be harsh; for, when medicine and injections do not work then surgery must be resorted to. This is a point where women are tortured (*tarhapti hain*) by the expression 'to hit' (*marne ke lafz se*), especially when it is read out in the Urdu translation. However did the Prophet of God ever hit a woman in his life? He did not lift a finger on any woman. It has not been encouraged.

Moreover, there are rules which must be followed. First, a wife cannot be hit on the face. She cannot be hit in such as way that leaves a mark on her body. The idea is more to frighten her than anything else (*danda dikhane vali bat hay*). One scholar of the Quran, Ibn Abbas, recommended not using anything more than a toothbrush (*miswak*) because the goal is to achieve a type of mental reform (*nafsiyati islah*). A man who has suffered injustice (*mazlum hua hay*) because his wife was rude or unfaithful has to have a 'catharsis' as well. Beating her is the last resort to save the home and family. Even here, divorce has not been recommended. There is a prophetic tradition that no one should beat his wife like he beats his slave. Once the Prophet even forbade the hitting of wives but it resulted in women becoming too bold and so the permission to hit them was given back to men. But even then it was said that those among you who are good (*ache*) will not hit their wives. The cause for women being beaten in the West is that when a woman starts to fight back (*marne par a jati hay*), she is the one who has to face the harsh consequences because, obviously, a man is more powerful than a woman and in a physical confrontation she is bound to be the loser.

It is important to understand that there is a difference between what is permitted, when the permission should be used and the ways in which it should be used. There are circumstances which must be met, rules which must be followed and parameters which should be adhered to. God has promised women the ultimate protection because it is said that He will take revenge from the husband who is cruel and unjust to his wife.

At the end of the lecture, Hashmi says that she learns a lot from interacting with women because it allows her to relate her explanation of the Quran to ordinary everyday experience. She gives the example of an 'awkward' case about a woman who had told her that she did not get 'satisfaction' until her husband hit her. She seems to imply that this anonymous woman's confession about enjoying her husband's beatings adds to her argument that, in the relation between husband and wife, the man is meant to be—as nature intended—the hitter and the woman the one to be hit.

Identity and Authority

In the introduction to his work, *Islam: The View from the Edge*, Richard W. Bulliet asserts that the 'eleventh century is as, if not more, important for understanding the origin of today's political and social forces than the nineteenth'.[11] Bulliet's goal is to expose the forgotten cultural processes that shaped the identity of medieval Muslims. These processes, Bulliet argues, are still at work in modern Muslim societies wherever there is an 'edge', that is, a social space—not a geographic or political one—where Muslim identity is in the process of taking shape:

The edge in Islamic history exists wherever people make the decision to cross a social boundary and join the Muslim community, either through religious conversion, or, under modern conditions, through nominal Muslims rededicating themselves to Islam as the touchstone of their social identity, or recasting their Muslim identities in a modern urban context.[12]

The quest for a stable identity can be a powerful force for both material and cultural change. As an example of the former, Bulliet shows that early Muslim converts in medieval Khurasan, who were non-Arab, migrated to the cities in order to learn more about their religion and this led to a rapid urbanization of eastern Iranian society.[13] More importantly, through such a quest in the early centuries, ordinary Khurasani Muslims shaped the institutions of Sunni Islam and their society by selecting, and re-selecting, the sources of authority to settle questions of identity. In this way the early Muslim laity played a central role in conferring authority on different social groups, elevating one group while demoting another. Bulliet argues that similar processes, driven by a quest for a stable social identity, are at work again in today's post-colonial Muslim societies.

'For me being a Muslim seems to be exceedingly difficult,'[14] says Riffat Hassan, in apparent agreement with Bulliet's thesis about the dislocated nature of post-colonial Muslim identity. A Pakistani-born academic and women's rights activist who taught Islamic Studies at the University of Louisville in Kentucky, Hassan writes in an essay on Islam and human rights in Pakistan that her difficulty lies in knowing precisely what it means to be a Muslim. Like Hashmi, Hassan is also a self-professed Muslim feminist. She is a scholar of Islam who has spent much of her professional life interpreting the Quran and re-evaluating the early religious traditions in order to arrive at a liberal and feminist reading of them. To overcome the epistemological obstacles of being Muslim in the modern age, she turns to two prominent thinkers of modern Islam in South Asia, Syed Ahmad Khan and Muhammad Iqbal.[15] To her, these intellectuals point towards a rational reinterpretation of Islam by individual Muslims:

> To me being a Muslim means carrying forward the message of the Muslim modernists who have raised the cry 'Back to the Qur'an' (which, in effect, also means 'Forward with the Qur'an') and insisted on the importance of 'Ijtihad'—both at the collective level (in the form of 'Ijma') and at the individual level—as a means of freeing Muslim thought from the dead weight of outmoded traditionalism.[16]

She goes on to explain that this means to not look towards the Quran as if it were an encyclopedia of religious knowledge or as a legal code but rather to view it as an ethical framework that provides guidance:

> It is vitally important for present-day Muslims to realize that they will receive the guidance they seek from the Qur'an not by looking for selected verses on specific subjects but by understanding its ethical framework consisting of universal principles which form the core of Islam.[17]

These universal principles, according to her, are those of 'human equality and the need to do justice to all of God's creatures'.

Hassan calls for a public debate between her and two other Pakistani women intellectuals: Farhat Hashmi and Asma Jahangir, a lawyer and leading human rights activist in Pakistan. Viewing her own position between that of Hashmi's religious revivalism and Asma Jahangir's secular liberalism, she laments that in Pakistan 'the discourse on Islam has been hijacked by "religious extremists" and the discourse on human rights has been hijacked by "anti-religious extremists"'.[18] She may well be right in that these three stances on religion are representative of the ones available to those educated Pakistani women who have questions about themselves and their status in the world.

Hassan's position conforms to the movement of Islamic modernism in British India. Her intellectual models, Syed Ahmad Khan and Mohammad Iqbal, are in fact the two most important thinkers for Indian Muslim, and now mostly Pakistani, nationalism. Their ideas provided the foundation on which the Indian Muslim nationalist elite attempted to erect a new identity. Islamic modernism was meant to provide a version of Islam compatible with the 'enlightened' notions of rationality and human equality. Accordingly, Hassan's critique of Hashmi is two fold: first, while Hashmi publicly claims to be a liberal, modern and feminist interpreter of Islam, her actual position, as it comes out in her teachings on Islam, does not match any of these categories; second, Hashmi's message to women does not include any reference to social justice or human rights.[19] Her criticism has had some effect: there is a lecture available now on 'Human Rights' (*Huquq al-'Ibad*), and 'Al-Huda International Institute of Islamic Education for Women' has been, quite recently, renamed 'Al-Huda International Welfare Foundation'.

However, as Hashmi alluded to in the BBC Online interview, the call to Islamic modernism or Muslim nationalism does not seem to attract the same crowd of educated Pakistani women as Hashmi's lectures (*dars*). The reason for this does not lie in Hashmi and Hassan's methodology. After all, both of them uphold scriptural Islam as the primary source of authority and appeal to reason in their arguments—Hashmi, as evidenced by her lecture, uses numerous references to science and social science studies done in the West. Rather, it is in the form of their arguments where the crucial difference lies. Hashmi's discourse exudes a confidence that invites Pakistani women to understand Islam via a literal reading of the Quran and her easy-to-understand explanations in Urdu and English. Indeed, she claims to have an answer, based on the Quran, for almost any question that most well-to-do Pakistani women may have. One can almost hear the question to which some of her 2004 audio lectures seem to be responding:

Can good Muslims celebrate April Fool's Day?
Lecture: April Fool.

Is it alright for Muslims to celebrate Valentines Day?
Lecture: How to Express Love, Sacrifice or Valentine?

Does Islam permit photography?
Lecture: Islam and Photography

April Fool's Day, Valentine's Day, photography. These are all pastimes of the affluent and bear little relevance to any of the major social issues confronting most women in Pakistan. However, these questions pertain to how prosperous Pakistani Muslim women should *be* in their daily lives. And Hashmi treats these themes at great length in her lectures, all of which start with the explication of a set of Quranic verses. Many of her answers are not to everyone's liking or convenience. In fact, as one can see in the lecture summarized above, she often alludes to women who become angry and tortured at some of her proclamations: do not celebrate April Fool's day, do not celebrate Valentine's day, do not take needless photographs; but rather, cover yourself, obey your husband, be submissive even if he beats you. But her instructions are firm, not too distant from her audience's lived reality, and seemingly derived straight from a literal reading of the Quran.

In contrast, Hassan professes an epistemological crisis with regards to being a Muslim. The Quran, for her, provides a framework of universal principles; but to construct from these the details of a modern Islamic orthodoxy and orthopraxy requires a deep intellectual commitment on the part of every Muslim, not to mention a lot of hard work. In other words, her approach towards understanding religion provides a guideline for asking questions rather than answering them; it does not resolve questions of identity, but conversely it affirms the crises of identity. To most affluent Pakistani women, living in the present and not particularly mindful of history, such an approach understandably seems less sure of itself—and less authoritative—than that of Hashmi.

But what about the third option available to educated Pakistani women, the alternative of secular liberal feminism as espoused by the human rights lawyer, Asma Jahangir? Riffat's main issue with this standpoint is its 'anti-religious extremism', and more specifically, its assertion that '"Islam" and "human rights" are mutually exclusive'.[20] Riffat attacks the Human Rights Commission of Pakistan, headed by Jahangir, as a Western-funded agency which cannot claim to represent 'the people of Pakistan who are near-universally "believers" and regard Islam as the matrix in which their lives are rooted'.[21] Putting the question of representation aside, the Islamic belief and identity of many elite Pakistani women certainly precludes Asma Jahangir from being selected as source of cultural authority. Nonetheless, her position, out of the three discussed, seems to be the one informed by the history of the evolution of Pakistani laws and customs regarding women.[22] Needless to say, this history is less than uplifting.[23]

Identity and Control

Since Pakistan's founding in 1947, time and again, the call for Islam has served both as a legitimizing strut for faltering governments and as a façade for local patriarchal customs and traditions.[24] In either case, unfortunately, women and their bodies have served as the ground on which power was negotiated. In order to understand how this occurred, it is worth paying attention to what this label hides rather than what it explicitly signifies; that is, how religion's role in identity formation enables it to be used in social control.[25] This is not to take away from the various normative doctrines of Islam that have taken firm historical shape but rather to investigate how the trope of 'Islam' gets deployed in the current Pakistani context.

As Gail Minault has shown, the cultural defensiveness of the Muslim elite in India deepened with the rise of British rule; elite Muslim men closely guarded their social practices governing women and most efforts at women's education and social reform were conducted within protected cultural boundaries.[26] Even though some upper-class women like Shaista Ikramullah[27] were able to gain social ground via the Muslim nationalist movement, the political use of religion at the time of the independence movement—voting for the Muslim League was termed a 'religious' duty—bequeathed a troublesome legacy for Pakistani secularists and women. After independence in 1947, the early governments, faced with calls for implementing the rule of Islam, simply followed a policy of non-action and allowed custom to prevail with regard to women in the broadly conservative Pakistani society.[28] This process has also been termed a 're-tribalization of society' where sub-state bonds of community became stronger than national bonds and custom prevailed over law.[29] Under the guise of upholding religious values, accommodations were reached between a weak state lacking legitimacy and a powerful patriarchal society defending its traditional customs.

In 1961, General Ayub Khan's Muslim Family Law Ordinance (MFLO) gave some legal advantages to women. Asma Jahangir traces the birth of this ordinance to the controversy over the second marriage of Prime Minister Mohammad Ali Bogra in 1953. Bogra's first wife had opposed his second marriage publicly. The embarrassed Prime Minister appointed a commission to look into the Islamic principles regarding the issue. The commission on the one hand claimed that 'so far as the basic principles and fundamental attitudes are concerned, Islam's teaching is comprehensive and all embracing',[30] but on the other hand stated,

> As nobody can comprehend the infinite variety of human relations for all occasions and for all epochs, the Prophet of Islam left a very large sphere free for legislative enactments and judicial decisions even for his contemporaries who had the Holy Qur'an and the Sunnah before their eyes.[31]

The commission's conservative recommendations were implemented, much later, only by decree of the secular minded Ayub Khan. The MFLO's main accomplishments were to override a few customs regarding marriage by providing some legal protection to women and children, and by erecting a handful of bureaucratic hurdles for men.[32] Even though the ordinance's effectiveness in granting rights to women was severely limited, it became and continues to be controversial as its opponents deem it to be against Islam.

After Ayub, Prime Minister Zulfiqar Ali Bhutto's populism offered little more than rhetoric in terms of women's rights. It was strongly opposed by a rising Islamic revivalism. In 1979, this broad feeling was tapped and exploited by General Zia who claimed to hold a 'direct brief from Allah'.[33] Zia legitimized his rule by declaring himself the champion of Islamization. So-called Islamic laws were defined and applied in two areas—criminal and personal law—both of which turned out to be extremely oppressive for Pakistani women. Under the Hudood (*hudud*) ordinances promulgated by Zia, women could be accused as rapists, rape victims could be convicted as adulteresses, and adultery became a crime against the state. The result was that the number of women in prison increased exponentially. Moreover, the state sanctioned a new manner of open violence against women; the Qisas and Diyat Ordinance which allowed for blood money to be paid as penalty for murder provided a legal umbrella for the honour killings of women. In addition, a woman's testimony as witness was declared unequal to that of a Muslim man. Jahangir, who as an activist lawyer opposed these measures publicly, sums up her views on the matter:

> Women's groups should not accept laws based on religion—whether they be family laws or Islamic criminal laws. It is now a foregone conclusion that a true liberal interpretation of Islam will never be widely accepted. On the other hand, the half hearted liberalisation of Islam will be more detrimental for women. Laws which violate the rights of women must be repealed. Those which give women no rights must be reformed.[34]

During Zia's rule there was not only an intensification of the politics of difference but also an escalation in conservative attitudes to the female body. Women's dress had always been a marker of national and religious identity, but under Zia, women were told how to dress: the *sari* was termed a Hindu dress and discouraged.[35]

In the 1980s, the religious establishment rose to political prominence by collaborating with Zia's military government. The government, in turn, was buoyed with arms and money from the US and Saudi Arabia against the Soviet occupation of Afghanistan. With Saudi aid, both formal and informal, came the conservative Wahhabi creed. The government used it to shape the official ideology and the country's laws as it was compatible with the version of Islam upheld by its political ally, the hitherto electorally insignificant Jamaat-i-Islami. Women were not completely absent from this process. Some, like Jahangir and the members of Women's Action Forum (WAF) opposed it. Others, often either members of the Jamaat-i-Islami or relatives of men in power, supported it. For example, in the parliamentary debate in 1983 on the Draft Laws of Evidence Bill that was going to depreciate the legal value of a woman's witness, eleven female legislators fought against the resolution while two actively defended it.[36] Moreover, women from religious political parties were active in opposing women's participation in athletics, and in lobbying for separate but equal universities for women. Even after the military dictator's demise in 1989, his legacy continued to shape the workings of the Pakistani state and society. It is in this context that Farhat Hashmi's discourse needs to be analysed.

Although presented with the aid of Microsoft PowerPoint, and broadcast via satellite television and FM radio (a relatively new phenomenon in Pakistan in 2004), the content of Hashmi's message was not very original. It matched quite closely the authoritarian commandments about women emanating from the Permanent Council for Scientific Research and Legal Opinions (CRLO) based in Saudi Arabia. This establishment represents the Wahhabi school of thought, termed by Khaled Abou El Fadl as the 'predominate school in contemporary Islam'. These Saudi CRLO opinions can be found in Pakistani bookstores under the English title, *Islamic Fatawa Regarding Women*.[37] In terms of legal and scriptural interpretation, the legal scholar Abou El Fadl offers a devastating critique of these injunctions. His central criticism of this type of discourse is that rather than attempting to speak in God's name, the speaker claims to speak for God; that is, instead of being authoritative, he or she becomes authoritarian.[38]

The first aspect that links together the Saudi CRLO discourse on women with that of Farhat Hashmi is the ahistorical and problematic use of religious sources to construct a religious or legal opinion. For example, as Abou El Fadl shows, many of the hadith traditions that seem derogatory towards women, and often cited in Saudi CRLO injunctions, can be traced to the transmitter Abu Hurayrah. A controversial figure of early Islamic history, his credibility has been under scrutiny since the earliest days of hadith sciences. Traditions related to him were considered 'weak' by a majority of Muslim jurisprudence scholars in the classical age. Aisha, the Prophet's wife, for instance is said to have reacted to a tradition circulated by Abu Hurayrah, in which he put women in the same category as animals, by saying, 'God confound you! You have made women the same as dogs and donkeys!'[39] It is noteworthy that Hashmi also states a prophetic tradition related by Abu Hurayrah regarding the sexual duties of a Muslim wife to her husband.[40] She does not provide the transmitter for the second tradition she states, but this one is also prominent in the official Wahhabi injunctions regarding a wife's duty to obey her husband.[41] What this amounts to is, in fact, an erasure of history regarding the gender negotiations and 'the contested territory of the role of woman in general, and wives in particular' in the early Islamic period.[42]

Another parallel between Hashmi's message and that of the Saudi CRLO is that both present a monolithic West questioning its liberal assumptions about gender. Hashmi cites a Protestant organization in America, a recent book by an American woman, and social science studies all of which supposedly show that Western science and Western women are widely questioning the value of gender equality. Similarly, the CRLO jurists say:

Considering that some people benefit more from the discourses of Eastern and Western scholars than from the words of God, the words of His Messenger (S), and the words of Muslim scholars, it is vital that we cite for them what Eastern and Western scholars admit about the harms and costs of loose interaction.[43]

They then go on to produce a variety of quotes against equality between men and women from Shopenhauer, Lord Byron, Samuel Smiles, 'one of the members of the United States Congress', and so on.

Finally, the most interesting harmony between the two discourses is the absence of women as positive role models. This is a marked shift from historical and contemporary efforts at reforming Muslim women in South Asia and around the world. A majority of the religious books for women in Pakistani bookstores in 2003 were in fact about women. There are numerous Urdu titles like, 'The Women of Islamic History' (*Tarikh-i Islam ki Khawatin*), 'The Mothers of the Believers' (*Ummahat al-Mu'minin*), 'Pure Wives: Lives and Services' (*Azwaj-i Mutaharrat: Hayat wa Khidmat*), 'The Life of Aisha' (*Sirat-i 'A'isha*), 'The Life of Khadija' (*Sirat-i Tayyiba Khadija al-Kubra*), 'The Life of Fatima' (*Sirat-i Fatima al-Zuhra*). A focus on the lives of the early Muslim women as models is evident in popular pre-independence Urdu works like *Bahishti Zewar*, aimed at 'perfecting' Muslim women in India.[44] Literary and historiographical references to Prophet's wives and daughters as women to be emulated is, indeed, found in the earliest Muslim sources.[45] However, in none of her lectures, pamphlets, or articles that I have read did Hashmi use the life of an early Muslim woman as a role model.[46] This absence is also conspicuous in the Saudi CRLO proclamations about women.

Conclusion

The BBC article on Hashmi's organization cited earlier in this paper is inconclusive as to why the sudden interest in Islam among the affluent women of urban Pakistan. The suggested causes range from 'curiosity and the academic approach' offered in interpreting Islam at these lectures to the phenomenon being little more than a social fad that attracts wealthy and jaded Pakistani women tired of 'coffee parties and sleeveless blouses'. Farhat Hashmi, however, gives a measured response to this question:

> I have never asked women why they come to hear me. . . . The expectations of Pakistanis have not been fulfilled in our 50-odd years of independence. . . . There is a feeling of betrayal and despair. Even political Islam has not been able to address people's grievances.[47]

Perhaps there is some validity in these observations. Religion, in combination with other markers of identity such as ethnicity, class, and gender, plays a key role in the self-definition of many Pakistani women.[48] Additionally, Pakistan's history of colonialism has bequeathed it with a legacy of dislocated socio-economic and cultural systems.[49] Often, the impotence and dysfunctional nature of the state tends to be interpreted by many citizens in cultural terms.[50] This implies a widespread belief that access to a certain 'authentic' source of culture has been lost and its recovery would lead to cultural and social stability. Thus many Pakistanis are drawn to religion as a source for rethinking and reaffirming their identity.

Moreover, for many urban Pakistani women, religious rituals often provide a space for women to meet, socialize, and get around the social barriers to mobility which they encounter in their daily lives.[51] These women's view of religion in terms of their private lives and individual experiences is often a positive one: most of them lack doctrinal understanding of Islam and are unaware or uncritical of how religion is used in the public space to construct laws and customs that perpetuate a hierarchy of gender.[52] In this way, a large segment of the Pakistani female society plays a central role in the rituals of reproducing their patriarchal society. By seeking to define themselves as good Muslims, they select scholars of religion like Farhat Hashmi as the authority to settle questions of identity; but, in doing so they give up the opportunity to be critical of their society's customs and laws that are perpetuated under the label of religion.

Imposing authoritarianism on Muslim women in South Asia, however, has not always been successful. In the fourteenth century, Ibn Batutah, the famous traveller who was also a learned religious scholar much interested in women (he married 23 times and had 70 offspring), left behind some insightful and amusing pre-modern reminders of this fact. On his 75,000-mile tour of the world, he also visited the western coast of India. He describes the women of a town there:

> The women in this town and in other towns of the coast do not wear stitched clothes but rather use an unstitched piece of cloth for their clothing. On one side they tie it on the waist and the other side they throw it across their heads and chests. These women are very beautiful and pious. They wear a golden ring in their nose. One of their distinctions is that they know the entire Quran by heart. In this town I saw thirteen madrasas for girls and twenty three madrasas for boys which I did not see in other towns.[53]

Both the learning and the beauty of the *sari*-wearing Muslim women of the Indian coast caught his eye as a traveller. Later in the Maldives, where he was appointed judge, he attempted to bring orthodoxy to the place. This included efforts, much like General Zia's attempts half a millennium later, to get women to wear clothes that met his standards of modesty. He boasted about his success in reforming many things—regular prayers in the mosques, proper divorce proceedings—but, unlike

Zia, Ibn Batutah admitted his failure in attempting to reform women's dress: 'And I also tried hard to force the women to put on [proper] clothes, but in this matter I did not find success.'[54]

Notes

1. A detailed study of Farhat Hashmi's organization based on ethnographic fieldwork conducted in 2003 and 2004, which is the time when the audio lectures studied in this essay also appeared on al-Huda's website, is in Sadaf Ahmad, *Transforming Faith: The Story of Al-Huda and Islamic Revivalism among Urban Pakistani Women*, Syracuse, NY: Syracuse University Press, 2009. A shorter and more recent overview is in Sadaf Ahmad, 'Al-Huda and Women's Religious Authority in Urban Pakistan', *The Muslim World*, vol. 103, no. 3, 2013. In 2005, Farhat Hashmi moved to Canada and set up her organization in Mississauga. See Khanum Shaikh, 'New Expressions of Religiosity: A Transnational Study of Al-Huda International' (Unpublished Doctoral Dissertation, University of California, Los Angeles, 2009).
2. Sahar Ali, 'Pakistan Women Socialites Embrace Islam', *BBC News*, http://news.bbc.co.uk/go/pr/fr/-/2/hi/south_asia/3211131.stm (accessed 31 March 2004).
3. This is based on informal interviews of booksellers in the Rawalpindi-Islamabad area in the summer of 2003. At least one book seller on his own suggested Al-Huda as a cause for a heightened interest in religious material for women.
4. 'Al-Huda International: Assorted Lectures', Al-Huda International, http://www.alhudapk.com/audio-video/assorted/, accessed 31 March 2004.
5. The English title of this lecture is Farhat Hashmi's translation. The lecture was available in recorded form from both Al-Huda's website as well as an audio tape that can be purchased from the organization. Farhat Hashmi, 'The Key to a Successful Family Life', Al-Huda International, http://www.alhudapk.com/audio-video/assorted/success-key/success.asp, accessed 31 March 2004.
6. This is not meant to be a transcription of the lecture. Rather, it paraphrases the key points of her argument and presents them in the order stated. When she makes the same points several times, I only give one or two examples. English words in quotes in this section imply that Hashmi uses these words in her lecture in English.
7. From surat al-nisa, with translation at: 'The Key to a Successful Family Life', Al-Huda International, http://www.alhudapk.com/audio-video/assorted/success-key/success.asp, accessed 31 March 2003.
8. Farhat Hashmi does not mention this American Protestant organization by name, but it is probably the Southern Baptist Church, given the reference to Bill Clinton who was raised a Southern Baptist.

9. Hashmi also gives examples from studies done in Russia which I have not outlined here for the sake of brevity. However, the point is that she gives examples from two nations representing the modern 'West'.
10. The implication being that she has to first ask him if he desires sex because once the wife starts her fast, sexual relations are forbidden from sunrise to sunset.
11. Richard W. Bulliet, *Islam: The View from the Edge*, New York: Columbia University Press, 1993, p. 12.
12. Ibid., p. 9.
13. Bulliet argues that in trying to find rare pockets of Arab Muslims who could explain the new religion of Islam, and in trying to escape the social ostracism of largely non-Muslim rural populations, the new Muslims began to converge in large numbers upon towns to live with their co-religionists. He supports his argument by showing a correlation between the rise in conversion and the rise in urbanization in Iran.
14. Riffat Hassan, 'Islam and Human Rights in Pakistan: A Critical Analysis of the Positions of Three Contemporary Women', http://www.webb-international.org/download/word/articles_riffat/ISLAM_AND_HUMAN_IN_PAKISTAN.doc, accessed 31 March 2004.
15. Ibid., p. 4.
16. Ibid., p. 5.
17. Ibid., p. 9.
18. Ibid., p. 29.
19. It is interesting to note that Hassan's indictment of Hashmi's religious message is based less on scriptural grounds and more on the notion that it does not meet the liberal ideals of Western modernity.
20. Hassan, 'Islam and Human Rights in Pakistan'.
21. Ibid., p. 28.
22. See Asma Jahangir, 'The Origins of the MFLO: Reflections for Activism', in *Shaping Women's Lives: Laws, Practices and Strategies in Pakistan*, ed. Farida Shaheed et al., Lahore: Shirkat Gah, Women's Resource Centre, 1998.
23. This history is detailed, from the perspective of women's rights activists, in Khawar Mumtaz and Farida Shaheed, *Women of Pakistan: Two Steps Forward, One Step Back?*, London; Atlantic Highlands, NJ: Zed Books, 1987.
24. Ayesha Jalal, 'The Convenience of Subservience: Women and the State of Pakistan', in *Women, Islam, and the State*, ed. Deniz Kandiyoti, Philadelphia: Temple University Press, 1991, p. 85.
25. Farida Shaheed, 'Constructing Identities: Culture, Women's Agency and the Muslim World', *International Social Science Journal*, vol. 51, no. 159, 1999, p. 66.
26. For a detailed treatment of this topic, see Gail Minault, *Secluded Scholars: Women's Education and Muslim Social Reform in Colonial India*, Delhi; New York: Oxford University Press, 1998.
27. Active in the pre-independence Muslim League, Shaista Ikramullah was one of the first Muslim women to make speeches from behind the *purdah* to male

audiences. Later, after 1947, for newly created Pakistan, she helped define the constitution, spoke at the United Nations and served as ambassador to Morocco. See her autobiography, Shaista Suhrawardy Ikramullah, *From Purdah to Parliament*, Rev. and exp. ed., Karachi: Oxford University Press, 1998.
28. Jalal, 'The Convenience of Subservience', p. 86.
29. 'In Pakistan, this continued fragmentation is perhaps best exemplified by the parallel systems of law and governance that continue to flourish, while, on the ground, the operational law is rarely that of the state, particularly in family and gender matters.' Farida Shaheed, 'The Other Side of the Discourse: Women's Experiences of Identity, Religion and Activism in Pakistan', in *Appropriating Gender: Women's Activism and Politicized Religion in South Asia*, ed. Patricia Jeffery and Amrita Basu, New York: Routledge, 1998, p. 144.
30. Jahangir, 'The Origins of the MFLO', p. 97.
31. From the Rashid Commission's report quoted in ibid., p. 98.
32. For example, it required marriage registration, enabled children to inherit from grandparents, and made the wife's permission mandatory for polygyny. Ibid.
33. Jalal, 'The Convenience of Subservience', p. 100.
34. Jahangir, 'The Origins of the MFLO', p. 103.
35. Shahnaz Rouse, 'The Outsider(s) Within: Sovereignty and Citizenship in Pakistan', in *Appropriating Gender: Women's Activism and Politicized Religion in South Asia*, ed. Patricia Jeffery and Amrita Basu, New York: Routledge, 1998, p. 58.
36. Khawar Mumtaz, 'Political Participation: Women in National Legislatures in Pakistan', in *Shaping Women's Wives: Laws, Practices and Strategies in Pakistan*, ed. Farida Shaheed et al., Lahore: Shirkat Gah, Women's Resource Centre, 1998, pp. 346–7.
37. Jamaal al-Din M. Zarabozo, tr., *Islamic Fatawa Regarding Women: Shari'ah Rulings Given by the Grand Mufti of Saudi Arabia Sheikh Ibn Baz, Sheikh Ibn Uthaimin, Sheikh Ibn Jibreen and Others on Matters Pertaining to Women*, ed. Muhammad bin Abd al-Aziz Al-Musnad (Riyadh: Darussalam Publishers & Distributors, 1996).
38. In this regard he says, 'In fact, the values of the interpreter are equated, completely, to the values of the Principal. There is a perfect unity between the will of the interpreter, and the Will of the Principal—whatever the interpreter feels, thinks, desires, or values is imputed to the Principal.' Khaled Abou El Fadl, *Speaking in God's Name: Islamic Law, Authority, and Women*, Oxford: Oneworld Publications, 2001, p. 200.
39. Quoted in ibid., p. 226.
40. See note 7 (this chapter).
41. Fadl, *Speaking in God's Name*, p. 282.
42. Ibid., p. 232.
43. Quoted in ibid., p. 294.

44. For a review of the literature which included women, both historical and fictional, as role models for Muslim women's reform and education in India see chapters one and two in Minault, *Secluded Scholar*, pp. 14–104. See also Ashraf 'Ali Thanvi, *Perfecting Women: Maulana Ashraf Ali Thanawi's Bihishti Zewar: A Partial Translation with Commentary*, tr. Barbara Daly Metcalf, Berkeley: University of California Press, 1990.
45. For an analysis of how the biographical images of Aisha (the Prophet's wife), Khadija (the Prophet's wife) and Fatima (the Prophet's daughter) developed in the early sources see the chapter entitled 'The Politics of Praise: 'Aisha and the Development of Islamic Female Ideals' in Denise A. Spellberg, *Politics, Gender, and the Islamic Past: The Legacy of 'Aisha bint Abi Bakr*, New York: Columbia University Press, 1994.
46. Al-Huda lectures were available on Ali (Fatima's husband and son-in-law of the Prophet) and Abu Bakr (Aisha's father and the father-in-law of the Prophet) but not on Fatima and Aisha. 'Al-Huda International: Assorted Lectures'.
47. Ali, 'Pakistan Women Socialites Embrace Islam'.
48. For a look at how women's identities are constructed in Pakistan and other Muslim countries, see Shaheed, 'Constructing Identities'. And also Shaheed, 'The Other Side of the Discourse'.
49. Shaheed, 'Constructing Identities', p. 63.
50. Shahnaz Rouse, 'Feminist Representations: Interrogating Religious Difference', *Gender & History*, vol. 10, no. 3, 1998, p. 550.
51. Shaheed, 'Constructing Identities'.
52. Jalal, 'The Convenience of Subservience', p. 77. Shaheed, 'Constructing Identities', p. 153.
53. My translation, 'Abd al-Hadi Tazi, ed., *Rihlat Ibn Batutah al-Musammah Tuhfat al-Nuzzar fi Ghara'ib al-Amsar wa-'Aja'ib al-Asfar/Ta'lif Shams al-Din Abi 'Abd Allah Muhammad ibn 'Abd Allah al-Lawati al-Tanji*, 5 vols., vol. 4, Al-Rabat, al-Mamlakah al-Maghribiyah: Akadimiyat al-Mamlakah al-Maghribiyah, 1997, p. 33.
54. My translation, ibid., p. 74.

References

'Al-Huda International: Assorted Lectures', Al-Huda International, http://www.alhudapk.com/audio-video/assorted/, accessed 31 March 2004.
'The Key to a Successful Family Life', Al-Huda International, http://www.alhudapk.com/audio-video/assorted/success-key/success.asp, accessed 31 March 2003.
'Instep Comment', *The News International*, http://www.jang.com.pk/thenews/jan2004-weekly/nos-18-01-2004/instep.htm#9, accessed 31 March 2004.
Ahmad, Sadaf, *Transforming Faith: The Story of Al-Huda and Islamic Revivalism among Urban Pakistani Women*, Syracuse, NY: Syracuse University Press, 2009.

Ahmad, Sadaf, 'Al-Huda and Women's Religious Authority in Urban Pakistan', *The Muslim World*, vol. 103, no. 3, 2013, pp. 363–74.

Ali, Sahar, 'Pakistan Women Socialites Embrace Islam', *BBC News*, http://news.bbc.co.uk/go/pr/fr/-/2/hi/south_asia/3211131.stm, accessed 31 March 2004.

Bulliet, Richard W., *Islam: The View from the Edge*, New York: Columbia University Press, 1993.

Fadl, Khaled Abou El, *Speaking in God's Name: Islamic Law, Authority, and Women*, Oxford: Oneworld Publications, 2001.

Hashmi, Farhat, 'The Key to a Successful Family Life', Al-Huda International, http://www.alhudapk.com/audio-video/assorted/success-key/success.asp, accessed 31 March 2004.

Hassan, Riffat, 'Islam and Human Rights in Pakistan: A Critical Analysis of the Positions of Three Contemporary Women', http://www.webb-international.org/download/word/articles_riffat/ISLAM_AND_HUMAN_IN_PAKISTAN.doc, accessed 31 March 2004.

Ikramullah, Shaista Suhrawardy, *From Purdah to Parliament*, Karachi: Oxford University Press, 1998.

Jahangir, Asma, 'The Origins of the MFLO: Reflections for Activism', in *Shaping Women's Lives: Laws, Practices and Strategies in Pakistan*, ed. Farida Shaheed, Sohail Akbar Warraich, Cassandra Balchin and Aisha Gazdar, Lahore: Shirkat Gah, Women's Resource Centre, 1998, pp. 93–106.

Jalal, Ayesha, 'The Convenience of Subservience: Women and the State of Pakistan', in *Women, Islam, and the State*, ed. Deniz Kandiyoti, Philadelphia: Temple University Press, 1991, pp. 77–114.

Minault, Gail, *Secluded Scholars: Women's Education and Muslim Social Reform in Colonial India*, Delhi; New York: Oxford University Press, 1998.

Mumtaz, Khawar, 'Political Participation: Women in National Legislatures in Pakistan', in *Shaping Women's Wives: Laws, Practices and Strategies in Pakistan*, ed. Farida Shaheed, Sohail Akbar Warraich, Cassandra Balchin and Aisha Gazdar, Lahore: Shirkat Gah, Women's Resource Centre, 1998, pp. 93–106.

Mumtaz, Khawar and Farida Shaheed, *Women of Pakistan: Two Steps Forward, One Step Back?*, London; Atlantic Highlands, NJ: Zed Books, 1987.

Rouse, Shahnaz, 'Feminist Representations: Interrogating Religious Difference', *Gender & History*, vol. 10, no. 3, 1998, pp. 549–52.

———, 'The Outsider(s) Within: Sovereignty and Citizenship in Pakistan', in *Appropriating Gender: Women's Activism and Politicized Religion in South Asia*, ed. Patricia Jeffery and Amrita Basu, New York: Routledge, 1998, pp. 53–70.

Shaheed, Farida, 'The Other Side of the Discourse: Women's Experiences of Identity, Religion and Activism in Pakistan', in *Appropriating Gender: Women's Activism and Politicized Religion in South Asia*, ed. Patricia Jeffery and Amrita Basu, New York: Routledge, 1998, pp. 143–64.

———, 'Constructing Identities: Culture, Women's Agency and the Muslim World', *International Social Science Journal*, vol. 51, no. 159, 1999, pp. 61–73.

Shaikh, Khanum, 'New Expressions of Religiosity: A Transnational Study of Al-Huda International', Unpublished Doctoral Dissertation, University of California, Los Angeles, 2009.
Spellberg, Denise A., *Politics, Gender, and the Islamic Past: The Legacy of 'Aisha bint Abi Bakr*, New York: Columbia University Press, 1994.
Tazi, 'Abd al-Hadi, ed., *Rihlat Ibn Batutah al-Musammah Tuhfat al-Nuzzar fi Ghara'ib al-Amsar wa-'Aja'ib al-Asfar / Ta'lif Shams al-Din Abi 'Abd Allah Muhammad ibn 'Abd Allah al-Lawati al-Tanji*, vol. 4, Al-Rabat, al-Mamlakah al-Maghribiyah: Akadimiyat al-Mamlakah al-Maghribiyah, 1997.
Thanvi, Ashraf 'Ali, *Perfecting Women: Maulana Ashraf Ali Thanawi's Bihishti Zewar: A Partial Translation with Commentary*, tr. Barbara Daly Metcalf, Berkeley: University of California Press, 1990.
Zarabozo, Jamaal al-Din M., tr., *Islamic Fatawa Regarding Women: Shari'ah Rulings Given by the Grand Mufti of Saudi Arabia Sheikh Ibn Baz, Sheikh Ibn Uthaimin, Sheikh Ibn Jibreen and Others on Matters Pertaining to Women*, ed. Muhammad bin Abd al-Aziz Al-Musnad, Riyadh: Darussalam Publishers & Distributors, 1996.

5
Syed Ahmad's Problems with Women

DAVID LELYVELD

SOMETIME CLOSE TO the end of his long life, Syed Ahmad Khan (Sir Syed) was visited in Aligarh by Syed Mumtaz Ali, a close disciple and protégé from Lahore, who wanted to show him the manuscript of *Huqūq-i Niswān*, the book he had written on women's rights. Syed Ahmad started to examine the text, 'but as he leafed through [the pages] his face turned red and his hands began to tremble. Finally, he tore up the manuscript and threw it into the wastepaper basket'. Gail Minault's vivid account of this incident goes on to tell us how Mumtaz Ali managed to retrieve the manuscript but to delay its publication until after Syed Ahmad's death in 1898.

The question I consider here is why Syed Ahmad was so upset. Why, with all his radical ideas for reform—shoes in the mosque, chickens slaughtered by wringing their necks—and his admiration for European ideas and ways of life, did he oppose the granting of full equality to women? My purpose here is not to judge, justify, or condemn Syed Ahmad, but to understand him and through him to document some of the tensions, contradictions and transitions that his attitude to women's issues represents. As with many issues that he addressed in his life, Syed Ahmad went through shifting ideas and goals: abandoning, for example his commitment to Urdu as the preferred language of instruction, his agenda for scientific advancement, his call for Indian representation in the colonial government, and his demand for educational autonomy free of British supervision. These changes in his ideas speak to the changing world he lived in and the balancing of competing goals. As a staunch defender of *parda* and opponent of women's education—that is, institutional education outside the home, and access to the curriculum of such schools—Syed Ahmad was hardly the man of 'modern' or enlightened ideas that we usually take him for. I think it would be a mistake to blame him, as has been done, for the low levels of female literacy in present-day Pakistan, for example;[1] all we can say is that he did not take a leadership role in this matter, not that things would have been different if he had. The issue isn't a personal one, but Syed Ahmad articulated the dominant male ideology of much of India of his times—if not the present—among Hindus as well as Muslims. (Women of the Nehru family, for example, were in parda till the early years of the twentieth century.)[2]

What so upset Syed Ahmad, based on his brief perusal, was that Mumtaz Ali's book called into question the standard reasons, both religious and practical, for confining women to a limited set of household roles and the raising of children. Written in what one might have thought to be the style and spirit of his mentor's extensive and often radical calls for social and cultural reform, *Huqūq-i Niswān* is grounded in a Syed Ahmad-like exegesis of Islamic scriptural and scholastic literature, and retains assumptions of social status and gender separation that hardly can be called a full-throated cry for equality.[3] If Rammohun Roy's defence of Hindu women many decades earlier has been found wanting by critics like Sumit Sarkar and Lata Mani for its alleged failures to break with religious orthodoxy, Mumtaz Ali was considerably more conservative.[4] Far bolder are the writings of the Egyptian reformer Qasim Amin, a contemporary of Mumtaz Ali and a more enduring influence in the Islamic world, though he too has been found wanting by more recent Muslim feminists like Leila Ahmed.[5]

One characteristic of almost all the sources for the study of the lives and status of north Indian Muslim women in the late nineteenth century is that they are to be found in the writings of men. Gail Minault has given a rich account of what men had to say about women, speaking for women and sometimes even attempting to depict women's voices. Following Minault's lead, the much exploited writings of Nazir Ahmad, Altaf Hussain Hali, Abdul Halīm Sharar, and Mirza Mohammad Hadi Ruswa have so far dominated research into the lives of women in the Urdu cultural milieu.[6] What Margrit Pernau says of Delhi applies more generally: 'there is hardly a single woman . . ., whose name is known, let alone her biography and the circumstances of her life.'[7] A notable exception is Nawab Shah Jahan Begum (1838–1901), the so-called Begam of Bhopal.[8] One might go farther afield to Bengal and the English language, but the extraordinary Rokeya Sakhawat Hossain is probably too distant and too exceptional to be relevant to the social milieu of Muslims in north India and the development of women's literary self-expression in Urdu.[9] From a more subaltern perspective, there is the case, found in court records, of a Muslim woman who ran a butcher's shop in Bombay, though that too is far afield.[10] Gail Minault's work, however, shows that the stage was set in the early twentieth century, however modestly, for women's educational institutions and a public sphere of Urdu print.[11]

Alongside and following Gail Minault's pioneering work in women's history, there has been much significant scholarship on the history of women, gender, and family in British colonial India, the Muslim world and the capitalist transformations of a Euro-American dominated world. Partha Chatterjee has warned against using the Euro-American example of changing bourgeois ideologies and institution as 'modular', and one can say the same thing about relying too heavily on the experience of the Bengali Hindu middle class to understand how the so-called 'women's question' played out in other regions and social groups. Nevertheless one can learn much from comparative and connected histories for the questions they raise and the sources they suggest. Chatterjee's argument was that late nineteenth-century Bengali Hindu nationalists, mostly men but also some women, marked off a private, feminine realm of cultural preservation in the face of the colonial challenge of male public sphere. He notes that even within Bengal, the experience of Muslims was different.[12] Tanika Sarkar extended and elaborated Chatterjee's discussion by examining how gender relations responded to the practical challenges, social and economic, of a changing, colonially dominated, society.[13] More recent scholarship deals with the interventions of colonial law with respect to marriage and family life.[14]

Returning then to Syed Ahmad and male discourse about women, one must realize its limited purchase on the wider society and the diverse sources that have yet to be explored with respect to the conditions of women. Nevertheless, Syed Ahmad's long life and his intellectual prominence serve to make his ideas about the roles and rights of women, including his ambivalences and inconsistencies, matters that have had to be reckoned with, if only as a point of departure for further research on the history of gender and family. How his leadership and the institutions he established may have reached beyond a limited stratum of Indian society or have been relevant to a larger population of Muslims and Hindus within or beyond northern India (whether they played a role in promoting or inhibiting social change), have become familiar topics in the literature on reform.[15] For now, I will review Syed Ahmad's public statements relevant to women and women's education and consider whether they were motivated by the pragmatic concerns of a public leader with other priorities and contradictory ideological commitments. I also want to consider the emotional roots of his furious outburst in response to Mumtaz Ali's manuscript.

Images and Ideas about Women before 1857

The span of Syed Ahmad's life, 1817–98, traces what scholars have identified as a period of substantial change in women's roles and conditions as well as ideas among men about what they should be, including an imposition of silence and invisibility that appears to become more pronounced in the later nineteenth century. The turning point as represented in the historiography is the Great Rebellion of 1857 and with it, the final erasure of the Mughal court as a symbol of authority. The earliest expression that I know of Syed Ahmad's opposition to women's education and women's rights can be found in the famous pamphlet he wrote in the wake of the 1857 Rebellion, originally titled *Asbāb-i sarkashi-i Hindustān kā jawāb mazmūn* (An Essay on the Causes of the Indian Revolt). Written to reconcile what he took to be mutual misunderstandings on the part of the British rulers and the wider Indian public, the work in fact enunciates a remarkably outspoken critique of British policies and even more British attitudes to their Indian subjects. One source of discontent was the British effort to see to it (in Fran Pritchett's translation) that 'girls should come to the schools, and obtain education, and become unveiled [*be-parda*]—which was utterly unacceptable to the Hindustanis'. Furthermore, women, 'even married women', were granted autonomy—*khud mukhtari*—in the courts; 'the guardianship [*vilāyat*] of the guardians over women was removed'. Even if the courts ruled that women who had run away from their husband's household had to be returned, this was rarely enforced.[16]

One can detect a few earlier expressions of Syed Ahmad's ideas about women in his most important early publication, *Āsār us-sanādid,* which dates back ten years before the Rebellion. This description of the buildings of Delhi includes respectful mention of mosques and gardens endowed by women. It also gives brief notice to women entertainers and saints among the notable personalities of the city. In his account of the Qutb Minar site he describes an encounter with a group of young, pretty girls at the iron pillar who were trying to wrap their arms around it to determine their marriage prospects. In describing the Qutb and its surroundings, the author says that the decorations carved on the stone were like the tresses of a thousand beloveds—and that the loose stones were like the teeth of an old hag.[17] These images suggest the ghazal world of love, desire, and the beloved's enticements, a world also represented in the extensive quotations of poetry in the last section of the book. We know from Hali's account of Syed Ahmad's youth that he was no stranger to this 'lively and colourful' (*zinda dil aur rangīn*) world. His uncle introduced him to gatherings of song and dance, and late in life he recalled with apparent pleasure the singing of Janna, famous for her *dhrupad* and *khayāl*, and the beautiful dancer Shirin Jan. He maintained such interests after he was married and posted to Agra. This is the world that Syed Ahmad grew up in with its bifurcation of the inner world of the household and the outer world of pleasure.[18]

But Syed Ahmad's reflections on his early life, including his moving account of his mother, may best be saved until we reach his late years, for it is only then that they became matters for nostalgic recollection. According to Faisal Devji, the Muslim reform movement associated with Syed Ahmad was characterized by the 'gendering' of the past. 'On the one hand, such a past had to be experienced and enjoyed by compelling women to speak out from within it. And on the other, this tradition had to be given up for modernity by forcing women to remain silent about it.' This 'dual gendering' he says, 'produces its own form of pleasure as nostalgia, . . . and even makes possible the ambivalent "preservation" of a rejected tradition.'[19]

Such a 'tradition' with respect to gender and family loomed large in Syed Ahmad's formation: the so-called Nasirean ethics of the thirteenth-century Persian scholar Nasir al-din Tusi. Muzaffar Alam and Rosalind O'Hanlon have examined the *Akhlāq-i Tūsī*, as elaborated by Abu'l Faz'l, and its abiding role in the ideological integration of the Mughal ruling class.[20] The 'household' or the 'management of the household'—*tadbīr-i manzal*—was nothing less than model of and model for society in general, for the whole imperial realm. In Wickens's English translation this comes out as 'Economics' since it is concerned with the accumulation and expenditure of wealth and property.[21] One part of this section is entitled, 'Concerning the chastisement and regulation of wives'. 'The purpose for taking a wife should be twofold, the preservation of property and the quest of progeny; it should not be at the instigation of appetites or for any other purpose.' Tusi warns against 'excessive' love for the wife. As O'Hanlon points out, these ideas are reflected in the opening of Abu'l Faz'l's *A'in-i Akbarī*, which starts with the *manzal*, the household, and speaks of the relationship of Emperor Akbar to the people of the realm as both father and husband.

The Nasirean tradition is reiterated in Shah Wali Ullah's *Hujjāt Allāh-i Bāligha*, a work of considerable importance to Syed Ahmad. According to this text:

the need for sexual intercourse necessitated relationship and companionship between man and woman, then affection for the children required their cooperation in raising them, and by nature the woman is the one ... more guided to bring up the children and the less intellectual of the two, the one less able to bear hardships and more totally modest and attached to the home.[22]

Later in 1870, Syed Ahmad was to adapt the terminology associated with the Nasirean tradition by naming his journal, *Tahzīb al-Akhlāq* (Refinement of Conduct).

After 1857: Conflicting Influences and Priorities

In the 1860s, as part of his efforts to adapt to and reconcile with British rule, Syed Ahmad took some interest in the dominant liberal ideology of his time. One of the books translated by the Scientific Society was John Stuart Mill's *Political Economy*, which put forth a very different concept of society from the gendered hierarchy of Nasir al-din Tusi. According to Mill, 'the feudal family, the last historical form of patriarchal life, has long perished, and the unit of society is not now the family or the clan, composed of all the reputed descendants of a common ancestor, but the individual or at most a pair of individuals.'[23] A major theme in Syed Ahmad's ideological project was to find commonalities between the Islamic intellectual tradition and contemporary European rationalist universalism. If this comes out as what Faisal Devji has called 'apologetic modernity', 'attempts to enter into conversation with someone speaking a different language',[24] it is only fair to note the ambivalences, contradictions, and conflicts that characterized social thought within

Britain itself. Mill was about as close as a male British liberal got to a concept of gender equality, at least with reference to British society, and very much on the outer fringe of his times. As for India, Mill's practical experience and historical relativism served to modulate and constrain the extension of radical reformism in the face of Indian resistance, particularly the 1857 Rebellion.[25]

Whatever Syed Ahmad's initial attraction to thinkers like Mill may have been, he was probably closer to Mill's intellectual adversaries, Henry Sumner Maine and James Fitzjames Stephen, successively legal members of the viceregal council and close associates of Syed Ahmad's mentor, John Strachey. Maine's *Ancient Law*, published in 1861 on the eve of his departure for India, famously developed the concept that societies progressed from status to contract, that is from collective identity based on kinship ties to voluntary agreements among individuals. But for India, especially as he came to know it over the following years, the role of the British legal regime was to assure stability by fixing it in its traditional institutions based on collective and ascribed identities.[26] Syed Ahmad may have faced linguistic obstacles in navigating the cross-currents of British controversy, but Maine and the rest were equally constrained by their own intellectual limitations and by the exigencies of practical experience. As Bernard Cohn wrote in an early essay, 'Failure to understand the nature of Indian society, assumptions based on British practice, mistakes and short-term practical considerations, rather than the unfolding of a social law or the implementation of a well thought through grand design on the part of the British rulers, lay behind the movement in Indian society of "status to contract".'[27]

For Syed Ahmad as well, intellectual explorations with respect to British social thought and Islamic intellectual traditions accompanied a life of practical experience among family and friends, as a judge in the British service, and after 1857 as a public leader dedicated to establishing new institutions starting with the Scientific Society in 1864 and its journal, the *Aligarh Institute Gazette*, in 1866.[28] Iftikhar Alam Khan has recently shown that Syed Ahmad was impressed by the status of British women, their independence, and independence, even before he went to England in 1869. The Aligarh collector's daughter, for example, won Syed Ahmad's praise for her role in supervising the design and planting of the Scientific Society's garden that was commemorated years later with a fountain and inscription on the site.[29] A number of articles appeared in the *Aligarh Institute Gazette* on the subject of women's rights, though at least one of them, reprinted from another source, insisted that women's education should not violate the rules of parda.³⁰ It is noteworthy that this is the only article that refers specifically to Muslim women.

In 1869, when Syed Ahmad travelled to England with his two sons, a young cousin and a servant, he reports in dispatches to the *Aligarh Institute Gazette* many direct encounters and conversations with women. In Bombay, he is impressed with the establishment of schools for Parsi girls, though he is sceptical about the trouble they take to learn English. Crossing the Mediterranean, he is delighted to encounter a Muslim woman from Kanpur, who has had a long and adventurous career as an ayah for British children. 'She was no less a wonder than the Suez Canal.' When questioned by a British fellow passenger, Syed Ahmad enthusiastically affirmed that the ayah and he belonged to the same *qaum* (community) and the same *mazhab* (religion).³¹

It was crossing the Indian Ocean that he became acquainted with Mary Carpenter, who was returning from one of her many trips to India on behalf of women's education. With the help of his son and young cousin, he discussed her work and responded to her request to write a comment in a book she kept for this purpose. Avril Powell has discovered and reproduced this document from the Bristol Record Office. Syed Ahmad is full of praise for Carpenter's brave and high-minded efforts to promote *tahzīb ul-akhlāq* for women, men's helpers, but expresses some doubt about the likelihood of her success. Well-intentioned efforts sometimes fail when they go against the habits and customs of the people they want to benefit and indeed against 'nature' (he uses the English word). It is like the biblical story of Joshua stopping the sun from setting: of course the sun doesn't really revolve around the earth, but people believed it did, so God indulged them by using the common understandings of the times.³² The discussion pertains to 'Hindustani' women, not specifically Muslims.

Arriving in France and then England, Syed Ahmad continues to be impressed with the intelligence and achievements of women: a Paris shop girl selling gloves, the servants attached to his lodgings in London, a woman who manages the Clifton Observatory. He was presented to Queen Victoria and was duly deferential. But it is only in England that the focus shifts to the condition of Muslim women and the need to respond to the disparagement of Islam by Christian evangelicals, notably his benefactor, Sir William Muir, Lieutenant-Governor of the North-Western Provinces. Far from the intellectual milieu of Maine or

Stephen, let alone Mill, Muir stands as a full-fledged orientalist, deeply learned in Arabic texts and unwilling to recognize variation and historical development from their essential authority.[33] His numerous writings, published in Urdu as well as English, particularly his two volumes *Life of Mohammed*, published in 1858 and four volumes in 1861—and many times since—were a challenge that came to occupy the major share of Syed Ahmad's time in England and stimulated his future work as religious thinker, educator, and public leader.

Soon after Syed Ahmad arrived in England, he threw himself into an urgent effort to respond to Muir, rushing into print in English at significant personal expense in what he hoped would be a persuasive refutation. The title page of his book, *A Series of Essays on the Life of Mohammad: And Subjects Subsidiary Thereto*, states, 'The original English of these Essays has been revised and corrected by a friend', and much of the text is lengthy quotations from an odd assortment of English writers from Milton and Gibbon to much less famous and reputable contemporaries. The preface states that he is wholly ignorant of English. An Urdu version of this text was not published for another seventeen years.[34]

Polygamy, divorce, and slavery, Muir had argued, were inherent flaws in Islam. Syed Ahmad's text offers in response a 'calm and candid investigation' of these matters. Polygamy, for example, is not actually promoted by Islam; it is allowed in response to special circumstances when a wife is unable to give birth to a child. He notes that it had been practised by both Jews and Christians, and the rules of Islam constrain the practice, particularly in contrast to the customs of pre-Islamic Arabia. Divorce is sometimes preferable to an unhappy marriage; much of the argument is then taken up by a lengthy quote from John Milton's *The Doctrine and Discipline of Divorce Restored to the Good of Both Sexes*. Slavery, which is condoned by the Bible but practised until very recently in the United States, was practised in early Islam only under special circumstances, such as war. Whatever slavery still exists in contemporary Muslim societies is against the basic principles of Islam.[35]

Scattered between this blur of lengthy and undigested quotations, one can discover some statements that capture Syed Ahmad's ideas about the condition of women. Social roles and emotions, he declares, are matters of changing historical, environmental and cultural variability, but an overarching principle is that woman are created to 'help' man, 'to increase his happiness and diminish his afflictions by her tender sympathy'. It is woman's natural duty to 'contribute, with himself, to carry out that all-important command "Increase and multiply, and replenish the earth"'. Islam responded to this imperative by regulating and constraining 'the brutal appetites of the male sex' that characterized pre-Islamic Arabia.[36]

So much for apologetic modernity. On his return to India, Syed Ahmad took offence at an article on women's rights that appeared in both the *Aligarh Institute Gazette* and the newly founded *Tahzīb ul-Akhlāq*. Claiming a belief in the equality of women and men, he pointed out, quite correctly, that British law, though newly and very partially reformed a year earlier during his visit to England, allowed far fewer rights to women than did Islamic law with respect to property and independent action. Paradoxically, he conceded, the condition of women in the more advanced (*tarbiyat yāfta*) countries was actually better than in Muslim ones. The solution to the poor conditions under which Muslim women lived in India, however, was not to end parda, which he affirmed was appropriate at least for Indian conditions. Nor would it be correct to blame Islam as such, but rather to cultivate adherence to what he claimed were the more enlightened rules of conduct that Islam proclaims.[37]

Sir Syed's major project at the time and for the rest of his life was the establishment of the M.A.O. College at Aligarh. And one of his chief purposes from the outset was to remove boys and young men from the influence of women and the household. 'Unless boys are kept at a distance from home . . . they will always remain ignorant, worthless and exposed to all sorts of evils.'[38] In 1876, Syed Ahmad published a highly negative article in the *Aligarh Institute Gazette* on the condition of Indian women, accusing them of attachment to old customs, superstition, and other irrational actions and beliefs and practices.[39] These shortcomings are a result, he says, of the confinement of women from childhood on, like birds in a cage, such that they have no real experience of the world. And yet, he doesn't propose to release them from this confinement. Oddly much of the article consists of an extended quotation from an unidentified source, a woman from a 'civilized' (*shāy'ista*) country, who turns out to be Hannah Catherine Mullins, a well-known Christian missionary from the pre-1857 era. The book he quotes, *Phulmani and Karuna*, first published in Bengali in 1852 but possibly originally in English, depicts Bengali women recently converted to Christianity, not the contemporary 'Hindustani' women referred to in Syed Ahmad's article and not Muslims. It is sometimes said to be the first Bengali novel. Syed Ahmad was no doubt relying on an Urdu translation, which may have omitted the Bengali connection.[40]

Syed Ahmad, of course, was not the only Indian caught between admiration for modern European civilization and a strong wish to maintain cultural autonomy. Citing the authority of a European woman did not mean that he wanted Indian women to emulate them—or for Indian men to marry them.[41]

In 1882, Syed Ahmad testified to the Hunter Education Commission against schools for women. Stating that women in his own family were in fact well-educated in Arabic and Persian and wrote Urdu poetry, he said that the general level of education had declined. Nevertheless, the colonial government has no role to play. Government schools for girls are disreputable. 'The fact is that no satisfactory education can be provided for Muhammadan females until a large number of Muhammadan males receive a sound education. The present state of education among Muhammadan females is, in my opinion, enough for domestic happiness considering the present social and economic conditions of the life of the Muhammadans in India.'[42] In an undated letter to Mumtaz Ali, published after Syed Ahmad's death, in *Huqūq-i Niswān*, Syed Ahmad expressed anxiety about the marriage prospects of educated women in the absence of a sufficient number of educated men.[43]

In 1884, on one of his tours to Punjab to raise funds and recruit students for the Aligarh College, he was confronted by a document prepared by a women's group, Muslim, Hindu, and Christian (and perhaps Sikh), that called upon him to turn his attention to the education of women. A woman's committee had been formed, collected funds in support of the Aligarh cause, and had hoped to meet with Syed Ahmad. The plan seems to have been that a young woman would present the formal address that the committee had prepared. It isn't clear why Syed Ahmad did not meet the women in person, but the address was delivered by his male host and Syed Ahmad responded in writing in a warm and conciliatory tone but also one that could be considered condescending. He addressed the women as sisters (*ai baheno*) in the familiar *tum* mode, pointing out that he was older and knew more than they did. As in his Education Commission testimony, he declared that the women of previous generations were better educated and that women should indeed be educated—at home and only in religious and practical texts, not the ones studied by men. There is, he said, no country in which women's education took priority over men's.[44]

Religion, Nostalgia and the Uses of the Past

If Syed Ahmad wanted to avoid the subject as a public leader, the question of women was unavoidable in his other large project, a multi-volume Urdu translation and commentary (*tafsīr*) of the Qur'an. His commentary on the fifth Sura, Al-Nisa' (the Women), returns to the themes of protection, mutual affection, and the regulation of sexual relations. He emphasizes the rights of young women, particularly orphans, to their own property and to consent to any marriage. Marriage must be a matter of mutual consent, not only as a matter of justice (*'adl*) but of a meeting of hearts (*mil qalbi*) and love (*muhabbat*). He condemns sexuality based on desire (*hirs*) and particularly the Shi'a practice of temporary (*mut'a*) marriage.[45]

In his testimony to the Education Commission in 1882, Syed Ahmad mentioned his mother, who had taught him Persian. We know almost nothing about individual Muslim women in late nineteenth-century India, but we have the striking account from earlier in the century of Azizunnissa Begum, Syed Ahmad's mother, which Gail Minault uses at the outset of *Secluded Scholars*.[46] The account is based on his short book on his maternal grandfather, Khwaja Fariduddin Ahmad, which concludes with Syed Ahmad's moving recollections of his mother as a woman of learning, independence, sense of justice and what Syed Ahmad would consider rational piety. Khwaja Farid of Kashmiri descent and something of a self-made man established the kind of extended household, a miniature Mughal court perhaps, that could well fit the Nasirean tradition. He appears to have married off his daughters to husbands of less wealth but higher religious status on the condition that the daughters remain in the household. In fact, Azizunnissa built her own separate house across a road but within the larger vicinity, and it was there that she remained until the tragic events of 1857. When the British recaptured Delhi, her brother was one of those they shot. The rest of the family escaped, but Syed Ahmad's mother remained in her house, surviving on horse grain. When Syed Ahmad finally reached her she had endured three days without water. She died shortly after that in Meerut.[47]

As for Syed Ahmad's wife, Parsa Begum, also from the family of

Khwaja Farid, she too died in 1861, leaving two young sons and a very young daughter. Syed Ahmad resisted the urging of friends to marry again because of his abiding attachment to her memory.[48] Years later he recalled a dream he had after her death:

... she was sitting in a very fine house, wearing a very fine green garment, and her body and face were glowing like the moon. Syed wanted to touch her with his hand. She said, no hand can touch this body. The body and dress are spiritual [*nūrāni*], they are not the body and dress of this world.[49]

It is with such memories and dreams that Syed Ahmad clung to the separation and seclusion of women, at least within his own social milieu and his own times. Rooted in an ideology of gender hierarchy, he also had the more recent experience of violence and victimization that inspired the need to protect what he took to be the vulnerability of women.

Syed Ahmad's long-standing struggle with the ideology of gender and family, therefore, doesn't fully explain his emotional response to Mumtaz Ali's manuscript. He had seen and admired what women in other places were capable of, but he feared that radical change in the most intimate relationships would undo all his other aspirations. Nostalgia for his earlier domestic life had been challenged by recollections of the violence and tragic displacements associated with the 1857 Rebellion. More recently conflicts with close relatives and erstwhile friends over the leadership of the Aligarh College were followed by a series of public scandals and falling enrolment. There were more intimate problems with the next generation in his family, including conflicts between his son Syed Mahmud and his wife; Syed Ahmad may well have been called upon to protect his daughter-in-law from her volatile husband.[50] Motivated by a wish to avoid additional opposition to his other projects, he now faced challenges from a growing number of people, many of them off spring of the college and cultural movement that he himself had set in motion. In his last days, Syed Ahmad had much to be agitated about.[51]

For many years, Syed Ahmad had an especially cordial relationship with Syed Mumtaz Ali. Their correspondence started in 1877, when the younger man was only seventeen. Two years later, he travelled to Calcutta to meet Syed Ahmad. From the large number of letters over the following decades Syed Ahmad appears to have treated Mumtaz almost as a son, encouraging his studies, advising him to travel to England, assisting in his publishing enterprise. As a later concession, no doubt after his outburst over the manuscript of *Huqūq-i Niswān*, Syed Ahmad wrote a letter suggesting that if the younger man had to publish a journal to promote women's education and social reform, he might call it, after *Tahẓīb ul-Akhlāq*, *Tahẓīb un-Niswān*.[52]

Notes

1. Tahera Aftab, 'Negotiating with Patriarchy: South Asian Muslim women and the appeal to Syed Ahmad Ahmed Khan', *Women's History Review*, vol. 14, no. 1, 2005, pp. 75–91.
2. Henriette M. Sender, *e The Kashmiri Pandits: A Study of Cultural Choice in North India*, Delhi: Oxford University Press, 1988, p. 268. As a young boy, Hashim Muhammad Ali, a grandson of Sayyid Ahmad Khan, attended a garden party in Allahabad c.1908, that was memorable as the first time the ladies of the Nehru family came out of parda (Interview, Karachi, September 1969).
3. Syed Mumtaz Ali, *Huqūq-i Niswān*, Lahore: Rafah-i 'Am, 1898, https://archive.org/details/HuqooqENiswan, accessed 18 May 2017; the book is ably summarized in Minault, 'Syed Mumtaz Ali and "Huquq Un-Niswan".'
4. Sumit Sarkar, 'Rammohan Roy and the Break with the Past', in *Rammohun Roy and the Process of Modernization in India*, ed. V.C. Joshi, Delhi: Vikas Publishing House, 1975; Lata Mani, *Contentious Traditions: The Debate on Sati in Colonial India*, Berkeley: University of California Press, 1998.
5. Qāsim Amīn, *The Liberation of Women and, the New Woman: Two Documents in the History of Egyptian Feminism*, Cairo: American University in Cairo Press, 2000; Leila Ahmed, *Women and Gender in Islam: Historical Roots of a Modern Debate*, New Haven: Yale University Press, 1993, pp. 155–64.
6. Gail Minault, *Voices of Silence: English Translation of Khwaja Altaf Hussain Hali's Majalis un-nissa and Chup ki dad*, Delhi: Chanakya Publications, 1986. See also Ruby Lal, *Coming of Age in Nineteenth-Century India: The Girl-Child and the Art of Playfulness*, Cambridge: Cambridge University Press, 2013; Margrit Pernau. *Ashraf into Middle Classes, 356–64*, Delhi: Oxford University Press; Faisal Devji, 'The Equivocal History of a Muslim Reformation', in *Islamic Reform in South Asia*, ed. Filippo Osella and Caroline Osella, Cambridge: Cambridge University Press, 2013, pp. 3–25.
7. Pernau, *Ashraf into Middle Classes*, p. 355.
8. Barbara Daly Metcalf, 'Islam and Power in Colonial India: The Making and Unmaking of a Muslim Princess', *American Historical Review*, vol. 116, issue 1, 2011, presidential address was delivered at the 125th annual meeting of the American Historical Association at http://www.historians.org/about-aha-and-membership/aha-history-and-archives/presidential-addresses/barbara-d-metcalf, accessed 18 May 2017.
9. Rokeya S, Hossain, *Sultana's Dream: And Selections from the Secluded Ones*, New York: The Feminist Press at CUNY, 2013.

10. Asiya Siddiqi, 'Ayesha's World: A Butcher's Family in Nineteenth-Century Bombay', *Comparative Studies in Society and History*, vol. 43, no. 1, January 2001, pp. 101–29.
11. Gail Minault, *Secluded Scholars: Women's Education and Muslim Social Reform in Colonial India*, Delhi: Oxford University Press, 1998.
12. Partha Chatterjee, *The Nation and its Fragments: Colonial and Postcolonial Histories*, Princeton: Princeton University Press, 1993.
13. Tanika Sarkar, *Hindu Wife, Hindu Nation, Community, Religion, and Cultural Nationalism*, Delhi: Permanent Black, 2001.
14. Radhika Singha, 'Colonial Law and Infrastructural Power: Reconstructing Community, Locating the Female Subject', *Studies in History*, vol. 19, no. 1, n.s., 2003, pp. 87–126; Veena Talwar Oldenburg, *Dowry Murder the Imperial Origins of a Cultural Crime*, Oxford: Oxford University Press, 2002; Mytheli Sreenivas, *Wives, Widows, and Concubines: The Conjugal Family Ideal in Colonial India*, Bloomington: Indiana University Press, 2008.
15. Asghar 'Abbas, 'Sar Syed tahrīk ki nisa'i jihāt', *Aligarh Megzin*, Khawatin Nambar, 2001, pp. 25–35; Nasreen Ahmed, *Muslim Leadership and Women's Education: Uttar Pradesh, 1886–1947*, Gurgaon: Three Essays Collective, 2012; Rahat Abrar, *Muslim Female Education: Veil to Moon*, New Delhi: Reference Press, 2014; Firdous Azmat Siddiqui, *A Struggle for Identity: Muslim Women in the United Provinces*, New Delhi: Foundation Books, 2014.
16. http://www.columbia.edu/itc/mealac/pritchett/00urdu/asbab/translation2005.html? Syud Ahmed Khan, *An Essay on the Causes of the Indian Revolt*, Agra: J.A. Gibbons, Mofusselite Press, 1859; http://www.columbia.edu/itc/mealac/pritchett/00urdu/asbab/urdutext1859.html?, accessed 18 May 2017.
17. David Lelyveld, 'The Qutb Minar in Syed Ahmad Khan's *Āṣār us-ṣanādīd*', in *Knowledge Production, Pedagogy, and Institutions in Colonial India*, ed. Indra Sengupta and Daud Ali, Houndmills, Basingstoke, Hampshire: Palgrave, 2011.
18. Altaf Husain Hali, *Hayāt-i Javīd*, 1901; repr., Lahore: Ishrat Publishing House, 1965, pp. 62–4.
19. Devji, 'The Equivocal History of a Muslim Reformation', p. 3.
20. Muzaffar Alam, *The Languages of Political Islam: India, 1200–1800*, Chicago: University of Chicago Press, 2004, pp. 68–80; Rosalind O'Hanlon, 'Manliness and Imperial Service in Mughal North India', *Journal of the Economic and Social History of the Orient*, vol. 42, 1999, pp. 47–93.
21. G.M. Wickens, tr., *The Nasirean Ethics by Nasir al-Din Tusi*, London: Allen & Unwin, 1964, pp. 153–84.
22. Marcia K. Hermansen, tr., *The Conclusive Argument from God: Shāh Walī Allāh of Delhi's Hujjat Allāh al-bāligha*, Leiden: E.J. Brill, 1996, p. 123.
23. Cited in Carole E. Pateman, *The Sexual Contract*, Stanford: Stanford University Press, 1988, p. 36. I thank Julia Stephens for sharing her unpublished M.Phil.

Cambridge dissertation, 'Ideas in Motion: *Syed* Ahmad Khan and Liberalism in Late-Nineteenth-Century India', 2006.
24. Faisal Devji, 'Apologetic Modernity', *Modern Intellectual History*, vol. 4, no. 1, 2007, p. 62.
25. Lynn Zastoupil, *John Stuart Mill and India*, Stanford: Stanford University Press, 1994.
26. Karuna Mantena, *Alibis of Empire: Henry Maine and the Ends of Liberal Imperialism*, Princeton: Princeton University Press, 2010; see also Zastoupil, John Stuart Mill and India, pp. 186–9.
27. Bernard S. Cohn, 'From Indian Status to British Contract', *The Journal of Economic History*, vol. 21, no. 4, December 1961, p. 628; reprinted in his *An Anthropologist among the Historians and Other Essays*, Delhi: Oxford University Press, 1987, p. 479.
28. D. Lelyveld, *Aligarh's First Generation: Muslim Solidarity in British India*, Princeton University Press, 1978; 2nd edn., New Delhi: Oxford University Press, 1996; repr. 2003; ACLS Humanities E-Book, 2009.
29. Iftikhar Alam Khan, 'Sar Syed aur taʻalim-i niswan', *Tahzib al-akhlaq*, vol. 33, no. 9, September 2014; see his *Sar Syed aur Scientific Society*, Delhi: Maktaba Jamiʻa, 2000, p. 99 (and photo).
30. 'Muslim Female Education', reprinted from the *Friday Review*, with an Urdu translation, *Akhbar Scientific Society (Aligarh Institute Gazette)*, 4 October 1867, pp. 615–17, http://www.sirsyedtoday.org/books/read/default.aspx?bid=40, accessed 18 May 2017.
31. Asghar ʻAbbās, ed., *Sar Syed Kā Safar Nāmah, Musāfirān-i Landan*, Aligarh: Educational Book House, 2009, pp. 101–2; for English translations, see George F. Graham, *The Life and Works of Syed Ahmed Khan*, Edinburgh, 1885, pp. 103–4, or Mushirul Hasan and Nishat Zaidi, eds. and tr., *A Voyage to Modernism*, Delhi: Primus Books, 2011, p. 120.
32. Avril Powell, 'An Unusual Shipboard Encounter: Mary Carpenter Quizzes Sir Saiyid Ahmad Khan on Education for Indian Women', SAALG Newsletter Issue 3, South Asia Archive & Library Group, British Library, pp. 20–5, http://www.bl.uk/reshelp/bldept/apac/saalg/issue3.pdf, accessed 18 May 2017; ʻAbbās, *Sar Syed Kā Safar Nāmah*, pp. 52–5.
33. Avril A. Powell, *Scottish Orientalists and India: The Muir Brothers, Religion, Education and Empire*, Woodbridge: Boydell Press, 2010.
34. Syed Ahmad Khan, *A Series of Essays on the Life of Mohammad: And Subjects Subsidiary Thereto*, London: Trübner & Co., 1870, Muḥammad Ismāʻīl Pānīpatī, ed., *Maqālāt-i Sar Syed*, vol. XI, Lahore: Majlis Taraqqī-yi Adab, 1963. See Powell, *Scottish Orientalists*, pp. 163–5, 211–12.
35. Khan, *A Series of Essays on the Life of Mohammad*, pp. 146–62.
36. Ibid., pp. 148, 150.
37. 'Auraton kē Ḥuqūq' (August 1871), in Pānīpatī, *Maqālāt-i Sar Syed*, vol. V, pp. 194–9.
38. *Translation of the Report of the Members of the Select Committee*, Benares: Medical Hall Press, 1872, p. 60.

39. 'Hindustan ki auraton ki halat' (April 1876), in Pānīpatī, *Maqālat-i Sar Syed*, vol. V, pp. 188–93.
40. Susie Tharu and K. Lalita, *Women Writing in India, Vol. I: 600 B.C. to the Early 20th Century*, New York: Feminist Press at the City University of New York, 1991, pp. 203–10; cf. Sisir K. Das, *A History of Indian Literature:1800–1910: Western Impact: Indian Response*, New Delhi: Sahitya Akademi, 1991, p. 114. For the Urdu translation, see *Conference on Urdu and Hindi Christian Literature, held at Allahabad, 1875*, Madras: The Christian Vernacular Education Society, 1875, p. 99.
41. *Aligarh Institute Gazette*, 3 January 1893.
42. *Aligarh Institute Gazette*, 5 August 1882, Supplement.
43. Syed Mumtaz Ali, *Huqūq-i Niswān*, pp.57–9.
44. Syed Iqbāl 'Alī, *Syed Aḥmad Khān Kā Safar Nāmah-Yi Panjāb*, Lahore: Majlis Taraqqī-yi Adab, 1973, pp. 138–48; see Aftab, 'Negotiating with Patriarchy'.
45. *Sar Syed kī tafsīr-i Qur'ān*, vol. 2, Paṭnah: Khuda Baksh Oriental Public Library, 1995, pp. 457–86; original publication, Aligarh: Institute Press, 1886, pp. 102–70, http://www.sirsyedtoday.org/books/read/?bid=193.
46. Ibid., pp. 14–17.
47. Syed Aḥmad Khān, *Sīrat-i Farīdiyah*, Karācī: Pāk akeḍīmī, 1964, pp. 135–48. See also Iftikhār 'Ālam Khān, *Sar Syed, darūn-i khānah*, Aligarh: Educational Book House, 2006.
48. Altaf Husain Hali, *Hayāt-i Javīd*, p. 125.
49. David Lelyveld, 'Young Man Sayyid: Dreams and Biographical Texts', in *Muslim Voices: Community and the Self in South Asia*, ed. David Gilmartin, Sandria Frietag and Usha Sanyal, New Delhi: Yoda Press, 2013, pp. 265–70.
50. Alan M. Guenther, 'Syed Mahmood and the Transformation of Muslim Law in British India', Ph.D. dissertation, McGill University, 2004, pp. 109–10. See also D. Lelyveld, 'Macaulay's Curse: Sir Syed and Syed Mahmood', in *Sir Syed Ahmed Khan: A Centenary Tribute*, ed. Asloob A. Ansari, New Delhi: Adam Publishers, 2000.
51. Lelyveld, *Aligarh's First Generation*, pp. 313–16.
52. Panipati, *Maktūbāt-i Sar Syed*, vol. 2, pp. 184–5; http://www.sirsyedtoday.org/books/read/default.aspx?bid=137, accessed 18 May 2017. The letter is undated, but the editor estimates that it was 12 March 1898, Syed Ahmad Khan died on the 27th of that month.

6

Intimacy and Marriage in Urdu Advice Literature, 1900–1910

ASIYA ALAM

MOVEMENTS OF SOCIAL reform amongst Indian Muslims in the late nineteenth century witnessed the emergence of women's education and conjugality as key issues that informed debates about gender and the role of women in society. While reformers like Nazir Ahmed and Altaf Hussain Hali discussed domesticity under the broad rubric of women's education, writers also treated conjugality autonomously. This chapter will consider two texts, Muhammadi Begum's *Rafiq-e Arus* (The Bride's Companion), published in 1901, and Saiyid Ali Asghar Bilgrami's *Falsafa-e Izdivaj* (Philosophy of Marriage), written in 1909, to highlight the discourse on conjugality as a distinct topic of public conversation and how it appeared independently as a question.

Muhammadi Begum (1878?–1908) was the daughter of Maulvi Ahmed Shafiq who was a government official in the state of Punjab. She was educated at home and learnt to read Urdu and memorize the Quran. She was married at the age of nineteen to Syed Mumtaz Ali, an Urdu scholar and pioneer of women's education who founded the weekly journal of *Tahzib-e Niswan* (The Women's Reformer) in 1898. Muhammadi Begum and Syed Mumtaz Ali together edited the journal and wrote several columns and articles on questions of family reform and women's education.[1]

The first line of *Rafiq-e Arus* illustrates the purpose of Muhammadi Begum's writing where she says that 'the real reason for the structure and composition of this book is the invaluable advice letter that my father wrote to me during the days of my marriage.'[2] After she became responsible for the editorial work at *Tahzib-e Niswan,* Muhammadi Begum writes that she began to reflect more on the nature of articles and columns that could be published in the journal. The more she read and re-read the views of her father, the more she realized that the letter was a microcosm of all that she wished to include in *Tahzib-e Niswan*. After much consideration, she decided to write a series of articles on each aspect of her father's advice. This was published in 1901 as *Rafiq-e Arus* and became extremely popular. The positive reception of the text led Muhammadi Begum to write a second edition in 1905,[3] with more columns and an extended commentary on previous chapters.[4]

Her father's suggestions on how to cope with married life shaped her view of marriage and influenced significant portions of her text, *Rafiq-e Arus*. The letter by Maulvi Ahmed Shafiq, Muhammadi Begum's father, was written on 2 August 1897, five months before her marriage, as a kind of advice manual. Ahmed Shafiq writes, 'it must be remembered that the relation between a man and a woman in the world is a strange one. The duty in this relationship is that one should love the other more than their own life'.[5] If this is not possible, he continues, 'then the purity and honour of this relationship has not been understood'. To fully explicate his feelings, Ahmed Shafiq constructs a triadic discourse around love, discretion and self-respect. Love, says Ahmed Shafiq, is related to the heart but some people degrade their beloved in expressing their affection. Love, therefore, must be balanced by the capacity of discretion and when they both combine, it gives rise to a 'curious remedy' that can comfort all sorrows.[6] Furthermore, according to Ahmed Shafiq, without self-respect, there can be no love. Only when one learns to respect oneself do others also begin to respect us.[7] A crucial aspect here in *Rafiq-e Arus* is the mention of self-respect as a criterion for respecting the husband and its implications for the fashioning of an autonomous self. Given its emphasis on self-respect, *Rafiq-e Arus* thus creates a greater space for the expression of female intimacy. In addition to self-respect, Ahmed Shafiq also asks his daughter to develop courage. Insisting that Muhammadi Begum should not change her opinion if it is correct, or remain silent in any assembly out of fear of reproach, he directs her to explain her reasoning regardless of anyone's reaction and to be afraid only of the reproach of her own conscience.[8]

Alongside advice about self and intimacy, Ahmed Shafiq's letter mentions general commentaries about the status of women in India. In a semblance to other reformers, he argues that housekeeping, in particular the management of the kitchen and cooking, is central to a good domestic life, and one in which Indian women are sadly inept. Emphasizing the obligations of living in a joint family, 'in our country, women have to face one more great difficulty, which is that the husband's family views their actions constantly with criticism'.[9] He counsels Muhammadi Begum not only to strive to keep her husband happy but also to be polite to the members of his family and the servants of the household. If there is any difference of opinion, it must be resolved politely through dialogue. If there are still problems in developing a relationship, he specifically warns her that she should not abandon her efforts for other friends outside the family.[10]

Ahmed Shafiq also reflects briefly on the status of women in other communities. Commenting on the religious practices of non-Muslims, particularly the Greeks and Hindus, he writes that he often wondered 'why women have been worshipped in the past and still are worshipped today'. Addressing his long-held rumination, Ahmed Shafiq argues that, unlike men, women have several qualities, especially beauty, empathy, sincerity, love, honour and care of the community, which are integral to them. Ahmed Shafiq's conclusion to his daughter is more striking than his essentializing of women in the letter. As a result of these qualities, he says 'women are not worshipped in Islam but if you fall in love with a woman, then there is greater reflection for her than for God'.[11]

There are two unique aspects of the letter with important historical implications. First is that Muhammadi Begum married Syed Mumtaz Ali, who had been married before and had two children who she needed to take care of.[12] Mentioning this crucial aspect of her married life, Ahmed Shafiq wrote that 'in your condition, the most difficult eventuality that you will have to confront is that you will have to deal with two small children'.[13] Advising that treating a motherless child with kindness and compassion is one of the best deeds of this world, he confidently adds that he is assured that she will treat them well because she is good with children. Muhammadi Begum's marriage and her father's advice reflects the diverse marital arrangements that women often encountered when they commenced their married life. A second marriage for a man after the death of his first wife was a permissible social practice in society and was different from marrying a childless young man who had not married earlier. In *Rafiq-e Arus,* Muhammadi Begum is more precise on the dilemmas of parenting children not one's own than on giving advice about it. If one tried to admonish or discipline the children, one ran the risk of being accused by others of stepmotherly treatment towards the child. On the other hand, if one hesitated to reprimand them, one could spoil them and raise them poorly. Muhammadi Begum's advice on such matters is simply to learn to love carefully and moderately so that one doesn't suffer from either extreme; achieving such a balance would nevertheless require struggle and accuracy of feeling.[14]

The prospect of marrying a man who had once been married was not limited to widowers but also included a polygynous marriage for the woman. The sensitive issue of polygyny comes under scrutiny during the late nineteenth century within the Muslim community in the context of debates raging between Christian missionaries, evangelical colonial officials like William Muir and Indian reformers such as Syed Ahmad Khan and Syed Ameer Ali. By the early twentieth century, concerned writers and activists such as Bashiruddin Ahmed, Rashid-ul Khairi and Akbari Begum were among those who offered advice to women on how to endure the tribulations of a polygynous marriage. Much like the counsels of Bashiruddin Ahmed and Akbari Begum, Muhammadi Begum acknowledges the pain of a woman who is the second wife to her husband but refrains from criticizing the institution. Her advice to second wives is to maintain a friendly relation with the first wife and strive to purge from themselves those traits that might disturb the husband.[15]

The second crucial factor, which has significant historical ramifications, is that Ahmed Shafiq asks Muhammadi Begum to read the father's letter in Nazir Ahmed's *Mirat ul-Arus* (The Bride's Mirror). Published in 1869 by Nazir Ahmed Dehlavi (1833?–1912), this didactic novel was on the benefits of female education. Born in a family of Islamic scholars, Nazir Ahmed received a classical Islamic education in Persian and Arabic from his father and later studied at Delhi College. After graduating from Delhi College, he briefly taught Arabic in the state of Punjab and then joined the colonial government as Deputy Inspector of Schools in the city of Allahabad in the North-Western Provinces.[16]

Mirat ul-Arus is a story of contrast between two sisters, Asghari, who is educated and well-mannered, and Akbari, who is uneducated and subsequently arrogant and ill-mannered. In the story, Durandesh Khan, their father, writes a letter to the younger daughter Asghari before her marriage. He informs her that her wedding will open a new world, whose responsibilities she must bear well. Specifically, he asks her to maintain amity and concord in domestic life and not blemish them with quarrels and disputes. Invoking the belief in the legend of Adam and Eve, Durandesh Khan says that the duty of a wife is to keep her husband happy and also be a vigilant guardian of his wealth. He advises Asghari not to gossip about her husband or his family and to respect them in all circumstances. After reading the letter, Asghari is emotionally overawed and promises to read it regularly everyday.[17]

Ahmed Shafiq's mention of Nazir Ahmed's letter points to the positive reception of *Mirat ul-Arus* amongst the Urdu-speaking *sharif* Muslims. At the same time, it highlights important elements of a social practice in the father-daughter bond, which appear crucial to understanding both parenting and marital relations. The letter becomes a rite of passage for the father as well as for the daughter and it ensures that the father's duties in preparing his daughter for her 'new life' are fulfilled. Thus, it is not only the norms of good mothering that are advocated in advice literature but notions of fatherhood and parenting by men. What is more significant is that the role of fathers in shaping women's views on marriage is more significant than that of their mothers.

It is also important to note that women followed the advice of their fathers not simply out of duty but also out of reverence. In response to her father, Muhammadi Begum writes that her 'modest intellect didn't have the words to express what she experienced upon examining the contents of the letter'.[18] She says that she read the letter of love several times but it wasn't sufficient to simply read it. She wished to imbibe the contents as if it were a talisman and promised to read it regularly and imprint each page in her mind. Like the letter, her book contains similar counsel for women, and Muhammadi Begum emphasizes respect towards husband and in-laws, care of the home and self-control and stoicism in wives.

The second text I analyse is *Falsafa-e Izdivaj* (Philosophy of Marriage) written by Syed Ali Asghar Bilgrami (1891–1961) in 1909. This tract is based on Sylvanus Stall's *What a Husband Ought to Know* from the popular Sex and the Self series published in the US during the late nineteenth and early twentieth century. Sylvanus Stall, a Lutheran pastor, was author of *What a Boy Ought to Know,* the first in the series in 1897. This was followed by *What a Husband Ought to Know* in 1899. A writer based in Hyderabad, Syed Ali Asghar Bilgrami (Bilgrami) was the son of Maulvi Syed Hasan Jashan. He completed his early education in Hyderabad and Aurangabad, and was trained in Islamic jurisprudence. Qualifying the revenue and judiciary examinations, he worked as an assistant revenue officer in the Nizam government. In October 1914, he was employed as an assistant in judicial court and later also worked as an assistant to the home secretary in the Nizam office. He was temporarily appointed as Director of Nizam's Archaeological Department when Ghulam Yazdani was on leave. In 1929, he became trustee and chief organizer of finance, and later continued to rise in the Nizam government. Besides *Falsafa-e Izdivaj,* he published *Ma'asir-i Deccan* in 1924, which provided a survey of the archaeology of Hyderabad and its surrounding areas. In 1927, Bilgrami translated *Ma'asir-i Deccan* into English as *Landmarks of the Deccan: A Comprehensive Guide to the Archaeological Remains of the City and Suburbs of Hyderabad. Ma'asir-i Deccan* was reprinted from Karachi in 1978 with an introduction by Moinuddin Aqeel. In addition to the archaeological history of Deccan, Bilgrami also edited in two volumes the Persian text of *Hadiqat al-Salatin-i Qutb Shahi* that was published in 1961 from *Idarah-i Adabayat-i Urdu.*[19]

In his work in *Falsafa-e Izdivaj,* Bilgrami writes that he has ignored irrelevant things in the original text to select only 'beneficial' ideas transforming *Falsafa-e Izdivaj* into neither an exact translation nor a new document but a trans-creation of literature from one language into another. My main aim in this analysis is to illustrate what *Falsafa-e Izdivaj* appropriated from Stall's manual and how it located itself within Urdu literature to resonate with its readers.

Deeming the publication of *Falsafa-e Izdivaj* necessary, Bilgrami argues that the tendency amongst elders to avoid discussion on the relationship between men and women had led to the spread of ignorance and misconceptions about these matters and the birth of endless social problems. Specifically, he added that through this text, he wished to address the dangerous developments that had become prevalent in Indian society following the introduction of modern education.

At a fundamental level, the primary aim of both *Falsafa-e Izdivaj* and *What a Husband Ought to Know* is the regulation of sexuality and the demarcation of socially acceptable norms, which locates sexual practices firmly within the domain of marriage and family. Informed by American Christian discourse, *Falsafa-e Izdivaj* thus aimed to discipline sexuality through the discourse of familial reform. *What a Husband Ought to Know* is divided into three sections—'husband', 'wife', and 'children'—whereas *Falsafa-e Izdivaj* eliminates the part on children and also adds some information to the section on 'wife'. More generally, Stall's publications were segregated along gender lines and addressed specifically to male readers whereas Asghar Bilgrami's text places no particular emphasis on men in its title, leaving the book open to a possible female readership.

Like Stall, Bilgrami begins the book with an exaltation of love celebrating it as the emotion that makes life worthwhile and allows a perfect union between two individuals.[20] Following this note, Bilgrami departs from Stall's texts and leaves out the illustration of life processes of growth and reproduction as well as details of biological differences between men and women. Although Bilgrami ignores biology, he endorses Stall's understanding of the 'complementary' nature of emotions and intellect amongst men and women, women being more amenable to feelings while men are seen to respond to 'reason'. But the primary appropriation in *Falsafa-e Izdivaj* from the Stall section on 'husband' is the emphasis on sexual moderation and mutuality in marital relationships.

Foregrounding the concern of sexual restraint against everything, Bilgrami writes that 'the greatest war is that which is fought against one's own sexuality'.[21] Relating the practice of sexual restraint to that of health and good living, Bilgrami argues that incontinence in sexuality injures physical health, harms the mind, and destroys good habits. For Bilgrami and Stall, marriage acquires its uniqueness through moderation and such moderation provides focus and discipline in life. Condemning in particular men who oppose marriage, Bilgrami writes that they belong to a class of individuals who hold low and debased views about women and engage in sexual activity purely for hedonism and regard women to be an instrument for their immoderate desires.[22]

In addition to moderation, Bilgrami endorsed Stall's concepts of mutuality and reciprocity in conjugal relationships. According to Bilgrami, out of selfishness, some men regard their wives as property and deprive them of their natural rights. Turning 'nature' into a politically discursive category from which 'rights' or *haq* originate, he adds that the rights which nature has given to each individual do not imply that one become a master of another. Well-mannered men, he says, nurture their wives with the same rights that they have been given.[23]

It is crucial to mention here that the concept of 'rights from nature', which Bilgrami draws upon to argue for mutuality, is not present in Stall. For Stall, the lack of reciprocal relations between husband and wife are not so much destructive of 'natural rights' as of happiness. According to Stall, in order to secure a comfortable home and a happy future, it was necessary for the husband to provide the same comfort and happiness to his wife and children, which they would reciprocate.[24] On the other hand, Bilgrami's appropriation of 'nature' for the defence of reciprocal conjugal relationships corresponds well with the larger trend in colonial Muslim thought in the late nineteenth century. Bilgrami's use of 'nature' constitutes a conversation with Syed Ahmed Khan's 'natural theology' and points to a continuous identification of concepts such as that of 'nature' drawn from an episteme of popular scientific knowledge available to reformers in colonial India.

Bilgrami says that 'if the husband thinks that the meaning of wife is obedience and if obedience means that he can rule over her, then this word (wife) should be eliminated from the record of civilization'.[25] Adding practices of domesticity and household management to the equation, he states, 'it is the duty of the husbands that they help their wives in the tasks of housekeeping. It is shameful that women be left alone in the war of housekeeping'.[26]

While sexual moderation and conjugal mutuality remain the main pillars of Stall's ideas, in the first half of *Falsafa-e Izdivaj*, Bilgrami does not include Stall's expositions on physical problems such as impotence which could hamper marriage, his concerns with addiction to tobacco or liquor, or even his discussion of various sexual diseases.

Stall begins the second section on the 'wife' with a discussion on the ignorance of women on the subject of sexuality. For Stall, the extensive preparations of the wedding along with this ignorance add to considerable stress and he advises men to be considerate to women especially immediately after the wedding. Following Stall, Bilgrami too warns his male readers against using force in post-marital sexual intercourse, emphasizing instead patience and caution. Although Bilgrami doesn't explicitly state the term 'consent', this stress on sexual restraint after marriage is one of the few censures of marital rape in reformist Urdu literature. While there was an incessant focus on acquiring a woman's consent to marry in debates of the early twentieth century, there was a strong silence on issues of female sexual consent following marriage. Bilgrami's emphasis on this point, albeit an import from Stall, remains a unique feature in Urdu discourse on conjugality in early twentieth century.

Digressing from Stall, Bilgrami in his discussion on the wife's role points to 'Eastern' thinking on marital relations. According to Bilgrami, for Eastern philosophers, there are three aspects of managing marital relations. In the first, the husband should establish such dignity as to instill awe in the eyes of the wife, so that she should consider her benefits and losses based on his commands; the second involves magnanimity where the husband should provide that support to his wife which becomes the basis of conjugal love; the third entails preoccupation with service where the wife should focus her attention on the management of the house and the care of her family.[27]

In addition to these qualities, Bilgrami also mentions three features which he felt should be avoided in conjugal relations. The first was that husband should not display unrestrained love for his wife, the second was that he should not discuss any matter that could cause hostility between them, and the third was that he should avoid the company of women who enthrall men with stories of love.[28]

Bilgrami's inclusion of characteristics that need to be cultivated as well as those elements that need to be avoided reveals contradictions and inconsistencies in the text of *Falsafa-e Izdivaj* in particular and marriage advice manuals in general during this period. Although adopted from Stall, it was not unusual in Urdu advice literature of the colonial period to stress emphasis on mutuality, on companionship and on the rights of both husband and wife. Simultaneously, much like Bilgrami's schema of conjugal traits, there was also a preponderance of reformist arguments against classical writing on love, counsels that instructed the wife to manage the household and remain obedient, even in awe, of the husband. The subject of the 'wife' that appears in Urdu print culture during the colonial period especially in advice manuals thus is an ambiguous one that seeks to both subvert earlier gender hierarchies and also re-establishes norms that placed women squarely within the mold of an unequal relation.

The ambiguous subject of the wife in *Falsafa-e Izdivaj* is not only constructed from Bilgrami's own comprehension of 'Eastern' views, but also from Stall's orthodox views on sexuality and gender. For Stall, the great majority of women are devoid of sexual pleasure and their purpose in the divine scheme is child-rearing.[29] Appropriating these views on female sexuality, Bilgrami reiterates his stance on obedience and domestic management, and venerates the home where the purpose of marriage is procreation and child-rearing, which is fulfilled dutifully in the role of motherhood.[30] Endorsing Stall, Bilgrami writes that 'the natural outcome of love is marriage and the necessary outcome of marriage is the continuation of species'.[31]

Another feature common between Stall and Bilgrami in their section on the wife is the overarching stress on health and physiology. While Bilgrami ignores illustration of biological processes from the section on the husband, he discusses the process of fertilization and pregnancy in detail and counsels the reader regarding diet, exercise and health prior to childbirth.[32] Bilgrami elaborates the connection between heredity, health and marriageable age. Opposing young marriage for women, he argues that when young girls are forced into marriage, their physiology cannot support child bearing and consequently the children inherit their incapacities. According to Bilgrami, the marriageable age in warm countries for women should be sixteen and for men should be twenty-one.[33]

In general, both Stall and Bilgrami share the belief that marriage characterized by sexual restraint or socially acceptable sexual behaviour is the essential component of good living in which a happy and useful life serves to raise healthy, strong children. Despite this common thread running through the two texts, it is necessary to point out that *What a Husband Ought to Know* and *Falsafa-e Izdivaj* were composed in different languages by authors hailing from distinct cultural backgrounds and were addressed to very different readership. The fundamental motivation for Stall in publishing the Sex and the Self series was not merely regulation of sexuality and the enforcement of gendered hierarchies, but the construction of a Christian identity within the crucible of family. Laden with illustrations from Scripture, *What a Husband Ought to Know* is a text aimed at religious conversion in which the publication of the entire Sex and the Self series can be associated with evangelical activity and is imbricated in transnational networks of Christian missionaries engaged in proselytization. What is different about *Falsafa-e Izdivaj*, especially given Syed Ali Bilgrami's own interest in Islamic culture and history, is that it desists almost completely from employing religious sources in its argument. There are no supporting quotations from the Quran or the Hadith or philosophers like Al-Ghazali, cited often in the modern discussion on conjugality. Even more unusual is the absence of any demands of piety in the life of a 'good' husband or wife. For a text produced specifically for an Indian Muslim audience, these features are a unique departure from the Urdu reformist literature of the colonial period.

But how does the text correspond with the Urdu reformist literature of the colonial period? I argue that it resonates with the larger discourse on marriage and family through its language particularly in its emphasis on cultural categories established in Urdu literary etiquette. The two terms which mark Syed Ali Asghar Bilgrami's approach to conjugality are *tahzib* or 'culture' and *tamaddun* or 'civilization'. Bilgrami says that *tahzib* and *tamaddun* are the products of the union achieved between two individuals in marriage.[34] Considered virtues of self-refinement, both *tahzib* and *tamaddun* were lynchpins on which reformist discourse articulated its claims in the colonial period. Translated as 'manners', 'politeness' or 'refinement', *tahzib* also carries associated meanings of education and culture, which acquired great stress in Muslim colonial socio-religious movements. Upon his return from England, for example, Syed Ahmed Khan started his journal *Tahzib-ul Akhlaq* ('The Training of Etiquette' or 'The Social Reformer') and one of the first journals devoted to the cause of women's education was *Tahzib-e Niswan* (Culture of Women). Similarly, *tamaddun*, translated as 'civilization', 'urbanity' and sometimes 'culture', was evoked repeatedly where ideas associated with reform could restore and rejuvenate *tamaddun* or 'civilization'.

Falsafa-e Izdivaj received favourable reviews and was endorsed by several writers and reformers in the Muslim community. Altaf Husain Hali called the publication of the book a favour for the community (*qaum*) and the country (*mulk*) and felt that every single and married person should read the book again and again, to follow all its counsels.[35] Muhibb-e Husain, editor of *Mu'alim-e Niswan* said that the book was not just a translation but a much-needed compilation composed after careful deliberation.[36] Shad Azeemabadi wrote that the book was as necessary as the institution of marriage, and hoped that people would read the book with care and act on its generous counsels.[37] Syed Ahmed Dehlavi praised Bilgrami for paying attention to the social conditions of Muslims and for providing an easy and simple method for reform.[38]

Conclusion

How do the texts of *Rafiq-e Arus* and *Falsafa-e Izdivaj* compare and contrast with each other? Perhaps the most crucial distinction that can be made is that Muhammadi Begum's text was drawn from her own personal relations with her father and highlighted an important rite of passage for young women. Counsels from parents or elders of the family about the roles and expectations of married life weren't unusual, and advice manuals were often gifted as part of dowry. Bilgrami's text, on the other hand, remains remote from lived familial practices. It operates as an impersonal text, which seeks to impart knowledge to the public about a particular aspect of life. Another important difference is that Muhammadi

Begum remains silent on sexuality whereas Bilgrami addresses sexual life but firmly domesticates it within the sphere of marriage. I would therefore argue that despite Muhammadi Begum's emphasis on family and obedience, and her silence on sexuality, Bilgrami's public discussion of sexuality, influenced by orthodox views of a Christian evangelical, generates new restrictions on intimacy and associates sexuality exclusively with health and conjugality instead of desire and love. Muhammadi Begum and Syed Ali Asghar Bilgrami thus highlight different sets of normative beliefs about intimacy and family, and demonstrate how elite Muslims valued alternate structures of social hierarchy within the family and everyday life.

Notes

1. Gail Minault, *Secluded Scholars: Women's Education and Muslim Social Reform in Colonial India*, Delhi: Oxford University Press, 1998, pp. 110–14.
2. Muhammadi Begum, *Rafiq-e Arus*, Lahore: Rifah-e Aa'm, 1906, Preface, p. 1.
3. The printing press mentions 1906 as the date of publication whereas Muhammadi Begum wrote the new preface to the text in 1905.
4. Muhammadi Begum, *Rafiq-e Arus*, Preface, pp. 1–2.
5. Ibid., pp. 98–9.
6. Ibid., p. 99.
7. Ibid., p. 100.
8. Ibid., pp. 108–9.
9. Ibid., p. 104.
10. Ibid., pp. 104, 106.
11. Ibid., p. 107.
12. Minault, *Secluded Scholars*, p. 112.
13. Muhammadi Begum, *Rafiq-e Arus*, p. 103.
14. Ibid., pp. 93–5.
15. Ibid., pp. 84–7.
16. Minault, *Secluded Scholars*, pp. 33–4.
17. Nazir Ahmed, *The Bride's Mirror*, tr. G.E. Ward, London: Oxford University Press, 1903, pp. 59–62.
18. Ibid., pp. 113–14.
19. Moinuddin Aqeel, introduction to *Ma'asir-i Deccan: mutazammin bar halat-i imarat va asar-i Baldah-yi Hyderabad* by Syed Ali Asghar Bilgrami (Karachi: Hafiz Muhammad Haider Memorial Academy, 1978), alif-te.
20. Syed Ali Asghar Bilgrami, *Falsafa-e Izdivaj*, Agra: Muhammad Ibrahim Khan Private Press, 1909, pp. 4–5.
21. Ibid., p. 36.

22. Ibid., p. 18.
23. Ibid., p. 26.
24. Sylvanus Stall, *What a Young Husband Ought to Know*, Philadelphia: Vir Publishing Company, 1899, pp. 52–3.
25. Bilgrami, *Falsafa-e Izdivaj*, p. 19.
26. Ibid., p. 15.
27. Ibid., pp. 49–50.
28. Ibid., p. 51.
29. Stall, *What a Husband Ought to Know*, pp. 118, 147.
30. Bilgrami, *Falsafa-e Izdivaj*, pp. 62–3.
31. Ibid., p. 67.
32. Ibid., pp. 85–90.
33. Ibid., pp. 73–4.
34. Ibid., pp. 14–15.
35. Ibid., p. 1.
36. Ibid., p. 8.
37. Ibid., pp. 11–12.
38. Ibid., p. 6.

7

Secluded Sovereign

Islam and Women's Empowerment in Nineteenth-Century India

BARBARA METCALF

GAIL MINAULT INTRODUCED her important book *Secluded Scholars: Women's Education and Muslim Social Reform in Colonial India* (1998) with a little anecdote about the beginning of her project. A British friend, she explained, hearing that she planned to undertake research on Muslim women's education and social reform in colonial India, offered the sceptical response, 'Oh, really. Was there any?'[1] The title of this essay pays homage to the title of the book that belied that skepticism. It is meant as a contribution not only to the general subject that Gail Minault pioneered, but it is also offered in the spirit of her work. At the heart of that spirit, not only in this book on education but in her many other writings, is a challenge to the kind of stereotypical conclusions about Muslim Indians that are often evident, and that are even more critical than the disbelieving quip she recorded.

The 'secluded sovereign' of my title is the third of the four Muslim women who successively held power in the princely state of Bhopal between 1819 and 1926.[2] She was Nawab Shah Jahan Begum (1838–1901) who ruled in her own right for roughly the last three decades of the nineteenth century. She was exactly, almost to the year, the contemporary of the Muslim social reformers of the late nineteenth century, the men whose Urdu texts would be read by many generations. Most celebrated among those writing specifically for and about women were Altaf Husain Hali (1837–1914)—known to many through Gail Minault's translation of his *Assemblies of Women* and *Homage to the Silent*[3]—and Deputy Nazir Ahmad (1836–1912), celebrated for his many didactic novels for girls and women. Trained by tutors at home, Shah Jahan shared the Persian and Arabic education that these writers and other literati of the day had had.[4] Like them, she was a prolific writer, taking advantage of newly available facilities for print and distribution of published materials. Most important for our purposes, in 1882 she published an extensive guide addressed to both women and men on the issues of women's health, education, entitlements, and obligations, all in the context of the well-ordered family life of the Muslim privileged classes. Shah Jahan's book was *Tahzibun niswan wa tarbiyatul insan*: 'Women's improvement and human development.'[5]

Shah Jahan was a lone female voice publishing a work like this in Urdu in an era when, as Gail Minault pointed out, '[the] writing of literature suitable for the edification of Muslim girls and women became a growth stock at the end of the nineteenth century and early in the twentieth'.[6] But only later did the activist women, whose lives Minault so well evokes, take up the social reform message themselves. Indeed, women's literary production in Urdu in the nineteenth century was typically associated with educated, cultivated courtesans, of whom the Hyderabadi Mah Laqa Bai was among the most famous.[7]

How did Shah Jahan's work differ from that of her male contemporaries? First off, not much when it came to issues related to women. Like them, she insisted that respectable women were to be 'secluded women'.[8] There were, in fact, a few rare voices who spoke out against parda, but the weight of respectable public opinion was against them.[9] In addition to favouring parda, Shah Jahan supported the other items on the basic reform list of the day: an end to child marriage, the importance of girls' education, the legitimacy of widow remarriage, the importance of marital compatibility and cooperation. She joined the reformist call, moreover, for hard work, time management, upright piety, and dissemination of the knowledge that all right-living people, male and female alike, required. Such practices were central to the reformist ideal of holding up a new model of respectability, *sharafat*, in contrast, typically, to the old extravagant, self-indulgent *sharafat* of the aristocratic, 'nawabi', class. Shah Jahan Begum, without making a point of it, imagined herself as simultaneously aristocratic and reformed. Like other reformers, her target consisted of the ignorant.

As a woman, Shah Jahan Begum faced a particular challenge in claiming to speak as an authority on matters of morality and behaviour.

At a time when elite Hindus and Muslims alike were imagining a 'new' woman defined by what Minault among others terms a 'bourgeois' vision of women's domestic respectability, Shah Jahan out of necessity had to play a public role. Here is where her support of parda helped her out. She may have played a role in public, but she did so as a veiled, married woman. This made her public role as ruler less outrageous. Indeed, she set an early precedent for women covering themselves as part of their entry into such public settings as formal education and employment.[10] Like later women, she experimented with new fashions for her 'portable seclusion', treating her voluminous robe of the Order of the Star of India, coupled with a scarf, for example, as suitable for some occasions.[11]

But what, besides respectability, made Shah Jahan credible as an authority? Unlike the two male contemporaries noted previously, she did not seek or display the stamp of approval of the colonial authorities. Shah Jahan, as a ruling princess under the Raj, was obviously a colonial figure, but unlike the reformers in government service, her role did not lead to a familiarity with European texts, or opinions, as theirs did. They wrote, moreover, very much aiming at a European audience as well as an elite Muslim one, designing their most influential texts to earn prizes and the advantage of textbook distribution.[12] Shah Jahan wrote outside the ever-judgemental European gaze. One implication of that autonomy was that she wrote a more Islamically-informed text than the male reformers wrote, who, in contrast, framed their texts at a more general level of morality.

Shah Jahan claimed her authority on the basis of Islamic learning. Not for Shah Jahan, Nazir Ahmad's fiction or Hali's fiction-like discourses.[13] Not even for her, the blockbuster *Bihishti Zewar*, a guidebook written by a seminary-based scholar a generation later. In that work, Maulana Ashraf 'Ali Thanawi (1863–1943), the most influential cleric of his day, laid out his instructions *tout court*. No need for him to provide elaborate citation and argumentation to prove his legitimacy. Shah Jahan's book was the opposite, every point documented by detailed quotations from sacred texts and commentaries; where appropriate, she also bolstered her arguments with reference to scholarly works including medical treatises. She did that, however, without the classic male imprimatur of having gained her learning from a succession of teachers, one teaching the next, and each receiving the *ijaza* or permission to teach a specific text in turn. To be sure, her book included approving verses and statements of various learned luminaries, and that is important. Primarily, however, her scholarship spoke for itself. Nawab Shah Jahan was thus, one might suggest, a pioneer, a new style of Islamic intellectual of the sort that would be influential in the coming century, the product of print and literacy and not of scholarly succession or what was coming to replace it, the formally organized *madrasa*.[14]

Anyone who argues, as Ruby Lal recently has, that women within the reformist orbit lacked 'critical reasoning',[15] surely needs to read Shah Jahan's book. On point after point Shah Jahan challenged conventional opinions and did so by making clear the scaffolding of her arguments. She did not just assert her opinion. She cited Qur'anic verses as well as the *hadith* reports of prophetic behaviour and sayings. She demonstrated her ability in the classic analytic skills focused on the historic chain of transmission for *hadith* (with authenticity claimed for those with proximity to the Prophet, known quality of character, and appropriate age and location). She noted how often a *hadith* appeared in what are taken as the sound compendia. At times, she invoked the occasion of revelation for a Qur'anic verse or of a tradition as part of discerning the heart or intention of a text to know what the issue was. She cited a stunning number of earlier commentators and scholars, and even an occasional poetic couplet, to make her point.

All this is an example of Islamic reasoning. As Shah Jahan's text makes clear, *difference of opinion is built into the system*. A scholar advising an inquirer on a personal problem conventionally ends every opinion with the phrase 'God knows better'.[16] At various points, Shah Jahan Begum prefaced *her* teaching with what can only be seen as a self-confident *meeree nazar main*, 'in my opinion'. This attention to context and variability is not the common image of 'Islamic law', shaped as it is today by the legal codification and programmes of the so-called Islamic states of the modern period.

One might think that Shah Jahan's work could be dismissed on the ground that her position as a ruler allowed her a wholly atypical opportunity to act in public and to take unconventional positions. To some extent that is true, and equally true for activist women later on; it is also true that she had the support of her reformist husband, himself a scholar of considerable repute. Certainly, her position gave her the resources that few other women or men would have had to publish and disseminate her works. But when it came to her opinions, they should not be taken as deviant exceptions. Not only did she share the basic outlook of the reformist writers of her time, it is important to note that Maulana Ashraf 'Ali Thanavi, even though belonging to a different sectarian orientation, included her book in his list of recommended reading in his own wildly successful guidebook for women, mentioned previously, published a quarter century later.[17]

Whereas the overall programme of reform suggested by Shah Jahan is like that of the male reformers, its range and tone differed significantly. Beyond her style of Islamic argumentation, there is yet another striking difference: Shah Jahan wrote with the pain and passion of first-hand experience. And even if her teachings were mainstream in the context of Islamic reform of the day, her emphases and glosses were very much her own.

Conventional reformist writings of the day were coloured by response to the colonial criticism that made women's issues the mark of India's inferior stage of civilization. Reformers wrote under that shadow, and they justified their reforms expediently as the foundation of social progress. Shah Jahan Begum too saw her teachings as key to worldly well-being, but she stood out for framing her positions in far more lofty terms. For her, women's rights and entitlements were properly understood as essential to women's procreative role, at once analogous and essential to *God's* own creative purpose.

Islamic texts always begin with an invocation that typically praises divine qualities that signal the text's subject or thesis.[18] Shah Jahan Begum praises God as Creator: 'unlimited praise to the best of creators who has made humans the noblest of creation'. It was, she points out, 'the *womb of Eve*' through which God allowed the noblest of creation to 'spread into all the corners of the world'. Similarly, the Prophet Muhammad, she continues, made procreation the means of increasing the number of followers (the blessed *ummat*). He conveyed to family and companions the right care and nurture of young children, she adds, so that *we* also acquire the ability to discriminate every good and ill. Shah Jahan thus takes what could be seen as a limitation—childbearing and child rearing—and makes that creative role, which is the gift shared with the Creator, her grounds for asserting women's many rights and entitlements. Shah Jahan, in short, puts women front and centre to the fulfilment of divine purpose, and she proposes to set out the teachings, based on Prophetic guidance, which allow readers to sustain women as they should.

She framed her book distinctively, and chose her topics distinctively as well. None of the other reformers, for example, launched their books with detailed discussion of issues of reproductive health as, indeed, fit her invocation. Shah Jahan organized her teachings in an order at once logical and practical, divided into twenty dense chapters, beginning with pregnancy and ending with death. She shared the premise of the day that this was an era of decline, and she shared as well the conviction that improvement depended on knowledge and skill. What one needed to know, first off, was the importance of women's health in the interests of offspring, an opportunity to reiterate the divine sanction given to human creation. Shah Jahan cites a Qur'anic verse whose agricultural metaphor of seeds and cultivation she interprets as a clue to the utter centrality of securing offspring. In it, as in the sacred texts of other religions, the Qur'an addresses men: 'Your wives are as a tilth [prepared soil] unto you; so approach your tilth when or how ye will . . . '.[19] This verse is often taken as giving men absolute control over their wives' bodies in a way that some regard as degrading to women. Shah Jahan ignored any such interpretation in favour of spelling out a range of teachings to foster women's strength and fecundity. Indeed, far from any interpretation that in terms of physical intimacy men can do whatever they want, Shah Jahan in the course of her book identified multiple occasions in the life cycle when women must *limit* sexual activity in the interests of their health and the health of the unborn child.[20]

If Shah Jahan's tone is distinctive, it is above all shaped by the need for women, and for the children whom women and men raise, to be informed, competent, and in control. For women, it is astonishing how much of that control is physical control of the body, not least during the objectively dangerous course of pregnancy and childbirth. Women, Shah Jahan insists, are entitled to particular foods during the reproductive cycle. They must be careful in terms of heavy labour or lifting weight. They must know, as noted, when to curtail male sexual access. They should exercise in order to be strong. Having stressed the religious scaffolding of the text, it is worth noting that extensive sections, for example on health, education, and physical exercises—including detailed instruction on horsemanship and even skilled handling of armaments, from guns to swords to bows and arrows—are presented without religious reference.[21]

This is a detailed and practical text. On the subject of girls' education, Shah Jahan's standards are high. She has no hesitation in contesting conventional practices. She urges serious learning in core Arabic and Persian traditions, as well as in the practical subjects of geography, arithmetic, literary texts, and so forth; she reviews specific titles and pedagogic techniques for boys and girls alike, concerned with the daily schedule of instruction, modes of fostering retention, and positive reinforcement. Notably, she insists that girls' education is *more* important than boys' since 'the poor things'—*bechaariyaan*—are constrained in gaining experience because of their limited opportunities to mix freely in public.[22] Shah Jahan may have insisted on seclusion, but she saw its problems and sought ways to mitigate its costs. The girl's teacher, she insisted, should be a man if at all possible—a true scholar, and not, as she puts it, just some *kath mulla*, a scholar who is really a quack.[23] Men in this society, Shah Jahan pointed out, were more likely to be learned and serious than women of the day. And just in case anyone was tempted to hire a woman anyway, she strategically added the stereotype that women, compared to men, were often designing and crafty.[24] It is important to note that her vision was of a family able to hire private tutors. When it came to girls' schools, increasingly embraced by reformers by the end of the century, Shah Jahan limited them to disadvantaged girls, like her own Victoria School (1891), intended to teach only basic skills and income-generating activities to female orphans and other needy.[25]

For her own audience, Shah Jahan writes with urgency and seriousness, the fruit of her own personal experience and of her observation of the world around her. Times change and personal fortunes, often thanks to forces beyond one's control, change as well. Against that, one could only be prepared, and for that knowledge and skills were essential. For example, Shah Jahan had no time for any woman who said she did not need to learn to sew because she could hire a tailor. She reports that she has seen at her own door members of the dispossessed Mughal nobility now reduced to begging.[26] Women need to know how to manage their household so they can be frugal if frugality is needed; and children need potentially income-earning skills against any day of hardship. Shah Jahan abhorred debility or dependence, a theme not unique to her in these years but one taken up for men, not women, notably by Nazir Ahmad.[27]

Shah Jahan herself never knew deprivation, but she knew intimately the experience of being forced into situations of frustration and helplessness. She was determined to foster in herself and her readers, knowledge and skills that offered protection and resources. She herself was born in exile where her mother and grandmother had taken refuge. Her grandmother had been regent for the state under an arrangement that required her to hand over power to a member of her late husband's family when he married her daughter. She delayed that marriage by every stratagem she could, even civil war. In the end, yielding to official British pressure, in 1835, her daughter, Sikandar Begum, Shah Jahan Begum's mother, was married off to a hot-headed incompetent who succeeded to the throne and seems to have tried to kill her on more than one occasion. Shah Jahan's first memories would have been of the precarious years in exile where she lived for her first seven years. She subsequently saw her mother, now widowed, by sheer will and competence secure the regency for herself and ultimately, the right to outright rule. Sikandar, however, organized a marriage for her daughter, Shah Jahan, that met the demands of *real politik* but not her daughter's happiness. Shah Jahan expected her situation to improve when she acceded to the throne upon reaching maturity some three or so years into the marriage. However, in 1859, she saw her mother negotiate outright power for herself. Shah Jahan then had to await her freedom almost an additional decade until the successive deaths of husband and mother. In Shah Jahan Begum's own life there was thus a quest for autonomy and self-reliance. She had seen helplessness; she had been helpless; and she never intended to be in that situation again. Hers is the passionate voice of hard experience.

Once in power, Shah Jahan intended to never lose her independence again. Three years after her accession, she made a second marriage to a husband of her own choosing, Sayyid Siddiq Hasan (1832–90), a munshi at the court who had risen to be her private secretary. This gave her the position of a married woman—the standard of respectability. It also gave her an absolute ally free of all familial pressures. But for a widow to remarry—and to choose her own husband—and to choose someone, as she did, of a different ethnic and economic background, went wholly against the behaviour of her class. Even her own grandmother broke off contact with her. Shah Jahan, however, insisted that every woman should have a choice and that every widow should be able to remarry, just as she did.[28] Thus, she brought the edge of tough experience to the social reform issues of the day, particularly the girl's age at marriage (and related issues of compatibility) and the remarriage of widows, two subjects she treats at length in her book.

Shah Jahan starts off her section on marriage—almost a quarter of the book—with discussion about the moral and physiological rationales for marriage and the criteria for choosing a spouse.[29] She provides an unusual density of Qur'anic verse and *hadith* citation in these pages, invoking in just the first three pages two Quranic verses along with a plethora of traditions from the classic compendia of *hadith*—Tirmizi, Bukhari, Muslim, Abu Da'ud, and Nisaa'ii. Shah Jahan finds *hadith* that make religiosity the most important consideration in spousal choice, over beauty, respectability, and wealth. But a tradition conveyed by the great Imam Bukhari adds another consideration. In that tradition, one Jabir is with the Prophet. The two are returning from battle and approaching Medina when Jabir asks permission to go directly home. The Prophet Muhammad asks: 'So—have you gotten married?' 'Yes.' 'A virgin, or someone previously married?' 'Previously married.' 'Why not a virgin, so you could laugh and play with her and she, with you?'[30]

The obvious interpretation of this *hadith* would be to say that the Prophet devalued marriage to a widow or divorcee. But Shah Jahan has a quite different angle, so important to her that she does not even quote the full *hadith*. (She stops before Jabir's explanation that he wanted an older woman because he had several daughters to raise.)[31] What mattered to Shah Jahan in this *hadith* was the prophetic sanction of *playfulness*. (Elsewhere in fact she did find *hadith* to explicitly equate virgins and previously married women as a choice.)[32] Shah Jahan uses the *hadith* about Jabir's marriage to segue into *multiple* traditions that emphasize the importance of intimacy, affection, love, and, yes, simple fun and pleasure between spouses. 'Companionate marriage' is usually understood to be a goal of the Western educated, but for Shah Jahan it is an Islamic entitlement with scriptural backing.

The proposed couple should meet in order to get a sense of what the other is like, hardly the usual view, but Shah Jahan has a *hadith* from five transmitters to back her up, with the Prophet's urging a companion to meet his intended in order to confirm the likelihood of intimacy and love.[33] Other *hadith* make clear, she claims, that parents need to scrutinize the family of the possible partner to see if the relationships within the prospective spouse's family are affectionate.

And couples should indeed be able to play and laugh together. For that, Shah Jahan argues, the girl and boy must be roughly the same age. If the difference is as much as ten or twelve years, she argues, a girl has no sensual pleasure at all, none of the savour of youthful experience. Her years will pass without pleasure (*be lutfi*), with no sensual pleasure (*hazz nafsani*), no worldly delight (*duniya ka 'aish*), no taste for living (*zindagani ka mazah*). There is, in short, none of the pleasure of youth (*lutf jawani*).[34] The young girl has to be shy and respectful towards her older husband, and she is deprived of the appropriate informal and unconstrained behaviour she should have. The man, Shah Jahan continues, is happy enough because in fact he absorbs her energy while the girl sees her strength sapped and feels herself becoming old and weak.

Her only hope is if he dies. Shah Jahan lays it all on the table: 'This was precisely my experience', she writes. 'My first husband was 16 years older than I, and I was his third wife. And now, since the person I married is the same age, I am happy as I never was in my youth.'[35]

Shah Jahan lists other objections to girls being married off young, namely, the serious harm to their health and even fertility that is at risk from early sexual relations.[36] These were arguments prominent in public life at the time across religious boundaries. But there is another issue rarely addressed—a young girl's powerlessness, a matter always at the heart of Shah Jahan's concerns. A girl married off young winds up not only subordinate to her husband, Shah Jahan argues, but to the household staff. Inevitably, uneducated and untrained in household management, the young bride falls prey to 'the maids, slaves, and servants', as she puts it, who rule the roost and terrify her.[37] They run roughshod over the household and win her with flattery to get what they want. 'Look at how wise the English are,' she writes. They devote the whole of childhood to education.[38]

Shah Jahan also takes up a theme important to the contemporaneous Bengali reformers and others that young girls married to older men are the more likely to soon find themselves widows. Shah Jahan fears nothing more than helplessness and no one, in her view, is more vulnerable than a widow. The widow faces neglect; she runs the mortal risk of winding up pregnant; she faces the treatment that makes her a pariah at every celebration because of her presumed inauspiciousness. She is wholly dependent on the will of the in-laws. Here is Shah Jahan:

> The widow is forced to sit silent in the house and throw the world and the afterworld and youth all in the dirt. She has to tell everyone that she doesn't even want to remarry; she doesn't want a man. Look at this fairly. She says this only to please the in-laws; otherwise she would want it. If her husband were alive, she'd have relations with him for fifty or sixty years and have children. . . . If, by chance, the husband were ill and they could not have relations, she'd complain about it. Instead a widow, even if twelve years old, says I have no wish for a man. She says this only because of the in-laws and because she's been taught to say so.[39]

The Qur'an has several verses on the waiting period required before a widow or divorcee remarries (the *'iddah* to allow confirmation of any pregnancy). For Shah Jahan, that provision is enough to make her point on the absolute legitimacy of remarriage. In fact, Shah Jahan adds, God abrogated an initial teaching that set the waiting period for a year, not four months, confirmation for her that a woman cannot live without a man that long and that God wants what is good for his creation.

Shah Jahan makes clear to her readers that her teachings on this controversial subject are not a matter of choice. *Jaanaa chaahiyee*—'you just need to know', as she always says—that exactly as Almighty God fixed the obligations of prayer, fasting, the *hajj*, *zakat* and so forth . . . for all Muslims, he also set out . . . the rules for the marriage of divorced women.' Remarriage of widowed and divorced women thus has exactly the importance of the fundamental ritual obligations of worship, including prayer and the fast. No guardian can forbid this, she says. And lest the point be missed: 'Not to accept [this teaching] and act on it, in fact to consider it a sin, makes a person a *munaafiq* (a fraud) and not a true Muslim.'[40] It was clear that even with statutory law passed in 1856 allowing the remarriage of Hindu women, to say nothing of the public approval of remarriage routinely made by Hindu and Muslim reformers alike, remarriage for elite women was rare.[41] Given the practice of the day, Shah Jahan brought out for Muslims the heaviest guns she could imagine—remarriage or, essentially, damnation.

Shah Jahan brilliantly navigated the ambiguity of multivalent texts to argue forcefully for what she believed to be the rights and entitlements of Muslim women. Take, for example, *hadith* which would seem to confirm a conventional misogynist view of female nature: she simply turns them on their head. A woman, she writes, is particularly prone to emotion and ill temper. But, as the *hadith* says, the woman's 'crooked nature' stems from her being made from man's rib. If a man tries to change a woman, he might break her. Thus, it is a man's duty, as affirmed in multiple *hadith*, to put up with whatever a woman may do, to be 'light-hearted', as she puts it, and good natured.

In any matter that is not against the *shari'a*, or a source of disgrace and sin, you *must* give priority to the happiness of your wife, and, to the extent that is possible, keep her comfortable, satisfied, and happy, and act toward her lifelong with gentleness and good nature so that love and intimacy grows every day and there is no sorrow or unpleasantness between you.[42]

It is *men* who need to bend over backwards to keep their wives happy. As this last comment made clear, Shah Jahan Begum spoke with a distinctive voice. To be sure, she worked within the same parameters as her fellow male reformers in these years. There was no question of challenging the basic patriarchal family structure nor the primarily domestic role of women, even if in this regard her own life was, indeed, an exception. There was every question, as they all agreed, of pushing, however limited the result, a range of reforms of contemporary practice affecting women like age of marriage, widow remarriage, and girls' education. All agreed, moreover, that disseminating knowledge was the key to change. Shah Jahan, however, was distinctive in the way she elevated the status of women, both in comparison with fellow Muslim reformers and the Hindu reformers who turned the 'new' woman into the 'goddess' of the home. Rather, as argued previously, Shah Jahan identified women as nothing less than agents of God's creative purpose in producing and shaping the world.[43] God's entire divine plan thus depended on women's reproductive health, on her learning, and on her skills in management. Anyone who ignored women's rights and entitlements did so at their own peril. Shah Jahan's teachings, informed by her own experience, driven by a commitment to self-reliance, and bolstered by scholarly argumentation, carried a commanding punch.

It is tempting to weigh in with a value judgement, measuring Shah Jahan's teachings in terms of what are often taken as universal values of egalitarianism and the presumption of an inevitable trajectory towards gender egalitarianism and isomorphism. By this standard, Shah Jahan Begum, a woman with a public role, committed to women's entitlements and promoting women's skills, might well be taken as a woman who was 'ahead of her times'. To make such a judgement, however, bumps up against Shah Jahan's acceptance of female seclusion and covering, her commitment to women's domestic role and presumed subordinate place in the family, and her ready repetition of stereotypes about women's emotionalism and cunning.

Indeed, as noted here, a historian like Ruby Lal sees the reformers of the period as the opposite of progressive. Imagining a better time before, she writes, 'Attention to these richer and less programmed lives [of the early nineteenth century] also troubles the typical progressive narrative of women's increasing liberation.'[44] As Lal writes,

Reformist writings of the late nineteenth century, British as well as Indian, often erase the potential for spontaneity and discovery ... while simultaneously constricting the space for the exercise of critical reasoning and the capacity for autonomy and self-governance that the 'new woman' could be expected to possess.[45]

This argument is, of course, disproved by Shah Jahan's own life, quite apart from the evidence about her reasoning set out here.[46] Moreover, any movement that included literacy, particularly at a time when few families fostered girls' education, inevitably would open up new opportunities precisely of the kind that Lal sees precluded.

To offer these caveats, however, does not mean that it is appropriate to apply a progressive label to the texts at stake. Such a judgement is also ethnocentric and anachronistic. Even to gloss Shah Jahan as a proto-'Islamic feminist', valuing choices like parda without ethnocentric bias, belies her own goals.

It is often assumed that once religious teachings, and especially Islamic teachings, are invoked, they have negative consequences for women,[47] especially as regards female covering. Ethnographic work among Muslim women in many regions of the world, in fact, makes clear that women's problems stem not from 'Islam', but far more likely from larger structures of state, society, and poverty.[48] A major study conducted in India, for example, showed that poverty, illiteracy, and discrimination impacted Muslim women's lives just as they did Hindu women's lives.[49] Poverty and 'structural discrimination' that minimized the availability of educational and health facilities as well as employment opportunities, in fact, harmed Muslim families disproportionately.[50] The answer to the title of anthropologist Lila Abu-Lughod's book, *Do Muslim Women Need Saving?* may be 'yes'; but salvation did not entail being saved from Islam.

Bodily covering, and in some cases seclusion, may in some cases be a tool to control women, but it need not be. The very fact that the 'secluded scholars' of Gail Minault's book and the 'secluded sovereign' of this essay turn out to be educated, spirited, and enterprising women is one reason that their stories need to be told. Many ethnographic accounts reveal similar stories of women who cover themselves in public but lead active and engaged lives.[51] Other studies have documented the pragmatic advantages of covering, from ease in moving in public space to identifying with movements of political and cultural resistance. Poor working women do not have the luxury of seclusion or even of buying extensive lengths of cloth: for them the practice of covering may become a route to respectability and social mobility.[52] All this is not to say that there is not extensive debate among Muslims on the necessity of this practice.

Rather than sanctioning or condoning Shah Jahan's choices, we do best to place them in the context of their times. As noted here, male reformers associated with the Westernizing, modern Aligarh movement favoured seclusion as well and, in fact, made it a characteristic of the new-style, educated woman they envisioned. For Shah Jahan Begum, such propriety was particularly important considering her public role. As an activist for one of the reformist religious movements of the day, moreover, covering served as a public statement of piety, the more powerful in her case since it was freely chosen against her mother's precedent and against official British pressure.

Hers was a time of considerable debate and challenge to received practice. Although Shah Jahan does not use a term like 'empowerment', it is fair to see her very act of choice as a source of satisfaction and 'agency' that is indeed empowering.[53] Beyond the empowerment that one must recognize in a choice (even) like accepting parda, Shah Jahan spells out multiple entitlements for women that empower them from girlhood on, starting with the superior education that she prefers and moving on to marriage arrangements and the entitlements of widows that defy conventional behaviour of the day.

Other times and places did not offer an opportunity for such challenges. By the turn of the twentieth century, Muslim spokesmen began to envisage the identity of 'Indian Muslim' as part of a larger Indian nationalism. Shah Jahan Begum, however, writing earlier as well as in the context of a princely state where issues of nationalism were long moot, had no such concern with 'Indian Muslims'. She wrote generally for women of her class, with reference to a vague and undefined Muslim *umma*. By the period of mass anti-colonial nationalism in the interwar period of the twentieth century, Muslim spokesmen for this 'community' espoused the newly salient global category of 'minority cultural rights' as they looked ahead to their place in a democratic society. Many Muslims came to take Muslim personal law as the constitutionally guaranteed hallmark of their minority identity, a conviction that persists for many till present. An embattled minority status risks a legal rigidity not evident in an earlier era and absent from the writings of Shah Jahan.

In Pakistan in recent decades, contestation over Islamic 'law' has taken on a rigidity of its own. The 1970 Pakistani edition of Shah Jahan's book, with its cover images of the sites of pilgrimage and *hajj*, suggests a focus on ritual that the book does not have. That the author is identified on its cover as '"Mrs" Shah Jahan Begum, wife of Nawab Siddiq Hasan Khan'—a proper bourgeois housewife?—is perhaps a clue to the orientation of the editor of this edition. He, in fact, periodically intervenes with footnotes to differ with Shah Jahan's interpretations, for example on such issues as the suitable age of girls' marriage.[54]

Shah Jahan Begum was not part of the imagining of a minority 'Indian Muslim community', let alone of the Islamist nationalism that came later. Freed of such confining identities, she espoused Islamic teachings as a resource to justify practices that asserted what she saw as a route to her own worldly and spiritual autonomy as well as practices that served the well-being of elite families like hers.[55] Her model of Islamic reasoning is very different from the rules and even laws that come into play when Islamic symbols are assigned the burden of preserving the identity of a permanent minority or defining the ideology of an 'Islamic state'. The content of her teaching, moreover, is different from the stereotypical assumptions that Islamic reform is limited to eliminating 'Hindu' practices, enhancing men's control of women, and depriving women of self-sufficiency, choice, and even pleasure. Instead, in her hopeful view, women who are the very centre of God's creation, deserve the education and other entitlements that would make them not only self-sufficient but happy as well. A secluded sovereign, like 'secluded scholars', may not be what she seems.

Notes

1. Gail Minault, *Secluded Scholars: Women's Education and Muslim Social Reform in Colonial India*, Delhi, New York: Oxford Univeristy Press, 1998. p. 1. Elsewhere Gail graciously thanks that friend, none other than Peter Hardy, for her 'opening line'. Minault, *Secluded Scholars*, p. vii. At this retrospective moment, it is good to remember how Peter Hardy's superb work in the field of Indo-Muslim history was invaluable for all researchers in the field, not least those of us working in the early years of attention to South Asia in the American academy.
2. For a general history of these women in the context of Bhopal's history, see Shahriyar Khan, *The Begums of Bhopal: A Dynasty of Women Rulers in Raj India*, London: I.B. Tauris, 2000.
3. Altaf Husain Hali and Gail Minault, *Voices of Silence: English Translation of Khwaja Altaf Husain Hali's Majalis an-Nissa and Chup ki Dad*, Delhi: Chanakya Publishers, 1986.
4. Shah Jahan Begum cites in the text at hand poets like Rumi and Saadi; medical works, Qur'an and Qur'anic commentaries, and, above all, *hadith* collections and commentaries on them. She would also have read classic works of ethics, like the *Akhlaq-i Nasir*, works that inculcate the moderation of emotions and discipline. Margrit Pernau contrasts Shah Jahan Begum with writers of this

era shaped in the Aligarh tradition and suggests that she rather writes in the akhlaq tradition of giving 'pride of place' to knowledge. Margrit Pernau, 'Asghari's Piety', in *Learning How to Feel: Children's Literature and Emotional Socialization, 1870–1970*, ed. U. Frevert et al., New York: Oxford University Press, 2014, p. 61.

5. Citations in this chapter are from a later edition. Shah Jahan Begum, *Tahzibun niswan wa tarbiyatul insan*, ed. Maulana 'Abdul Khaliq Quddusi, Gujranwala, Urdu Bazar: Maktaba No'maniya, 1970. My translation of the title is only one of many possiblities. Gail Minault, for example, takes *Tahzibun Niswan*, also the title of a periodical launched in 1998 to be 'The Muslim Reformer', and the phrase could as easily be translated as 'Civilizing Women'. I use the word 'improvement' to signal the contemporaneity of the enterprise since improvement—self-improvement, social improvement, improvement of customs—was so central to public life at the time. For a study that puts the study of a different reformer into the larger 'improving' culture of the day, see Brian A. Hatcher, *Idioms of Improvement: Vidyasagar and Cultural Encounter in Bengal*, New Delhi: Oxford University Press, 1996.

6. Minault, *Secluded Scholars*, p. 103. For a review of several of the texts written by the Urdu 'men of letters' (an appropriate term in this context), see Chapter 4, 'A Suitable Literature', in Minault, *Secluded Scholars*, pp. 58–104.

7. See Scott Kugle, 'Courting 'Ali: Urdu Poetry, Shi'i Piety and Courtesan Power in Hyderabad', in *Muslim Cultures in the Indo-Iranian World during the Early-Modern and Modern Periods*, ed. Denis Hermann and Fabrizio Speziale, Islamkundliche Untersuchungen Band 290, Berlin: Klaus Schwarz Publishers, 2010, pp. 125–66. See also Kugle, 'Mah Laqa Bai and Gender: Language, Poetry and Performance of a Courtesan in Hyderabad', *Comparative Studies in South Asia, Africa and the Middle East*, vol. 30, no. 3, 2010, pp. 365–85. The genre of this production was primarily poetry, although John Malcolm recorded the gift to him of an Urdu history ('of the Nizam and his ancestors, to which she had added a general essay on universal history') on the part of a courtesan in Hyderabad; Malcolm did add that he knew the compilation had been made for her. John William Kaye, *The Life and Correspondence of Major-General Sir John Malcolm, G.C.B.*, vol. 2, London: Smith, Elder, and Co., 1856, pp. 164–5. Both Mah Laqa Bai (1768–1824) and the Hyderabadi courtesan flourished earlier in the century.

8. Seclusion of elite women was not limited to Muslim women and that of the Rajput *rani's* was regarded as particularly extreme. Rameshwari Nehru (1886–1996), an activist and editor of the important journal for women, *Stri Darpan*, was secluded from the age of 12 and only left off the practice when she came to Allahabad and married into the Nehru family in 1902. Manesha Lal, '"The Ignorance of Women is the House of Illness": Gender, Nationalism, and Health Reform in Colonial North India', in *Medicine and Colonial Identity*, ed. Bridie Andrews and Mary P. Sutphen, London and New York: Routledge, 2003, p. 17.

9. Moulvi Mohibb-i Husain, for example, part of the service elite in Hyderabad, was a translator attuned to Middle Eastern publications that may well have influenced him. By the 1890s, his journal, *Mu'allim-i Niswan*, 'The Women's Teacher', spoke out against women's seclusion. He largely wrote the journal's articles himself, but did serialize a novel of Abdu'l Halim Sharar that took a position against purdah. He wrote on sufferance, and when in 1901 he compared purdah to the medieval European chastity belt, the Hyderabad government closed the publication down. Minault, *Secluded Scholars*, pp. 107–10.
10. Fadwa El Guindi early on documented the modern use of veiling on the part of urban women representing a first generation with university education who found their movement in public space facilitated by covering. See, for example, El Guindi, *Veil: Modesty, Privacy and Resistance*, New York: Berg, 1999. Similarly, at a different class level, Aihwa Ong has shown the utility of covering for Muslim women factory workers in Malaysia; see Ong, *Spirits of Resistance and Capitalist Discipline: Factory Women in Malaysia*, Albany: State University of New York Press, 1987.
11. The phrase was introduced by Hannah Papanek. See her 'Afterword', in *Sultana's Dream and Selections from the Secluded Ones by Rokeya (Begum)*, tr. Roushan Jahan, New York: The Feminist Press, 1988, pp. 64–6. For an image of the Begum wearing her robe, see the *Supplement to the Illustrated London News*, 5 February 1876, p. 137. The occasion was the most important visit made by any member of the royal family in the nineteenth century. Chandrika Kaul, 'Monarchical Display and the Politics of Empire: Princes of Wales and India, 1870–1920s', *Twentieth Century British History*, vol. 17, no. 4, 2006, pp. 464–88. For an image of her less covered on the same occasion in a more informal setting, see Sir William Howard Russell, *The Prince of Wales' Tour: A Diary in India*, London, 1878, p. 321.
12. On the didactic Urdu publications that garnered government support, see C.M. Naim, 'Prize-winning *ADAB*: A Study of Five Urdu Books Written in Response to the Allahabad Government Gazette Notification', in *Moral Conduct and Authority: The Place of adab in South Asian Islam*, ed. Barbara Daly Metcalf, Berkeley: University of California Press, 1984, pp. 290–314.
13. That is not to say that other texts concerned with girls' behaviour did not call for generalized piety: they certainly did. Nazir Ahmad, moreover, in his later years became a serious writer on religious questions, including a translation of the Qur'an and his own guidebook, *al Huquq wa al Fara'iz*, 1906. See Mushirul Hasan, *A Moral Reckoning: Muslim Intellectuals in Nineteenth-century Delhi*, New Delhi: Oxford University Press, 2003, pp. 146–50.
14. Dana Sajdi for an earlier period in the Levant similarly raises the question of the claims of authority on the part of several writers who lacked *ijaza* but still asserted the authority of critiquing the behaviour of elites and ruler alike. In the case of the barber of her book's title, he made clear his association with the revered and learned in a context—the barbershop—that, like the

similar coffee shop of the day, was a site of social mixing and conversation. Shah Jahan Begum, similarly, framed her book with verses and statements of approval by those with appropriate credentials, including among them her own husband. Dana Sajdi, *The Barber of Damascus: Nouveau Literacy in the 18th Century Ottoman Levant*, Stanford: Stanford University Press, 2013.

15. Ruby Lal, *Coming of Age in Nineteenth-Century India: The Girl-Child and the Art of Playfulness*, Cambridge: Cambridge University Press, 2013, p. 37.

16. See Muhammad Khalid Masud, Brinkley Messick and David Powers, eds., *Islamic Legal Interpretation: Muftis and Their Fatwas*, Cambridge: Harvard University Press, 1996.

17. Maulana Ashraf 'Ali Thanavi, *Perfecting Women: Maulana Ashraf 'Ali Thanawi's Bihishti Zewar*, ed. and tr. Barbara Daly Metcalf, Berkeley: University of California Press, 1992, p. 377. 'This is a very good book, but its legal points are not in accord with the law school of our Imam [the Hanafi legal tradition in contrast to that of the Ahl-i Hadith]. Therefore, act on those points with the *Bihishti Zewar* as guide. . . . Other points written here are all ones that encourage a good disposition, offer good counsel, and are conducive to comfort. All these are worth acting on.' The late nineteenth century saw the emergence of new sectarian orientations among Sunni scholars, including the Deobandi, that of Maulana Thanawi, 1863–1943, the Barelvi, and the Ahl-I Hadith. See Barbara Daly Metcalf, *Islamic Revival in British India: Deoband, 1860-1900*, 2nd edn., New Delhi: Oxford University Press, 2002.

18. With thanks to Professor Shahid Amin. After a talk about the begums at the Centre for the Study of Democratic Societies, Delhi, he sent me back to the text to check on the invocation, which to that point I had only skimmed. Shah Jahan Begum, *Tahzibun niswan wa tarbiyatul insan*, p. 12.

19. Surah Baqra (2: 23). 'Tilth' refers to prepared soil. This is the translation of Abdullah Yusuf Ali, tr., *The Holy Quran*, Lahore: Sh. Muhammad Ashraf, 1973. The translation and commentary were first published in 1938.

20. Among the occasions to avoid intercourse are during illnesses that 'originate from the womb', which is regarded as the source of most of women's diseases. Shah Jahan Begum, *Tahzibun niswan wa tarbiyatul insan*, pp. 13–14.

21. See for example, ibid., pp. 125–40.

22. Ibid., p. 120. She did say that more attention should be given to boys in terms of writing, the *munshi gari* ('business of a *munshi*, a writer/secretary') that could earn them employment. She insisted, however, that girls needed to be able to write Urdu, a position that even Thanawi, who personally favoured writing, was willing to waffle on since some feared that girls who could write could, for example, conduct secret correspondence. On the education of a *munshi*, see Muzaffar Alam and Sanjay Subrahmanyam, 'The Making of a Munshi', *Comparative Studies of South Asia, Africa and the Middle East*, vol. 24, no. 2, 2004, pp. 61–73. Nazir Ahmad had made the same point

about the need for girls' education to compensate for seclusion. Nazir Ahmad, 1903, *The Bride's Mirror: A Tale of Life in Delhi Forty Years Ago*, tr. G.E. Ward, reprinted with an Afterword by Frances W. Pritchett, New Delhi: Permanent Black, 2001, p. 15.

23. Ahmad and Maulavi, *The Bride's Mirror*, p. 118. The definition is from Duncan Forbes, *Dictionary, Hindustani and English*, 2nd edn., London: W.H. Allen & Co., 1858.
24. Shah Jahan Begum, *Tahzibun niswan wa tarbiyatul insan*, p. 118. They were *makaar* and *chaalaak*.
25. For the debate over private tuition and schools, see Minault, *Secluded Scholars*, pp. 216–28, 239, for example, on the efforts of Syed Karamat Husain and the challenges of establishing what would become Aligarh Women's College. In 1908, the Victoria School had 180 pupils who were instructed in reading, arithmetic, Qu'ran, and needlework. C.E. Luard, *Bhopal State Gazetteer, Volume III: Texts and Tables*, assisted by Munshi Kudrat Ali, Calcutta: Superintendent Government Printing, 1908, p. 73.
26. Shah Jahan Begum, *Tahzibun niswan wa tarbiyatul insan*, p. 135. 'Up until today', she writes, 'they have nothing to rely on except begging'.
27. See, for example, Christina Oesterheld's analysis of Nazir Ahmad's novel, *Ruya'-i Sadiqa*, written a quarter century later than his celebrated book for women, *Mir'atul 'Arus*. A work focused largely on religious instruction, it also made a new-style, economically self-sufficient male its hero. Christina Oesterheld, 'Nazir Ahmad and the Early Urdu Novel: Some Observations', *Annual of Urdu Studies*, vol. 16, 2001, pp. 27–42.
28. As for ethnicity, she orchestrated a suitable Pathan marriage for her daughter but defended her own outside marriage on the ground that her new spouse was a *sayyid* claiming Prophetic descent and thus enjoyed an elevated status.
29. Shah Jahan, *Tahzibun niswan wa tarbiyatul insan*, devotes four of her 20 chapters and some seventy-odd jam-packed pages (pp. 152–226) to marriage: Chapter 13, on maturity and suitability for marriage; Chapter 14, on requirements for selecting a spouse; Chapter 15 on widow remarriage; Chapter 16 on divorce.
30. Shah Jahan, *Tahzibun niswan wa tarbiyatul insan*, pp. 166–7.
31. 'I said, "My father died, leaving seven or nine girls (orphans) and I did not like to bring a young girl like them, so I married a woman who can look after them". He said, "May Allah bestow His Blessing on you."' This is from the *hadith* compendium of Sahih Bukhari, vol. 8, book 75, no. 396, http://www.searchtruth.com/searchHadith.php?keyword=jabir&book=&translator=1&search=1&search_word=&start=280&records_display=10, accessed 26 August 2014.
32. Shah Jahan Begum, *Tahzibun niswan wa tarbiyatul insan*, p. 189. She makes this equation on the basis of the Qur'anic surah (66:5).
33. Shah Jahan, *Tahzibun niswan wa tarbiyatul insan*, pp. 167–8.
34. Ibid., p. 168.

35. Ibid., pp. 168–9.
36. The issue of the age of girls at marriage was widely debated in the late nineteenth century, culminating in the passage of an 'Age of Consent' law in 1893. There is considerable scholarship on this and related issues, with the work of Tanika Sarkar particularly important. See, for example, her 'A Prehistory of Rights: The Age of Consent Debate in Colonial Bengal', Points of Departure: India and the South Asian Diaspora, *Feminist Studies*, vol. 26, no. 3, Autumn 2000, pp. 601–22.
37. The terms used are *naukar, laundi, ghulam*. Shah Jahan Begum, *Tahzibun niswan wa tarbiyatul insan*, p. 170.
38. Ibid.
39. Shah Jahan Begum, *Tahzibun niswan wa tarbiyatul insan*, p. 192.
40. Ibid., p. 188.
41. Tanika Sarkar, however, makes the important point that however little followed, the debate on these reforms contributed to the development of new perspectives on women's well-being and rights. A collection of several valuable interventions on nineteenth-century social reform is Sumit Sarkar and Tanika Sarkar, eds., *Women and Social Reform in Modern India*, Bloomington: Indiana University Press, 2008.
42. Shah Jahan Begum, *Tahzibun niswan wa tarbiyatul insan*, pp. 200–1.
43. See, for example, Judith Walsh, *How to be the Goddess of your Home: An Anthology of Bengali Domestic Manuals*, New Delhi: Yoda Press, 2005.
44. Lal, *Coming of Age in Nineteenth-Century India*, p. 33.
45. Ibid., p. 37.
46. For poetry, see especially her first *diwan*, Janab Nawab Shahjehan Begam, *Diwan-Shiriin*, Kanpur: Matba' Nizaami, 1288/1871–2, whose poetry Syed Akbar Hyder judges as original and accomplished (personal communication). On architecture, see Barbara D. Metcalf, 'The Buildings of the Begums of Bhopal: "Islamic" Architecture in a Nineteenth-century Indian Princely State', in *Woman's Eye, Woman's Hand: Making Art and Architecture in Modern India*, ed. D. Fairchild Ruggles, New Delhi: Zubaan Press, 2014. According to her great-grandson, she 'had given Bhopal a new, liberal dimension adding colour, gaiety and panache . . . [she] built glorious palaces and the largest mosque in India; there was always the sound of music in the palaces, endless festivity and more than a whiff of decadence'. Khan, *The Begums of Bhopal*, p. 153.
47. Although Lal includes some Hindu texts of the period in her study, the book is framed by Muslim voices and they dominate the argument. The text rewarded for government were each designed for either Muslim or Hindu girls.
48. See Abu-Lughod's report of a conversation with a woman in southern Egypt. When asked if Muslim women were oppressed, she readily answered yes: the government oppresses people, it does nothing to provide work or jobs, prices are too high. Lila Abu-Lughod, *Do Muslim Women Need Saving?*, Cambridge: Harvard University Press, 2013, pp. 1–2.

49. Even Islamic teachings allowing such practices as easy divorce on the part of men and polygyny did not figure. Zoya Hasan and Ritu Menon, *Unequal Citizens: A Study of Muslim Women in India*, Delhi: Oxford University Press, 2004.
50. Jeffery and Jeffery (1988) demonstrate that higher fertility among rural Muslims correlates with their lack of opportunities apart from manual farming and other labour.
51. See Mukulika Banerjee, ed., *Muslim Portraits: Everyday Lives in India*, Bloomington: Indiana University Press, 2008, p. xix; Patricia Jeffery, Roger Jeffery and Craig Jeffrey, 'Aisha, the Madrasah Teacher', in *Muslim Portraits:Everyday Lives in India*, ed. Mukulika Banerjee, pp. 56–68.
52. See, for example, Fadwa El Guindi, *Veil: Modesty, Privacy, Resistance*, Oxford: Berg Publishers, 1999. Contemporary veiling practices are a modern phenomenon, whether among educated urban women or among factory workers, whose covering enables their work, as shown by Aihwa Ong, 'State versus Islam: Malay Families, Women's Bodies, and the Body Politic in Malaysia', *American Ethnologist*, vol. 17, 1990, pp. 558–82.
53. Such an argument fits with the interpretation, associated with the work of the anthropologist Saba Mahmood, which understands an active embrace of Islamic 'piety' as a source of *agency* that empowers women. Thus, for example, when women willingly accept male familial authority, seclusion, and so forth, their doing so is not a mark of their servitude to males, but of their chosen submission to God. To see this as an inferior life choice, Mahmood argues, is to exercise an act of cultural ethnocentrism. Saba Mahmood, *Politics of Piety: The Islamic Revival and the Feminist Subject*, Princeton: Princeton University Press, 2005.
54. Or on p. 119, he warns that a male tutor should be elderly, not a young man, however upright he might appear to be. He also is more stringent in his disapproval of customs, for example in relation to mourning the dead. Thus, although Shah Jahan Begum disapproves of excessive mourning and fixed days after the death for assembling and feeding fellow mourners, she considers it acceptable to distribute food to the poor and read the Quran to transfer merit to the departed's soul as long as the day for this is not fixed. The editor does not agree. Shah Jahan Begum, *Tahzibun niswan wa tarbiyatul insan*, p. 296.
55. Margrit Pernau points out that the work presupposes a world of servants, personal tutors, access to transport animals, and so forth. See Pernau, 'Asghari's Piety'. This was, as noted previously, an era geared towards 'improvement' at many levels and Shah Jahan was part of this.

References

Abu-Lughod, Lila, *Do Muslim Women Need Saving?*, Cambridge: Harvard University Press, 2013.

Ahmad, Nazir, 1903, *The Bride's Mirror: A Tale of Life in Delhi Forty Years Ago*, tr. G.E. Ward, reprinted with an Afterword by Frances W. Pritchett, New Delhi: Permanent Black, 2001.

Banerjee, Mukulika, ed., *Muslim Portraits: Everyday Lives in India*, Bloomington: Indiana University Press, 2008.

Begum, Shah Jahan, *Tahzibun niswan wa tarbiyatul insan*, ed. Maulana Abdul Khaliq Quddusi, Gujranwala, Urdu Bazar: Maktaba No'maniya, 1970.

Hali, Altaf Husain and Gail Minault, *Voices of Silence: English Translation of Khwaja Altaf Husain Hali's Majalis an-Nissa and Chup ki Dad*, Delhi: Chanakya Publishers, 1986.

Hasan, Mushirul, *A Moral Reckoning: Muslim Intellectuals in Nineteenth-century Delhi*, New Delhi: Oxford University Press, 2003.

Jeffery, Patricia, Roger Jeffery and Craig Jeffrey, 'Aisha, the Madrasah Teacher', in *Muslim Portraits: Everyday Lives in India*, ed. Mukulika Banerjee, Bloomington: Indiana University Press, 2008, pp. 56–68.

Lal, Manesha, '"The Ignorance of Women is the House of Illness": Gender, Nationalism, and Health Reform in Colonial North India', in *Medicine and Colonial Identity*, ed. Bridie Andrews and Mary P. Sutphen, London and New York: Routledge, 2003, pp. 14–40.

Lal, Ruby, *Coming of Age in Nineteenth-Century India: The Girl-Child and the Art of Playfulness*, Cambridge: Cambridge University Press, 2013.

Luard, C.E., *Bhopal State Gazeteer, Volume III: Texts and Tables*, Assisted by Munshi Kudrat Ali, Calcutta: Superintendent Government Printing, 1908.

Oesterheld, Christina, 'Nazir Ahmad and the Early Urdu Novel: Some Observation', *Annual of Urdu Studies*, vol. 16, 2001, pp. 27–42.

Pernau, Margrit, 'Asghari's Piety', in *Learning How to Feel: Children's Literature and Emotional Socialization, 1870-1970*, ed. U. Frevert et al., New York: Oxford University Press, 2014, pp. 57–73.

———, *Ashraf into Middle Classes: Muslims in Nineteenth-Century Delhi*, New Delhi: Oxford University Press, 2013.

8

Raja Bhagvatsinh and Rani Nandkunvarba of Gondal

'Valiant Champions of Female Emancipation'

AARTI BHALODIA

RAJA BHAGVATSINH (1865–1944), a Jadeja Rajput, was the ruler of Gondal state in western India from 1884 to 1944. His contemporaries referred to him as the 'maker of modern Gondal' and 'valiant champion of female emancipation'.[1] During his long reign over Gondal, Bhagvatsinh made great advances in the fields of education, irrigation and transportation. He was a champion of women's education, sending his daughters to boarding schools in England and encouraging them to become role models for the girls of Gondal. Current and former residents of Gondal state still sing praises of Bhagvatsinh and refer to him affectionately as 'Bhaga Bapa'.

Literature on princely states tends to focus heavily on rulers, overwhelmingly male. Influenced by Gail Minault's scholarship, especially *Secluded Scholars*, I decided to bring the women of princely states into conversation. In early stages of my research I noticed the important role played by the elite women of Gondal in furthering female education. It was an effort to track down documents that focused on the women of Gondal or else authored by them. Originally, my project was focused solely on Bhagvatsinh as I believed he was the only architect of Gondal's education policy. I wanted to study educational reforms carried out in Gondal state during Bhagvatsinh's time as I had heard about this illustrious ruler as a child growing up in the vicinity of the state. It was part of public culture, especially in Gujarat, to praise Bhagvatsinh for the various reforms he had carried out, especially his promotion of education for boys and girls. It was only after I started conducting my research that I learnt the important contributions of women in promoting female education. The focus of my project changed as I realized that if I wanted to provide a complete picture of female education in Gondal, I would have to examine the contributions of both Bhagvatsinh and also Rani Nandkunvarba, his wife.

Those of us who study the history of female education are careful not to take it at face value. As I studied my material in greater depth I asked who the proponents of female education were, and about the motivating factors. How did the women of Gondal view the state's educational policy? Were there any other female reformers besides Bhagvatsinh's wife, Rani Nandkunvarba, and how did they fit into the picture?[3]

The Century of Reform

In tune with the reformist tradition of the nineteenth century, Bhagvatsinh placed great emphasis on women's education. In South Asia, reform focused on social issues such as ending female infanticide, allowing widow-remarriage, discontinuing child marriage, and promoting literacy. Both the liberal reformers of the 1820s–1870s and the cultural revivalists who started showing their influence after the 1870s had strong opinions on gendered topics. Locating women as the grounds for revival of the community, be it along caste, religion, or national lines was an idea widespread across India.[2] The goal of both Hindu and Muslim social reform was to educate not just men but also women, as both needed to be uplifted in order to ensure the regeneration of the community. Rammohun Roy argued women's enlightenment was the answer to moving India away from its 'degenerate state'. This belief resulted in reformers across the spectrum (the Deoband *ulama*, the Aligarh movement, the Arya Samaj and the Brahmo Samaj) encouraging the spread of literacy among women, which would give them the ability to read scripture and become better Muslims and Hindus.[3]

While studying at Elphinstone College, the novelist Govardhanram Tripathi had the following to say about women: 'Women are the very source of human happiness, one of the principal means of the improvement of society, the centre of our domestic bliss and the easy delight of the human heart.'[4] Tripathi identifies women as the 'principal' agents of reform. For reformers, both Hindu and Muslim, the 'backwardness' of women symbolized the degenerate state of their religion.[5] However, women also symbolized all that was worth preserving and embodied qualities essential for revival. In the reformist mind, uplifting women from ignorance was a prerequisite for reinstating the 'Golden Age'.[6] Reformers treated women as victims to be rescued or as backward people who needed to be uplifted.

As expected, Gondal state came under the influence of the prevailing reformist climate. An examination of educational policy of Gondal state highlights the fusion of modern and traditional ideas.[7] Like his contemporaries, Bhagvatsinh believed women were central to the reformist project and in order to bring back the Golden Age, women needed to be uplifted to the level of their counterparts in ancient times. The women of Gondal's royal family were not silent observers of Bhagvatsinh's reformist project. In their capacity as *rani* (queen), *rajkumari* (princess), mother, wife, and daughters, they played an instrumental role in shaping Gondal's educational policy.

Despite heavy emphasis on the plight of women and ways to improve their miserable condition, reformist movements during the nineteenth century were dominated by men. Female voices were either absent or silenced in reformist debates.[8] Women were the grounds on which the reformers, the orthodoxy, and the colonial state debated what constituted authentic Indian tradition.[9] Male reformers engaged in public debate with the conservative elements over what should be the position of women in Indian society. Meanwhile women remained silent as it was their job to be reformed, but not act as reformers. Although women did not actively participate in reformist activities until the late nineteenth century, they did influence male reformers, men influenced by strong maternal figures in their lives.[10] In her research Minault has shown us that female voices were not completely silent; women influenced the world outside the *zenana* through the power they exercised over the men in their lives.

Female Education, Patronage and State Policy

Rani Monghiba, Bhagvatsinh's mother, supported women's education, as she believed an educated woman could better discharge her conjugal and maternal responsibilities. In 1858, the Monghiba School for Girls was established in Gondal. In matters of female education, Bhagvatsinh was following in the footsteps of his mother. Under the influence of Swaminarayan saints, Monghiba developed a positive view towards female education, differing from other Rajput women of her times.[11] She believed that education should not be the exclusive privilege of men.

Following her husband's *death*, and while her son was a minor, Monghiba dealt with the British. Her relations with the Kathiawar Agency were often contentious as she struggled to limit the British political agent's control over young Bhagvatsinh.[12] Monghiba's personal experience in political affairs played a role in shaping her views on education. For her, being a mother often meant she had to venture out of the safety of the female sphere into the male world of politics to ensure her son's political future. Monghiba felt that women could not afford to remain uneducated, as they needed to acquire crucial skills to prepare them for motherhood, and so she continued to support the vernacular girl's school throughout her life.

After Monghiba's death, Bonjiba, Bhagvatsinh's widowed sister-in-law, became the main patron of the girl's school now named after Monghiba.[13] This was a time when there still was considerable opposition to girls' schools. Male education was accepted among middle class families, as it was seen as a steppingstone towards administrative and professional jobs. The prevailing argument in the nineteenth century in favour of modern education for Indian men was the financial benefits. Education for middle- and upper class women was regarded as superfluous, since they were not required to contribute to the family economy. Additionally, the opponents of female education held that educating a woman was such a great sin (*pap*) that bad karma would befall anyone partaking in such an activity, even leading to the woman in question becoming a widow at an early age, widowhood being the greatest calamity for women in a deeply patriarchal society. In such an environment, upper class women publicly declaring their support for female education had a positive impact. In 1893, Bonjiba set up a trust that would distribute annual prizes to deserving female students in an effort to encourage female education.[14]

Bonjiba's life as a widow made her realize the importance of education for girls, as it was a means to provide them with tools to deal with hardships. In addition, her widowhood made her more attuned to the life of other widows. As an aristocrat, despite her status as a widow, Bonjiba led a materially comfortable life, as is evident from the various organizations she patronized. But she was sensitive to her middle-class sisters who did not have similar material resources. Support for female education rose from her acknowledgement of the reality that in the absence of men, women often had to provide for the family. Thus women could not be barred from school on the basis that educating them had no financial payback. Encouraging widows to become teachers was also a way to give widows a purpose in life.[15] In some ways this mindset was similar to the one espoused by Sahajanand, the founder of Swaminarayan Hinduism, who allowed widows to join his group of male ascetics.[16] Under the influence of Sahajanand's teachings, after all Gondal has one of the oldest Swaminarayan temples, the Monghiba School for Girls welcomed widows from its earliest days and encouraged them to become teachers on completing their education.[17]

In addition to the Monghiba school, Monghiba, Bonjiba, and Nandkunvarba (Bhagvatsinh's wife) patronized various other institutions with private funds. Monghiba was a follower of Swaminarayan and donated money to the temple in Gondal and frequently gave alms to holy men of various faiths. Bonjiba started an asylum for mentally and physically handicapped people. Nandkunvarba started the Bhagvatsinhji Orphanage, which was supported exclusively from her private purse.[18] During the famine of 1897–1901, she and Nandkunvarba donated to Hindu *mahajans* and Muslim *jamats* who were organizing relief efforts. Dhoraji, the principal city of Gondal state and home to the prosperous Muslim mercantile community, started the Nandkunvarba Zenana hospital for women to show their appreciation for the queen's generosity towards madrasas and hospitals in the city.[19] In the Rajput tradition these women patronized various charitable causes.[20] It was their political as well as religious duty to aid those in need. Sultan Jahan, the Begum of Bhopal, was another royal who addressed multiple audiences and assumed different roles. The Begum navigated being a woman, a Muslim, and a royal.[21] Similar to the women of Gondal, Sultan Jahan patronized all subjects, irrespective of their religion.

All the donations by the women of Gondal were sanctioned by religion as acts of *seva* (service). The idea was to not just help the poor and needy, but to also accumulate good *karma* while doing so. Where they differed from their ancestors was in the sponsorship of educational institutions. This was a result of the nineteenth-century reformist climate. While the colonial state praised these women for their philanthropic activities, the British government viewed philanthropy as a secular activity. Indian elites on the other hand regarded supporting educational institutions as an extension of their political and religious duties. The religious and the secular were intertwined for these women. In the nineteenth century, education became another arena in which one could perform *seva*. Not educated in Western schools, Nandkunvarba, Monghiba, and Bonjiba did not see any distinction between patronizing orphanages, hospitals, temples, and schools. All these institutions provided services beneficial to society and it was one's duty to support them.

State policy reflected Bhagvatsinh's views providing every form of support to educational institutions. When Leilaba, Bhagvatsinh's daughter got married, he started the Leilaba scholarship for any student of Monghiba girl's school who wanted to pursue college education.[22] This was a marked change from previous years as rulers much like merchants preferred to donate to places of worship, orphanages, and hospitals. It was common for upper class families to commemorate joyous occasions such as birth of a child or marriage by sharing some of their wealth with the less fortunate. Schools were unlikely recipients of princely or mercantile philanthropy. But with reformist influence this mindset changed, and the elites began to consider donating to schools as a form of *seva* equivalent to or even greater than religious service.

In 1913, the Monghiba school was converted into a high school, the Monghiba Girl's High School, the first girl's high school in all of Saurashtra (formerly Kathiawad).[23] A decade earlier English had been added to the curriculum. Students graduating from Monghiba High School appeared for Bombay University's matriculation exam. In its first year Manibai B. Udani, a Vania girl, passed the exam for which she achieved the Bhagvatsinh Silver Jubilee prize.[24] She went on to join the staff of the Monghiba school as a teacher. Manibai faced opposition from orthodox sections of the Gondal community, but refused to bow before the conservative elements. She was well remembered among reformist circles, a role model for students at Monghiba and other schools in the state. Leilaba, Bhagvatsinh's daughter, congratulated Manibai on her achievement and encouraged other girls to follow in her footsteps.[25]

Leilaba and her sister Bakuverba were former pupils of Monghiba girl's school. Educated in India and England, the sisters would frequently visit their alma mater in Gondal and share their worldly experiences with the young girls. When the high school started a science laboratory to teach elementary physics, chemistry, and physiology, Bakuverba attended the opening ceremony.[26] Together with the rest of the family the two sisters worked to promote education, especially female education, in Gondal state. Needless to say neither Leilaba nor Bakuverba observed parda in any form. In this they benefited from the radical steps taken by their mother. The royal family hoped the decision by their women to not observe parda would be emulated by the rest of society. They wanted their educated daughters to serve as examples to the women of Gondal, but the people of Gondal were slow to change. Enrolment in girl's schools was lower than expected. Bhagvatsinh came to the conclusion that the only way to get people to send their daughters to school was to use compulsion. Baroda state had made primary education compulsory for boys and girls in 1907. Gondal made primary education for girls compulsory in 1917.[27] Many wondered why Bhagvatsinh did not make primary education compulsory for boys too. Why the sole focus on girls? The state explained that there were multiple factors that led to such a decision. Foremost was the discrepancy in literacy levels leading to men having uneducated wives. Intellectual inequality between husbands and wives could result in unstable marriage and it was important to establish parity between couples by providing educated men with educated wives.[28] In this Bhagvatsinh and Nandkunvarba's thinking was similar to reformers across India. The push for formal education came from the upwardly mobile for who formal schooling was the way to adjust to the modern world. Education for women was a part modernization.

Another reason for focussing on girls was to prepare them for motherhood. An educated woman would pass on her learning to her children.[29] Educating a girl meant educating the whole family, thus making female education a worthy investment for the state and society at large. This second reason was an outcome of society treating women as nurturers and caregivers, as those in charge of the domestic sphere. In a colonial society it was their job to ensure that the family did not go astray under the influence of a foreign culture. Women were the guardians of tradition in a rapidly modernizing world. After primary education was made compulsory in 1917, the number of school going girls rose fourfold in one year.[30]

A New Form of Union: Companionate Marriage

Nandkunvarba married Bhagvatsinh in 1882 when she was fifteen years old. Raised in a conservative household and given primary education, she quickly assimilated to her husband's reformist views on coming to Gondal. Within six years Nandkunvarba stopped observing parda and attended public events. She was the first Rajput woman in Gujarat to step out of parda[31] as she wanted to keep up with her husband and travel unrestrained in his company.[32] This resulted in the first of many trips to England. Two years later she took a world tour with Bhagvatsinh and visited Europe, America, Japan, China, Australia, and Sri Lanka.[33] This was unusual for a Rajput woman. Using her position as the queen she encouraged other women to discard the veil.[34]

Though Nandkunvarba took a radical step by stepping out of seclusion, she attributes her decision to wifely devotion. She saw herself as being a *pativrata* woman following Hindu tradition and not a radical. Like many Hindu reformers Nandkunvarba viewed parda as a custom introduced by Muslims: since ancient Indian women did not observe parda, she saw no need to do so, she said. She described the decision to stop living in seclusion as reinstating the past and not as a break from tradition. In writings about Nandkunvarba she is celebrated as a woman who achieved many firsts.[35] She was one of the first Rajput women to discard the veil and travel to England. In 1892, the Queen conferred on her membership of the Imperial Order of the Crown of India. Not only did she go on a world tour with her husband, she also published her travel diary entitled *Gomandala Parikrama* (A Tour around the World). Besides descriptions of Nandkunvarba as a trailblazer, are comments about her love for Puranic literature, the *Ramayana*, the *Mahabharata*, and household management. The Gondal state took pains to paint a picture of Nandkunvarba as a traditional queen and a good Hindu woman.[36] Her actions are valorized but explained as simply mimicking the lifestyle of ancient Indian women. Nandkunvarba would say that her globetrotting to be a constant companion to her husband and her reading of religious epics constituted a lifestyle that was more Indian and more Hindu than that of her contemporaries living a cloistered life in the *zenana*.

In writings about Gondal, all written by men, Bhagvatsinh is depicted as the sole reason for Nandkunvarba's radical lifestyle. No attention is paid to the other women of the Gondal family, especially Monghiba, who was alive when Nandkunvarba came out of seclusion. It is hard to imagine the new queen at the age of twenty leaving the *zenana* without her mother-in-law's support.[37] The reformist Monghiba who patronized female education because it prepared women to become better mothers and wives saw the merit in her daughter-in-law sharing her son's reformist outlook as it would only strengthen their marriage. It is safe to say Bhagvatsinh was not the only influence on the young queen.

Nandkunvarba's decision to adapt with time came from a desire to be her husband's partner in all his endeavours. Though an aristocrat she had a middle-class understanding of companionate marriage; a relationship where husband and wife were partners and supported each other.[38] In a speech on the merits of female education Nandkunvarba stated:

Education is a great ornament to our class. It is a more valuable and beautiful possession than jewels and rich clothing. . . . Men and women may be variously mis-mated, some in age, some in disposition; but those who are mis-mated in education are the worst-mated of all, and are more unhappy than any of the others. . . . Where the mother is educated, there the children are better trained.[39]

For Nandkunvarba the primary purpose of female education was to shape women to become compatible companions for their educated husbands. Educated men across India desired educated wives. The primary reason behind educating women was to build a stable family, a stable community. Education would turn women into more suitable wives and effective mothers, thereby strengthening society. The promotion of female education was a step to modernity, to adjust to the new sociopolitical climate that required middle and upper class men to have received formal schooling. As expected of a queen, Nandkunvarba took a leadership role in furthering state policies. Being a dutiful wife she supported her husband's reformist policies. By promoting female education, Nandkunvarba was fulfilling her duties as a wife and queen.

Nandkunvarba believed in separate spheres for men and women and cautioned Indian women against blindly following their Western counterparts. She did not approve of the new woman of Britain who had acquired 'masculine spirits'.[40] Nandkunvarba had strict views on the appropriate roles for men and women, roles that were not interchangeable. In 1888, in a speech before students of the Barton Female Training College[41] at Rajkot, Nandkunvarba stressed the important differences between men and women.

You must remember that the provinces of males and females are quite distinct, and consequently the ways of educating the two must necessarily differ. There may be some points in common. But the most important part of our education lies in creating good, obedient wives, devoted to their husbands in both prosperity and adversity. The good wives will prove good mothers and will be impressed with the duty of bringing up their children carefully. . . . Neatness also forms a part of female education. In this as well as in other civilized countries a clean and tidy house reflects no small credit on the housewife. . . . Attention to household matters tends not only to the savings of money but also gives excellent physical exercise to the women of this country. I do not advocate females neglecting the duties in their proper sphere, and, for want of such exercise, taking to manly sports, as is done in some of the countries of Europe.[42]

Indian women were not to mimic their Western counterparts but to look within Indian culture for role models. Nandkunvarba constantly used Sita as an exemplar of wifely devotion, virtue, and purity. She encouraged women to model themselves in Sita's image and become good, obedient wives. While excellence in sports was crucial to public school education for boys in Britain and India, Nandkunvarba cautioned against same aspiration for girls. The female sex did not need sports for exercise as they had housework to keep them healthy.

Much like her views on companionship in marriage, Nandkunvarba's description of a woman's domestic duties was middle class. This is surprising from an aristocratic woman. Since when did frugality, neatness, and attention to household matters become a virtue among aristocrats? Nandkunvarba's views show the influence of middle class reformers on Indian aristocrats. Indian middle class reformers and imperial voices too criticized Indian aristocrats for their wasteful spending, their inattention to the lives of their subjects, and their unwillingness to change with time. Princely states are often depicted as being isolated from colonial India, their rulers not keeping pace with the advent of modernity. Yet Gondal, Bhavnagar, Mysore, and Baroda[43] show us a considerable number of princes being aware of the sociopolitical climate beyond their state boundaries. They enacted policies accordingly. In the field of social reform, there was cooperation between aristocrats and middle class social reformers. Not only did princes support middle class reformers, they also adopted their values. Nandkunvarba's definition of a good wife and mother was similar to that of the middle class reformers. While in political matters there might have been a disconnect between the middle class and the aristocrats as witnessed by the hostile relationship between nationalists and princes, in social matters the two supported each other's agendas. Many princes were sympathetic to middle-class desires for modernity and supported such efforts in their own states as well as outside.[44] Though the middle class depended on aristocrats and upper-class merchants as patrons for their causes, they maintained considerable intellectual independence. Instead of donors shaping the reformist message, the reverse happened with the monied groups adopting, or at least promoting, middle class values.

With male reformers setting the agenda one wonders how women responded, especially the generation educated in formal schools. How did women respond to their assigned roles as wives and mothers? For the most part it appears that they were happy with the status quo. As examined above, Nandkunvarba firmly believed in men and women not infringing on each other's domain. Women limited themselves to civic and charitable causes. For aristocratic women this was a continuation of their traditional duties as women of the royal family, patronizing learning, religion, orphanages, hospitals, and other social causes. What changed under reformist influence is the addition of educational institutions and reformist organizations as beneficiaries of royal patronage.

Conclusion

The women of Gondal who were beneficiaries of state education bestowed upon Bhagvatsinh the title 'valiant champion of female emancipation' and thanked him for introducing compulsory female education in the state.[45] These reformed women of the new generation were grateful to their male reformers. Vidyagauri Joshi, a graduate of Monghiba High School, credited Bhagvatsinh with recognizing from an early age that 'the woman's cause is man's cause'.[46] But these women did not limit themselves to the domestic arena. By the 1930s, women from prominent families were present and active at official state functions. They made public speeches at these events in the name of the women of Gondal. Just as English-educated Indian men claimed to represent the rest of the population, the English-educated women appointed themselves as spokespersons for all women. They asked for continuing efforts to spread female education and the removal of impediments faced by girls in going to school, cultural or economic. Women spoke out against the evils of seclusion and praised Bhagvatsinh for providing scholarships to women who wanted to pursue further education outside Gondal state.

Bhagvatsinh adjusted to the changed social climate and recognized the presence of educated women. He appointed Jamnabai Rathod, the first woman from Saurashtra to receive a B.A. from Bombay University, to the position of secretary in state administration.[47] The mood of these reformed women is captured in a speech made by Godavri Pandya (also a graduate of the Monghiba school) in 1934 during the golden jubilee celebrations of Bhagvatsinh's rule.

In an age when the youth challenge the authority of elders, women challenge the authority of men-folk, and the proletariat challenge the authority of those who govern them, out-of-date social customs and ill-founded prejudices will hold no good at all. They are largely to blame for the still-existing absence of uplift in the case of female education in some parts of Kathiawar.[48]

These are not the words of a submissive woman, but that of one who is aware of the ongoing changes in India as well as other parts of the world. Pandya knew that women in other countries were fighting for equal citizenship and wanted the same for Indian women. While women were grateful to reformers of the previous generation, they did not necessarily hold the same viewpoint. Nandkunvarba might have wanted women to concentrate on their husbands and children, but her daughter's contemporaries were not satisfied with being tied to the house. They asked for equal rights in the political arena and charted a path unforeseen by their reformers.

Notes

1. Ms. Vidyagauri Joshi referred to Bhagvatsinh as the 'valiant champion of female emancipation' in a speech she gave during Bhagvatsinh's Golden Jubilee Ceremony on 24 October 1934. *Gondal's Cherished Treasures: An Account of Shree Bhagvat Sinhjee Golden Jubilee Celebrations*, Gondal: Shee Bhagvat Sinhjee Golden Jubilee Committee, 1934, p. 13.
2. Gail Minault, *Secluded Scholars: Women's Education and Muslim Social Reform in Colonial India*, New Delhi: Oxford University Press, 1999; Geraldine Forbes, *Women in Modern India*, Cambridge: Cambridge University Press, 1999; Neera Desai, *Social Change in Gujarat: A Study of Nineteenth Century Gujarati Society*, Bombay: Vora and Co., 1978.
3. David Kopf, *The Brahmo Samaj and the Shaping of the Modern Indian Mind*, Princeton: Princeton University Press, 1979; Kenneth W. Jones, *Arya Dharm: Hindu Consciousness in Nineteenth Century Punjab*, Berkeley: University of California Press, 1976; Barbara Metcalf, *Islamic Revival in British India: Deoband, 1860–1900*, Princeton: Princeton University Press, 1982; David Lelyveld, *Aligarh's First Generation: Muslim Solidarity in British India*, Princeton: Princeton University Press, 1978.
4. Sudhir Chandra, *The Oppressive Present: Literature and Social Consciousness in Colonial India*, Delhi: Oxford University Press, 1992, p. 75.
5. Minault, *Secluded Scholars*, p. 6
6. Uma Chakravarti, 'Whatever Happened to the Vedic Dasi? Orientalism, Nationalism and a Script for the Past', in *Recasting Women: Essays in Indian Colonial History*, ed. Kumkum Sangari and Sudesh Vaid, New Brunswick: Rutgers University Press, 1999, pp. 27–87; J.T.F. Jordens, *Dayanand Saraswati: His Life and Ideas*, New Delhi: Oxford University Press, 1978; Charles H. Heimsath, *Indian Nationalism and Hindu Social Reform*, Princeton: Princeton University Press, 1964; David Kopf, *British Orientalism and the Bengal Renaissance: The Dynamics of Indian Modernization, 1773–1835*, Berkeley: University of California Press, 1969.

7. The blending of traditional and modern ideas was prevalent in various princely states. Pamela G. Price, *Kingship and Political Practice in Colonial India*, Cambridge: Cambridge University Press, 1996; Manu Bhagvan, *Sovereign Spheres: Princes, Education and Empire in Colonial India*, New Delhi: Oxford University Press, 2003.
8. Rosalind O'Hanlon, *A Comparison Between Women and Men: Tarabai Shinde and the Critique of Gender Relations in Colonial India*, Oxford: Oxford University Press, 1994.
9. Lata Mani, 'Contentious Traditions: The Debate on Sati in Colonial India', in *Recasting Women: Essays in Indian Colonial History*, ed. Kumkum Sangari and Sudesh Vaid, New Brunswick: Rutgers University Press, 1999, pp. 88–126.
10. Minault, *Secluded Scholars*, pp. 14–57.
11. St. Nihal Singh, *Shree Bhagvat Sinhjee: The Maker of Modern Gondal*, Gondal: Golden Jubilee Committee, 1934, pp. 20–1.
12. Singh, *Maker of Modern Gondal*, pp. 26–7.
13. Singh, *Maker of Modern Gondal*, p. 228; Administration Reports of Gondal State, various years.
14. Administration Report of Gondal State, 1893–4.
15. Forbes, *Women in Modern India*, pp. 32–63.
16. To give widows a purpose in life Sahajanand allowed those who wanted to live as ascetics to become his disciples. While formal initiation into asceticism was limited to men, female ascetics (unlike lay women) were allowed in the company of male ascetics provided they kept a physical distance. Raymond B. Williams, *An Introduction to Swaminarayan Hinduism*, Cambridge: Cambridge University Press, 2001.
17. Major W.M.P. Wood, Political Agent in Administration Report of Gondal State, 1913–14.
18. The asylum accepted orphans from all castes and communities. A few of the orphans were from neighbouring states but most were from Gondal. Administration Report of Gondal State, 1909–10.
19. The hospital was open to all women needing medical attention irrespective of their caste and religion. Administration Report of Gondal State, 1915–16; Singh, *Maker of Modern Gondal*, pp. 258–72.
20. Ramusack, *Indian Princes and their States*, pp. 132–69; Barbara Stoler Miller, ed., *The Powers of Art: Patronage in Indian Culture*, Delhi: Oxford University Press, 1992.
21. Siobhan Lambert-Hurley, *Muslim Women, Reform and Princely Patronage: Nawab Sultan Jahan Begam of Bhopal*, New York, Routledge, 2007.
22. Administration Report of Gondal State, 1919–20.
23. Monghiba Girl's High School attracted many visitors over the years, including British officials, neighbouring princes, and reformers such as Lady Vithaldas Thackersey who was impressed by the school's performance. Sir Vithaldas Thackersey was a prominent Gujarati philanthropist and financier of the

SNDT University (named after his mother), the first Indian women's university.
24. Administration Report of Gondal State, 1913–14.
25. Ibid.
26. Administration Report of Gondal State, 1915–16.
27. Singh, *Maker of Modern Gondal*, pp. 340–2.
28. Ibid., pp. 339–40.
29. *Highness Nandkuverba, C.I., Rani Saheb, Gondal* (Rajkot, date unknown), p. 8.
30. Singh, *Maker of Modern Gondal*, p. 343.
31. Charles Allen and Sharda Dwivedi, *Lives of the Indian Princes*, New York: Crown Publishers, 1984, p. 90.
32. Singh, *Maker of Modern Gondal*, p. 8; *Highness Nandkuverba*, p. 5.
33. *Highness Nandkuverba*, p. 7.
34. *The Times of India*, December 1888 and February 1890.
35. *A Review of 25 Years' Administration of Gondal State*, Bombay: The Times Press, pp. 38–9; *Highness Nandkuverba*, pp. 6–7; Singh, *Maker of Modern Gondal*, pp. 238–43; Administration Reports of Gondal State, various years.
36. *Highness Nandkuverba*, pp. 5, 7–8.
37. Singh, *Maker of Modern Gondal*, p. 156.
38. Aparna Basu, 'The Reformed Family, Women Reformers: A Case Study of Vidyagauri Nilkanth', *Samya Shakti: A Journal of Women's Studies* IV–V, 1989–90, pp. 62–82.
39. *Highness Nandkuverba*, p. 8.
40. Singh, *Maker of Modern Gondal*, p. 239.
41. The Barton Female Training College was set up in 1885 to train female teachers for schools in Saurashtra. Various princely states of Saurashtra contributed to the trust that ran the Barton College. *A Manual of Karbharis' Meeting of Kathiawar States, 1870–1940*, Rajkot: G.K. Shingala Printing Press, 1940, pp. 89–91.
42. *Highness Nandkuverba*, pp. 9–10.
43. Bhagavan, *Sovereign Spheres*.
44. Satadru Sen, *Migrant Races: Empire, Identity and K.S. Ranjitsinhji*, New York: Manchester University Press, 2004, pp. 24–5.
45. *The Bombay Chronicle*, 27 August 1934.
46. *Gondal's Cherished Treasures*, p. 13.
47. Ibid., p. 15.
48. Ibid., p. 19.

9

The Maharaja Grants the Brahman a Boon

The Subordination of History to Myth

LEAH RENOLD

A POPULAR STORY IN Varanasi concerns the origin of Banaras Hindu University. It explains how the founder of the university obtained the land on which the university was constructed. There are several versions of the story, all of which are elaborations on the theme of the Maharaja of Banaras granting a boon of a gift of land to a brahman. The story is not supported by documented historical evidence of the event and could be dismissed as a tale of little consequence. The popular story, though, is now as common in Varanasi as any of the ancient stories of the Sanskrit epics or Puranas. The fact that the account of the Maharaja granting a gift of land is told and retold, elaborated upon, and offered as a true account, encourages analysis of the relationship of the story to the truth claims of history. The story has mythic elements, and as this paper will show, the mythic aspect of the story has predominated in local memory over the historical details of British involvement in the founding of the university. The rich tapestry of ancient Hindu myth

*Our beloved mentor brought me to the topic of Banaras Hindu University, first with her work with David Lelyveld, 'Campaign for a Muslim University', published in *Modern Asian Studies,* then with her amazing course on Social and Religious Reform Movements, and finally with her guidance of a Ford Foundation project, in which four of her graduate students participated, on Religious Pluralism and Educational Reform in India. My part in the project focused on BHU and, with Professor Minault's encouragement, I set out for Varanasi and expanded my work into a dissertation and book, *Hindu Education: The Early Years of BHU* (OUP).

serves as a kind of sieve through which historical events are filtered. What remains as a local claim of truth serves to erase the memory of colonial presence and to legitimate certain features of the social structure of Varanasi. This paper considers the oral account of the founding of the Hindu University as a modern myth, and explores the relationship of the account to the wider nexus of Hindu mythology and the function of the myth in relation to history.

This case study of a local narrative applies to a larger question: Could the sustaining influence of South Asian mythic traditions, which have little to do with factual truth and much to do with the construction of meaning and group identity, reflect an indigenous epistemology that subordinates the truth claims of history to the truth claims of myth? Do the persistence of myth and the subordination of history to myth demonstrate that the realities expressed in myth are regarded on some level as higher truth than historical evidence? The truth claims of myth exist in relationship to the believers. Can the opposite hold true in regard to historical evidence? Can historical facts be devoid of meaning and value and as such untrue, having no relationship with a people? It is apparent that while history is a means of knowing in certain societies, not all structures of meaning and value include appreciation of the role of evidence in the historical method. In India today, history is at the centre of important debates between those falling on opposite sides of a broad range of secularist and religious nationalist positions. These largely educated middle class factions make opposing claims based on differing perceptions of what constitutes reliable evidence and analysis, but both have accepted the historical paradigm as the legitimate means of interpreting the past. A larger segment of the population, though, regards not history, but myth as the authentic witness to the past.

Of this wide gap in perspectives, Vinay Lal writes, 'The disconnect between the two Indias can also be read as the gulf between those Indians who are comfortably attuned to discourses of history and have embraced the historical sensibility, if only as one of the indispensable accoutrements of modern citizenship, and those Indians who still dwell largely in the house of myth.'[1] For many in South Asia, the personalities and events of ancient mythology continue to be malleable and rich sources for interpreting the truth claims concerning past and present events. Vinay Lal sets forth a challenge to consider Puranic and mythic literature of South Asia as a 'corpus of literature that might yield an aesthetics and epistemology which might be deployed to question a modern aesthetics of time, memory, history, narrative, and chronology, or modern notions of events, occurrence, and repetition'.[2] The truths of South Asian mythic traditions could be employed, then, in the rejection the historical paradigm.

There are multiple understandings of the definition and function of myth to be considered in locating the modern story of the Maharaja of Banaras and the Brahman within the mythic realm. Ivan Strenski writes that a wide variety of stories have been identified as myth:

Myth is everything and nothing at the same time. It is the true story or a false one, revelation or deception, sacred or vulgar, real or fictional, symbol or tool, archetype or stereotype. It is either strongly structured and logical or emotional and pre-logical, traditional and primitive or part of contemporary ideology. Myth is about the gods, but often the ancestors and sometimes certain men. . . . It is charter, recurring theme, character type, half truth, tale or just plain lie.[3]

While some scholars do not distinguish between legends, folktales, and myth, Mircea Eliade viewed myths specifically as tales that explained how something came into being.[4] He defined creation stories, stories of the origin of things, as myths. Claude Levi-Strauss viewed myths as structured stories that could reveal much about the thought of the creators of the myths. Levi-Strauss writes of myth:

They [myths] teach us a great deal about the societies from which they originate, they help us lay bare their inner workings and clarify the *raison d'etre* of beliefs, customs and institutions, the organization of which was at first slightly incomprehensible; lastly, and most importantly, they make it possible to discover operations modes of the human mind, which have remained so constant over the centuries.[5]

In his analysis of myth, Levi-Strauss was not concerned with the association of myths to specific religious traditions, but with how the internal structure of the myth reflected the particular logic of the mind that constructed the myth. While Levi-Strauss believed that the phenomenon of myth making resulted from the need of the human mind for order, Carl G. Jung believed that myths represented universal archetypes in the collective consciousness of humanity. Other scholars have put forward other explanations of myth. Ivan Strenski, though, holds that there is really no such thing as a 'myth'. He regards myth as a modern construction. He writes, 'There may be the word "myth", but the word names numerous and conflicting "objects" of enquiry, not a "thing" with its name written on it. "Myth" names a reality that we "cut out", not one that "stands out". It is the camel in the cloud, the profile of the Rorshach test.'[6] Strenski's position, though, is only one among many on myth.

Wendy Doniger's definition of the term 'myth' seems particularly applicable to the story in Varanasi concerning the creation of Banaras Hindu University:

(A) myth is not a lie or a false statement to be contrasted with truth of reality or fact or history, though this usage is, perhaps, the most common meaning of myth is casual parlance today. But in the history of religions, the term *myth* has far more often been used to mean 'truth'. What makes this ambiguity possible is that a myth is above all a story that is *believed*, believed to be true, and that people continue to believe despite sometimes massive evidence that it is, in fact, a lie. . . . In its positive and enduring sense, what a myth *is* is a story that is sacred to and shared by a group of people who find their most important meanings in it; it is a story believed to have been composed in the past about an event in the past, or more rarely, in the future, an event that continues to have meaning in the present because it is remembered; it is a story that is part of a larger group of stories.[7]

In dealing with the story of the Maharaja giving the land for Banaras Hindu University, historical documents exist that would lead a historian to consider the tale as a 'lie or false statement to be contrasted with truth of reality or fact or history'. Yet, the story is believed and, as the paper will demonstrate, contains truths or values deeply held by many in modern Varanasi and can thus be considered as a modern myth.

The creation of myth is not confined to the ancient past, but extends into the present. Haripriya Rangan, for example, examines the construction of a myth surrounding the Chipko movement to save trees in the Garhwal Himalaya in recent history. He writes, 'Myths are not just ancient tales of gods and heroes . . . nor is their production an activity confined to "primitive" societies and religious minded-folk. . . . Myth-making occurs in the present, within rational, secular, and non-exotic worlds, and through contemporary modes of communication.'[8] Rangan refers to myth as an allusion to a particular kind of narrative, and in the case of Chipko an environmental narrative, that shapes social and political realities:

Environmental narratives are particular forms through which social power is gained, asserted, and reinforced by narrators in various spaces of political discourse. Each environmental narrative aims to reshape social and material life by authorizing particular experiences, people, and events... by seeing them as natural, as integral parts of nature and the natural world, and in so doing, dismissing other social practices and experiences by deeming them artificial, illegitimate, or inauthentic.[9]

The narrative of the acquisition of the land on which Banaras Hindu University was built can be understood as an environmental narrative, particularly in versions of the story which have the brahman of the story traversing the boundaries of the land on which the Hindu University was to be built, symbolically sanctifying the land as part of the Hindu holy ground of Varanasi.

The chartering of Banaras Hindu University was a significant moment in the history of modern South Asia. During the colonial period, the British envisioned higher education in India as a means of breaking down barriers of religion, language, caste, and regionalism. English education was a means of producing a cadre of subjects who were rational, scientific, secular, and cosmopolitan in outlook. As part of British strategy, religion was not taught in Indian universities. Yet in an abrupt change in policy, in 1915, the British Government of India chartered the establishment of Banaras Hindu University, proposed by the most active promoter of Hindu causes during the period, Pandit Madan Mohan Malaviya. In the royal charter for the major national institution, a stipulation was included that called for compulsory education in the Hindu religion for all Hindu students. While the university is now a secular institution, administered by the Central Government of India, many Hindus, especially local residents of Varanasi, regard the university as a Hindu institution belonging to the ancient tradition of learning of the city. The weaving of Banaras Hindu University into the mythic fabric of Hindu tradition is supported by the popular story of the founding of the institution.

The Myth

The story of the Maharaja of Banaras, Prabhu Narayan Singh (1855–1931), giving the land for the Hindu University to the brahman, Pandit Madan Mohan Malaviya (1861–1946) is well known to the citizens of Varanasi, a city of over one million people. The story is not confined to certain social circles or caste groups, and is told in multiple versions. According to one version, Pandit Malaviya was present at a religious festival when the Maharaja was feeding the brahmans of the area. When asked by the Maharaja what more he would like, Pandit Malaviya said he would like a large area of land on which to build a university:

One time, the Maharaja held a great feast and invited brahmans of the city to attend. Pandit Malaviyaji was called to the feast. During the meal, the Maharaja approached the Pandit Malaviyaji and asked if he would like anything more. Malaviyaji told him that he would like to ask a boon of the Maharaja. The Maharaja told him to ask whatever he liked and it would be granted. Then Malaviyaji pointed to the land on the opposite side of the river and told the Maharaja that he would like all of the land so that he could build a great university. The Maharaja gave the gift of the land to Malaviya. This is how the Banaras Hindu University came to be.[10]

Another version of the story has the Maharaja at the bank of the Ganga when Pandit Malaviya asks him for a boon. According to the tale, one morning Pandit Malaviya was standing at the waters of the Ganga saying his prayers. In one account of this version, the narrator said that Malaviya was at particular location, Assi Ghat. While the brahman was saying his prayers, the Maharaja came along in his boat and noticed the serene look on his face and recognized him to be an enlightened person. The Maharaja went to the brahman and told him that he would like to grant him a boon. It was then that Malaviya asked for the land and the Maharaja granted him the gift.[11]

In one telling of this particular story, the meeting in the river occurs only after Malaviya had gone repeatedly to the palace to ask for the land for the university, but had been ignored by the Secretary of State, who refused to give him access to the *raja*.[12]

In yet another version of the story, when Pandit Malaviya asks the Maharaja to give him land, the Maharaja responds by telling Malaviya that he can have as much land as he can walk around in twenty hours.[13] In one day the brahman walked around the large piece of land that is now the campus and the Maharaja gave him the land. In yet another version, told by the owner of a travel agency, the Maharaja told the brahman that he could have all the land he could cover if he ran without stopping. In this story, Malaviya was standing at what is now Lanka Gate, the main entrance to BHU. He ran all the way to Hyderabad Gate (which is at the opposite end of the campus), and the Maharaja gave him the land.[14]

In its various forms, though, the story of the Maharaja and Malaviya has become part of the mythic fabric of Varanasi.

The Wider Tapestry of Hindu Myth

Aspects of the story of the *maharaja* giving the land to the brahman link the tale to Hindu myths of ancient origin. In this regard, the story of how the land for the Hindu University was acquired has been woven into the wider tapestry of Hindu myth. The account of the Maharaja of Banaras giving the land for the Hindu University to Pandit Malaviya corresponds to a common theme in Hindu myths of Sanskrit literature in which a righteous *raja* bestows upon a poor, pious brahman a generous boon. In the *Mahabharata*, the poor brahman sage Atri, for example, before forsaking his worldly duties and retiring to the forest, approaches King Vainya to ask for wealth to leave to his sons. The king dutifully granted the boon.[15] According to the *Mahabharata*, the figures of the righteous *raja* and the brahman sage are complementary. A section of the *Mahabharata* is devoted to expounding upon the necessity and benefit of the relationship between the brahmans and *ksatriyas* (rulers/warriors).[16] In the *dharmashastra* (Hindu law) text, the *Manusmriti* (or Laws of Manu), a section on the duties of the *raja* states that the holier a Brahman, the greater the gift the *raja* should bestow on him and, likewise, the greater the gift given by the *raja* to the brahman, the greater would the *raja's* reward after death.[17] Feeding of brahmans, providing for their protections, gifting of various forms or wealth, including land, are considered meritorious acts for *rajas*. The authority of the *raja* in the physical realm is used to support the authority of the brahman in the realm of the spiritual, and vice versa.[18] The spiritual powers of the brahman, as in the myth of the sage Bharadvaja, can powerfully affect the success of the *raja*. In the *Saukhyana Srauta Sutra*, Bharadvaja receives gifts and wealth from the three *rajas* Prastoka Srnjaya, Abhyavartin Cayamana and Bribu Taksan and in return gives them all victory in battle.[19] When *rajas* refused to grant boons they were cursed.[20]

A second theme present in two versions of the story is the traversing of the land. In these accounts, the *maharaja* stipulates that he will grant the boon of the gift of the land for the university, but that he will give only as much land as the brahman can walk around in 20 hours or run around without stopping. This theme seems to echo accounts of the *ashvamedh* (horse sacrifice ritual), found in several ancient Sanskrit texts, in which ancient rajas allowing a consecrated horse to roam free for a year, accompanied by attendants. At the end of the year, the land over which the horse had roamed became the *raja's* at the conclusion of the ritual when the horse was sacrificed. The ritual was basically a means of sanctifying the gaining of new land. An example of the theme is found in the myth of the descent of the Ganga from the heavens included in the Bala Kanda of Valmiki's *Ramayana* and the Vana Parva of the *Mahabharata,* in which King Sagara sends out the sacrificial horse to roam.

A twist to the roaming of the horse element tells of a king granting a boon to a dwarf brahman to have all the land that he can cross in three steps.[21] It is told in several versions in different texts of King Bali, who was preparing to sacrifice the horse. King Bali invited brahmans to attend the sacrifice. When Vamana, a dwarf brahman, arrived, the king asked him to name whatever he desired. The dwarf replied that he only wanted three strides of land. Unbeknownst to King Bali, the dwarf was a manifestation of Vishnu, who in taking the three strides covered the earth, the heavens, and the underworld. So Vishnu, in the form of a dwarf, takes the role of the sacrificial horse. After taking three giant steps to claim the worlds, Vishnu sanctifies the universe. In the light of these myths, the story of the Maharaja of Banaras telling the brahman that he can have all the land he can cross gets another dimension, associated with the mythic acquisition and sanctifying of new lands. The themes of the ritual traversing of land and of a beneficent raja granting a pious brahman a boon are found in a variety of myths from different Sanskrit sources spanning hundreds of years. The inclusion of these themes in the modern story imparts a mythic quality to the explanation of how the land for Banaras Hindu University was acquired.

The Function of the Myth

A mundane event becomes a potent source of meaning when enmeshed in a powerful mythic tradition. The origin of the university as a gift from a maharaja to a brahman places the establishment of a modern Western institution, a university, within the Hindu realm, while at the same time denying the historical reality of the colonial context for its establishment. The myth not only subordinates the fact that the ruling authority of the time was not the Maharaja, but the British Raj, but that the leading supporters of Malaviya's plan were British officials, not the Maharaja of Banaras.[22] The actual extent of the British role in the establishment of the university was voiced in a letter written by Viceroy Hardinge to Harcourt Butler, the Member for Education. The Viceroy wrote, 'It is very satisfactory to feel that this venture in Indian education, for whose birth you and I are chiefly responsibly, has been successfully launched.'[23] The intention of these officials for Hindu education at the institution to be used to promote loyalty to the Government of India is obscured entirely.[24]

The myth not only erases the colonial presence, but also Muslim participation in the creation of the Hindu University. In fact, in another myth that is equally popular in Varanasi, Pandit Malaviya approachs another ruler, the Nizam of Hyderabad, for a donation to the university, but the miserly Nizam, who is a Muslim, sends him one of his old shoes on a platter to the brahman.[25] There are variations to the story, all narrating how the Pandit Malaviya was successful in publicly humiliating the Nizam by one means or another into giving a sizeable donation to the institution. The narrative, like that of the maharaja and the brahman, is told and retold in Varanasi. The myth of the Nizam, also has its parallels in episodes in Sanskrit literature in which disrespectful kings deny the requests of brahmans. The effect of the Nizam myth in Varanasi, though, is to discount the actual substantial Muslim support for the university, including the well-documented generous financial support of the Nizam of Hyderabad, Mir Osman Ali Khan (1886–1967) to the Hindu University.[26]

In contrast, the myth of Pandit Malaviya and the Hindu Maharaja of Banaras affirms the figures of the maharaja and the brahman in their correspondence to key social positions in Varanasi. The Maharaja of Banaras is given a prominent role in the myth, which corresponds to the significance the current Maharaja continues to play in the ritual life of city. Regarded as the central Hindu figurehead of the area, he presides over the major public rituals of Varanasi.[27] The myth reinforces the legitimacy of the Maharaja of Banaras as a beneficent Hindu figurehead. At the time of the founding of the Hindu University, there were many subjects who would have contested this portrayal. In the early years of the century, when the students of BHU were becoming involved in the independence struggle, the subjects of the State of Banaras, over which the Maharaja ruled, were fighting their own struggle against the tyranny, not of the British, but of the Maharaja. The agitation of the Praja Mandal Movement,[28] a democratic movement against the tyrannical rule of the Maharaja, which continued from 1921 to 1947, is now largely forgotten. The maharaja of the myth, the beneficent ruler and supporter of brahmans predominates.

Additionally the popular narrative affirms the place of brahmans in the society of Varanasi, which has long had a reputation as a centre of brahmanical tradition. In Varanasi, many still point to Pandit Madan Mohan Malaviya as the exemplar brahman, referring to his simple lifestyle, strict adherence to rules of purification, and knowledge of the scriptures. The myth expresses the maharaja's reverence for the spiritual superiority of the brahman and the brahman's dependence upon the beneficence of the maharaja. The myth also puts Hindu education in the hands of Pandit Malaviya, a role traditionally claimed by brahmans, but one that was contested in the early years of the Hindu University.

The myth obscures from view the acquisition of the land, the protests against the acquisition, and the suffering caused by the displacement. The fact is that villages were dispossessed and people were forced to leave their homes, wells, crops and orchards. But this is forgotten. Some versions refer to the displacement, but wrap it in a cloak of benevolence. For instance, one story version says that in compensation for their loss, Pandit Malaviya offers employment at the university to the former inhabitants of the land.[29] In another account, Malaviya promises the poor inhabitants that he would employ one person from each family at the university.[30] In another version, Malaviya relocates the inhabitants in two other neighbourhoods outside the university gates. The most common versions of the story, though, leave out any mention of displacement of former residents of the land on which the Hindu was constructed.

The mythologizing of a historical event has political significance. In this case, we see the erasure of colonial influence from the history of the Hindu University, the diminishing of Muslim contribution, the buttressing of an idealized social order in the prominence of the brahman and the legitimization of the maharaja as figure-head of the community and the supporter of brahmans. Such use of myth for political purposes is not a modern phenomenon. Indian kings, for instance had specific myths expressed in art that would serve to legitimate their rule. For instance, as Heinrich von Stietencron illustrates, the first image of Gangadhara (Shiva as the deity who carries Ganga) was created after the victory of king Mahendravarman I (c.610–30), who was a worshipper of Shiva, over the Ganga dynasty, who were Jains. The Gangadhara image was based on a specific variation of the descent of the Ganga story in which

Ganga tries to destroy Shiva, but Shiva punishes her.[31] The myth of the descent of the Ganga was given political meaning within a particular historical context.

Another instance of the connection of myth to power relates well to the myth of the origin of the Hindu University. As historian Vasudha Dalmia has written in *The Nationalization of Hindu Tradition*, the legitimacy of the lineage of the Maharaja of Banaras as the traditional Hindu lord of the land is based on a myth of a raja granting a brahman a boon of a gift of land.[32] In a twist upon the theme of the maharaja granting the boon to the brahman, the raja bestows the boon upon the brahman, but against his wishes. The brahman curses the raja, telling him that his own brahman descendants would become the rulers of Banaras. The myth of the raja granting the boon of land locates the origin of the lineage of the Maharaja of Banaras in a distant mythical Hindu past, thus providing legitimacy for the maharajas as the rightful Hindu rulers of Banaras. The establishment of the lineage of the Maharajas of Banaras was actually brought about by the granting of land by Muslim Mughal rulers, but this information is obscured by the myth.[33] In similar manner, myth of the gift of the land for the Hindu University does not correspond well with the historical events surrounding the creation of the university.

The History

The story of the Maharaja giving the land to Pandit Malaviya is not supported by historical evidence. British documents attest to the fact that the land was not donated by the Maharaja, but was acquired from the previous inhabitants only by force through the execution of a land acquisition order. These documents are from the local records of the British Government at the time of the foundation of the university, which are now housed at the Banaras Regional Archives. The records show that the land Pandit Malaviya and the other founders of the university desired was already inhabited. The forced evacuation of the site was protested by owners and tenants of the very valuable and fully cultivated land.[34] The acquisition order was issued on 17 November 1915 by the Government of the United Provinces for the acquisition of approximately 1,164 acres from the *pargana* of Dehat Amanat, including the *mauzas* (villages) of Sri Gobardanpur, Khizirhi, Jangampur, Siswahi, Chettopur, Bhagwanpur, Dhanarjaipur, and Naria for the site of the Hindu University.[35]

The acquisition of such a large tract of land was extremely unusual. Sheo Karan Nath Misra, the Special Land Acquisition Officer assigned to consider the amount to be paid in compensation to the proprietors and tenants, wrote to the Collector of Banaras, explaining that such a tract of land, of about 2 sq. km., consisting of first rate cultivated land, under permanent settlement and so close to the city had seldom been taken by forced acquisition.[36] According to the officer, the Hindu University could hardly have chosen a more valuable plot of land from the agricultural point of view. There was hardly any portion of the area which could be called actual waste or barren land—over three quarters of the total twelve hundred acres was regularly cultivated land yielding two, and in some cases, three crops each year. In addition, fixed rate tenants or occupancy tenants had occupied most of the land for some time and were privileged to retain a very low rent. These villages were practically losing all that they possessed in the world. Their houses, groves, their tenures and their wells, in fact everything they possessed had been taken.[37]

After the initial acquisition of land for the campus, the university required additional plots of land. In 1917, the university officials wanted to expand the boundary of the university. As the proprietors of the land were unwilling to part with it, the university obtained another land acquisition order from the local government.[38] Again in 1921, the university made an application for yet another acquisition of land. It was in connection with this acquisition that the Maharaja of Banaras was involved. The Maharaja owned a 75-acre plot of land that the university wanted for the purpose of building a canal to irrigate some 2,100 acres of land.[39] The Maharaja would only agree to lease the land. In 1923, Pandit Malaviya still had not acquired the land through private negotiations and wrote to the Commissioner, Benares Division asking that 'the Government to take the necessary action for the acquisition of the land in question as early as may be practicable'.[40] By 1924, J.B. Darwin, the Deputy Collector for Banaras reported that the additional land had been acquisitioned for the university.[41]

The land acquisition records at the Banaras Regional Archive reveal that all of the acreage for the site on which Banaras Hindu University is now located was not received as a gift, but was acquired by land acquisition orders, including land under the proprietorship of the Maharaja of Banaras. Former owners and tenants of the land protested the action, but nevertheless were forced to leave their homes, fruit trees, and wells. The story that is revealed in the 'official' records of the land acquisition would appear to a historian to be the more reliable account. Yet the official version of how the land for the Hindu University was acquired is given no hearing in Varanasi. The myth prevails in local memory.

Distinguishing Myth from History

The untangling of history and myth has been a topic of scholarly concern. Early Western scholars in South Asia found that its literature was extensive and diverse, covering a number of subjects from drama, to politics, to medicine. They could detect little, though, that they regarded as historical. They also perceived the apparent lack of historical work as a deficiency of South Asian culture. Indians responded by making efforts to write their own histories. Another development occurred which involved attempts to historicize myths and to prove that myths contained modern scientific truths. In the early twentieth century, at the time of the establishment of the Hindu University, the Maharaja of Banaras, Prabhu Narayan Singh, and Pandit Madan Mohan Malaviya were members of an association in Varanasi called the Kashi Bharat Dharm Mahamandal. In one of the publications of the organization, *The World's Eternal Religion*, an argument was made against the attempt to historicize ancient mythology, explaining that the inhabitants of the subcontinent deliberately did not construct a historical record:

As regards the historical test, it is worthwhile to observe that India did not, nay, in the view of the truth, could not, care to record a history in the modern sense which means narrations limited to particular periods and geographical tracts, to certain select great names and localities arranged in a chronological order, all intended to picture forth a past to vivify the present. India's wisdom transcended the wisdom of every other country's, and it had a vivid knowledge of the past, the present, and the future. How could the Seers of old take account petty details which are forgotten as soon as given, as by school boys on leaving school? Countless ages, countless places, countless personages have come and gone, and will come and go. The Seer adheres to the truth. 'History but repeats itself'—this is what they have brought out in the Grand Epics. In the play of human character in its birth and development and ideals and consummation common to all ages in all conditions, the essence is there, the chaff is thrown off. India has always referred itself for light and guidance to such ideals of lofty character as Bhishma, Rama, Krishna, Vyasa, etc. What higher ideals are necessary to govern human conduct by example and precept?

The wisdom deduced from the epic record is preserved, and will never be lost, while modern historical works will have their day and vanish into 'oblivion's uncatalogued library'.[42]

The authors interpreted India's past lack of historical literature not as a deficit, but as cultural difference and claimed historical research to be of limited utility in guiding people toward the true goals of human existence. The details of history fell into the realm of the mundane and were given scant respect in the wider scope of the wisdom of countless ages, the wisdom exemplified in the lofty characters of myth.

In *Textures of Time*, Narayana Rao, David Shulman, and Sanjay Subrahmanyam refute this view that Indians rejected history and argue that a significant body of historical literature exists from late medieval and early modern south India.[43] They explain that the historical material has not been recognized as such because the history appears in different genres from folk-epic to poetry that do not correspond to the formal features of historical narrative prose.[44] Nevertheless, the authors argue, there is a clear distinction between factual and fictional accounts within a single genre of literature indicated by variations, sometimes subtle, in language, which could be detected by the intended audience. History and myth co-existed then and were distinguished one from the other.[45]

The distinguishing of the language of history and myth can be applied to the modern accounts of the founding of Banaras Hindu University. In oral accounts of the founding of the university, the mythic story of the Maharaja granting the Brahman a story is told, but curiously, in official records of the Hindu University, the story of the Maharaja giving the land is not included. Also, the official history of the university, *History of Banaras Hindu University*,[46] published by Banaras Hindu University Press, does not include any mention of the story of the Maharaja of Banaras giving the land to the brahman, Pandit Malaviya. In a chapter, 'University Site and the Holy Kashi', which details the selection of the site, the author only vaguely states that, 'necessary steps for the acquisition of the land were initiated'.[47] In the prevalence of the myth in local oral accounts and the absence of the myth in official papers and historical account, there appears to be clear distinction between history and myth. A difference can also be detected between the language used in the official history of the university and that of the oral accounts. The oral accounts, for instance, set the scene for the maharaja and brahman outside of history with a beginning much the same as the 'once upon the time' of fairy tales.

The myth, though, being commonly accepted as the true origin of the Hindu University, has made its way into books and other sources of information as history. For instance, in her book on Varanasi, *Banaras: City of Light*, Diana Eck mentions the founding of the Hindu University. She writes, 'The Maharaja of Banaras donated the land for the university.'[48] In another book on the history of the city, *Kashi: The City Luminous*, in a section on the Maharajas of Banaras, the author writes that Prabhu Narain Singh 'donated 1300 acres for the starting of the Banaras Hindu University'.[49] Is this mistaking of myth for history due to the lack of understanding of language of which Rao, Shulman, Subrahmanyam wrote? Are these instances of the often-told claims of truth of the mythic oral accounts being confused or combined with the truth claims of historical accounts?

Myth has little to do with factual truth and much to do with the construction of meaning and identities. The story of the maharaja giving the university land to the brahman, in one regard, is a lie or a false statement contrary-to-fact. Yet it is a story shared and believed by many who embrace the social norms, hierarchies, and the politics affirmed by the story. In this regard the story of the giving of the land can be regarded as myth. As Wendy Doniger maintains, a myth is a part of a larger group of stories of a people.[50] In this case, the corpus of Hindu myth is massive, with themes that continue to be woven into modern events, as this paper has demonstrated. Local accounts of historical events, especially when told in various versions and having mythic elements, can easily be discounted. This paper, although drawing attention to various dimensions of such stories and connecting them to myth, is not a call for historians to become mythologists. It is only in the difference between the historical record and the mythic record, that what is left out of the story and what is added, becomes apparent. As Rao, Shulman, and Subrahmanyam write:

To distinguish the fictive from the factual, is perhaps, the work of history; to distinguish false from true is the work of poetry, or of logic or of myth and music. Still there are kinds of history, and great historians are open to that dimension of reality that we call 'myth', in the sense of being more deeply saturated with meaningfulness and also more creative of the reality that they purport to describe than are other expressive modes.[51]

Myth also often serves to portray the ideal imagined by the myth-makers. Myth can be a narration of idealized events, one that reshapes or masks realities. The popularity of a myth can point to the existence of a less than ideal situation behind the myth and suggest that there is much more to the story than is being expressed.

Modern myths such as the Maharaja of Banaras granting the boon of the land for Banaras Hindu University can be understood as narratives of events as they *should have* happened (at least according to those who prefer the myths to history). In this, myths may be considered in the light of Jonathan Z. Smith's analysis in the 'Bare Fact of Ritual'.[52] In his examination of a bear hunting ritual, Smith concluded that the ritual, which was performed before an actual hunt, was an enactment of a bear-hunt as the hunters imagined an ideal hunt, as a hunt *should* happen. The fact that the idealized bear hunt was performed before the actual hunt was 'eloquent testimony' that actual hunts did not correspond to the ideal.[53] In a similar manner, modern myths can be understood as idealized oral accounts of events. Importantly, the fact that the myths are remembered and repeated in much the same way that ritual is repeated to imbed the ideal in community, can also be testimony that the actual events did not correspond to the ideals expressed in the myths.

Instances of the interpretation of a historical event in mythic terms may provide insights that may be entirely absent in the historical record. Revealing the truth of an event for the people may be the boon that such mythic accounts grant historians. As in the case of the Maharaja granting the land to the brahman, the myth illustrates the importance of the Hindu University in the eyes of the people of Varanasi, the insignificance accorded to the role of the British and Muslims in the history of the university, the continued social affirmation of the ascribed roles of the maharaja and the brahman during a time when those roles are being contested by other segments of society, and the absorption of a modern institution into the mythic Hindu past. Understanding the existence of such a myth as an expression of an ideal that is contrary-to-fact, can also lead to what is obscured by the truth claims of the myth. Such truths can enrich historical interpretation.

Notes

1. Vinay Lal, *The History of History: Politics and Scholarship in Modern India*, Delhi: Oxford University Press, 2003, p. 281.
2. Ibid., p. 282.
3. Ivan Strenski, *Four Theories of Myth in the Twentieth Century: Cassirer, Eliade, Levi Straus and Malinowski*, London: Macmillan Press, 1987, p. 1.
4. Mircea Eliade, *No Souvenirs: Journal, 1957–1969*, translated from the French by Fred H. Johnson, Jr., New York: Harper and Row, 1977, p. 16.

5. Claude Levi-Strauss, *The Naked Man: Introduction to a Science of Mythology 4*, Translation of *L'Homme Nu,* 1971, London: Harper and Row, 1981, p. 639.
6. Strenski, *Four Theories of Myth*, p. 1.
7. Wendy Doniger, *The Implied Spider: Politics and Theology in Myth*, New York: Columbia University Press, 1998, p. 2.
8. Haripriya Rangan, *Of Myths and Movements: Rewriting Chipko into Himalayan History*, Delhi: Oxford University Press, 2000, p. 10.
9. Ibid., p. 19.
10. Vibhuti Narayan Singh, Maharaja of Banaras and grandson of the maharaja of the story, interview with author, Varanasi, September 1997.
11. S. Somaskandan, interview with author, Varanasi, November 1996.
12. Pushpa Pratap, interview with author, Varanasi, March 1997.
13. Rajendra Prasad, interview with author, Varanasi, September 2006.
14. Salil Tiwari, interview with author, Varanasi, August 2006.
15. *Aranyakapurva* 3.183.1–32, in *Mahabharata*, vol. 1, Poona: Bhandarkar Oriental Research Institute, 1971, pp. 636–8.
16. *Shantipurva* 12.73–7, in *Mahabharata*, vol. 3, Poona: Bhandarkar Oriental Research Institute, 1974, pp. 2085–98 and 'The Necessary Complementarity of Ksatriyas and Brahmins', Book 12, pp. 73–7, *Mahabharata*, vol. 7, James L. Fitzgerald, translator and editor, Chicago: University of Chicago Press, 2004, p. 350 fols.
17. Chapter 7, pp. 82–7, Wendy Doniger, translator, *The Laws of Manu*, London: Penguin Books, 1991, p. 137.
18. John E. Mitchiner, *Traditions of the Seven Rsis*, Delhi: Motilal Banarsidass, 1982, p. 224, writes of the mutual necessity of brahmans and kings: 'In several instances, Rsis are depicted as giving instruction on the necessity for and duties of kings. Thus Bharadvaja is said to have composed a *raja-sastra*, or treatise on the duties of kings; in a similar manner Vasistha instructed king Mucukunda on the interrelations between kings and their Purohitas—to the effect that a king depends on his Purohita for success, while a kingdom depends on a king. This question of the political involvement of the Rsis generally conform to—and may be considered in connection with—the more general theory of Brahmin-Ksatriya relations, where it is the duty of the king or ksatriya to rule to and to protect the Brahmin, while it is the duty of the Brahmin to legitimate and sanctify the power of the king.'
19. Ibid., pp. 228–9.
20. *Mahabharata* 13.53.20 tells of a king's reaction to a *rishi's* request for meal; 'Through fear of the *rishi's* curse, the king had caused all kinds of foods to be gathered and got ready for his guest.' Also see 'Cursing Kings', in John E. Mitchiner, *Traditions of the Seven Rishis,* pp. 230–3.
21. Deborah A. Soifer, *The Myths of Narasimha and Vamana: Two Avatars in Cosmological Perspective*, New York: State University of New York Press, 1991, p. 3.

22. Leah Renold, 'Chapter Two: A Leap In the Dark: The Chartering of the Hindu and Muslim Universities', *A Hindu Education: The Early Years of Banaras Hindu University*, Delhi: Oxford University Press, 2005, pp. 29–63.
23. Letter from Lord Hardinge to Harcourt Butler, 18 February 1916, India Office Library, Butler Collection, MSS.EUR.F.116/42.
24. Renold, *Hindu Education*, pp. 52–60.
25. Maqsood Ali, interview with author, Varanasi, April 2015; Jokhan Singh, interview with author, April 2015. A version of this story is also told in Krishnadatta Dvivedi, *Bharatiya Punarjagarun aur Madan Mohan Malaviya*, Varanasi: Vishvavidyalaya Prakashan, 1962, pp. 19–20.
26. S. Somaskandan and S.L. Dar, *History of the Banaras Hindu University*, p. 778.
27. Vasudha Dalmia, *The Nationalization of Hindu Traditions: Bharatendu and Nineteenth-century Banaras*, Delhi: Oxford University Press, 1997, p. 77.
28. An unpublished Ph.D. thesis, 'Cultural History of Varanasi in the First Half of the Twentieth Century', completed at BHU by S.K. Singh in 1990, includes a chapter on the Praja Mandal Movement.
29. Rajendra Prasad, interview with author, Varanasi, September 2006.
30. Vidya Varidhi Upadhyaya, interview with author, Varanasi, September 2006.
31. Heinrich von Stientencron, *Hindu Myth Hindu History: Religion, Art, and Politics*, Ranikhet: Permanent Black, 2005, pp. 10–11.
32. Vasudha Dalmia, *The Nationalization of Hindu Tradition*, pp. 65–6.
33. In another instance of a Muslim ruler granting lands to brahmans, an interesting twist is given to the myth of the maharaja granting the boon to a brahman in the story of the origin of the lands of the Maharaja of Darbhanga, who coincidentally played an important role in the establishment of Banaras Hindu University. One of the versions of the story goes that Akbar, the Mughal emperor, granted a land to a poor brahman student who had the power of being able to see the new moon of Eid even when it was entirely obscured by cloud. The poor student, in turn, made a gift of the land to his guru. The guru, then, became the first Maharaja of Darbhanga. The myth provides a means for the maharajas of Darbhanga, who were particularly pious Mithili brahmans who would have been polluted by the gift from a Muslim, to situate the origin of their lands in a ideal context as a *gurudakshina*, a traditional gift of a brahman student to his guru.
34. Y.P. Dubey, interview with author, Varanasi, January 1995.
35. No. 1843/XV-292, Educational Department, 17 November 1915, Appropriation of Land for a Public Purpose, Government, United Provinces, Banaras Regional Archives.
36. Sheo Karan Nath Misra, Special Land Acquisition Officer, to the Collector, Benares, 22 May 1916, Banaras Regional Archives.
37. Ibid.
38. No. 1226 of 1917, from G.H. Lambert, District Officer of Benares to the Commissioner, Benares District, 15 January 1917, in Banaras Regional Archives.

39. S. Somaskandan and S.L. Dar, *History of the Banaras Hindu University*, Banaras: Banaras Hindu University, 1966, p. 463.
40. Madan Mohan Malaviya, Vice-Chancellor, Benares Hindu University, to J.C. Smith, Commissioner, Benares Division, 3 March 1923, in Banaras Regional Archives.
41. Letter from J.H. Darwin, I.C.S., Deputy Collector of Benares to the Commissioner, Benares District, 17 January 1924, in Banaras Regional Archives.
42. *The World's Eternal Religion*, 2nd edn., Varanasi: Bharat Dharm Syndicate, Ltd., 1924, pp. 2–3.
43. Velcheru Narayana Rao, David Shulman and Sanjay Subrahmanyam, *Textures of Time: Writing History in South India, 1600–1800*, Ranikhet: Permanent Black, 2001, Kindle Edition, p. 158.
44. Rao, Shulman, and Subrahmanyam, *Textures of Time*, p. 166.
45. Ibid., p. 190.
46. S.L. Dar and S. Somaskandan, *History of Banaras Hindu University*.
47. Ibid., p. 317.
48. Diana Eck, *Banaras: City of Light*, London: Routledge and Kegan Paul, 1983, p. 91.
49. K. Chandramouli, *Kashi: The City Luminous*, New Delhi: Rupa & Co., 1995, p. 283.
50. Wendy Doniger, *The Implied Spider*, p. 2.
51. Rao, Shulman and Subrahmanyam, *Textures of Time*, pp. 343–4.
52. Jonathan Z. Smith, 'The Bare Facts of Ritual', *History of Religions*, vol. 20, no. 1/2, 1980, pp. 112–27, accessed 20 June 2016, http://www.jstor.org.libproxy.txstate.edu/stable/1062338.
53. Smith, 'The Bare Facts of Ritual', p. 127.

References

Chandramouli, K., *Kashi: The City Luminous*, New Delhi: Rupa & Co., 1995.
Eck, Diana, *Banaras: City of Light*, London: Routledge and Kegan Paul, 1983.
Eliade, Mircea, *No Souvenirs: Journal, 1957–1969*, translated from the French by Fred H. Johnson, Jr., New York: Harper and Row, 1977.
Dalmia, Vasudha, *The Nationalization of Hindu Traditions: Bharatendu and Nineteenth-century Banaras*, Delhi: Oxford University Press, 1997.
Doniger, Wendy, *The Implied Spider: Politics and Theology in Myth*, New York: Columbia University Press, 1998.
———, ed. and tr., *The Laws of Manu*, London: Penguin Books, 1991.
Dvivedi, Krishnadatta, *Bharatiya Punarjagarun aur Madan Mohan Malaviya*, Varanasi: Vishvavidyalaya Prakashan, 1962.
Fitzgerald, James L., ed. and tr., *Mahabharata*, vol. 7, Chicago: University of Chicago Press, 2004.
Lal, Vinay, *The History of History: Politics and Scholarship in Modern India*, Delhi: Oxford University Press, 2003.

Levi-Strauss, Claude, *The Naked Man: Introduction to a Science of Mythology 4*, translation of *L'Homme Nu*, 1971; repr., London: Harper and Row, 1981.

Mitchiner, John E., *Traditions of the Seven Rsis*, Delhi: Motilal Banarsidass, 1982.

Rao, Velcheru Narayan, David Shulman and Sanjay Subrahmanyam, *Textures of Time: Writing History in South India, 1600–1800*, Ranikhet: Permanent Black, 2001, Kindle Edition.

Renold, Leah, *Hindu Education: Early Years of Banaras Hindu University*, Delhi: Oxford University Press, 2005.

Singh, S.K., 'Cultural History of Varanasi in the First Half of the Twentieth Century', Unpublished Thesis, Banaras Hindu University, 1990.

Smith, Jonathan Z., 'The Bare Facts of Ritual', *History of Religions*, vol. 20, no. 1/2, 1980, pp. 112–27, http://www.jstor.org.libproxy.txstate.edu/stable/1062338, accessed 20 June 2016.

Soifer, Deborah A., *The Myths of Narasimha and Vamana: Two Avatars in Cosmological Perspective*, New York: State University of New York Press, 1991.

Somaskandan, S. and S.L. Dar, *History of the Banaras Hindu University*, Banaras: Banaras Hindu University, 1966.

Strenski, Ivan, *Four Theories of Myth in the Twentieth Century: Cassirer, Eliade, Levi Straus and Malinowski*, London: Macmillan Press, 1987.

Von Stientencron, Heinrich, *Hindu Myth Hindu History: Religion, Art, and Politics*, Ranikhet: Permanent Black, 2005.

OTHER SOURCES

Banaras Regional Archives, Varanasi, India.
Butler Collection, Indian Office Library and Records, British Library.
Mahabharata, vols. 1 and 3, Poona: Bhandarkar Oriental Research Institute, 1971.
World's Eternal Religion, 2nd edn., Varanasi: Bharat Dharm Syndicate, Ltd., 1924.

10

The Case of the 'Holy Dacoit'

C.M. NAIM

GAIL MINAULT'S STILL indispensible account of the Khilafat Movement—that almost quixotic political campaign of the 1920s led by the curious triad of a Farangi Mahall maulana, an Oxford graduate, and a would be Mahatma—ends on a note of pathos.

The Ali brothers and Abdul Bari had come to a parting of the ways, breaking a religious and political partnership that had begun in 1912. Muhammad Ali finally publicly renounced his allegiance to his preceptor in *Hamdard* on January 13, 1926. Abdul Bari suffered a stroke a few days later and died on January 19. Muhammad Ali rushed to Lucknow and wept at his grave, but it was too late. It was also too late for the caliphate.[1]

Had Professor Minault taken her account of Muhammad Ali's public life only ten months further—there was no need for her to do so, I hasten to add—she would have come upon a scene involving Muhammad Ali that smacked of nothing other than bathos. It also involved another, equally prominent Muslim public figure of Delhi of the time, and its chief significance now lies only in the fact that it enabled another remarkable 'Old Boy' of the M.A.O. College, Aligarh—Muhammad Ali's first *alma mater*—to create one of Urdu's most memorable literary villains—arguably, he is also its 'holiest'.

I begin with the 'Old Boy'. Zafar Omar (1884–1949) was born in the small town of Bharoth in Meerut District, not very far from Rampur, Muhammad Ali's birthplace six years earlier. After graduating in 1902, Omar, worked for a few years as a personal secretary, first to Nawab Mohsinul Mulk and then to the Begam of Bhopal. He then successfully competed for selection in the Imperial Police—it later became the Indian Police Service—and rose to a high rank despite a tragic hunting accident in which he lost a leg.

Omar also started publishing essays in prominent Urdu magazines, mostly on politics and history. In 1910, he published a small book entitled *Mustaqbil-e Islām* ('The Future of Islam'), a finely done translation of the similarly titled final chapter of Armin Vambéry's *Western Culture in Eastern Lands*. A year later, in 1911, Omar published a very different book, perhaps the first of its kind in India, called *Pulīsmain* ('The Policeman'). A short notice in the *Adīb* (Allahabad) commended the book in this manner: 'Mr Zafar Omar, in this small book, has laid out the true duties, manners, morals, and modes of behaviour of a policeman in such a thoughtful and engaging manner that the Indian police would turn into "angels of mercy" were they to follow his advice.'[2]

The book was based on the lectures Omar gave to in-training constables as a part of his job. It drew the immediate attention of his superiors, who encouraged him to put it into English. Omar obliged, and the English version, *The Indian Policeman*, came out the following year, followed by translations into several Indian languages. The book still makes for delightful reading, as could be expected of a text originally inspired by Lord Baden Powell's classic, *Scouting for Boys*.

Five years later, in 1916, Omar became sensationally famous when he published a mystery novel entitled *Nīlī Chhatrī* ('The Blue Parasol'). Not an original piece of writing, it was nevertheless a remarkable 'transcreation' or adaptation in Urdu of *The Hollow Needle* by Maurice Leblanc (1864–1941). Omar turned Leblanc's immortal creation, Arsène Lupin: Gentleman-Burglar, into an equally memorable, gallant Indian thief named Bahram. The book became an instant hit, and went through seven printings in ten years—a rare feat in Urdu. Three years later, Omar published *Bahrām kī Giriftārī* ('The Arrest of Bahram'), an adaptation of Leblanc's other major book, *813*. It too was equally popular, and established the name 'Bahram' in the annals of Urdu mystery fiction, so much so that soon many hack writers were publishing their own stories about that man of many disguises. By 1936 there were at least 40 books with the name Bahram in their titles.

Ten years passed before Omar published another novel, his last—also his best in my view. He called it *Lāl Kathor* ('The Red Hoard'). It was an adaptation—though unacknowledged this time—of *The Three Just Men*, a minor novel by Edgar Wallace (1875–1932). Bahram and his acolyte Masud, an 'Old Boy' of what by then had become Aligarh Muslim University, along with a third friend, were now turned into public avengers, who went about, at great risk to themselves, protecting the innocent and punishing the criminal whenever the state machinery failed to do so.

Wallace's novel features a particularly nasty villain named Dr Eruc Oberzohn, whose ostensible business involves export and import of innocuous merchandise but who secretly sells weapons to warlords in various countries, particularly in Africa. He also has in his service in London two private assassins who kill his enemies with a poison gun of his invention, besides a small army of agents who do his bidding across the world. As the book opens, Oberzohn is plotting to get his hands on a hoard of gold in Africa that legally belongs to a young woman who does not know about it, but whom the three 'Just Men' are equally determined to help in acquiring that inheritance since they despise the evil doctor and his nefarious activities. Wallace's book, expectedly, is full of murder and mayhem; it is also replete with racial slurs and caricatures. Omar turned it into a milder book, devoid of racism and short on mayhem; in particular, he rather neatly turned Wallace's overblown fiend Oberzohn into a coldly evil Mirza Bilgirami, whom one watches in action as fascinated as when watching a king cobra.

Omar goes to great lengths to introduce Bilgirami in stages, only gradually bringing to our attention his physical appearance and preferences in clothes, his secret vocations and the public life that stands in vivid contrast to them. We first see him in his old-fashioned office, where he sits on a *takht*, amidst a scatter of magazines and newspaper, doing some writing. Next we learn that besides running a girls' school he also owns a press, where he publishes books and pamphlets on national, communal, and religious matters, and that he had once been engaged in the 'deceptive business' (*gorakh-dhandā*) of *tablīgh* (proselytization). As Bilgirami explains in a soliloquy, he gave up the latter business only because 'it doesn't sell anymore. May God's curse be on the editor of

Anīs—he looks like a *maulavī*, but is a Christian at heart. He has so exposed me that now that particular source of my income is almost gone.' We also discover that until recently he had also been working as an informer for the colonial authorities in order to keep them from prying into his own nefarious affairs.

Soon we discover that Bilgirami, much in the manner of a Sufi master, also had several 'disciples', and that one of them named Bundu worked as Bilgirami's favourite assassin, killing any perceived enemy with a poison gun devised by Bilgirami. Eventually comes the moment when Omar almost gives up every pretence, and his readers are left with no doubt about the identity of his target.

Mirza Bilgirami, always keen to think through an issue meticulously, had given much thought to the usefulness of marrying Hira Bai once he had found her. There was only one problem, his wife 'Bilgirami Bano,' in whose praise the Mirza had filled countless pages of his magazine, in the daily diary he regularly serialized—not that he loved her, but for his own publicity. How would she react if he married this young Parsi woman? He was afraid she might grab his beard with one hand and use the other to play a tattoo on his baldpate with a slipper.[3]

The last sentence sounds crude and cruel now, but in 1929 most readers of it would have exclaimed, 'Why, that is Hasan Nizami he is talking about!' And many would have done so rather gleefully.

Omar's target, Khwaja Hasan Nizami (1878–1955), was a controversial figure all his life, much more so during the 1920s and 1930s, when those who knew of him either loved him or despised him. Over five busy decades, he edited and published several magazines and countless books and pamphlets, and developed a much-admired distinctive style of his own in Urdu prose. But he also hobnobbed with the rich and the famous, and sold himself to the general public in a manner no one had done before. He peddled apocalyptic prophecies and miracle cures, claimed to be a Sufi master initiated in Indian and North African *tariqa*s, while also being regularly accused of being a paid police informant. Some even accused him of blackmail, and at least one attempt was made on his life. Nizami also called his second wife Khwaja Bano, and regularly featured her in the diary he serialized in one of his journals.

No doubt in the 1920s Nizami stood for everything that the straight arrow graduates of the M.A.O. College condemned as unworthy, reactionary and orthodox. So the question is not that Omar made fun of him, but rather: 'why did he feel compelled to do so in a most cruel fashion in 1927–8?'

It all began with a falling out between Khwaja Hasan Nizami and a Shaikh Zia'ul Haq of Hapur.[4] According to Zafarul Mulk, a public figure and the editor-publisher of an important monthly, *Al-Nāzir*, Haq was a notorious pamphleteer and a close confidant of Nizami. Over a decade or more, the two had shared many moneymaking schemes that involved colonial authorities and princely states. In one such conspiracy, the two had allegedly managed to terminate the professional career of Zafar Ali Khan—a multitalented writer, journalist and public figure, who later became famous as Maulana Zafar Ali Khan, the editor of *Zamīndār*—when he was in Hyderabad. Zafarul Mulk writes, 'In August 1918, Maulana Zafar Ali Khan was invited to Hyderabad a second time, where he gained many favours from the Nizam. The people who were opposed to him and wished him away then sought a way [to get rid of him] by getting the Government of India involved.' Accordingly, they contacted Haq, who in turn got in touch with Nizami. The latter then went to the Chief Commissioner of Delhi, and told him that Zafar Ali Khan was in Hyderabad and 'giving lessons in Pan Islamism to the Nizam'. Very soon, allegedly under pressure from the colonial authorities, the Nizam ordered both Zafar Ali Khan and his son to leave Hyderabad immediately and go back to British India. Then, in 1926 when the two conspirators had a falling out—reasons unknown—Haq sought to disgrace Nizami publicly. What happened subsequently has come down in two versions.

According to Nizami, Haq sent a letter and some documents to the owner of a press in Delhi, asking him to publish them as a pamphlet. The owner brought the matter to Nizami's notice, who, having nothing to fear as an honest man, gave him the go ahead. The owner, however, did not publish the pamphlet. Haq then sent the same material to Muhammad Ali, who had been a detractor of Nizami in the past and was also at the time the editor-publisher of an influential daily, *Hamdard*. Nizami, 'always desirous of not causing bitter dissent among Muslims on minor matters', called on Ali in person, but failed to dissuade him. He then immediately published a note of his own in *Munādī*, a journal published by a close friend, condemning the betrayal of his confidence, and explaining his own sincere reasons for the action in 1918. In the note, Nizami did not name Haq, but instead referred to him as the *Muhazzab Dākū* ('The Refined Dacoit').

According to the detractors of Nizami and admirers of Ali, Haq initially wrote Ali a long letter making the charge against Nizami, in which he copied the short note he had received from Nizami in 1918. When summoned by Ali to a face-to-face meeting, Haq gave him the original note and also some additional material. Ali, nevertheless, remained hesitant—given the gravity of the charge—preferring to consult with several notables of Delhi before publishing anything about the matter in his journal. Meanwhile Nizami learned of the meeting with Haq from his own sources, and came and gave Ali his version of the matter. Then, sensing that he had failed to convince Ali, Nizami rushed home and published—as a peremptory strike—his article in *Munādī*. Ali then published the incriminating letter in the *Hamdard* and also several commentaries of his own.

Both sides agree on the authenticity of the incriminating letter, dated 12 August 1918, and the following damaging sentences in it:

> It wouldn't surprise me if the Government [of India] wrote [to the Nizam]. I had personally stated all the details to the Chief Commissioner of Delhi, and formally (*bā-zābita*) informed him about the lessons (*sabaq*) in Pan Islamism that the Nizam was being given. I know that he had alerted the Punjab government to this danger. This letter is purely personal. Please destroy it; do not tell anyone about it. In other words, no one else but you should know what I have done.[5]

While Nizami had labelled his nemesis, Haq, the *Muhazzab Dākū*, Ali in his notes called Nizami the *Muqaddas Dākū* ('The Holy Dacoit'), and also brought out a pamphlet by that name. That title was also used by Zafarul Mulk for his two long editorials in *Al-Nāzir*, in which he severely criticized the doubly 'traitorous' activities of Nizami. What Nizami had done, Zafarul Mulk declared, was as much a betrayal of Islam as of Indian nationalism.

The mighty battle of words raged in Urdu journals of north India for several months, starting in November 1926 and ending—probably—in May 1927. How fierce and extensive it was can be gauged by the fact that when Nizami put together in April 1927 a 'selection' of the articles and letters his supporters had published in various journals it came to nearly 700 pages. (Nizami promptly hiked the price to Rs.2 per copy, though originally he had desired to sell it for much less.) The full text on the title page reads as follows:

The Mental and Scribed Replica of the Battle of Siffin, i.e. a complete account of that Battle of Words between Mr Muhammad Ali, Editor of *Hamdard*, and Khwaja Hasan Nizami, which was started by Mr Muhammad Ali on November 17, 1926, and ended by Khwaja Hasan Nizami of Delhi on December 24, 1926. This also includes articles from certain Islamic journals as well as letters from Muslims about that conflict.

The reference to the Battle of Siffin is interesting. Nizami claims the phrase was first and repeatedly used by Muhammad Ali. One can easily imagine the latter's rhetorical strategy: Ali was a part of his name; he was a nationalist Muslim and an enemy of imperialism; and the historical battle at Siffin in 657 CE, between Ali ibn Abi Talib and Mu'aviya ibn Sufyan, had been a battle between a champion of 'democratic' rule against one who preferred 'dynastic kingship'. Now how could he lose, Ali might have thought, in any exchange of rhetorical flourishes? But Nizami, very cleverly, turned tables, claiming that he, Nizami, was a Sayyid and thus a direct *descendant* of Ali ibn Abi Talib, which Ali was not—he was a Pathan, two ranks below a Sayyid—and that, in fact, Ali in attacking him was only imitating Mu'aviya, the enemy of the Prophet's family.

According to Abdul Majid Daryabadi, a notable writer, scholar, and journalist given to polemics, there was never much love lost between Ali and Nizami. Daryabadi greatly admired Ali, and wrote a superbly readable and informative book of memoirs about him. It includes a useful account of the 1926 incident, and mentions some of the things that the 'Khwaja Party' did in print to tarnish Ali's name. These included a fake photograph showing Ali prostrating himself before Pundit Madan Mohan Malaviya, and an equally wild allegation that Ali had described his bathroom to be cleaner than the Prophet's tomb in Madinah! Daryabadi, however, fails to report how the 'Ali Party' reciprocated, though he allows that Ali was not slow to retaliate.

I have not had access to the entirety of the aforementioned tome published by Nizami, but judging from what Nizami wrote in the 'Introduction' Ali could have written only blistering critiques of Nizami's public actions and their negative consequences for the two causes dear to his, Ali's, heart: nationalism and Hindu-Muslim unity in public life. Nizami begins with the charge that Ali always put his politics above his religion. Consequently, Nizami claimed, Ali was angry with him due to the *tablighi* work Nizami was doing to counter the *shuddhi* activities of the Arya Samaj. Nizami also charges Ali with being extremely jealous of anyone who gained any public recognition, and claims it was his inherent jealous nature that had led Ali in the past to 'declare war' on Abul Kalam Azad, Zafar Ali Khan, Abdul Bari of Firangi Mahal, Gandhi, Nehru, and many more. In between, Nizami, very cleverly, repeats the *ad hominem* charges mentioned above, and further accuses Ali of interceding with government officials on behalf of the Raja of Nabha and making money from it. As for the specific charge of causing the ejection of Zafar Ali Khan from Hyderabad, Nizami boldly claims that whatever he did was motivated only by his supreme desire to serve the cause of Islam and protect the Nizam from any British reaction.[6]

Muhammad Ali's *Hamdard* was a popular read for Muslims in north India at the time, and particularly so for the young Muslims who had gone to Aligarh and now forged forward in many professions, away from their familial roles as petty landholders or retainers to the Muslim landed elite. They were, generally, enthused with some spirit of nationalism. Most 'Old Boys' of Aligarh, be they of the old Mohammedan Anglo-Oriental College or the new Aligarh Muslim University, regarded themselves the champions of progress and modernity in all public matters, social or political. Most importantly for our purpose, all 'Old Boys' of Aligarh were honour-bound to side with one of their kind against any outsider.

Omar must have followed the 1926 brouhaha in the pages of *Hamdard* and *Al-Nāzir*—in those days, Muslim college graduates read Urdu journals and contributed to them much more than (sadly) is the case now—when he was working on his Urdu transposition of an English novel that had come out in 1924 and caught his attention. Perhaps due to the bandying of such expressions as *Muhazzab Dākū* and *Muqaddas Dākū*, or perhaps independently, Omar realized he could lend a hand to a 'senior' 'Aligarian' in a most unusual manner. And so Omar's Mirza Bilgirami sports a beard and shoulder-length curly hair, is a Sufi journalist, and writes and publishes a daily diary in which he mentions his wife, calling her Bilgirami Bano (Nizami did the same, calling his wife Khwaja Bano). He works as an informant to the colonial authorities in order to hide his many more nefarious activities. And though Bilgirami's nemesis in the press is an unnamed person—Nizami denounces him only as 'that maulavi-looking but Christian-natured editor'—his paper's title,

Anīs, is synonymous with Muhammad Ali's *Hamdard*. That Omar was eminently successful in his effort is affirmed by a contemporary review of *Lāl Kathor* by none other than Abdul Majid Daryabadi. It originally appeared in *Al-Nāzir* in 1930, and like Daryabadi's other polemics makes a delightful read.[7]

Majid begins with an interesting aside.

In the West, the acme of intellectual achievement is to present lies disguised as truth, whereas in the East, the peak of high thinking was to tell truths disguised as lies. The fact-chronicles out of London—[he means all realistic fiction]—were truth in appearance but deceitful at heart, while the tall tales from Delhi were nothing but truth at heart though an artifice on the outside.

He then segues into a discussion of Sufis, highlighting the Malamatis, i.e. the Sufis who deliberately pretended to be worldly and sinful in appearance but were at heart piously devoted to Truth, and cheerfully declares that Zafar Omar was an 'Aligarh Malamati', for though he was an 'Old Boy' of Aligarh and served in the Police, 'the most "kindly-reputed" department of the government', his heart was filled with a genuine concern for Islam and Muslims. He then moves to praise of his novels, and declares that though now he had no time to spare for novels he was moved to order Omar's new book when a friend told him about it. The rest of the essay, some five pages, is exclusively devoted to the villain of the book, Mirza Bilgirami, to tacitly establish that Bilgirami was the same as Hasan Nizami without ever mentioning the name. 'No reader should now complain,' Daryabadi triumphantly writes near the end, 'that the reviewer has failed to pull the mask off Mirza Bilgirami's face'.

Nizami, in his mind, may have 'ended' the mock 'Battle of Siffin' on 24 December 1926, but the fact that he published a massive compendium of all the shots his side had fired tells us that minor skirmishes continued for a while longer. Unfortunately, the files of *Hamdard* are not available, and so we don't know what, if any, Ali's response was to Nizami's book. Nevertheless, Omar's novel and Daryabadi's review of the same, clearly show that Ali's supporters were eager to launch a verbal sortie or two even four years later. Nizami, however, must have had the last laugh. His reputation and businesses did not suffer any damage, and he outlived not only Muhammad Ali (d. 1931) and Zafarul Mulk (d. 1946), but also Zafar Omar. At his death in 1955, Nizami was widely honoured as a Sufi master and a man of peace, as well as for being a brilliant stylist in Urdu prose.

As one goes over the documents of this long forgotten brouhaha, one is struck by the fact that some eighty years back things were not much different among South Asian Muslims when it came to verbal warfare. *Ad hominem* attacks were as common then as are now, and passionate accusations could equally commonly range from spying and extortion to 'non-Islamic' behaviour and 'insulting the Prophet'. But one must also note that falsely accusing Ali of 'claiming his bathroom to be cleaner than the Prophet's tomb' did not lead to his murder. He remained the leader that he was, and died a tragic but natural death away from India. Even as late as 1954, when Yagana, a great but eccentric Muslim poet in Lucknow, was accused of writing quatrains that were insulting to the Prophet—Daryabadi, was a major instigator against him—he was not lynched; he was only roughed up and paraded in the streets with a blackened face. Obviously new and also utmost frightening is the habit now of readily killing a person even if he is merely accused of such 'blasphemy'. The sectarian and communal violence perpetrated by the Muslims of Pakistan and Bangladesh is only too well known. But the same unholy passions can be noticed as barely controlled among an expanding number of Indian Muslims too, as can be discovered in the pages of Urdu newspapers most weeks. Why this development has happened is another matter, but it is sad to see that our amusing little case of the 'holy dacoit' can now be read as a sobering lesson in mutual toleration.

Notes

1. Gail Minault, *The Khilafat Movement: Religious Symbolism and Political Mobilization in India*, New York: Columbia University Press, 1982, p. 207.
2. *Adib*, September 1911, p. 122.
3. Omar, p. 155.
4. The narrative that follows has been pieced together from the writings of Zafarul Mulk, Abdul Majid Daryabadi, Shaikh Ziaul Haq and Khwaja Hasan Nizami listed in the bibliography. I'm grateful to Ms. Maritta Schleyer of Bonn for making available copies of Haq's and Nizami's books.
5. Haq, p. 15.
6. Nizami, *passim*.
7. Daryabadi, *Inshā-e Mājid*, pp. 354–61.

References

Abdul Majid Daryabadi, *Inshā-e Mājid yā Latā'if-e Adab*, edited by Abdul Qavi Daryabadi, Calcutta: Idarah-e Insha-e Majidi, 1991.

———, *Muhammad 'Alī: Zātti Dā'iri ke Chand Varaq*, Lucknow: Sidq Foundation, 2005, repr.

Gail Minault, *The Khilafat Movement: Religious Symbolism and Political Mobilization in India*, New York: Columbia University Press, 1982.

Khwaja Hasan Nizami, *Namūna-e Jang-e Siffīn*, Delhi: Kakrun-e Halqa-e Mashaikh, 1927

Shaikh Zia'ul Haq, *Hasan Nizami kī Ghaddārī va Jāsūsī kī Kahānī: Akhbār Madīna, Al-Khalīl aur Mukhbir-e 'Ālam kī Zubānī*, Delhi: Sh. Ziaul Haq, 1927.

Zafarul Mulk, *Muqaddas Dākū*, pts. I and II, included in *Silsila-e Intikhāb-e Al-Nāzir, Lakhna'ū*, vol. 3, Patna: K.B. Oriental Public Library, 2001, pp. 243–58.

11

From Despair to Divinity

Legacies of Sadat Hasan Manto and Yās Yagānah Changezī

SYED AKBAR HYDER

TWO OF SOUTH ASIA'S greatest iconoclasts died lonely deaths one year apart: Sadat Hasan Manto, the acclaimed craftsman of Urdu prose, died in Lahore in 1955; and Yās Yagānah Changezi, the most original versifier of the Urdu lyric in the twentieth century, died in Lucknow in 1956. Both were inspired by the legacy of Mirza Asadullah Khan 'Ghālib' (1797–1869), the virtuoso who evinced the spirit of Urdu poetic culture for hundreds of thousands. Both braved scorn, violence, and censorship upon rejecting outright the 'sacred' of their time. They faced financial woes, combined with the anguish of the new nation states foisted on them. Both experienced disciplinary institutions in post-Pakistan Lahore: Manto spent time in its mental asylum; and Yagānah in prison. They admired Oscar Wilde—a man who was no stranger to prisons and asylums of his own time.

The self-referential epitaphs of Manto and Yagānah further capture their intertwined legacies: 'He still believes his name is the letter that could not be repeated on the slate of time.'[1] Gracing Manto's tombstone is this variation on a line of Mirza Ghalib: *lauḫ-e jahāṅ pe ḫarf-e mukarrar nahīṅ hūṅ maiṅ* (On the tablet of the world, I am not a repeated letter). Yagānah's tombstone is etched with a couplet the poet repeatedly invoked to convey his self-pride: *khūd parastī kījīye yā ḫaqq parastī kījīye, āh kis din ke liye nā ḫaqq parastī kījīye* (Either praise your self, or praise the Truth: May that day never come when Untruth wins our praise). The student of Urdu literature will notice at once how the Urdu rhetorical question *kis din ke liye (for what day)*, charged with futility, resignation, and irony, falls short of an idiomatic English translation. It must be remembered from the outset that Yagānah and Manto afford us an extraordinary access to Hindi-derived phrases and words of Urdu that did not feature prominently in the existing Persian-laced ghazal world.

The year 2012 marked Manto's birth centenary. If there was any doubt about his place in the literary canon, it has been put to rest by the many university courses that focus on him, by the seminars organized across the continents in his honour, by the books devoted to his life. Who can argue with those who say that Manto not only documented the breaking down of the moral order around him, but also humanized villains and monsters, breathing new life into loony asylums and brothels? Moreover, Manto, at least in Urdu literature, has rightfully acquired the status of the commentator par excellence of 1947.[2] He stands apart as a witness to the traumas that followed the births of the nations of India and Pakistan. Notwithstanding his value to South Asian history, Manto has also shaped a modern literary aesthetic that intersects with age-old mystical Islamicate idioms. That is, Manto would be relevant to our discussion of aesthetics even if 1947 had not happened, just as Muhammad Iqbal would be a poet of consequence if Pakistan had not been created, Ghalib would engage Urdu poetry and prose if 1857 had not happened, and Mir Anis would stand tall as the master of the Urdu epic even if the Battle of Karbala had never been fought.

In this essay, I hope to recover a dimension of Manto that is rooted in classical Perso-Indic ghazal aesthetics; one which is not necessarily bound to the context of 1947. Concurrently, as a tribute to Manto, I tell the story of Yagānah, a poet who has fallen into relative neglect because he does not heed the calls and submissions of the hegemonic Urdu literary movements of the twentieth century and beyond.

Manto and Yagānah relished the figure of the reprobate: one who is aloof from the conventions around him, be they human conventions or divine ordinances. Bishan Singh is perhaps Manto's most endearing character: a loner in a Lahore asylum who chants incomprehensibly. Time is irrelevant to him; he does not sleep. Resonating in Bishan Singh is *āyat al-kursī*, the Quranic Chapter 2, Verse 255, which begins with the affirmation of God's tributes: 'no slumber can seize Him nor sleep'. Manto closes his renowned short story *Toba Tek Singh*, the stellar satire on the 1947 Partition, with the collapse of Bishan Singh.[3] Manto is well aware that in his tradition, gods may fall, even be shamed. After all, Mir Taqi Mir, the greatest Urdu ghazal writer, also Yagānah's source of emulation, had wondered:

Ilāhī kaise hote haiñ jinhen hai bandagī khwāhish,
hameñ to sharm dāmangīr hotī gar khudā hote[4]

Oh Lord, what sort of beings are those who desire servitude,
Shame would collar me, had I been god

The Islamicate ghazal world (to which Mir subscribed) and its attendant transgressive spirit, often but not always springing from its mystical traditions, gave Manto an uncanny impetus. Manto values *insān dostī* (humanism) while not bypassing the mystical spirit omnipresently operative in the ghazal paradigm. Manto augments this paradigm as a locus of ethics, particularly when he forfeits religious exclusivity or self-righteousness. Remember that Bishan Singh, who stands with the weight of sleeplessness much like that of the Qur'anic God, is not Muslim.

The transregional ghazal genre, with the backing of a thousand years, supplies us not only with the stock characters of the reprobate lover (*'āshiq* or *rind*), the beloved (*ma'shūq*), the rival (*raqīb*), the censor (*nāsih*), the preacher (*shaikh*), but also affords certain enduring tenets (*usūl*) to its audience. Whereas a copious discussion of annihilation in love (*fanā fil 'ishq*) or annihilation in the teacher (*fanā fil shaikh*) is familiar to students of Islamicate cultures, discussions pertaining to annihilation in the principles of and from the margins must be discerned more systematically. It is annihilation in these principles (*fanā fil usūl*) that lends weight to Manto's memorable characters: Bishan Singh, Basit, Mummy, Karim Dad, and Tapish Kashmiri. Let us consider two of them here.

Manto begins his story *Tapish Kashmīrī* with: *mujhe un kā asal nām abhī tak ma'lūm nahīñ—hālāñkeh maiñ un ko bārah baras se jāntā hūñ. Sāth baras to ham ikaTThe sāth rahe* (I do not know his real name to this day, even though I have known him for twelve years; so much so that for seven of those years we lived together).[5] Tapish can invoke poetry at the drop of a hat; he relishes red chilies; and he falls in love with a boy from one Islamiya school: 'this is the platonic-kind of love', the narrator insists. Tapish, who was not inclined to pray till this moment of his infatuation, begins going to the mosque to see this lad; he then assumes leadership of this mosque so that the boy may pray behind him. The narrator even catches Tapish naked, reading the Qur'an. When questioned about approaching god's text without any clothes, Tapish simply draws attention to the fact that nowhere does the Qur'an require its readers to wear clothes.[6] Tapish at this time has no interest in women; in fact he says that the 'delicate gender' and the 'coarse one' simply do not mix. Tapish's beloved soon abandons him for another friend. Tapish quickly moves on to his next love, who happens to be a woman. Apart from financially supporting this woman, he purchases furniture for her family house. He believes that this woman would be happier if both of them lived with her family rather than moving in with him. In the meantime, her father is struck with cholera and she is abducted by a wrestler. On his bicycle, Tapish chases the car in which the girl is being carried away. If it were not for the Victoria car that crashes into his bike, he would have rescued the girl. (Recall the familiar scenes of Indian movies in which the hero risks his life through such feats.) Tapish ends up in the hospital but escapes from there in a few days. He then comes to the narrator, asking for advice about the future course he should take in life. When the narrator bows out of giving advice, Tapish appreciates the gesture with the statement: 'It is ok. Every person knows his own affairs well.' From the next day onwards, Tapish begins to dress in women's clothes. 'These are the very same clothes that he had gotten stitched for that girl.'[7]

This is an annihilation in the beloved but not an annihilation occasioned by the erasure of the individual; rather, it intimates an altogether different mode of existence, wherein Tapish remains Tapish, but with different clothes. When the story draws to a close, Tapish Kashmiri's real name ceases to be of interest, although we are reminded of the unlikely association between tapish (heat) and Kashmir, a land known for its coolness.

Karim Dad from Manto's 'Yazid', like Bishan Singh and Tapish Kashmiri, stands out in his surroundings, for he engages the world in a manner that is incomprehensible to those around him. It is not the language of 'upaR di' but rather the language that denounces the hailing of the Other as the 'enemy'. Even when his father and other relatives are brutally murdered and the water supply of his village is blocked, the only voice of protest that comes from Karim Dad is not to curse the enemy but admonish his own family and community about the self-defeating nature of the mere identification of the enemy as such. When the enemy is named as an enemy, he must live up to the signification of the name. Once named as such, the enemy could not retreat into the friend's position. Karim Dad turns the etiquette of naming on its head when he names his newborn son Yazid—the name of the most loathed tyrant of the Muslim world, whose forces devastated the household of the Prophet of Islam. Reacting to his wife's agony upon seeing Yazid stamped on her child, Karim Dad says: 'It is not necessary that this will be the same Yazid. That Yazid cut off the the river's water; this Yazid will restart it.'[8]

Ghalib had also weighed in on the bounteous lover's heart: it is actually the enemy's friend and that is the reason it does not impart enough momentum for the sights and laments (that rise from it) to reach their destination. Using the charming poetic device of *husn-e ta'līl* (beauty in assigning a cause), Ghalib tells us why no amount of complaining against the enemy or shedding tears over the enemy's cruelty has any effect. We must remember here that the heart of the believer is also the Divine abode, open to all, indiscriminate with the categories of the friend and the foe:

> *dostdār-e dushman hai 'etimād-e dil ma'lūm*
> *āh be asar dekhī nālah nā rasā pāyā*

> It's a friend of the enemy, the trustiness of the heart is known
> I saw sighing to be ineffective, lamentation futile

Manto keeps close company with such a heart/enemy/beloved and alters facile polarities of the self and the other.

In other places, I have explained how Manto's *Yazid* resonates with the ethical concerns of the fourteenth-century master poet of Persian, Shamsuddin Hafiz. Hafiz rescues from Yazid a line of poetry and it is this line that constitutes the opening of the most celebrated divan of Persian: 'O cupbearer, pour more wine, and send one more round of drinks.'

> *a lā yā ayyaha 'l-sāqī adir kā'san wa nāwil ha*
> *ki 'ishq āsān namūd valī uftād mushkilhā*

Hafiz compares the line of poetry to a diamond in the impure mouth of a dog; it does not matter how dreadful the carrier of beauty is. The aesthete is required, like the man of God, to go beyond hero worship and benefit from the beauty of the message.[9]

Manto's principled characters are thus not self-generating (in that their genealogy takes them back into the ghazal tradition) and yet they gain the readers' favour after coming into being through their own actions, not a priori. God has issues with prostitution, we know. But knowing Mummy the way we know her, can God demote her in good conscience? It is Mummy, the madame who overseas flesh trade while being protective of her girls, who is the yardstick by which morality, both in its god-given form and the state sanctioned one, is measured. Mummy provides the sustenance for thirsty libidos, protects the vulnerable, and exposes the hypocrites. Her abode is akin to the Ghalibian brothels that must exist in the shadow and the 'protection' of every mosque that gives the mosque its unique identity: *masjid ke zer-e sāyā kharābāt chāhiye, bhauṅ pās āṅkh qibla-e hājāt chāhiye*.[10] Ghalib builds his couplet by providing an analogy: a brothel is essential to the protection of a mosque, just as the eye, the organ of vision, deservedly stands under the brow. Note that the eye is aligned with the brothel and the brow with the mosque.

Not only did Manto write short stories for publication, he also wrote stories for films in Bombay before he migrated to Pakistan in 1948. His greatest hit was *Mirza Ghalib*, the 1954 film made by Sohrab Modi. *Mirza Ghalib* won India's national best film award the year Manto died in Pakistan. In my work on Ghalib, I argue that Manto helps Ghalib enter the canon of modern progressive/liberal politics by projecting him as a rebel figure. Ghalib, the court poet of the last Mughal ruler Bahadur Shah Zafar, refers to the assembly of royal poets as 'wanting in appreciation', and walks out of the darbar. Anyone who has studied the etiquette of the Mughal court would know that such an act would be considered more crude than rebellious.[11]

Manto quoted Ghalib profusely, for he grew up in a world where Abdul Rahman Bijnauri's panegyric, *Mahāsin-i Kalām-Ghālib* (1921) was becoming a component of the Urdu syllabus. Bijnauri made the claim that India had two sacred books: the Vedas and the *dīvān* of Ghalib.[12] Bijnauri's book in praise of Ghalib becomes a creedal statement to such an extent that the most important Indian Marxist literary reformist movement in the 1930s, the Progressive Writers Movement,[13] held up Ghalib as the founding figure of the movement.

One of the challenges that Manto, the writer, faced, is that of opting out of names. In a playful essay, *kuch nāmoṅ ke bāre meṅ* (A bit about names), Manto proposes that children should remain nameless until they become writers. And then they should have the liberty to select their name so as to protect their parents' sentiments and pride.[14] It would have been much more proper had the Progressives taken the name 'Progressives' after they had demonstrated their progressiveness, rather than at the time of their birth.

Yagānah concurred with the spirit of Manto's suggestion two decades before Manto captured it in writing. In 1926, Yagānah moved from Lucknow to Lahore, to a neighbourhood near Bhāti Darvāzah. The house to which Yagānah moved had a strange look, hence its low rent. Yagānah named it *teRhā banglah* (crooked mansion). On the return address of his letters, he noted this name. He told the postman to watch out for letters that carried the name of this house in their address: 'Remembering this address will cause trouble only until a few letters arrive—after that, it will have become registered on its own.'[15] Repeating the name ensures its permanence. Names leave shackle-like marks not just on the named ones, but also those who contribute to the naming process and witness its unfolding.

Yagānah, named by his father Mirza Wajid Husain, moved from Azimabad to Lucknow around 1914. All good poets in the Perso-Indic world experiment with their names. Mirza Wajid Hussain gave himself names that would eventually lead him into isolation and contribute to his notoriety for decades to come. He first called himself 'Yās', meaning despair. Yās Azimabadi—Despair from Azimabad. Azimabad is the earlier name of today's Patna, the capital city of Bihar. Yās married into a Lucknow family but never received the treatment owed to a South Asian son-in-law—or so he felt for the rest of his life. Lucknow was a difficult city; the canon guardians of the city believed their Urdu to be superior to all other Urdu modes. Even though Azimabad was only 300 miles away, the establishment in Lucknow looked down on Azimabad for accommodating local dialects in the lofty Urdu language. Yās never lived down this Azimabad connection. He hankered to be accepted by Lucknow and his émigré experience in this city provided a sideshow to all his writing for the rest of his life.

As soon as Yās moved to Lucknow, he prepared for a long fight with the existing literary establishment.

jān se baRh kar samajhte haiñ mujhe yās ahl-e dil,
ābru-e lucknow, khāk-e 'azīmābād hūñ[16]

The people of heart hold me, despair, more dear than their life.
I am the glory of Lucknow, the dust of Azīmābād

The Lucknow establishment split into two factions over Yās. Pyare Saheb Rashid, the grandson of Mir Anis, the acclaimed elegist from nineteenth century, showered Yās' poetry with praise, as did Masud Hasan Rizvi Adib, a young Urdu student at the time who later became Urdu's finest literary critic from Lucknow. Unfortunately, in Yās' early years in Lucknow, he was forced to confront forces much more powerful than Rashid and Adib, those of the literary fraternities, the *adabi anjuman*s. Although these fraternities have dominated several Urdu cultures that operated on the interface of (often literary and political power) the ones from Lucknow stood out for their gatekeeping, whether it was on the publication front or on the performative. Anjuman-e Me'ār-e Adab (founded *c*.1910) was one such fraternity. Gracing the cover of their monthly journal, *Me'ār*, were the sun and the moon—inscribed in the first was Mir Taqi Mir and in the second was Mirza Ghalib. Under the auspices of these names was the map of India, a nation-state that had not yet come into being as a political unit. Whereas Yās did not mind Mir's designated station, he could not bear the name of Ghalib alongside Mir's. He felt a cult had been created around Ghalib and the members of this cult got political mileage out of anachronistically turning Ghalib into an anti-colonial hero. A rite of the hero-making process, Yās felt, was vacuous praise showered on Ghalib's poetry and life—praise that acutely damages Urdu's critical enterprise and sets disconcerting precedent: it did not spring from verifiable and transparent aesthetic standards. A sacralization of Ghalib was taking place, Yās proclaimed. Subsequently, much of his poetry was born in a protest against the Ghalib cult. The incipient scourge that began to build up around Yās in the *Me'ār* circles became unrelenting with time. The dwellers of Lucknow, known for their impeccable *ādāb*, relinquished their civility very quickly and lapsed into vicious attacks on Yās's regional background, class, art, and religion.

In 1914, with his very first publication, *Nishtar-e Yās* [1914], Yās Azimabadi had snubbed the *Me'ār* and its ilk. The book begins with a statement from Ibn Khaldun: 'A Persian man, by appropriately utilizing the discourse of eloquent Arabs, may become worthy of being classified as a native speaker.' Yās draws our attention to a different standard of Lucknow: 'After all, I am not even foreign to Urdu, but because of regional prejudices I am left out of the establishment.' In the same preface, Yās commends the Swedes for rightly honouring Tagore. The people of Lucknow, Yās proceeds to say, trample on their own poets. Yās ends his preface in the voice of the prophets spoken through God in the Qur'anic chapter Yāsin, verse 17:[17]

w mā 'alaynā illal balāgh al-mubīn

and we are not responsible except for clear notification.

The first ghazal in *Nishtar-e Yās* shares its metrical and rhythmic pattern with one of Ghalib's famous ghazals:

chup lagī mujh ko gunāh-e 'ishq sābit ho gayā,
rañg chehre kā uRā rāz-e dil-e muztar khulā
ashk-e khūn se zard chehre par hai kyā turfah bahār,
dekhiye rañg-e junūn kaisā mere muñh par khulā
khanjar-e qātil se jannat kī havā āne lagī,
aur bahār-e zakhm se firdaus kā manzar khulā[18]

From the slayer's dagger blows the breeze of heaven
from the spring of the wound, the heavenly vistas come into view
The tears of blood on the sallow face—what a spring they bring,
behold how the colour of madness bedecks my face
A silence fell upon me; the sin of love was proven;
the colour of my countenance fled; the secret of the restless heart
    was divulged

phir gaiñ ānkheñ merī kūcha-e jānāñ ki taraf,
shukr hai marte dam itnā to mujhe hosh rahā[19]

Once again my glances turned toward the beloved's lane,
thankfully, this much awareness I had at the moment of death

kyā jāne āj yās ne kyā dekhā khāb meñ,
kyūn chunkte hi āp se begānah ho gayā[20]

Who knows what Yās has seen in his dream today,
Waking up startled, why has he become a stranger to himself

Divānā ban ke un ke gale se lipaT bhi jāo,
Kām apnā kar lo yās bahāne bahāne meñ

Feigning insanity, throw yourself in his embrace
Finish your work Yās, with one excuse or the other

Yās begins to experiment with different names to ascertain if his fortune would change with them. In many poetry assemblies, he wished to be addressed with the epithets of Imam ul-Ghazal (the leader of the ghazal establishment) and Abul Ma'ni (the father of meaning). Of course Abul Ma'ni is also the epithet of his fellow Azeemabadi and Mirza from the seventeenth century, Abdul Qadir Bedil, one of the most turgid of Persian poets and a foremost influence on Ghalib's Persian as well as Urdu poetry. The casualness with which Yās played with his names trickled down into his critiques of poets, past and present, and into his expressions about revered institutions, in his ghazals as well as *rubāʿīs* (quatrains):

Hai aur bhī ek rāh mazhab ke sivā
Mantaq ke sivā ʿilm-e muzabzab ke sivā
Bāz ā gaye manzil se kahāñ kī manzil
Matlab nahīñ koī tark-e matlab ke sivā[21]

There is a road, other than that of religion
Other than that of logic; other than the science of doubt
I am fed up with the destination—what destination
I do not mean a thing, save for the disavowal of meaning

Matlab nahīñ koī tark-e manzil ke sivā
Maqsad nahīñ koi tark-e bātil ke sivā
Kaʿbe kā huā maiñ nah sanamkhāne kā
Sar jhuk nah sakā kahīñ dar-e dil ke sivā[22]

I do not mean a thing, save for the disavowal of the destination
I do not intend a thing, save for the refusal of falsehood
Neither did I become the one of the Kaʿba nor of the temple
My head could not bow, save at the door of the heart

dard apnā kuch aur hai davā hai kuch aur
Tū Te hue dil kā āsrā hai kuch aur
aise vaise khudā to buhtere haiñ
maiñ bandah hūñ jis kā voh khudā hai kuch aur[23]

My pain is something else, the medicine is something else
The refuge for the broken heart is something else
This and that god are many out there
The one to whom I submit, that god is something else

From the pen name despair, Yās rose, in his estimation, to become Yagānah—one of a kind, unique, unrivalled. The new name instantly reminded the literate community around him of a well-known couplet from Ghalib's ghazal:

use kaun dekh saktā keh yagānah hai voh yaktā
jo dūī kī bū bhī hotī to kahīñ do chār hotā

Who can see him, for that unique one is peerless
If there had been a whiff of duality, he would become visible

This is a ghazal couplet that bows to the time-honoured concept of *wahdat al-wujūd*, Oneness of Being, in Arabic, or *hamā ūst*, All is He, in Persian. That the unique being can be seen, suggests the existence of the faculty of vision that would have to be unique in itself to behold the Unique one. And by its very essence this second uniqueness would run counter to the first one. Yagānah's gift for intertwining his autobiography with the story of a more dignified ghazal love transfixed Urdu aficionados and critics alike, turning his legacy into sneaking admiration, gossip and innuendos.

mazah gunāh kā jab thā ke bā wazū karte
butoṅ ko sajdah bhī karte to qiblahrū karte
mazār-e yās peh karte haiṅ shukr ke sajdeh
du'ā-e khair to kyā ahl-e lakhnaū karte[24]

The delight of sinning:
I could only procure it in the state of ritual purity
Even when I kneeled to the idols,
I did so facing the Ka'ba
At Yās's grave, they prostrate in gratitude [for the loss of his life]
How could the people of Lucknow wish him well [even in death]

Yagānah would build a small but dedicated following around him, even though his poetry and person were both galling to the larger Lucknow establishment. Whether he intended or not, seemingly innocuous words from his poetry caught the moment—and ire of poets much more influential than he was.

yās ab zalīl ko hī samajhte haiṅ sab 'azīz,
kānTe chaman ke tulte hain phūlon ke bār se[25]

Yās, nowadays everyone holds the wretched to be dear
Thorns of the garden are weighed against the flowers

These verses backfired as the word *'azīz* (dear) was read as a pointed reference to Lucknow's senior Me'ār poet, Aziz Lakhnavi. This was just the beginning of the feud between the two, to which I shall return later.

Yagānah frequently attached the Islamic *radī allāhu anhū* (may God be pleased with him) to his name, an honorific reserved for prophets and authorities of Islam. *Radī Allāh anhū* was followed by *jallā jalāluhū* (His glory is great), an honorific, that follows God's name. Under the banner of these names were Yagānah's couplets, provocative but meticulously crafted:

sab tere sivā kāfir, ākhir is ka matlab kyā,
sar phirā de insān kā, aisā khabt-e mazhab kyā

Everybody but you is an infidel, what exactly does this mean?
That which makes humans lose their mind, what is this obsession with religion

samajh meñ kuch nahīñ ātā paRhe jāo to kyā hāsil
namāzoñ kā kuch matlab ho to pardesī zabān kyūñ ho

Not a word can be understood, what will come of all such recitation
If 'namaz' is to have some meaning, why is it in a foreign language

khūdī kā nashā chaRhā āp meñ rahā nah gayā,
khudā bane the yagānah magar banā nah gayā[26]

The drunkenness of the self grew, it was not possible to stay within the self
God had tried to turn unique, but he could not pull it off/
yagānah had become God, but he could not pull it off

butoñ ko dekh ke sab ne khudā ko pahchānā
khudā ke ghar to koi bandah-e khudā na gayā[27]

Having seen the idols, all and sundry recognized god
No slave of god has ever been to the house of god

pukārtā rahā kis kis ko Dūbne vālā
khudā the itne magar koi āre ā nah gayā[28]

Who all did the drowning one beseech
So many gods were out there, but none came to his rescue

krishan kā hūñ pujārī 'alī kā bandah hūñ
yagānah shān-e khudā dekh kar rahā nah gayā[29]

I am the worshipper of Krishna and the slave of Ali
Yagānah, having seen god's glory, I simply could not hold myself back

nah khudāoñ kā nah khudā ka dar ise 'aib jāniye yā hunar
vahī bāt āi zabān par jo nazar pe chaRh ke kharī rahī[30]

Neither do I fear gods, not god, take this to be a fault or a virtue
Only that comes to my tongue, that which rises as the truth in my sight

āñkhoñ āñkhoñ men le liyā va'dah
kānoñ kān ek ko khabar nah huī[31]

A word was pledged so deep within the eyes
that not a hint of it reached listening ears.

*Ka'ba nahīñ ke sārī k͟hudāī ko dak͟hl ho
dil men sivāe yār kisī kā guzar nahīñ*[32]

It is not the Ka'ba, where all of god's creation meddles
Through the heart, no one but the friend proceeds

*mujhe dil ki khatā par yās sharmānā nahīñ ātā
parāyā jurm apne nām likhvānā nahīñ ātā*[33]

Yās, I do not know how to succumb to shame at the mistake of my heart
I do not know how to take the blame for someone else's crimes

*'ilm kyā 'ilm kī haqīqat kyā
jaisī jis ke gumān meñ āī*[34]

What is knowledge? What is the truth behind knowledge?
It is whatever anybody wants it to be

Yagānah was obsessive when it came to protecting Urdu as Urdu—not as Persian or Arabic, but as a composite language. Yagānah, like Manto, captured Urdu's populist spirit by writing in a language with a vocabulary accessible to the masses.[35] He found tremendous value in Urdu's aspirations and retroflexes, which are missing in writing heavy with Persian excesses. It was this concern over the Persianization of Urdu that helped Yagānah launch his earliest critiques of Ghalib. Just when the divan of Ghalib was rendered on a par with the divine vedas, Yagānah began to discern idioms in Ghalib's Urdu poetry that were acceptable in Persian but not in Urdu. As proof of this, Yagānah began with a series of essays and quatrains that found fault with Ghalib's language. These critiques ultimately formed the book Yagānah which is most closely associated with, *Ghālib Shikan*, The Ghalib breaker. Manto's Ghalib was a misfit on the silver screen. Yagānah was a spectacular misfit who projected himself as a destroyer of the Ghalib myth.

Yagānah attacked Ghalib on two fronts: the aesthetic and the moral. On the aesthetic front, Yagānah discerns slips of prosody, reigns of verbosity, paraphrasing of old masters like Bedil and Mir, and most importantly, the pretentious Persianization that makes the ghazal experience tedious and contrived. For instance, in a tongue-in-cheek remark on an Urdu couplet, he suggests that the couplet would be much more meaningful if we read its Urdu words as though they were Persian:

کون ہے جو نہیں ہے حاجتمند
کس کی حاجت روا کرے کوئی

kaun hai jo nahīñ hai hājitmañd,
kis kī hājitravā kare koī.[36]

Who is there who is not needy
Whose need might anyone fulfil

This is the most common reading of the Ghalib couplet; however, since classical Perso-Urdu poetry is usually not written with diacritical marks, readers have the prerogative of adding their own marks to certain words that are ambiguous. Thus, another way of reading this couplet is:

کُون ہے جو نہیں ہے حاجت مند
کس کی حاجِت روا کرے کوئی

kūn hai jo nahīñ hai hājitmañd
kus kī hājitravā kare koī

It's the ass that is not needy
Someone fulfil the vagina's needs!

Yagānah spins the polemics around Ghalib's personal life choices and actions by first rendering him an opportunistic sycophant. He calls into doubt Ghalib's patriotism by reminding Ghalib's followers, whom he calls 'Ghalibchis (petty Ghalibians), that Ghalib basked in wine and revelry while his patron Bahadur Shah was dying in Rangoon. Ghalib ingratiated himself with the British by writing a *qasīdah* for Queen Victoria.

angrez chupaR meñ kahīñ āte haiñ janāb
kyā dūr thā ā jātā koī aur 'itāb
kyā 'abd-e vafādār bane the mirzā
kaisā sūkhā milā qasīdeh kā javāb.[37]

Do the British ever fall prey to flattery, Mister
It wouldn't have been too far-fetched for another wrath to descend
Oh how Mirza became the slave of the faithful
What a flat refusal came in return for his praise

Yagānah's critiques of Ghalib began as objectively constructive, then became venomous and personal as Yagānah was boycotted by the admirers of Ghalib in Lucknow, especially by the Anjuman-e Me'ār-e Adab of Aziz and Safi Lakhnavi. Ghalib, rather than being the object of critical appreciation, was turned into a weapon, especially when it came to patriotism and mysticism.

ghālib bhī hai vallāh anokhā sūfī
angrez ke darbār kā bhūkā sūfī
penshan jo hu'ī band to bhūk aur khulī
hai aisā ko'ī peT kā bandah sūfī[38]

By god Ghalib is a rare Sufi
A Sufi who starves for the British court
When his pension was stopped, his hunger grew
Is there a Sufi so chained to the stomach?

To add fuel to the fire, Yagānah cast a critical gaze toward Muhammad Iqbal, who had raised Ghalib to the sphere of Mansur al-Hallaj in his heavenly journey *Jāvīdnāma,* and then toward the Progressives. Iqbal occupied an unrivalled position in the twentieth-century Muslim community as a thinker, spokesperson, and poet. Yet Yagānah accused him of sullying the language of Urdu with banal political slogans. Since Iqbal hailed from the Punjab, a region that the Delhi and Lucknow Urdu establishment mocked for not doing justice to particular Urdu letters like the *qāf* (which is pronounced in the Urdu circles of Delhi and Luckow as a uvular consonant from the back of the throat), Yagānah mocked Iqbal accordingly:

istage kā shā'ir hai nah chaurāhe kā,
letā hai qalam se kām charvāhe kā,
maiń bhī yahī kahtā hūń jo tum kahte ho,
ik bāl to ik bāl hai par kāhe kā[39]

Neither is he a poet of the stage nor of the street corner,
he makes the pen do the work of a shepherd,
I say exactly what you say,
a piece of hair is just a piece of hair, but of what!

Iqbal, if its q comes from deep down the throat in Lucknow and Delhi, means glory. However, if the q is read as a k, as it is by many in the Punjab, then it means a string of hair (*ikbāl*). How unfortunate it was that a man like Yagānah, who attributed his own persecution to regional prejudices—rather than accepting Urdu's cultural zone as polycentric—would feed into acute internecine regional hierarchies, hierarchies that have cost Urdu dearly. So while his attacks on Iqbal's Urdu pronunciation were unwarranted in the larger ecumenical interests of Urdu, Yagānah was on the mark when expressing his fear of Iqbal's literary criticism being taken into the custody of hagiographical praise ad nauseam.

As Iqbal was becoming a hallowed figure in the 1930s, Yagānah forewarned his readers that very soon Iqbal too would become immune to literary criticism and circulated indiscreet. When Manto was asked to pay tribute to Iqbal in a cultural programme he expressed apprehension at the mass production of Iqbal's legacy. That Iqbal appeared in the advertisements of soaps, oils, hotels and detergents could very well distort his vision in the narrow alleys of ignorance and parochialism.[40] Moreover, Manto felt that Iqbal had also been monopolized by self-appointed custodians of culture and literature.

Yagānah not only took umbrage at Iqbal's critics as legitimate judges of poetry but also at his poetry as good poetry, or even as reformist for that matter. Perhaps Iqbal was a successful motivational speaker; he certainly did not care about consistency of thought when tinkering with Islam of the Indian subcontinent variety. Religion and spirituality are specific to the society that gives birth to them and, in turn, is shaped by them. Reformers like Iqbal attempt to remedy Muslim society by ignoring the broader historical conditions of Indian Muslims, with reference to an Islam that is exogenous to South Asia. Yagānah thus accused the 'Poet of the East' for not just turning to the seventh-century Hijaz for twentieth-century solutions but for actually turning his back on the subcontinent. It is worth recalling here that as Rahi Masum Raza, a fine critic of Yagānah's thought, points out, the self-pride that Yagānah harbours is resonant with the pride that Iqbal attributes to Iblis, who being created by God refuses to bow to Adab, hence becoming the devil to many. Iqbal captures a remark from Iblis to God's good angel, Gabriel:

> *maiñ khaTaktā hūñ dil-e yazdāñ meñ kāñTe kī tarah*
> *tū faqat allāh hū allāh hū allāh hū*[41]
>
> I throb in the heart of the Almighty like a thorn
> And you: God is he! God is he! God is he.

This statement suggests that the devil is much more colourful and dynamic than the angel Gabriel. To Raza, this devil approximates Yagānah's hero. What must also be pointed out here is that within the world of the ghazal, poets frequently took to task god's angels and prophets and derided them for their inability to hold their liquor or provide proper guidance when asked to do so. For example, Ghalib writes:

girnī thī ham pe barq-e tajallī nah tūr par
dete haiñ bādah zarf-e qadah khār dekh kar

The lightning of manifestation should have struck me, not Mt. Tur
Wine is given according to the capacity of the cup drinker

Legend has it that Moses went up on Tur and wished for a glimpse of the Almighty. He received it in the form of lightning, which he simply could not withstand. Ghalib here sets himself up as Moses's rival and suggests that his own zarf (capacity) would have been much more expansive than that of Moses. Or, consider this:

lāzim nahīñ keh khizr ki ham pairavī kareñ
jānā ke ik buzurg hameñ hamsafar mile

It's not necessary that we follow the footsteps of Khizr
We know! We encountered an elderly gentleman as our fellow-traveller

Khizr is the guide par excellence in the world of devotion. Some take him to be a saint and others as a wise soul who came to the rescue of the likes of Alexander the Great. Ghalib in the above couplet tips his hat to Khizr's status as an elderly statesman of the literary world but also makes it clear that bowing in respect is not tantamount to emulation or blind following. Men of legends, Khizr and Moses, end up becoming adjuncts to Ghalib in his nineteenth-century ghazals. What Yagānah does is make Ghalib an adjunct to himself. To those who raised Ghalib to the status of a prophet, he has a brilliant response:

maiñ payambar nahīñ yagānah sahī
is se kyā kasr shān me āī[42]

If I am not a Prophet, at least I am one of a kind
How would this possibly shortchange my glory?

According to the Muslim lore, 124,000 Prophets were dispatched to the earth at the command of God. When poets like Ghalib took on Moses or Jesus as rivals, they were after all only contending with prophets who were two of the many. Yagānah here is the One, the one who by definition does not have competition and all Prophets are at his command. The poet bypasses the competition with the prophets, as though to say he had bigger fish to fry.

> *taqlīd kā bandah nahīñ k͟hudsar hūñ maiñ*
> *vallāh ik āzād sukhanvar hūñ maiñ*
> *voh mauj nahīñ hūñ jise sāḥil roke*
> *dhārā hūñ āj kal samandar hūñ maiñ*[43]

I am not a slave of emulation, I am headstrong
By god, I am a free designer of words
I am not that wave which can be stopped by the shore
I am a stream today, and the ocean tomorrow

Such a stream could not be dammed by any force, especially those of a myopic preacher:

> *jaise dozakh kī havā khā ke abhī āyā hai*
> *kis qadar vā'iz-e makkār Darātā hai mujhe*[44]

As though he has just returned from the flames of hell—
How the sly preacher bullies me!

The Urdu poetry assemblies responded by simultaneously pathologizing Yagānah and by rendering him heretical. They pitted Yagānah against the poets of Lucknow by issuing bellicose rhetoric. Soon, he was systematically boycotted and unemployed. He had to sell his precious book collection in order to provide for his wife and children. He compared Lucknow to Karbala:

> *vatan ko choR kar jis sar zamīñ ko maiñ ne 'izzat dī,*
> *vahī ab k͟hūn kī pyāsī hūi hai karbalā ho kar*[45]

After leaving my homeland, the land I had honoured
It has turned thirsty for my blood, having become Karbala

Yagānah's fame by the late 1920s had spread in the Urdu world. He was invited by a well-wisher in Hyderabad to work in the state bureaucracy; he was also offered a position in the court of the Nizam, but he politely bowed out of it by saying that his disposition was not suited for royal service—he would be compelled to recant his dignity and God forbid, might end up like Ghalib. When Hyderabad's popular literary icon and minister, Maharaja Kishan Parshad suggested that Yagānah write a few verses of praise for the Nizam, he responded: 'My benefactor, it's not in my control to undertake such tasks. If you see any shortcoming in my work, please mark me down for it. Qasidah writing is beyond the realm of my skills. This genre of writing stands against my disposition.'[46]

The dynamic literary establishment of Hyderabad greeted Yagānah warmly. Osmania University had just been established as the first Urdu-medium university in South Asia and the intellectual milieu of the Hyderabad state was thriving with Josh Malihabadi, Fani Badayuni, Ali Haidar Nazm Tabatabai, Turab Yar Jung, Shaheed Yar Jung, Mehdi Navaz Jung, and the various Bilgramis, Rashid Turabi, and Najam Afandi. Although Hyderabad bore its own share of tensions between natives and outsiders, Yagānah was held in high esteem by both sides. Along with his poetry, Hyderabadis were charmed with his forthrightness and austere lifestyle. They took pride in providing a sanctuary for a man shunned in the city of Lucknow, Hyderabad's Urdu rival. After lively discussions surrounding Ghalib and Mir, the poets of Hyderabad and Yagānah moved on to weightier issues: how does the *wuzu* of an elephant become invalid? Would the Muslim heaven have the same appeal to the inhabitants of Iceland as it does to the desert Arabs?[47]

As the 1930s drew to a close, the Progressive Writers Movement gained more appeal due to its alliances with anti-colonial movements. While maintaining a respectful distance from Yagānah, Progressive writers such as Sajjad Zaheer, Sardar Jafri, and Kaifi Azmi sought clarifications from Yagānah on matters of language. This should not come as a surprise, since even Iqbal sent linguistic and poetic queries that dealt with extremely technical aspects of Urdu to Yagānah.[48] In 1945, Sajjad Zaheer offered to publish the collection of Yagānah's poetry through the Qaumi Ishath Ghar of Lahore, a publishing house established to patronize Marxist literature. When Yagānah saw the results, he was devastated. He realized that an editor had made changes to certain verses and at times the sacred metrical conventions had been violated. The Progressives fell even lower in his esteem.[49]

For Yagānah, the ideological claims of these poets, including the claims they made for their poet-predecessors, and the principles by which they lived at a practical level did not correspond with each other; rather, they obfuscated progress and history for the masses by setting a pattern of working backward from one's own ideological privilegings.

When shown the popular poem slogan written by Faiz, *Bol*, Yagānah simply wondered if a lower division student could obtain even five points out of a hundred for clumsily stringing words in this manner. Not only was this not poetry but it was not even good prose.[50] As far as the 'Poet of Revolution', Josh Malihabadi was concerned, Yagānah conceded that Josh was a 'genius', although misguided and a neophyte. Even though Josh held Yagānah in high esteem, received clear inspiration from him even when writing film songs,[51] and came to Yagānah's rescue during the most dire times, Yagānah said he could not see himself growing tall by standing on his toes, the way Josh had.[52] Yagānah chided the popular Jigar Muradabadi for singing poetry that was crafted with a gross disregard for the varying contextual significance of synonyms.

shabāb maikash jamāl maikash khayāl maikash nigāh maikash
khabar voh rakhenge kyā kisī kī unheñ khud apnī khabar nahīñ hai[53]

Youth, wine-bibber, beauty, wine-bibber, thought, wine-bibber, glance, wine-bibber
How would he remain attentive to others, he who is unaware of his self

Yagānah suggests that Jigar should have used 'mast' (intoxicated/tipsy) instead of 'maikash' (winebibber). He gives a prose example: '*Mahmūd sharab meñ mast rahtā hai*' (Mahmud is intoxicated with wine) as acceptable and not '*Mahmūd sharāb meñ maikash rahtā hai*' (Mahmud is winebibber with wine). He cites a couplet by Khwaja Haidar Ali Atish as an example of how the same word could be used three times in a single line for a real potent impact on the audience:

maikadeh meñ nashah kī 'ainak dikhātā hai mujhe
āsmāñ mast o zamīñ mast dar o dīvār mast[54]

In the tavern, he shows me the spectacles of intoxication
Skies drunk, land drunk, doors and the walls—all drunk

Rather than studying the art of poetry by assaying the verses of Atish, Mir Anis, and Mir Taqi Mir,[55] the poets of his time, Yagānah claimed, suffered from a surfeit of thought that was mechanical (for instance, generated by technical imperatives of rhyme and meter) and ideologically dubious (Marxist for display purposes and capitalistic when put into practice). He lumps these poets either as unimaginative composers of verse (Aziz Lakhnavi, Saqib Lakhnavi, Fani Badayuni, Jigar Muradabadi), as pseudo-Sufis (Asghar Gondavi),[56] or as Progressives (Faiz Ahmed Faiz). By invoking this last group, he bemoans the state of Urdu in his time: 'By God, the art of poetry had not been disgraced at the hands of Chirkin (a nineteenth-century poet known for scatological verses) the way it is being disgraced in the hands of the Progressives.'[57]

Moreover, Yagānah says poetry of his time had become fodder for personality cults and if this continued, aesthetic discretion would die a painful death in Urdu. He was very much against poetic factionalism—just as he was against the religious one. He discouraged the formation of a cult around himself. The great romantic poet Majaz showed up at his doorstep. Yagānah inquired who he was. Majaz introduced himself: 'I am known as Majaz.' Yagānah inquired: 'What brings you here?' Majaz responded: 'I was extremely interested in meeting you.' Yagānah: 'Now that you have fulfilled your desire, please take leave.'[58]

Urdu literary 'critics' sought shelter in parochial fraternities, nepotistic educational institutions like the Aligarh Muslim University,[59] and unscrupulous journals (like Shahid Ahmad Dehlavi's *Sāqī*) to shield themselves from accountability.[60] Rather than judging poetry as though it were art, valuable in itself, critics have created distractions by drawing from the poet's religion, ethnicity, and ideology. Slogans are strong arming mass audiences into deflecting their gaze from the aesthetic merits, he wrote. Yagānah was put off by rhetorical grandstanding that did not correspond to actions. It was as though the Qur'an had created an opening for Yagānah's critique of the Progressives:

wā annahum yaqūlūna mā lā yafaʻlūn

And that they say what they practice not? (26:226)

Yagānah wondered about verses of devotional poetry that were thoughtlessly sung: '*mere maula bula lo madinah mujhe*' (my master, summon me to Medina). This is a popular poem in which the devotee pines for city of the Prophet Muhammad's burial, Medina. Yagānah said that Muslims are not worshippers of the Prophet; unless they have the traits and ethics of Muhammad, what will they achieve in just going off to Medina.⁶¹ Such a tradition of devotion fuelled cults of personality and ironically even those movements, like the Progressive Writers Association, devoured the ethos of the cults springing from blind devotion. The fashion of 'progressivism' and mere rhyming (foisted on the Urdu community by the likes of Muhammad Iqbal and Fani Badayuni), Yagānah hoped, will also come to pass and the new generation will be able to say:

> *voh daur rahā nah voh zamānah bāqī*
> *hai aur ko'ī din yeh fasānah bāqī*
> *kaisa idbār aur kahāñ kā iqbāl*
> *dunyā fānī magar yagānah bāqī*⁶²

> That era subsists, nor those times
> This is another day—the tale of this one subsists
> What came of those declines of good fortune (idbār),
> and where did that good fortune (Iqbal) go?
> The world is mortal (Fānī) but the Unique one (Yagānah) subsists

Here is another punch at Iqbal: the poet who sang of the lost glories of Islam (idbār); and at Fānī Badayuni (d. 1961), the poet so closely tied to the 'nocturnal' princely court of Hyderabad's Moazam Jah, the second son of the Nizam.

Much of Yagānah's judgement of his own art hinged on the opinion of his wife, notwithstanding his tiffs with her.⁶³ Yagānah wrote letters to his friends, in which it is clear that his wife appeared to be his hero. His older daughter recalled that when Yagānah would write poetry late in the night, he would wake up his wife and recite the *she'r*. With a smile, he would ask her if she thinks it is her husband reciting the poetry or if the source of this poetry was divine. Friends tried to persuade Yagānah to take a drink but he refused its asymmetrical delight, saying:

I cannot subject my innocent wife to such mental torture. If drinking is what is required to retain love and friendship, *to generate poetry*, then I bid goodbye to such friendships and enterprises from a distance.⁶⁴

In 1947, many a romance ended. Manto left his beloved Bombay behind soon after Partition. Yagānah's son, who worked for All India Radio Bombay, left for Pakistan, followed by his mother. Yagānah was persuaded by his dear friend, the leading Shia *zākir*, Rashid Turabi, to move to Pakistan as Turabi had.

In his personal notebook Yagānah wrote:

vatan ko choR ke pahunchā gharīb pākistān
yahān se aur kahāñ jāye kis jagah jāye[65]

After leaving his homeland, the poor one reached Pakistan
Where else does one go from here, where exactly does he go

When a loonie in Manto's Toba Tek Singh was asked about the whereabouts of Pakistan, he said that it was a kind of place in Hindustan where large razors are made. Yagānah substituted Pakistan with jannat, heaven, when he published the ghazal. And as all the students of ghazal know, jannat is where the lover's growth is stagnated, his playfulness suffocated; it is the least desired destination, even for the dead.

Yagānah arrived in Karachi and stayed with Rashid Turabi, who liberally quoted Yagānah from the pulpit as a man who questions superficial religiosity, a man who holds on to his devotion for Ali while questioning God himself.

'alī kā bandah ho ke bandagī kī ābrū rakh lī
yagānah ke liye kyā dūr thā mansūr ho jānā[66]

After becoming Ali's slave, he rescued the honour of slavery
It was not difficult for the One to turn into Mansur

Devotion to the Imam Ali (as opposed to god) leads Yagānah, yet again, to the claims of distinctiveness; by becoming the slave of Ali, Yagānah is spared the problems that beset the worshippers of God, the likes of Mansur al-Hallaj. Every other poet in the Islamicate world had compared himself to Mansur by raising cries of God's inseparability from himself and rhetorically opening the possibility of severe punishment, including execution. Expressions of being God's slave and lover, like Mansur, were commonplace. It was much more outrageous to claim to be the slave of Ali, in a language that would cast doubts on the 'Muslim' credentials of the speaker.

After staying with Turabi for a few weeks, Yagānah visited a friend in Lahore. While there, he realized how much he missed Lucknow. He tried to persuade his wife to move back to Lucknow but she refused, citing her skepticism about India's relationship with its Muslims and the presence of her children in Pakistan. Yagānah undertook the journey back to Lucknow on his own; when he approached the Wagah border, he was immediately arrested for not having the proper documentation to travel from Karachi to Lahore. Yagānah had worked in Lahore just thirty years earlier. He had written syllabi for the students of Lahore. He had even named a house in Lahore.

After spending two weeks in a Lahore prison, Yagānah was freed at the behest of his old students and patrons—the most important of whom is Dwarka Das Shola, a wealthy pharmacist from Lahore who moved to Delhi in 1947. Shola had been Yagānah's most consistent financial supporter. When Shola asked the poet in an Urdu letter what was the highest compliment Yagānah had ever received, Yagānah wrote back in English: 'He means what he says.'[67] In another letter, Yagānah quotes Shelley: 'Poets are the unacknowledged legislators of the world.'

More scourges awaited Yagānah in Lucknow, as many of his past confidants turned against him. What followed is a shameful episode in Urdu literary history: Yagānah had a long-standing friendship with Niyaz Fatehpuri, the editor of Lucknow's most prominent literary journal, *Nigār*. Fatehpuri was no stranger to religious controversies himself, for he had raised questions about several tenets of faith. Yagānah sent some of his intimate thoughts about religion to Fatehpuri, confident that these would stay between the two friends. Fatehpuri forwarded Yagānah's writing to a leading Sunni scholar of Lucknow, Abdul Majid Daryabadi, claiming later that he thought of this as a prank. Whether his intentions were mischievous or malicious, we shall never know. The consequences for Yagānah were devastating.

In addition to being an authority on the Qur'an, Daryabadi was also close friends with the Mi'ar party poets who had earlier caused Yagānah grief over his treatment of Ghalib. Daryabadi at the time controlled one of north India's renowned Islamic journal, *Sidq-e Jadid*. Daryabadi lambasted Yagānah in his editorial, accusing the poet of insulting the Prophet and the Qur'an. The rubā'ī circulated by Daryabadi was thus:

> *sachchā naqqād aur sachchā shā'ir,*
> *mardānah sifat but shikanī meṉ māhir,*
> *kis dil se yagānah ko bhulā de ko'ī,*
> *qurān pe bhi choT dhamak deṉ ākhir*[68]

A true critic and a true poet;
possessor of manly attributes, expert in breaking idols;
with what heart can anybody forget Yagānah;
he can even strike the Qur'an, if need be.

Other charges that Daryabadi levels against Yagānah with a clear objective of inciting violence against the poet follow:

(a) Yagānah was a Muslim in name only and was in reality from Bihar;
(b) Yagānah was born into the Shi'i sect;
(c) Yagānah first spewed smut against Ghalib and Aziz Lakhnavi and then proceeded to venomously attack Iqbal;
(d) Yagānah's duplicity was evident in the way he changed his name and concocted a genealogy going back to Chengiz Khan;
(e) Yagānah had the audacity to write *jallā jalālahū* after his name, thereby compromising God's unity.[69]

Apart from this litany of censures, Daryabadi implied to his readers that Yagānah had sent the insulting verses to Daryabadi himself. In the Perso-Urdu ghazal tradition, the identity of the letter's recipient is forever veiled. The most basic tenet holds that the beloved shall never be named in the ghazal, lest it brings disgrace to him. Here the recipient was not only named, but deliberately misnamed to humiliate and endanger the sender.

Given the chancy political atmosphere of the post-partition subcontinent, and the pressure on the representatives of Muslims to toe univocal sectarian lines, could it be that Daryabadi, through his attacks on Yagānah, was trying to undo the lingering sultry effects of his own atheistic discourses of the past? After all, Daryabadi had admired the likes of the American agnostic Robert Ingersoll, and lapsed into atheism in his 20s. He came out of this phase with the help of Buddhism and Sufism, eventually to become a stronger Sunni religious authority in north India.[70] Perhaps Daryabadi's growing communal celebrity status in the 1940s and 1950s was compelling him to procure more legitimacy from the Sunni community by attacking this easy target, Yagānah.

Regardless of the difficulty of ascertaining Daryabadi's precise motives, what becomes clear is that he shamelessly played the sectarian card in Lucknow, a city where the Shii-Sunni relations had remained volatile from the opening of the century. Daryabadi roused the Shias by saying that he has known them to be people who behold the honour of *tawhīd* and respect for the messenger. He summoned the prominent Shia personalities of Lucknow by name: Maulana Sayyid Ali Naqi, Shams ul-Ulama Maulvi Mehdi Hasan, advocate Sayyid Kalb-e Mustafa, and more. Daryabadi acknowledged that Yagānah had reached the stage of *junūn* (madness) and lost his senses. Having pathologized the poet, Daryabadi publicly implicated him in insulting the prophet and his revelation: 'If a non-Muslim had the nerve to launch such a contemptuous attack, Muslims would have raised hell. Let us wait and see what actions are taken against the atheistic writings of a Muslim.'[71] In his autobiography written two decades after Yagānah's death, Daryabadi proudly claims that his own waywardness during his atheistic phase never yielded any attacks on Islam's sacred personalities nor hurt the sentiments of Muslims.[72] Those who have a soft spot for Yagānah would certainly disagree considering the kind of hell that broke loose when Daryabadi's attack on Yagānah was published verbatim in the popular Shii newspaper *Sarfarāz*, for the purposes of disincentivizing blasphemy. Some young men then went in a procession to Yagānah's house, made him mount a rickshaw, blackened his face, put a garland of shoes around his neck, and dragged him through the markets of old Lucknow. They spat on him and cursed him at every step. The procession that intended to humiliate Yagānah created a jingle with their curse: '*Yagānah, dīvānah, la'n allāh la'n allāh* (Yagānah, the mad one, may Allah curse him, may Allah curse him). The revilers split into two teams: one of them wondered aloud—*yagānah?* The other one responded: *dīvānah*. Then both sides in unison said Allah damn him Allah damn him. The police saved Yagānah—after a few hours.'[73]

When an American journalist residing in Lucknow asked Yagānah about his religious beliefs after this incident, he responded: 'I am a follower of Muhammad. At times I say my prayers. I do not go to the mosque.'[74]

When Shola wrote his concerned letter to Yagānah after learning about the fate of his beloved teacher, the poet responded:

'*izzat jise kahte haiñ voh apnī zāt meñ maujūd hotī hai, ko'ī khārijī chīz nahīñ hai.*[75]

That which is called honour exists in one's essence; it's not an extraneous matter.

Yagānah died in Lucknow in 1956. He summoned three witnesses the night before he died, recited Islam's creed of God's unity, Muhammad's prophecy, and Ali's guardianship and asked them just two questions: Am I a Muslim? Am I a Shia? Upon hearing an affirmative answer to these questions, Yagānah fell silent.[76] Knowing well his frayed relationship with Islam, few would have thought that this would be the course Yagānah would set for his departure, that the poet would want the epilogue of his life to be written in such conventionally devotional terms.

Maut māngī thī khudāī to nahīṅ māngī thī
Le duā kar chuke ab tark-e du'ā karte haiṅ[77]

I had asked for death, not for divinity
All right, I am done with prayer, I now renounce prayers

And the tale does not end here: Some young men in Lucknow had sworn that they would make sure that Yagānah is not buried in a Muslim graveyard. As Yagānah was given his *ghusl-e janāzah* (final ritual bath), some of these men arrived at the site of the bath and told the corpse washer (*ghassāl*) that the poet should not be washed in accordance with Islamic law since he was an apostate. The washer responded by saying that it was against his principles to stop washing a corpse once he had begun. This is another voice of ethics. The voice of a *ghassāl*.[78]

The legacies of Yagānah and Manto help us retrieve another set of archive of 'progressivism' in South Asia. The two of them did not say that which was not said before; rather, they refused to cede power to the gatekeepers of literary and cultural canons. Neither of them could settle into an affable relationship with slogans or hagiographies. In the later part of his life, when Yagānah was asked about his mockery of Ghalib, smilingly he recited a couplet of Bismil Sandelvi:

yeh rāz kī bāteṅ haiṅ ko'ī inheṅ kyā samjhe
but sāmne rakh lenā aur yād-e khudā karnā[79]

These are the matters of mystery, how will anyone comprehend them:
Placing in the fore the idols, and remembering god

Yagānah never failed to mention that which he shared with Ghalib, whose name means triumphant:

donoṅ dīvāne haiṅ 'alī ke tālib
jān ek hai go judā judā haiṅ qālib
mazhab meṅ shā'iri meṅ qaumiyyat meṅ
ghālib haiṅ yagānah aur yagānah ghālib[80]

Both are insane, seekers of Ali
Their soul is one, although their bodies are separate
In faith, in poetry, and in community
Ghalib is peerless (Yagānah) and Yagānah is triumphant (Ghalib)

What a tribute this is to one's rival—a clear identification of that which binds Yagānah and Ghalib, Ali ibn Abi Talib, the first Shii Imam and the most formidable force of Islamic spirituality; this tribute also represents a setback for those who pitted Yagānah against Ghalib in oversimplified terms.

The reprobate that Manto creates and Yagānah becomes, is an old reprobate. We cannot reify this reprobate. Rather, we simply witness how he authoritatively, with each generation, sets himself apart from his surroundings. After all, do we not have the age-old Sufi idea so lovingly embraced by Ibn al-Arabi: *tajdīd al-khalq bil anfās* ('the renewal of creation with each breath'). The Manto-Yagānah reprobate is renewed with each breath and stands in competition with God and his prophets. Yagānah and Manto through this reprobate engaged gods—metaphysical and ideological, the gods of canon, progress, and naming. These stalwarts of Urdu hardly fell prey to nostalgia—unlike many contemporaries of theirs, including the Progressive ones, there is no lament in the work of either writers of the golden age that had come to a pass.

kahne ko to ka'ba bhī khudā kā ghar hai
dekhā to vahī inTh hai ya paththaar hai
haqq kā markaz hai haqshināsoṅ ke liye
yeh sīnah-e be kīnah 'ajab mandir hai[81]

In a manner of speaking, the Ka'ba is also the house of god
When I noticed it: it had the same bricks or stones
The pivot of truth is for those who are truth-knowing
The breast without a grudge—*this* breast is a wondrous temple

It's unlikely that the paths of Manto and Yagānah ever crossed in their lifetimes; but as we celebrate Manto's questioning spirit with well-deserved nostalgia, it is only fair that we remember the less fortunate, whose legacies are not celebrated to the same extent.
To recall a couplet of Yagānah's:

kise ummīd thī zālim keh hogā khātimah bilkhair,
terā karvaT livānā aur merā dam nikal jānā[82]

O Tyrant! Who could have hoped for a more fitting end:
you causing me to turn, and me? Dying at once

Notes

1. 'Here lies Saadat Hasan Manto. With him lie buried all the arts and mysteries of short story writing. Under tons of earth he lies, wondering if he is a greater short story writer, than God.' Concerned that such an epitaph might lead to the desecration of the grave, Manto's sister had it overwritten by another epitaph for which Manto had shown a liking; it's a variation on a line of Mirza Ghalib, Urdu's most well-known poet:

   Ya rabb zamanah mujh ko miTātā hai kis liye
   Lauh-e jahān pah harf-e mukarrar nahiñ huñ maiñ

   [Oh Lord! Why does time erase me
   On the tablet of the world, I am not a repeated letter]

   I am grateful to Manto's niece and biographer, Professor Ayesha Jalal, for enhancing my knowledge about Manto and South Asia in the course of various conversations we have had since 1997.
2. In this essay, I use 1947 as a metonym for the events that led to the creation of India and Pakistan, as well as for the events of the immediate aftermath. See Ayesha Jalal, *Manto and Pakistan,* Karachi Literary Festival 2012, Moderated by M.R. Kazimi, 11 February 2012: http://www.youtube.com/watch?v=p7nObBA-ZEw.
3. Sadat Hasan Manto, *Mantonāmā*, Lahore: Sang-e Mil Publishers, 2000, p. 18.
4. See Mir Taqi 'Mir', *Kulliyāt-e Mīr,* ed. Zill-e Abbas Abbasi, New Delhi: Taraqqi Urdu Bureau, 1968.
5. Manto, *Mantonāmā,* p. 765.
6. Ibid., p. 769.
7. Ibid., p. 773.
8. Syed Akbar Hyder, *Reliving Karbala: Martyrdom in South Asian Memory,* New York: Oxford University Press, 2006, p. 198.
9. Ibid.
10. Imtiaz Ali Arsh, ed., *Divān-e Ghālib, Nuskhahā-e 'Arshi,* Aligarh: Anjuman-e Taraqqi-e Urdu, 1958, p. 219.
11. See Syed Akbar Hyder, 'Ghalib and His Interlocutors', in *Heterotopias: Nationalism and the Possibility of History in South Asia,* ed. Manu Bhagavan, New Delhi: Oxford University Press, 2010, pp. 90–113
12. Abdul Rahman Bijnauri, *Mahāsin-e kalām-e Ghālib,* Islamabad: Abdul Rahman Bijnauri Trust, 2001.
13. Urdu's Progressive Writers Movement, formed in the 1930s, was conceived in the spirit of ethical utilitarianism: Literary aesthetics should expand to appreciate that which has been denied entry in the past—issues of class, gender, and sexuality; it must ultimately address social ills.
14. Manto, *Mantonāmā,* p. 413.

15. Ziya Azimabadi, *Mirzā Yagānah Changezī: Hayāt aur Shaʻirī*, Lucknow: Urdu Publishers, 1980, p. 161.
16. Nayyar Masud, *Yagānah Ahval o asar*, New Delhi: Anjuman Taraqqi-e Urdu, 1991, p. 9.
17. See Yaganah Changezi, *Kulliyāt-e Yagānah*, Karachi: Akadami Bazyaft, 2003, p. 94.
18. *Kulliyāt-e Yagānah*, Delhi, p. 412.
19. Ibid., p. 116.
20. Ibid., p. 130.
21. Mirza Yaganah Changezi Lakhnavi, *Kulliyāt-e Yagānah*, ed. Mushfiq Khaja, Karach: Akadami Bazyaft, 2003, p. 344.
22. Ibid., p. 345.
23. Ibid., p. 336.
24. *Kulliyāt-e Yagānah*, Delhi, pp. 301–3.
25. Ibid., p. 304.
26. Ibid., p. 409.
27. Ibid., p. 410.
28. Ibid., p. 409.
29. Ibid., p. 410.
30. Ziya Azimabadi, *Mirzā Yagānah Changezī: Hayāt aur Shaʻirī*, Lucknow: Urdu Publishers, 1980, p. 88; Yagānah, *Kulliyāt*, Delhi, p. 508.
31. *Kulliyāt-e Yagānah*, Delhi, p. 296.
32. Ibid., p. 274.
33. Ibid., p. 222.
34. Ibid., p. 502.
35. See Najeebuddin Jamal, 'Yaganah Shakhsiyat aur Fan', Dissertation submitted to Bahaudin Zakariya University, Multan, p. 403.
36. Mushfiq Khwaja, Pasha Rahman and Amna Mushfiq, eds., *Mirzā Yagānah Shakhsiyat aur Fan*, Aligarh: Asif Publications, 1992, p. 109.
37. *Kulliyāt-e Yagānah*, Delhi, p. 534.
38. Ibid., p. 533.
39. Sahil Ahmad, *Yagānah*, Allahabad: Urdu Writers' Guild, 1986, p. 262.
40. Manto, *Mantonāmā*, p. 433.
41. Rahi Masum Raza, *Yās Yagānah Changezī*, Allahabad: Shahin Publishers, 1967, p. 92.
42. *Kulliyāt-e Yagānah*, Delhi, p. 502.
43. Ibid., p. 529.
44. Ziya Azimabadi, *Mirzā Yagānah Changezī: Hayāt aur Shaʻirī*, Lucknow: Urdu Publishers, 1980, p. 120.
45. *Kulliyāt-e Yagānah*, Delhi, p. 252.
46. Dwarka Das Shola, *Shola Zar*, Delhi: Urdu Writers Cooperative Society, 1962, p. 23.
47. *Kāināt-e Najm*, New Delhi: Shahid Publications, 2006, p. 135.
48. Waseem Farhat Karanjvi, *Yagānah Changezī: Shakhsiyat o fan ma intikhāb-e kalām*, Jhelum: Book Corner, 2015, p. 50.

49. Changezi Lakhnavi, *Kulliyāt-e Yagānah*, p. 80.
50. Nayyar Masud, *Yagānah ahvāl o āsār*, p. 46.
51. Karanjvi, *Yagānah Changezī*, p. 337.
52. Rahi Masum Raza, *Yās Yagānah Changezī*, p. 183.
53. Ibid., p. 186.
54. Ibid.
55. See Yaganah Changezi, *Kulliyāt*, Delhi, p. 180: *āsār paidā kiyā chāho sukhan meñ tarz-e dil kash se*, to *andaz-e bayān sikho Anīs o Mīr o 'Atish se*.
56. Ziya Azimabadi, *Mirzā Yagānah Changezī: Hayāt aur Sha'irī*, Lucknow: Urdu Publishers, 1980, p. 106.
57. Rahi Masum Raza, *Yās Yagānah Changezī*, p. 189.
58. Ziya Azimabadi, *Yagānah Changezī: Hayāt aur Sha'irī*, Lucknow: Urdu Publishers, 1980, p. 181. The pages of this book are a mess. From p. 113 the page jumps to 193. And from p. 208 to p. 169.
59. Aligarh Muslim University is also complicit in such parochialism. Yagānah, *Kulliyāt*, Delhi, p. 480.
60. See Karanjvi, *Yagānah Changezī*, p. 299.
61. Azimabadi, *Mirzā Yagānah Changezī*, p. 90.
62. Nurul Hasan, *Urdu ka ma'tub sha'ir*, p. 41.
63. See Karanjvi, *Yagānah Changezī*, p. 254.
64. See Khwaja, Rahman and Mushfiq, *Mirzā Yagānah Shakhsiyat aur Fan*.
65. Yaganah dissertation, p. 376.
66. Yaganah Changezi, *Kulliyāt*, Delhi, p. 460.
67. Khwaja, Rahman and Mushfiq, *Mirzā Yagānah Shakhsiyat aur Fan*, p. 225.
68. Khwaja, Rahman and Mushfiq, *Mirzā Yagānah Shakhsiyat aur Fan*, Mirza Y. Shaksiyat aur fan, the rubai printed in sidq-e jaded.
69. See Rahi Masum Raza, *Yās Yagānah Changezī*, pp. 54–7.
70. See Abdul Majid Daryabadi, *Āp Bītī: Urdu ke mashhur sahib-e tarz adib aur mufassir-e Qur'an Maulana 'Abdul Majid Sahib Daryabadi*, Lucknow: Maktabah-e Firdaus, 1978, pp. 234–45.
71. Rahi Masum Raza, *Yās Yagānah Changezī*, p. 54.
72. Daryabadi, *Āp Bītī*, p. 242.
73. Najib Jamal, *Yagānah: Tahqīqī o Tanqīdī Mutaleah*, Lahore: Izhar Sons, 2013, p. 108.
74. Rahi Masum Raza, *Yās Yagānah Changezī*, p. 61.
75. Mirza yagaanah Shakhsiyat aur fan, edited by Mushfiq Khwaja, Pasha Rahman, Amna Mushfiq, Aligarh: Asif Publications, 1992, p. 208.
76. Rahi Masum Raza, *Yās Yagānah Changezī*, p. 65.
77. Waseem Farhat Karanjvi, *Yagānah Changezī: Shakhsiyat o fan ma intikhāb-e Kalām*, Jhelum: Book Corner, 2015.
78. Jamal, *Yagānah*, p. 118.
79. Nurul Hasan, *Urdū kā ma'tub Shā'ir*, p. 29.
80. Yaganah Changezi, *Kulliyāt*, p. 461.
81. Changezi, *Kulliyāt*, p. 588.
82. *Mirzā Yagānah Changezī*, p. 135.

12

Learning for the Glory of God *v.* 'Useful' Knowledge

A Scholarly Muslim Family and Western Schooling in Nineteenth-Century Madras

SYLVIA VATUK

THE DEVELOPMENT AND spread of Western education through the medium of English contributed more than any other single factor to the cultural transformation of India in the nineteenth and early twentieth centuries. However, throughout the country there were marked disparities of access and receptivity to Western schooling associated with both regional differences and demographic variables—such as gender, occupation, income, urban or rural residence, caste, and religion—within regions. Already in the second quarter of the nineteenth century the British rulers were opening up increasing numbers of salaried government jobs to Indians, and, over time, schools offering the kind of Western-style education that was required to qualify for such positions and to enter the professions of law and medicine became more numerous.

Naturally, those social groups that were best positioned for and most receptive to developing competency in the English language and studying Western subjects came to dominate the new occupations. The new Western-educated class drew heavily from segments of the population whose male ancestors had been literate in the indigenous administrative and religious languages and had been in the employ of pre-colonial rulers, those whom Bayly has termed the 'service gentry'.[1] As more and more English-medium schools offering a Western-style curriculum were set up—through the combined efforts of foreign missionaries, local philanthropists and, to some extent, the British authorities—they attracted children from families of middle- and even low-income, but typically high-caste, backgrounds. The indigenous aristocracy and wealthy landholding or merchant classes generally tended to be less convinced of the advantages of exposing their offspring to these new educational opportunities.[2]

In many—though not in all—parts of India, the number of Muslims in this emerging Western-educated middle class was relatively small and they were, consequently, poorly represented in the higher ranks of government service and in the professions, both absolutely and relative to their community's proportion of the total population. In the second quarter of the nineteenth century, the educational and occupational disparity between Hindus and Muslims began to become a matter of concern for some British officials. Especially after the 1857 uprising, for which Muslim 'disaffection' with colonial rule was held by many to have been largely responsible, a rhetoric developed according to which 'Muslims'—typically referred to as if they were a monolithic and internally undifferentiated social category—were characterized as implacably 'hostile' to Western learning for deep-seated religious, cultural, and historical reasons. Resentment at having been dislodged from their former position as rulers of India was one of the main factors that was said to lie at the root of their alleged reluctance to learn the colonizer's language and benefit from the increasing opportunities to acquire 'useful knowledge' in the European mode.

W.W. Hunter's 1871 polemic on the condition of Indian Muslims and its political implications was especially influential in promoting the thesis that Muslims, as a group, were 'lagging behind' Hindus in the educational sphere, and that more needed to be done to both enable and encourage them to acquire the skills necessary to qualify for government employment and the professions.[3] Hunter and others therefore urged the government—for reasons of self-interest as much as for the benefit of Muslims themselves—to take special measures to promote their access to secular schooling and to the public posts for which such schooling was a prerequisite.[4] Soon, similar demands began to be made by some segments of the Muslim population as well. Thus, in 1882 the National Mohammadan Association, based in Calcutta, submitted a petition to Lord Ripon to this effect,[5] setting in motion an extended official enquiry into the matter in all three Presidencies.[6]

A number of scholars have questioned the empirical basis for the stereotyped view of 'Muslim backwardness' in education in this period, pointing out that Muslims constituted a very diverse population, whose members responded—and should reasonably be expected to have responded—in very diverse ways to the challenges of the new educational and occupational order.[7] Granted that some were actively opposed to Western education, most were not so much opposed as indifferent. For them, the real question, to paraphrase Lelyveld, is not 'why they did not take to Western education?' but 'why should they have wanted to, given its irrelevance to the everyday realities of their lives?'[8] On the other hand, significant numbers of Muslims, differentially situated in the social order, *did* quickly grasp opportunities to learn the tongue of the new rulers and eagerly sought salaried employment in their service. In some parts of the country, indeed, the number of Muslims responding in this way was greater than that of Hindus.

Those who have contributed to this revisionist view provide an important and needed corrective to the idea that Muslims, as a body, were averse to learning English and benefiting from the new forms of knowledge brought to India by the British. However, having had it so convincingly demonstrated that important segments of the Muslim population strongly favoured, and indeed actively participated in, Western forms of education or innovatively adapted what they understood of it to what they saw as the special needs of their religious constituency, it may be time to remind ourselves that the issue was, especially for some of the *'ulama,* a hotly contested one. As David Lelyveld suggests, in order to sort out the variety and complexity of Muslim responses to Western education in the nineteenth century, one needs to determine their linkages to 'the position of an individual or group in relation to the distribution of wealth, power, prestige, ideas, and symbol'. This can best be done, he maintains, by looking at the experience of particular families, with a focus on the multiplicity of considerations that entered into actual decision-making at the family level for or against sending children to English schools and having them work for their foreign rulers.[9]

Here, following Lelyveld's suggestion, I will examine the experience of a prominent *'ulama* family of Madras whose members began in the early 1850s to actively resist British attempts to provide Muslim youth with an opportunity to acquire Western learning. I will ask how their strong and long-lasting hostility to Western schooling and the English language is to be explained. What was the nature of the dialogue between them and the British officials who were trying to promote Western education? What kind of arguments, framed in what form of rhetoric, did each party use to justify its position on the education issue? Also relevant are the strategies employed by family members in subsequent generations as they tried to hold at bay the new modes of learning and new curriculum content that threatened the survival of their 'traditional' Islamic forms of knowledge and accustomed modes of transmission.

When one compares this family's strongly negative attitude towards the English language and Western knowledge with what has been written about the responses of similarly placed *ulama* families in other parts of India to the growth and spread of European-style educational institutions, they appear to have been somewhat atypical. It is difficult to be certain of this, however, because most of the available historical literature on *ulama* families in India and the schools of religious thought that they founded—or followed—deals with a time period later than the one in which my story is set.[10] Furthermore, the authors of such works have rarely described in much detail how the forebears of those individuals and groups with whom they are primarily concerned responded when Western-type schools first began to be appear on the scene. From what *has* been written on *ulama* reactions to British educational innovations, it appears that instead of using their energies to fight the British directly, most of them concentrated on trying to strengthen the *umma*, as a body, internally, by promoting among the faithful the 'reform' of customary Muslim devotional practices and beliefs and devising means of adapting to modern conditions their own traditional modes of transmitting religious knowledge, in order to ensure that its substance would be preserved for future generations.[11]

Early Concerns in Madras about Muslim 'Educational Backwardness'

Although at this time the Muslims probably constituted at least 13 per cent of the population of Madras town—and perhaps 6.50 per cent or more of the population of the Presidency[12]—they were poorly represented, in proportion to their numbers in the population, in schools that offered a Western type of curriculum. Muslims were especially scarce at the higher levels of the educational system. Notwithstanding the public appearance of the Nawwab Regent of the Carnatic at the inauguration in 1841 of the new Madras University High School— and the presence on its governing board of two leading Muslim nobles close to the court—when the last Nawwab (Ghulam Ghaus Khan) died in 1855, not a single Muslim was to be counted among the thirty-six students who had thus far completed the school's course of study.[13]

The issue of Muslim 'educational backwardness' had, in fact, been raised in Madras long before Hunter brought it to national attention. As early as 1826, the then-governor of the Madras Presidency, Thomas Munro, called special attention in a Minute of that year to the educational needs of the Muslim population. Implying that the community had been neglected in the past, he urged 'extend[ing] to our Mahomedan the same advantages of education as to our Hindoo subjects, and perhaps even in a greater degree, because a greater proportion of them belong to the middle and higher classes'.[14] Subsequently he ordered the setting up of special primary schools for Muslim boys all over the Presidency. But this did not lead to an appreciable rise in the number of children of that community studying English and Western subjects.

By the mid-1840s, the foundations of Western education—at least for males—had been well-laid in Madras, though not so much through government efforts as by missionary and private endeavours.[15] The Hindu elite, in particular, had begun to respond with enthusiasm to the increasingly available opportunities for the formal study of English and other Western subjects. Indeed, they were exerting growing pressure on the Government to expand such educational facilities, to meet the needs of the many young men who wished to qualify for public employment. But Muslims were neither participating in these Hindu-led movements nor actively lobbying on their own towards similar ends. Few Muslims were studying in those institutions that did exist, and those who were enrolled rarely continued beyond the primary level. This naturally led to a notable paucity of Muslims in those ranks of the public service that required some knowledge of English.

By this time, some representatives of British officialdom in the Madras Presidency had come to define 'the meager representation' of Muslims in Western education and public employment as a problem. The rhetoric used by the Nawwab in some of his communications with the Government suggests that he too had come to share their concern to some degree—or that he considered it politic and of possible strategic advantage to voice such sentiments when seeking favours from the foreign rulers.[16] Thus, in 1846, at the instigation of the then Acting Government Agent at Chepauk, the young Nawwab Ghulam Muhammad Ghaus Khan formally proposed to the British that a special school for young men of the Muslim nobility be established.

He expressed in his letter to the Government the wish that, by this means, Muslims might be enabled to qualify in larger numbers for state employment. Whereas his words suggest that he agreed with the British that training for public-service jobs was the solution for the poor economic situation of the Madras aristocracy, he nevertheless outlined a curriculum for the proposed school that consisted solely of religious subjects and the Arabic and Persian languages. The British authorities' response indicated that while they welcomed his proposal in principle, they could not provide any funds to implement it. Consequently, nothing concrete resulted from the Nawwab's plea.

Edward Balfour and Muslim Education in Madras

Dr Edward Green Balfour (1813–89) was the British official who played the most central role in formulating and promoting the discourse according to which Muslims were 'falling behind Hindus' in the acquisition of 'modern knowledge' and in leading efforts to develop a practical solution to the problem. Balfour had studied medicine in Edinburgh and came to India in 1834 in the medical service, first in the Bombay and then in the Madras armies. He rose to the rank of Assistant Surgeon in the Madras Army and after a time was invited to serve as Persian Translator to the Government as well. Probably because of his facility in that language and in the local Dakkhani Urdu,[17] he was appointed Paymaster of Carnatic Stipends, then Acting Government Agent to the Nawwab of Arcot and, in 1851, Government Agent at Chepauk. In the course of his official duties he therefore had more frequent access to the Nawwab and was probably on more familiar terms with the royal entourage and other members of the Muslim elite of Madras town than any of his compatriots at the time.[18]

Susan Bayly has characterized Balfour as an 'orientalist polymath who directed his prolific literary output [and, I would add, his considerable energies and powers of oral persuasion!] towards the reform and moral "regeneration" of the south Indian Muslim elite'.[19] He was a man of wide-ranging scientific and literary interests, writing extensively on many different aspects of Indian society, culture, and natural history.[20] He also devoted considerable time and effort to a myriad of organizational activities, setting up government museums in Madras (in 1851) and later in Mysore (in 1866), where curiosities of the country of all kinds—natural and artifactural—were put on display.[21] He also founded India's first zoo. In 1854, having persuaded the Nawwab to donate his personal menagerie for the purpose, he noted the great enthusiasm with which the live animal exhibits were received by the local populace, and later saw to the addition of many other animals.[22] As Bayly has observed, another of Balfour's major preoccupations during the period with which I am concerned here was working for the intellectual, economic, and moral 'uplift' of the 'Mahomedan race'. His efforts in this direction included spearheading a campaign to induce the Nawwab, the *'ulama* and other elite segments of the community to set up a public library for the Muslims of Madras. This crusade culminated in the establishment, in 1851, of the Muhammadan Public Library (Kutub Khana-i 'Am Mufid Ahl-i Islam).[23] He was less successful in a later attempt to persuade some of the same individuals of the desirability of establishing a 'Society for Arts and Sciences', where the intellectually minded could come together on a regular basis for intellectual discussions and exchange of ideas on topics of common interest.[24]

Arguing from quite different premises than those of Munro, Balfour linked the need to encourage schooling for Muslims to their distressed economic condition. In his view, the community's dire poverty was a result of the insufficiency of suitable employment opportunities for those educated only in the traditional Islamic manner. Few Muslims having obtained any Western education, employment in the colonial civil service remained out of reach for them. The reason Muslims were falling so far behind Hindus in the acquisition of 'modern' knowledge, he opined, was that their religious leaders were too backward-looking. Fearing that their religion would be undermined if their children were exposed to Western learning, they not only refused to send their own youngsters to school but also discouraged other Muslims from doing so. Balfour recommended that instead of allowing Muslim boys to waste their time on religious study and on learning languages like Persian and Arabic that had no relevance to the modern world, the government should provide special facilities wherein they could acquire 'useful' knowledge.

Balfour was not, of course, unmindful of the extent to which it was also in the political interest of the British to educate the Muslims of the younger generation along Western lines. Such schooling, as he wrote in 1853, would help to imbue 'the youth of this Mahomedan community . . . with other feelings and other principles than those that their fathers are now actuated by. . .'.[25] Here we have what appears to be a thinly veiled allusion to a British view—which he apparently shared, or at least wished to exploit strategically in order to obtain official support for his plans—of the Indian Muslims as 'fanatical and implacably opposed to British rule', and of the *'ulama* as especially prone to fomenting public sentiment against the government.[26]

Balfour occasionally deigned to acknowledge some of the accomplishments of earlier generations of Islamic scholars, but his overall message was that the body of learning created by those men of the past was entirely inferior to European scholarship and science and therefore deserved to be superseded by it. This was so self-evident that he felt no compunction about forthrightly expressing his disdain for the Islamic scholarly tradition when addressing those who most cherished it, conveying in the process his poor opinion of the latter as well. Thus, for example, in a letter addressed to the Nawwab in 1851, a man well known for his generous patronage of Islamic scholars, literary men, and religious figures, he wrote:

[F]or anyone to compare . . . [Islamic knowledge] with the knowledge in Europe at the present day would be to compare the toys of children with the finished productions of grown up men. What Greece and its literature was to the Arabs, England should be today. Any education that does not embrace this knowledge is not only objectionable, but is injuriously occupying the golden time of youth with inadequate instruction . . . preventing [them from] acquiring an education suited to the wants of the present day.[27]

These remarks are, of course, reminiscent of Macaulay's famous 1835 *Minute on Education*, in which he argued—against the then-influential advocates of 'Oriental' learning—for the use of English as the language of instruction in government schools and colleges. Admitting that he has 'no knowledge of either Sanscrit [*sic*] or Arabic' and that he has, therefore, had to rely for an assessment of their value upon conversations with persons—presumably he meant British persons—who *do* know these languages, Macaulay proceeds to assert that it is a matter of general agreement, even among [British] 'Orientalists', 'that a single shelf of a good European library [is] worth the whole native literature of India and Arabia'.[28]

The *Khandan* of Muhammad Ghaus[29]

The extended family (*khandan*) that I discuss here might well have provided the model upon which British stereotypes about the Muslim '*ulama's* hostility to Western education were constructed. In the early 1850s, the two most influential senior men of this prominent *'ulama* family not only argued vehemently against Western knowledge when it was first proposed to be taught in a newly established school for Muslim boys, but actively tried to sabotage British attempts to introduce instruction in English and indigenous languages into its curriculum. Moreover, their descendants persisted for decades in remaining aloof from 'modern' forms of schooling, refusing to enrol their sons in Western-type schools or allow them to learn their rulers' language.[30] They continued to reject Western education even when the numbers of Muslim boys (and even girls) attending such schools were rising more rapidly in the Madras Presidency than in many other parts of British India.

The *khandan* belongs to a community (*qaum*) called Nawwayat or Naiti,[31] which today is found mainly in Karnataka and parts of Tamil Nadu and Andhra Pradesh. The Nawwayats are Sunni Muslims of the Shaf'i school (*mazhab*) of Islamic law, and trace their ancestry to Arab traders and missionaries who came by sea from Arabia to the western coast of India as early—according to their own traditions—as the eight century CE.[32] This family's forebears had later occupied judicial and other administrative posts in the Bijapur sultanates and subsequently under the Mughals. Several among them were distinguished Islamic scholars as well.

The founding ancestor of the *khandan* was a man named Muhammad Ghaus,[33] who was born in 1753 in the town of Arcot (in present-day Tamil Nadu), then the capital of the Carnatic under Nawwab Muhammad Ali Walajah.[34] Muhammad Ghaus's paternal grandfather had been the chief judge, *qazi-ul qazat*, of Arcot; his own father later served as superintendent (*serishtedar*) of the Nawwab's court of law in the same town.[35] After completing his education, Muhammad Ghaus obtained a court appointment as tutor to one of the Nawwab's grandsons. Upon the East India Company's annexation of the territory of the Carnatic in 1801 this royal pupil, who later went by the title 'Azim-ud Daula, unexpectedly succeeded to the Arcot *masnad* as the only member of the Walajah family willing to accede to the terms laid down by the British for allowing the Nawwabi to remain in existence.[36] Under the treaty he was persuaded to sign, he and his descendants would thereafter be rulers of the region in name only, though allowed to keep extensive personal properties and to receive an annual income of one-fifth of the revenues of his late grandfather's erstwhile realm. Because his succession had been strongly opposed by most members of the late Nawwab's extended family lineage, he had to assemble his own retinue of loyal supporters to manage the affairs of his court. He asked his former tutor Muhammad Ghaus to serve as his chief officer, his *diwan*.

The royal court was reduced even further than it had been in Nawwab Muhammad Ali's time, to a largely ceremonial entity. But it retained considerable symbolic importance for the Muslim population of Madras and provided livelihoods for thousands of people, chief among them those whose household heads were employed by the Nawwabi government (*sarkar*) in a wide variety of capacities, from the lowliest slave or free servant to the top administrative officials. The court also indirectly supported a large number of tradesmen, moneylenders, craftsmen and other independent providers of services to the court and its members. In addition, the treaty had provided for monthly stipends of varying amounts to be paid out of the East India Company coffers to each individual in the large circle of relatives and chief retainers of previous Nawaabs.[37]

Muhammad Ghaus served as *diwan* for a number of years and, after his death, both his sons were awarded appointments at court. The elder, 'Abdul Wahab (later titled Madar-ul 'Umra), followed in his father's footsteps as *diwan* under later Nawwabs, while the younger (Muhammad Sibghatullah Badr-ud Daula) eventually became *qazi-ul qazat* of the Nawwabs' Islamic law court, the *mahakama*.[38] Their distinguished lineage, their high scholarly achievements, and their official positions, ensured them a place of prestige among the leading religious authorities of the town. They and their two sisters produced more than thirty grandchildren for Muhammad Ghaus, most of whom married first cousins or other close relatives. Most of the men in the third generation also obtained positions at court and some—like their fathers, their grandfather and many more distant ancestors—became serious Islamic scholars as well. Over time the *khandan* came to constitute a large, solidary, and influential group within the circle surrounding the Nawwab of the Carnatic and his palace at Chepauk in the town of Madras. When, in 1846, Government Agent Balfour first proposed to the Nawwab that he fund a 'modern' school for Muslim boys, it was inevitable that these two men would be drawn into the ensuing discussions and debates.

A 'Modern' School for Muslim Boys

When the British declined Nawwab Ghulam Ghaus Khan's request that they fund the school for Muslim boys that he proposed to set up in his palace, Balfour continued to pressure him on the subject. But it was not until five years later that his urgings bore fruit. In 1851, a school for Muslim boys opened its doors on the grounds of Chepauk Palace. The Nawwab had finally agreed to fund the new school entirely out of his share of the Carnatic revenues. He chose its name, Madrasa-i 'Azam, after his own *takhallus*, 'Azam, the 'pen name' under which he wrote Persian poetry. This was the same name that he had earlier bestowed upon a favourite dancing girl when he took her into his household as a concubine (*haram*).

The first board of directors for the new school included Qazi Badr-ud Daula as chairman, with his older brother, Diwan Madar-ul 'Umra, and three of their nephews, as well as Government Agent Balfour, among the members. Approximately seventy pupils enrolled in the first year were all orphaned Carnatic stipendiaries, for whose education Balfour, in his capacity as Paymaster, considered himself particularly responsible.

Balfour's plans for a 'modern' secular, English-language institution notwithstanding, the curriculum ultimately agreed upon by the Board was a traditional Islamic one. As a member of the Board, he continued to press for the inclusion of history, geography, and other such subjects, and for the teaching of English and the most widely spoken local languages. But after only three meetings he felt it necessary to submit his resignation, because, as he later explained, 'from the intenseness of their dread of proselytism . . . [the other members] refused to allow instruction to be given in the English, Tamil, and Teloogoo languages, which, as the only useful branches of education, it was my chief object . . . to have taught'.[39]

Abandoning for the time being all hope of inducing the Nawwab to overrule the Board's decisions, he redirected his efforts towards trying to persuade some other influential Muslims of the town, who he believed were more sympathetic to his views, to set up their own schools for Muslim youths. Two of these men—Haidar Jang and Nasir-ul-Mulk, both relatives of the Nawwab—consented to do so. One of them allotted space within his own house for a small school.[40] Balfour then called a meeting of Muslim nobles and began collecting subscriptions for a larger school, which he envisioned locating in Triplicane, near the palace compound, where the bulk of the Nawwab's followers resided. He intended that this school would mainly teach English, Tamil, and Telugu, English literature and the European sciences. However, he remarked, 'as I discovered that the exclusion . . . of the Mahomedan languages was likely to excite feelings inimical to its prosperity, I found it necessary to provide, also, for instruction . . . in their own languages, though they are worthless, in my opinion, from the point of view of livelihood'.[41]

In the meantime, he was apparently continuing to pressure the Nawwab to accede to his wishes in terms of the curriculum and management of Madrasa-i 'Azam. In these efforts he was able to secure the cooperation of at least two members of the Nawwab's close circle of courtiers in a concerted campaign to remove from the board the *diwan* and the *qazi*, the two men most staunchly opposed to his views. Interestingly, one of those who worked with him in this effort was Qadir Murtuza Husain, the Nawwab's *bakhshi* (Paymaster), who was not only a nephew (sister's son) of the *diwan* and the *qazi* but was also the *diwan's* son-in-law!

At this point, apparently getting wind of the plan to ease them out of their positions on the board, the two senior men went on the offensive. On 14 August 1852 they addressed a vaguely worded letter to Balfour, indicating that, for various unspecified reasons pertaining to the *shari'at*, they were not willing to continue to participate in the management of Madrasa-i 'Azam.[42] When pressed by Balfour for their reasons, they responded with another brief note, saying, in effect, that the purpose of education should be to serve God, not to enable one to earn a livelihood. The curriculum Balfour proposed would give precedence to crass job preparation over the attainment of religious knowledge, which should be the true purpose of education.[43] They closed their letter with a request that they please not be bothered with the matter any further.

But the *qazi* did not leave the matter at that. Instead, he carried the controversy forth into the public arena, sending out a formal enquiry (*istiftah*) in the standard form of a request for a *fatwa* to a number of the local *'ulama*, soliciting their opinion as to whether Balfour's proposal to teach Muslim children English, Tamil, and Telugu in order to prepare them for employment in the British administration was permissible according to *shari'at* or not.[44] Having collected some statements supporting his own opinion that it was *not* permissible, he wrote to Balfour again. This third communication presents in fuller detail the argument that, according to Islamic doctrine, knowledge is to be acquired for the glory of God, not for worldly benefit. To learn for the purpose of making a more comfortable living is forbidden, an abomination (*haram*). The *qazi* agrees with Balfour and other Britishers that the Muslim community is poor. But he attributes this to 'our not having adhered firmly to our faith',[45] and to the tendency of some of his co-religionists to have become entangled in worldly temptations—perhaps a veiled allusion to the Nawwabi lifestyle he so abhorred. He asserts that neither the British nor the Hindus have any qualms about making a living by any means whatsoever. Because they lack discrimination in this respect, the Hindus of Madras have become very rich and are able to support schools through public subscription, something that the Muslims are in no financial position to do. He clinches his argument against English education by asking rhetorically, 'Let us assume that there are 20,000 Muslims in Madras. If 200 or 400 acquire the qualifications for government employment, will this alleviate the poverty of all?'[46]

On 14 March 1853, by which time Balfour had amassed towards his separate new project the sum of Rs.14,000—an unspecified portion of which had come from his own pocket—the Nawwab, 'influenced by better feelings or a more correct notion of his duties'[47] apparently had a change of heart. He wrote to Balfour asking him to place advertisements in the newspapers for English, Tamil and Telugu teachers for Madrasa-i 'Azam and invited him to rejoin the Board of Directors. He appended a request that Balfour obtained for the students of the school seventy tickets to the upcoming Madras Exhibition of Works, scheduled to be held in the Governor's Banqueting Room![48]

Balfour wrote back, expressing pleasure at His Highness' decision to restructure the curriculum of Madrasa-i 'Azam, adding—in phrases that he no doubt felt would strike a warm chord in the Nawwab's heart—that this move would 'spread your fame in this world and bring its reward in that which is to come'.[49] He assured the Nawwab that he was honoured to be asked to rejoin the committee but, before deciding whether to accept the invitation, he wanted to know who the other members would be, for formerly they had been nearly all 'aged men so utterly unacquainted with the way of the world as it is, and with its wants',[50] that it had been impossible to continue working with them. Now, he insisted, the Nawwab should form a committee of 'gentlemen of liberal minds, acquainted with the condition of Madras, with the wants of its youth and with the state of education, here, of the present day'.[51]

Within four days the *qazi* had submitted his resignation from the Board.[52] It was accepted two weeks later, just before the Nawwab informed Balfour that he had reconstituted the Board with members evidently selected with Balfour's express strictures in mind. Only one of the original members remained: the Nawwab's *bakhshi*. Tirazish Khan, another sister's son of the two brothers (who, like the *bakhshi*, was a son-in-law of the *diwan*), had been added to the list, along with a somewhat more distant agnatic relative of theirs, Nadimullah Khan. Four of the nine members of the new board were Britishers—one of them Balfour's own brother, Major George Balfour.[53]

By the end of June, a Hindu had been appointed to teach Tamil, and teachers of English and Telugu were later employed as well. The language courses did not supplant but merely supplemented the existing curriculum. At the end of 1854, the school reported 25 students learning English, ten attending classes in Telugu and six in Tamil, as against 82 studying the Qur'an, 46 studying religion, and 63 studying Arabic.[54]

Subsequent Developments at Madrasa-i 'Azam

In October 1855, upon the Nawwab's untimely death without issue at the age of thirty-one, the British refused to recognize a successor and abolished the Nawwabi as an institution. Madrasa-i 'Azam continued for a few years to operate on more or less the same basis as before. In 1857, the Director of Public Instruction for the Madras Presidency, Alexander Arbuthnot, reported that the institution consisted of a collection of practically independent units, teaching English, Arabic, Persian, Telugu and Tamil, respectively. The total number of students was 250 and the principal emphasis of the school continued to be Arabic, Persian and Islamic religion. He was of the view that very little 'useful knowledge' was being imparted there and recommended a major reorganization of the school and its curriculum.

In 1859, Madrasa-i 'Azam became a government school and a British headmaster was appointed. As in other government schools, English reading, writing, and grammar, arithmetic, geography, and history made up the core of the new curriculum. In addition, all pupils were required to study 'Hindustani' and either Tamil or Telugu. Arabic and Persian were made optional subjects. Teachers of Islamic religion and related subjects were pensioned off, notwithstanding Balfour's arguing for their simple dismissal. Some of these men left Madras soon thereafter, joining other *'ulama* in an exodus from the city that had begun shortly after the Nawwab's death and continued through the next three or more decades.

By the following year, out of a total enrolment of 242 students, only seven pupils each were studying Arabic and Persian.[55] By 1862 only two of the 257 students then enrolled were studying Arabic, though the number taking Persian classes had increased to 27. The teaching of Arabic was consequently discontinued and Persian began to be taught after regular hours, so as not to conflict with those courses of instruction that were deemed by the authorities to be more important.[56] From the point of view of the student's demand, the emphasis had apparently shifted dramatically. Within a period of five years the number of pupils desiring to pursue the study of the languages traditionally associated with Islamic learning—at least within this particular setting—had markedly declined. However, this trend must be seen within the context of a severe reduction in the amount of time given to the teaching of those languages. Not more than one hour a day was given over for this purpose and both languages were evidently taught at the same time, making it necessary for students to choose between them. Clearly any who wished (or whose parents wished them) to study the classical Islamic languages seriously would have been forced to go elsewhere for instruction.

There are unfortunately no numerical data available on the demographic makeup of the student body at Madrasa-i 'Azam, either before or after its re-constitution as a government school. Official reports after 1859 make reference—in the context of proposals to raise its fees—to the widespread poverty of the Muslim population of the town. For example, in 1866 the Director of Public Instruction remarked, in the course of an otherwise highly critical report on the functioning and academic standing of the school, that, despite all of its failings, Madrasa-i 'Azam did provide a valuable service by providing an education for many who would otherwise have little or no access to formal schooling. Then, in 1867, he argued against a doubling of the existing fee to 4 annas a month, on the basis that the Muslim community was poor and that the parents of some of the present pupils of the school would not be able to pay even that minimal amount.[57]

Western Education for Madras Muslims in Later Years

By the mid-1850s there were, in addition to Madrasa-i 'Azam, two other schools in the town of Madras that were designed specifically for Muslim boys: one government school—the Mylapore Middle School—and one private mission school, established in 1856 with the proceeds of a donation to the Church Missionary Society from the Honourable Sybilla Harris, wife of Governor Robert Harris.[58] Starting with only three pupils, the Harris School had grown slowly at first, then rapidly increased its enrolment from nine to seventy in the 1858–9 academic year, levelling off to between forty and fifty pupils in the subsequent decade. The curriculum included English and other standard Western subjects, as well as Hindustani. In 1866 it attained the status of a high school and began to be subject to regular government inspections.[59]

In 1872 Lord Hobart was appointed Governor of Madras. In the words of a contemporary European observer, the new Governor was, 'unlike most Britishers', especially favourably disposed towards Muslims[60] and was concerned about their relative backwardness as a community, both educationally and in terms of their representation in public service employment in the Presidency. He ordered an enquiry and, on the strength of its findings, instituted a number of special steps to encourage more Muslims to acquire Western education. He was convinced that the main reason why Muslims did not enrol in larger numbers in schools of the modern type—and typically failed to excel when they did—was because the existing system of education was not well suited to their linguistic and cultural needs. He therefore directed that special elementary schools for Muslims be set up throughout the Presidency, with instruction to be given in Urdu as well as in English, to prepare pupils for entrance into the higher classes of district, provincial, or other government or government-aided private schools.[61] Other measures instituted during the following decade to encourage Muslim education included fixing school fees for Muslims at half the rate charged to those of other religions, the award of special merit scholarships for Muslims, the appointment of a Deputy Inspector for Muslim schools, and the establishment of a Normal School for Muslims in the town of Madras.[62]

By this time the Government of India, in response to solicitations from Muslim leaders in Bengal and in line with recommendations set forth in the Hunter Commission Report,[63] had stepped up its pressure on the various Presidency governments to take active measures to further the cause of Muslim educational advancement. In 1881 there were already 20 government and municipal schools specifically designed for Muslim boys in the Madras Presidency and an additional number run by missionary organizations but receiving government aid.[64] There were also 102 government primary schools for Muslim children.[65] Whether because of these special government efforts or for other reasons, the next two decades saw a significant spurt in Muslim school enrolments. In 1881 there were reported to be 21,117 Muslim boys (and 958 girls) enrolled in schools of all levels in the Presidency—almost a five-fold increase since 1871. Not surprisingly, all but 838 of these pupils were in primary schools.[66] But by 1893, Muslim enrolment in government institutions alone had increased to 70,488, of whom 12,373 were girls. The number of Muslims studying above the primary level had also risen markedly, to 4,445. During this period Hindu school enrolments were of course also rising, but at a considerably slower rate. Indeed, to the surprise of some observers, by 1881 the proportion of Muslim boys of school-going age who were actually enrolled in school had reached 15.10 per cent, exceeding the aggregate rate for Hindus (of all castes), which was then 13.70 per cent. The Report on Public Instruction for 1885–6 showed Muslim enrolments continuing to rise, such that 22 per cent of Muslim boys of school age were now in school. And, by the time of the 1901 Census, Muslims constituted 9.70 per cent of all pupils in public institutions of the Presidency, well over their 6.50 per cent share of the population.[67] Understandably, given the recency of this trend, Muslim students were still very little in evidence at the secondary and college levels, though, as time went on, their representation there too continued to increase.

It should be noted that, as the idea of studying English and Western subjects became more acceptable and indeed desirable, the Muslims of Madras did not limit themselves to availing themselves of schools that had been set up specifically for their community. They went in increasing numbers to government and missionary schools that welcomed students of all religions. Indeed, as time went on, the number of Muslim boys (and girls) in such mixed schools greatly outstripped the number attending all-Muslim schools. One reason may have been that, as reported by some observers, Muslim pupils did better academically in the former than in the latter type of school.

Were Madras Muslims 'Indifferent' to Western Education and, if so, Why?

It is not difficult to understand why, in the mid-nineteenth century, interest in acquiring a Western education would at first have been relatively slight among Muslims of the Presidency. The vast majority—like the vast majority of Hindus—had no family tradition of learning. Largely a rural population, they had, in the context of their accustomed means of livelihood as unskilled labourers, farmers, or artisans, no obvious motive to seek an education, still less a Western education, for themselves or their children. There were indeed some fairly prosperous Muslim trading communities in the towns of the Presidency, but these had no reason to enrol their sons in schools where a new language, new forms of knowledge and new skills were being imparted. They had little motivation for sending their sons to such schools: they much preferred to train them from an early age to help in the family trade and prepare to take it over once they reached adulthood.

The Muslim aristocracy of the Madras Presidency was a small, largely urban, minority, centred around the ruling family: the Nawwab and his relatives, and proliferating numbers of descendants of earlier Nawwabs and their former senior retainers, many of whom were, as noted, in regular receipt of official British stipends. Even when these stipends were very small—as they almost invariably were after the lapse of several generations and the resulting subdivision among heirs—most of their recipients had little interest in having their sons qualify for gainful employment. This was in part because they considered it inappropriate to their rank and damaging to their dignity to work for a living. Another factor, without a doubt, was hostility to the foreigners who had taken control of the Carnatic and reduced the power of their former rulers to almost nothing. In a period in which almost the sole attraction of Western schooling, whether for Muslims or other Indians in Madras and elsewhere, was that it enabled one to obtain the necessary qualifications for a job with the colonial government, the Muslim aristocracy understandably saw little point in acquiring it and, in fact, regarded it as a betrayal of their own people to do so.

As for the old Muslim scholarly class, the *'ulama,* their widespread avoidance of and—as in the case of this family—even active opposition to learning English and acquiring a Western education was doubtless related to somewhat different factors. One was their conviction that the system of knowledge on which they were the acknowledged authorities was vastly superior to that of the *firangi*. Another was their perception that the latter presented a dangerous threat to the survival of the substance and values of their own religion and culture and to their own social position, cultural influence, and community leadership. Furthermore, as long as the Nawwabi *sarkar* remained a going concern, there was for most of them no pressing economic motive to capitulate to the beckonings of the new educational order. There were still job opportunities for men with their traditional educational qualifications in and around the royal court, where the working milieu was familiar and congenial for social, cultural, and religious reasons. Outside of this arena, they could find a niche in those sectors of British public service employment where their Islamic educational training was still relevant and of some value. They could work, for example, as teachers of Persian or Arabic or of Islamic law at the East India Company's College of Fort St. George, as personal assistants and language tutors (*munshis*) to British civil servants, or as law advisers (*muftis*) or lower-court judges (*sadar amins*) in the British judicial service. Thus men of this class, insofar as they were willing to work for the rulers at all, tended to gravitate towards such jobs, rather than attempting to prepare themselves or their sons for the kind of posts that required Western educational qualifications.[68]

The Traditional Educational System

It was usual among the south Indian Muslims of the upper classes—as it was in similar social strata in other parts of India—for children to receive their early education from family members, or, in some cases, to study privately at home with tutors (*ustad* and *ustani*). Well-to-do families often engaged such tutors on a long-term basis to live in and take charge of the education of the younger generation in the household. At the more advanced levels, boys would be sent to study with local scholars known for their expertise in particular subjects. Mosque schools, *maktabs*, and the like existed, but were attended largely by poor children and those whose families were not sufficiently well educated to be able to teach themselves and could not afford to hire private tutors.[69]

This preference among the elite for private instruction was, among other things, associated with considerations of class and status. An educated man of *sharif* ('respectable') lineage was not inclined to send his children to be taught by someone who was very likely less well-qualified for the task than he or other adult members of his family were. Furthermore, he would not want to throw them into close contact with boys from families of inferior rank and breeding. Home education ensured the transmission not only of a high standard of religious and scholarly knowledge, but also of the standards of morality and comportment considered appropriate to a man of his social standing.

In Muhammad Ghaus's *khandan,* as in other religiously observant Muslim families, children usually began their studies some time after their fourth birthday. First, they were taught to recite by rote the first verse of the Qur'an, in preparation for the *bismillah* ceremony, ideally celebrated at the age of four years, four months, and four days, marking their initiation into the world of religious learning.[70] After the *bismillah* a child's education began in earnest. Mothers, aunts and grandmothers often assumed the role of teacher in these early years. He (or she—for in this *khandan* girls were given the same early education as boys) learned to recognize the Arabic letters and the sounds associated with them, in order to 'read' the Qur'an aloud, without necessarily comprehending its meaning. After the child had completed a first reading of the entire Holy Book, a second gathering of family, friends and associates took place for the ceremony of *khatm-i qur'an.*[71]

The fundamental tenets of the Islamic faith, the rules of ritual cleanliness, and methods of prayer were also taught in these early years. The child then began to study Persian, the language of government administration, literary expression, and most other written communication—even within the family. It was, therefore, imperative for a cultured Muslim man to become fluent in it. The Dakkhani language customarily spoken in the home and informally among friends and associates was written in the same script, so the acquisition of literacy in the mother tongue required little additional instruction.

Some young men stopped at this point in their studies, but others embarked on the study of Arabic in order to be able to read the advanced texts of the Islamic curriculum in the so-called 'traditional' (*manqulat*)[72] and 'rational' (*ma'qulat*) sciences.[73] This phase of education did not have a fixed duration. A student went through a conventional syllabus, reading its books, but in no prescribed order, at his or her own speed, and usually with a variety of different teachers. When the contents of each book had been absorbed to the teacher's satisfaction, a personal certification (*sanad*) to that effect would be awarded, giving 'permission' or 'authorization' (*ijazat*) to teach the book to others.

A custom had developed in north India of formally marking a scholar's completion of the prescribed course of study with a feast and a ceremony in which a special turban (*dastar-i fazilat*) was bound around his head in the presence of family, friends, and fellow-scholars. At some point—probably not before the 1850s—this ritual began to be followed in Madras as well.[74] While not all men of Muhammad Ghaus's *khandan* reached this high level of scholarly achievement, those who did exemplified the most valued masculine ideals. Such men were accorded special respect and honour (*'izzat*), both within their own families and by society at large.

Learning in this system took place on a one-to-one basis or in small groups, and the relationship between teacher and pupil was a personal one of mentor and disciple, modelled upon that of parent and child.[75] Indeed, in *'ulama* families, the teacher was very often the child's own father or a close kinsman. In any case, students of the same teacher typically developed a close identification with one another and with the intellectual heritage that their teacher represented, and had an almost moral obligation to strictly follow his teachings in later life.[76]

Muhammad Ghaus's own educational career followed this same pattern. For the first 23 years of his life, his paternal grandfather took direct charge of his education and was, as long as he lived, his only teacher.[77] Afterwards, since there was no-one else of comparable scholarly stature residing locally, he was sent to study theology, philosophy, and rhetoric with a famous *'alim* in Sivaganga, Ramnad District. When this man died, Muhammad Ghaus moved on to Trichinopoly, where he studied mysticism under another noted scholar. When he eventually found employment in the Nawwab's household in Madras, he did not cease his pursuit of learning, but continued to study further under the guidance of the famous Islamic scholar 'Abdul 'Ali Bahr-ul 'Ulum, who had come to Madras from Lucknow's Farangi Mahal in the late eighteenth century at the invitation of Muhammad 'Ali Walajah, to become principal of a new royal school, Madrasa-i Kalan.

Muhammad Ghaus provided for his sons an education very similar to his own, although, since they were living in Madras, the centre of intellectual life for the Muslims of the Deccan at the time, it was not necessary for them to travel far and wide, as he had done in his search for qualified teachers. Following the death of their mother in 1798 and during their father's protracted absences while engaged in his search for steady employment, the boys' elder sister and their paternal grandmother gave them whatever instruction they could. Once their father became *diwan*, however, he employed tutors (*ustads*) to teach them at home. The younger brother, Muhammad Sibghatullah, progressed much more quickly than the elder, finishing his first reading of the Qur'an at the age of eight; his brother's *khatm-i qur'an* was celebrated three years later. The two received further instruction from several knowledgeable kinsmen, including their elder sister's husband, their stepmother's brother, their father's second cousin, and another more distant relative. They also studied for varying periods of time with well-known Madras *'ulama* unrelated to their family, including—towards the end of his life— Bahr-ul 'Ulum. Later they were taught by his son-in-law and successor, Allauddin Ahmad. All this while they continued to read various important Islamic texts (*darsi kitab*) under their father's guidance. It was from him that they received *sanads* in most of the branches of knowledge to which they applied themselves.[78]

During the 1840s and 1850s, Qazi Badr-ud Daula is known to have engaged at least one live-in tutor to instruct the younger boys of his household.[79] When his children were sufficiently advanced to benefit from *his* expertise, he began teaching them himself. Other young men from outside of the family also came to the house to study subjects on which he was an acknowledged authority, particularly *fiqh* (Islamic jurisprudence) and *tibb* (Unani—or Greek—medicine). One of his younger sons, the only surviving child of his second wife, studied *tibb* under him and later continued his training with a well-known Madras *hakim*. He eventually moved to Hyderabad, where he practised medicine as his profession.[80]

Education in the *Khandan* after the Dissolution of the Nawwabi

Long after many south Indian Muslim families of similarly elite origins and background had proved the popular stereotype of Muslim opposition to Western education misguided or at least outdated, the descendants of the *qazi* and the *diwan* remained ambivalent, at best, about the wisdom of allowing their sons to acquire the new forms of knowledge, particularly through the medium of English. For the time being, their families were economically secure. After the last Nawwab's death the British had pensioned off all of his family members and close relatives, as well as those holding high-ranking positions in his administration, including the *diwan*, the *qazi* and the *bakhshi*, three of the late Nawwab's chief officers. Each was awarded a lifetime pension, equal in amount to his former salaries. Those of their sons and nephews who had held lesser, but still responsible, official posts in the Nawwabi *sarkar* were given smaller amounts.

However, by the late 1860s both of the senior men and their eldest nephew had died and their pensions had consequently lapsed, leaving the living standards of their survivors greatly reduced. The men of the family had been educated solely in the Islamic tradition. None of them knew English, so their opportunities for careers under the new order were very limited. True to their elders' teachings, most remained vehemently opposed to acquiring—or allowing their sons to acquire—the kind of training that would have qualified them either for government service under the British or for the modern professions that many men of the corresponding Hindu learned classes (in particular the brahmans) were beginning to enter in ever-increasing numbers.

They had, therefore, to find ways to support themselves by other means. Early on, a group of senior men and women joined together to invest some of their assets in the purchase of a market in an area of the city occupied mainly by so-called Untouchables. This market is still in family hands and earns a small but regular income for its shareholders from fees paid by the traders who sell there. Other *khandan* members invested individually, on a small scale, in residential rental property or set up retail shops in their homes. Those of a more cerebral bent continued to occupy themselves with Islamic scholarship, striving to stem the tide of its decline against the growing popularity of Western learning.

The princely state of Hyderabad was a particularly attractive destination for those Madras *'ulama* forced to seek employment elsewhere after the demise of the last Carnatic Nawwab. The state was still under Muslim rule, with Persian as the language of administration. The Nizam's Prime Minister, Salar Jung I, was actively recruiting educated outsiders to man a newly modernizing administration, on the British model.[81] None of the men of Muhammad Ghaus's *khandan* had the kind of 'modern' education or administrative experience that the Nizam's Prime Minister was primarily seeking. But their family reputation and long association with the late Carnatic ruler nevertheless enabled a few of the more ambitious younger men to obtain government jobs in Hyderabad.[82] There, the nucleus of a branch settlement of the family was formed that, by the time I encountered it in 1984, totalled almost 250 men, women and children, slightly under half of the number then residing at the family's original home base in Madras.[83]

The Beginnings of 'Modern' Education in Muhammad Ghaus's *Khandan*

Until the 1880s, all young men (and young women) of the *khandan*, whether in Madras or in Hyderabad, continued to be educated at home or in the homes of close relatives. One of the first to attend a formal educational institution was Safiuddin Muhammad Nasir, a young man whose father had died shortly after his birth in Madras in 1863. His widowed mother had seen to her sons' early education, first employing private tutors and later sending them to study in the home of one of her cousins, a well-respected Madras scholar. When he was in his teens, Safiuddin left for Hyderabad, where his elder sister and her husband were already living. At his brother-in-law's suggestion, he enrolled in Dar-ul 'Ulum, a state-supported school established in 1854 by Salar Jang I.[84] Although ostensibly modelled upon British Indian schools and offering classes in the local Indian languages and in English, Dar-ul 'Ulum's curriculum at that time consisted mainly of Qur'anic studies, Arabic, and Persian.

One of the teachers of Arabic at Dar-ul 'Ulum was married to a grand-niece of the late Qazi Badr-ud Daula. This relative's presence may have made the school more acceptable to the *khandan* elders than it would otherwise have been. In any case, neither Safiuddin nor any of the cousins who followed him to Dar-ul 'Ulum enrolled in the school's English-language curriculum; instead each pursued advanced Islamic studies. Nonetheless, their attendance represented the opening of a slight crack in the *khandan's* united front against formal schooling.

During the decades of the 1880s and 1890s several more young men of the family—grandsons and great-grandsons of the *qazi* and the *diwan*—enrolled in Dar-ul 'Ulum. Their fathers were well-educated in the traditional manner but stood out from the majority of *khandan* men at the time, in that they were employed in responsible positions in the Nizam's administration. Their relative wealth and the respect and influence it engendered, enabled them to act counter to the majority opinion within the *khandan*, which was still strongly opposed to the English language and to 'modern' educational forms.

Safiuddin's brother-in-law, Husain Ataullah, one of the *qazi's* younger sons, was one of these influential men. In 1869, some years after the death of his father and his father-in-law, he had come to Hyderabad with an older stepbrother and had embarked upon a successful and lucrative career, first in the Nizam's service and later as administrator of the private estate of one of the Nizam's senior nobles. He was one of the first men of the Hyderabad branch of the *khandan* to enrol his own sons in a Western-type school other than Dar-ul 'Ulum and to have them study English there. While he himself had had a strictly Islamic education, Husain Ataullah is said to have studied some English on his own as a young man, helped informally by a Muslim neighbour who knew the language well. He pursued his studies in secret, in view of his father's strong opposition to the tongue of the foreign rulers. It is not clear from the sources how far he advanced in his study of English or how long he continued learning the language. However, his sons were among the first young men of the *khandan* to receive instruction in English in a 'modern' school setting, at a time when a great majority of their peers in the family were still being tutored at home, taught mainly by family members or close relatives, as their fathers and grandfathers had been.

At the end of the century, a small *madrasa* was built in Madras on the premises of a mosque within the *khandan's* residential compound.[85] Here boys and young men of the *khandan*, as well as some outsiders, proceeded through the standard Islamic curriculum in a more formally structured setting than had been customary for family members in earlier generations. The establishment of this *madrasa* provided the *khandan* with a family-approved setting where boys could be educated outside of the home by teachers who were also, for the most part, their close relatives. *Khandan* boys from Hyderabad were sometimes sent to Madras to stay with kinsmen for several months—or for however long it took—to complete their *hifz-i qur'an*.

Madrasa Muhammadi, as the school was named, is still operating, but it now offers little in the way of advanced religious instruction. Most of its pupils attend simply to gain a basic reading knowledge of the Qur'an. Some remain for a longer period in order to complete the memorization of the entire Holy Book (*hifz-i qur'an*). This accomplishment entitles a man to be called 'Hafiz' and qualifies him to earn modest amounts by teaching privately or doing religious recitations on ceremonial occasions and life-cycle rites.

Family sources suggest that for decades *khandan* elders not only continued to regard Western education with suspicion and disdain, but were even extremely reluctant to allow their sons to study advanced Islamic subjects—or even to do *hifz*—with scholars from outside of the family. It is not entirely clear whether this insistence on educating their own children stemmed simply from a belief in their own superior competence as scholars and teachers, or whether it reflected theological or other disagreements or conflicts within the local scholarly community. It is possible that, feeling their own scholarly traditions under attack, they were especially sensitive to the possibility that other *'ulama* were beginning to succumb to Western influence and might transmit undesirable notions to their sons.

It was only around the turn of the century that significant numbers of *khandan* boys began to be sent to other kinds of formal educational institutions. Entries in the family biographical register show that, among males born before 1890, only 12 received any kind of formal schooling and most of these studied in institutions offering only an Islamic curriculum. Thereafter the numbers began to rise. By 1915 over 50 male members of the *khandan* were cited in the biographical register as having had some formal schooling, mostly in institutions of a Western type. The family's opposition to the English language and European forms of knowledge was gradually weakening, first in Hyderabad and then, somewhat later, among those living in Madras. By the 1940s it had become a quite accepted practice to send one's sons to school when they reached an appropriate age, though it took somewhat longer for the practice of sending daughters to school.[86] By the 1980s, when I was doing my initial field research, most children, of both sexes, were going on to high school and many went on to college and entered the professions. This upward educational and occupational trend has continued—and has even accelerated significantly—up to the present day.

Conclusion

In his analysis of the political rhetoric of elites in Surat during the colonial period, Douglas Haynes shows how the colonial language of debate was adopted by many indigenous leaders in the course of pressing their various local agendas.[87] Those who wished to be heard in the civic arena were compelled—perhaps without always fully realizing it—to frame their arguments within the discourse of the ruling power. While this made it possible for them to be taken seriously, it also had the negative effect of constraining them from 'constructing formulations that more fully challenge colonial rule and the underlying moral principles on which it is based'.[88] Those who tried to directly assert the validity of moral and cultural values contrary to those of the British, who attempted to 'operate outside the critical vocabulary of this arena', were marginalized, their opinions and ambitions ignored.[89] I have shown that a similar dynamic was operating in Madras in the mid-nineteenth century. Thus, whereas Nawwab Ghulam Muhammad Ghaus Khan, in dealing with British authorities, adapted quite well and with some success to the new forms of rhetoric, the leading establishment *'ulama* of Madras took the opposite course, and with predictable consequences. Speaking from within a system of religious meaning, in a discourse of the permissible and the forbidden according to holy law, they talked past Balfour's and others' calls for modernization and progress. The result was an almost complete absence of dialogue between them and their foreign rulers.

The positions taken by the *diwan* and the *qazi* were complicated by divisions within the ranks of the Muslim elite. There is evidence that the Nawwab and many members of his extended family were more receptive than were the leading *'ulama* to the idea of Western schooling. The Nawwab himself was said to have acquired a limited knowledge of English and some of his nobles learned English at an early stage: one of them (Haidar Jang) learned it well enough to be able to travel to Britain as an emissary of the Nawwab and the Carnatic stipendiaries and to negotiate on their behalf—though with little success—with representatives of the British government. But, for the *'ulama*, maintaining boundaries of cultural identity between themselves and those associated with the Nawwabi milieu and lifestyle—and trying to influence the latter to become more abstemious and religiously observant—had been a central preoccupation at least since the time of Muhammad Ghaus and continued to be so for his offspring. The question of whether it was desirable to accommodate to the new forms of knowledge was only one of several cultural/religious issues on which the two parties held differing views, although in this matter, as in others, the Nawwab clearly hesitated to come out and confront the *qazi* and other *'ulama* directly. Balfour's speeches and writings suggest that he was well aware of this cleavage between the *'ulama* and the nobility and exploited it by openly deriding the pretensions of the religious establishment and flattering the Nawwab, while being harshly critical of the latter's lavish lifestyle and impecunious habits when communicating with his own countrymen.

The Government Agent repeatedly reminded the Nawwab—who was then in his twenties—of the advanced age of his advisers, clearly implying that this disqualified them from being taken at all seriously. Generational differences of opinion about the value of Western learning were developing at the same time within the two brothers' own extended family, as we have seen from the events surrounding Balfour's successful efforts to alter the make-up of the Board of Directors of Madrasa-i 'Azam. If the Nawwab had lived, it is not unlikely that these younger men, who had lent support to Balfour's ambitions for the school, would have continued to flout the authority of their elders over the issue of English and a Western-style curriculum. They might have even decided to send their own sons to a re-organized school, which would have led to more open dissension within the family. But instead, the disruptions created by the Nawwabi's death, the dissolution of the Nawwabi and the financial distress and uncertainty that it caused for all members of the *khandan*, seems to have made these younger men retreat from their former positions, reaffirm the solidarity of the extended family, and line up behind their elders on the issue that for a time had threatened to divide them.

Notes

1. Ms. Vidyagauri Joshi referred to Bhagvatsinh as the 'valiant champion of female emancipation' in a speech she gave during Bhagvatsinh's Golden Jubilee Ceremony on 24 October 1934. *Gondal's Cherished Treasures: An Account of Shree Bhagvat Sinhjee Golden Jubilee Celebrations*, Gondal: Shee Bhagvat Sinhjee Golden Jubilee Committee, 1934, p. 13.
2. Gail Minault, *Secluded Scholars: Women's Education and Muslim Social Reform in Colonial India*, New Delhi: Oxford University Press, 1999; Geraldine Forbes, *Women in Modern India*, Cambridge: Cambridge University Press, 1999; Neera Desai, *Social Change in Gujarat: A Study of Nineteenth Century Gujarati Society*, Bombay: Vora and Co., 1978.
3. David Kopf, *The Brahmo Samaj and the Shaping of the Modern Indian Mind*, Princeton: Princeton University Press, 1979; Kenneth W. Jones, *Arya Dharm: Hindu Consciousness in Nineteenth Century Punjab*, Berkeley: University of California Press, 1976; Barbara Metcalf, *Islamic Revival in British India: Deoband, 1860–1900*, Princeton: Princeton University Press, 1982; David

Lelyveld, *Aligarh's First Generation: Muslim Solidarity in British India*, Princeton: Princeton University Press, 1978.
4. Sudhir Chandra, *The Oppressive Present: Literature and Social Consciousness in Colonial India*, Delhi: Oxford University Press, 1992, p. 75.
5. Minault, *Secluded Scholars*, p. 6.
6. Uma Chakravarti, 'Whatever Happened to the Vedic Dasi? Orientalism, Nationalism and a Script for the Past', in *Recasting Women: Essays in Indian Colonial History*, ed. Kumkum Sangari and Sudesh Vaid, New Brunswick: Rutgers University Press, 1999, pp. 27–87; J.T.F. Jordens, *Dayanand Saraswati: His Life and Ideas*, New Delhi: Oxford University Press, 1978; Charles H. Heimsath, *Indian Nationalism and Hindu Social Reform*, Princeton: Princeton University Press, 1964; David Kopf, *British Orientalism and the Bengal Renaissance: The Dynamics of Indian Modernization, 1773–1835*, Berkeley: University of California Press, 1969.
7. See, among others, Aparna Basu, *The Growth of Education and Political Development in India, 1898–1920*, Delhi: Oxford University Press, 1974; Imtiaz Ahmad, 'Muslim Educational Backwardness: An Inferential Analysis', *Economic and Political Weekly*, vol. 16, no. 36, 1981, pp. 1457–65.
8. David Lelyveld, *Aligarh's First Generation: Muslim Solidarity in British India*, Princeton: Princeton University Press, 1978, pp. 89–92.
9. Ibid., p. 92.
10. Those who do deal with these matters in the context of an earlier period include Farhan Ahmad Nizami, 'Madrasahs, Scholars and Saints: Muslim Response to the British Presence in Delhi and the Upper Doab 1803–1957', Unpublished D.Phil. Thesis, Faculty of Modern History, University of Oxford, 1983; and Margrit Pernau, ed., *The Delhi College: Traditional Elites, the Colonial State, and Education before 1857*, Delhi: Oxford University Press, 2006.
11. See, for example, David Lelyveld, *Aligarh's First Generation*; Barbara Daly Metcalf, *Islamic Revival in British India: Deoband, 1860–1900*, Princeton: Princeton University Press, 1982; Francis Robinson, *The 'Ulama of Farangi Mahall and Islamic Culture in South Asia*, London: Hurst and Company, 2001; Usha Sanyal, *Devotional Islam and Politics in British India: Ahmad Riza Khan Barelwi and his Movement, 1870–1920*, Delhi: Oxford University Press, 1996.
12. These are estimates, as no census figures are available before 1871.
13. P.J. Thomas, 'History of Education in Madras', in *The Madras Tercentenary Commemoration Volume*, Madras Tercentenary Celebration Committee, Madras: Oxford University Press, 1939, p. 65.
14. *Report from the Select Committee of the House of Commons on the Affairs of the East-India Company, 16th August 1832, and Minutes of Evidence. I. Public. Appendix (I.) Papers Respecting the Education of Natives*, London: Printed by Order of the Honourable Court of Directors, by J.L. Cox and Son, 1833, p. 359.

15. For the early history of Western education in Madras see Robert Eric Frykenberg, 'Modern Education in South India, 1784–1854: Its Roots and its Role as a Vehicle of Integration under Company Raj', *The American Historical Review*, vol. 91, no. 1, February 1986, pp. 37–65; McCully, *English Education*; S. Satthianadhan, *History of Education in the Madras Presidency*, Madras: Srinivasa, Varadachari & Co., 1894; R. Suntharalingam, *Politics and Nationalist Awakening in South India, 1852–1891*, Tucson: University of Arizona Press, 1974; Thomas, 'History of Education'.

16. Douglas Haynes's discussion of the rhetoric of local leadership in Surat during the colonial is suggestive for interpreting the dialogue between the Carnatic Nawwab and the British on the topic of education during this period. Douglas Haynes, *Rhetoric and Ritual in Colonial India: The Shaping of a Public Culture in Surat City, 1852–1928*, Berkeley: University of California Press, 1991.

17. In the nineteenth century this language was usually called 'Hindi' or 'Hindavi' by its own speakers and 'Hindustani' by the British. See Ruth Laila Schmidt, *Dakhini Urdu: History and Structure*, New Delhi: Bahri Publications, 1981. See also Muhammad Yusuf Kokan 'Umari, *Khanwada-i Qazi Badr-ud Daula*, Madras: Dar-ul Tasnif, 1963, pp. 475–7, on the use of this nomenclature in Madras in the nineteenth century. Translations of this and other Urdu passages in the text are mine.

18. When the Nawwabi was abolished upon Nawwab Ghulam Ghaus Khan's death in 1855, Balfour became the key figure in the lengthy process of dismantling the administrative apparatus of the Nawwabi *sarkar*, disposing of its properties and arranging for the settlement of the Nawwab's debts and those of his uncle, who had served as Regent during his minority. In 1871, Balfour was appointed Surgeon General of the Madras Presidency and served in that capacity until his retirement and return to Britain in 1876. See Douglas M. Peers, 'Balfour, Edward Green (1813–89)', in *Oxford Dictionary of National Biography*, London: Oxford University Press, 2004.

19. Susan Bayly, *Saints, Goddesses and Kings: Muslims and Christians in South Indian Society, 1700–1900*, Cambridge: Cambridge University Press, 1989, p. 228.

20. Balfour's major and best-known work is the five-volume *The Cyclopaedia of India and of Eastern and Southern Asia: Commercial, Industrial and Scientific Products of the Mineral, Vegetable, and Animal Kingdoms, Useful Arts and Manufactures*, 3rd edn., London: B. Quaritch, 1885.

21. B.S. Baliga, 'The Government Museum, Madras', in *Studies in Madras Administration*, vol. I, Madras: Government of Madras, 1960, pp. 80–195.

22. A. Raman, 'The Zoo that Balfour Developed', *Madras Musings*, vol. 20, no. 18, January 2011.

23. In this effort he received financial help and donations of books and manuscripts from the Nawwab, from other prominent Muslims of Madras and from the then Governor Henry Pottinger, among others. Cf. S. Anwar, 'The Balfour Contribution to Muhammadan Modernism', *Madras*

Musings, vol. 19, no. 23, March 2010. The library continued to operate until 1980, when the historic building in which it had been housed was demolished to make way for a multi-storey shopping complex. Its large collection of Arabic, Persian and Urdu books and manuscripts were put into storage and many were damaged, destroyed or lost in the process. The library re-opened in 2005 in a room on an upper floor of the new building.

24. 'Umari details how Balfour tried—but failed—to persuade the *'ulama* to go along with this proposal. See 'Umari, *Khanwada*, pp. 415–17; Umari, *Arabic and Persian in Carnatic 1710–1960*, Madras: Printed at Ameera & Co., 1974, pp. 365–7.
25. *Madras Political Consultations* (hereafter *MPC*), 29 April 1853, no. 17, pp. 1564–5.
26. Francis Robinson, 'Ulama, Sufis and Colonial Rule in North India and Indonesia', in *Two Colonial Empires*, ed. C.A. Bayly and D.H.A. Kolff, Dordrecht: Martinus Nijhoff Publishers, 1986, p. 15.
27. *MPC*, 29 April 1853, no. 17, Appendix A.
28. Thomas Babington Macaulay, *Speeches by Lord Macaulay, with his Minute on Indian Education: Selected, with an Introduction and Notes by G.M. Young*, London: Oxford University Press, H. Milford, 1935.
29. This discussion of Muhammad Ghaus's *khandan* draws heavily from 'Umari, *Khanwada*, and several published and unpublished writings about the family by some of its members. Particularly informative were Muhammad Afzal[uddin] Iqbal, ed., *Tazkira-I Sa'id*, Hyderabad: Sayeedia Library and Research Institute, 1973 and Muhammad Mazhar, 'Maulana Muhammad Murtuza ki Halat', *Ruh-i-Taraqqi* (*Hyderabad*), pp. 8–9 (Special Edition), 1949. I have also used findings from my own ethnographic and archival research carried out in Chennai (formerly Madras), Hyderabad and London between 1983 and 1998 and from interviews in the United States and Canada with other descendants of its founding ancestor. I am particularly indebted to the late Dr Zakira Ghouse for sharing her extensive knowledge of her *khandan's* history with me. Her sisters, Dr Nasira Begam and the late Dr Shakira Begam were also extremely helpful, as have been, more recently, her daughter, Rafeth Yasmin, and her son, Muhammad Javed.
30. For more details about education in the *khandan* in later years, see Sylvia Vatuk, 'Schooling for What? The Cultural and Social Context of Women's Education in a South Indian Muslim Family', in *Women, Education, and Family Structure in India*, ed. C.C. Mukhopadhyay and S. Seymour, Boulder: Westview Press, 1994, pp. 135–64. See also Vatuk, 'The Cultural Construction of Shared Identity: A South Indian Muslim Family History', in *Person, Myth and Society in South Asian Islam*, ed. Pnina Werbner, Special Issue, *Social Analysis*, vol. 28, no. 1, 1990, pp. 114–31; Vatuk, 'Identity and Difference or Equality and Inequality in South Asian Muslim Society', in *Caste Today*, ed. C. Fuller, Delhi: Oxford University Press, 1996, pp. 227–62.

31. See Victor S. D'Souza, *The Navayats of Kanara*, Dharwar: Kannada Research Institute, 1955; Aziz Jang Wila, *Tarikh-un Nawwayat*, Hyderabad: 'Aziz-ul Matbu'a, 1904.
32. This *khandan* possesses written genealogical records (*shajre*) that trace its ancestry back to the fourteenth century.
33. Elsewhere, when writing about this family, I have referred to Muhammad Ghaus by the pseudonym 'Ghulam Mahmoud'.
34. See N.S. Ramaswami, *Political History of Carnatic under the Nawabs*, New Delhi: Abhinav, 1994.
35. The principal published source for this section is 'Umari, *Khanwada*. I have also drawn upon the *khandan's shajre* and other unpublished material in family archives.
36. He was the nephew (brother's son) of the recently deceased Nawwab 'Umdat-ul 'Umra.
37. These individuals were referred to as the Carnatic Stipendiaries. Under the terms of the 1801 treaty, stipends were to be paid only during the lifetime of the holder, but the rules were later modified so as to allow, in some cases, all or a portion of the original amount to be continued to the individual's legitimate descendants.
38. This court had official jurisdiction over disputes among Carnatic stipendiaries and other relatives of the Nawwab. However, other Madras Muslims often came to have the *qazi* adjudicate their disputes as well.
39. *MPC*, 29 April 1853, no. 17, pp. 1558–9.
40. Thomas, 'History of Education', p. 445.
41. *MPC*, 29 April 1853, no. 17, p. 1562.
42. 'Umari, *Khanwada*, p. 419.
43. Ibid., p. 420.
44. Ibid., pp. 421–2.
45. Ibid., p. 421.
46. Ibid., p. 422.
47. *MPC*, 29 April 1853, no. 17, p. 1565.
48. Ibid., p. 1566.
49. Ibid., p. 1581.
50. Ibid., p. 1582.
51. Ibid., pp. 1582–3.
52. 'Umari, *Khanwada*, p. 422.
53. For a biographical note about George Balfour see C.E. Buckland, *Dictionary of Indian Biography*, London: Swan Sonnenschein & Co., Ltd., 1906, p. 24.
54. 'Umari, *Arabic and Persian in Carnatic*, p. 362.
55. *Report on Public Instruction in the Madras Presidency for 1859–60*, Madras: Public Instruction Press, 1861, p. 33.
56. *Proceedings of the Madras Government, Educational Department*, 9 June 1862, no. 36. See also *Report on Public Instruction . . . for 1862–63*, Madras: Public Instruction Press, 1864, pp. 18–19.

57. *Proceedings of the Madras Government, Educational Department*, 31 July 1867, no. 83. This is consistent with Seal's observation that most of the school and college students in Madras in the late nineteenth century came from families of modest income. He notes, for example, that in 1883–4, 98.50 per cent of the fathers of secondary school students in the presidency earned less than Rs.5,000 per year, while 62.10 per cent earned under Rs.200. The majority of these fathers were relatively low-ranking government servants, among whom Hindus, particularly Tamil brahmans predominated. Anil Seal, *The Emergence of Indian Nationalism*, Cambridge: Cambridge University Press, 1968, pp. 108–9 and Table 59, p. 363.
58. *Report on Public Instruction . . . for 1859–60*, Table V, pp. xvii–xx; Satthianadhan, *History of Education*, p. 78. The latter source gives the date of the opening of this school as 1857. See also 'A Reputation Won against Odds', *The Hindu*, 11 February 2011, http://www.thehindu.com/todays-paper/tp-features/tpmetroplus/a-reputation-won-against-odds/article1475782.ece, accessed 11 June 2015.
59. *Report on Public Instruction . . . for 1859–60*, Table XII.
60. J.H.S.V. Garcin de Tassy, *La Langue et la Littérature Hindoustanies en 1875*, Paris: Librairie Orientale de Maisonneuve et Cie, 1876, pp. 104–5 (my translation).
61. Suntharalingam, *Politics and Nationalist Awakening*, p. 255; Satthianadhan, *History of Education*, pp. 118–19. The governor does not seem to have considered the fact that most Muslims in the presidency spoke Tamil, not Urdu, as their mother tongue.
62. Satthianadhan, *History of Education*, p. 122.
63. National Mohammadan Association, *The Memorial*; Indian Education Commission, *Report*.
64. Satthianadhan, *History of Education*, pp. 121–2.
65. Ibid., p. 270.
66. Satthianadhan, *History of Education*, pp. 78, 269–70; *Correspondence on the Subject of the Education of the Muhammedan Community in British India*, H.B. Grigg, Esq., D.P.I., to the Chief Secretary to Government, Ootacamund, 13 June 1882, p. 248.
67. See, for example, Basu, *Growth of Education*, p. 148.
68. See Sylvia Vatuk, 'Islamic Learning at the College of Fort St. George in Nineteenth-century Madras', in *The Madras School of Orientalism*, ed. Thomas Trautman, New Delhi: Oxford University Press, 2009, pp. 48–73.
69. Cf. Nizami, who, with reference to northern India, similarly indicates that the sons of the 'rich and respectable' were customarily taught at home by private tutors rather than being sent to school. Nizami, 'Madrasahs, Scholars and Saints', p. 13.
70. For a description of this ceremony as it was observed in the Deccan in the 1830s, see Jaffur Shurreef, *Qanoon-e-Islam, or, the Customs of the Moosulmans of India; Comprising a Full and Exact Account of Their Various Rites and*

Ceremonies from the Moment of Birth till the Hour of Death, tr. G.A. Herklots, Madras: Higginbotham, 1863 [1832], pp. 27–9.

71. See Shurreef, *Qanoon-e-Islam*, pp. 32–4, for a description of the latter rite. The author uses the term 'huddeea' (hadiya) for this rite, referring to the gift offered in gratitude on this occasion by the parents of the child to his or her teacher.

72. Including such subjects as 'exegesis' (*tafsir*), 'traditions of the Prophet' (*hadith*), 'theology' (*kalam*) and 'jurisprudence' (*fiqh*).

73. Including logic (*mantiq*), philosophy (*hikmat*), etymology (*sarf*), syntax (*nahw*), medicine (*tibb*), and mathematics (*riyazi*). For details about the traditional Islamic curriculum in India and the changes it underwent during the nineteenth century, see S.M. Jaffar, *Education in Muslim India*, Delhi: Idarah-i Adabiyat-i Delli, 1973 [1936]; G.M.D. Sufi, *Al-Minhaj, Being the Evolution of Curriculum in the Muslim Educational Institutions of India*, Delhi: Idarah-i Adabiyat-i Delli, 1977 [1941]; Kuldip Kaur, *Madrasa Education in India: A Study of its Past and Present*, Chandigarh: Centre for Research in Rural and Industrial Development, 1990; Barbara Metcalf, 'The Madrasa at Deoband: A Model for Religious Education in Modern India', *Modern Asian Studies*, vol. 12, no. 1, 1978, pp. 111–34; Robinson, *The 'Ulama*, pp. 42–68.

74. I have only negative evidence of this, as in none of the published or unpublished sources on the educational careers of Muhammad Ghaus and his sons is the ritual mentioned, though their receipt of *sanads* in particular subjects from various teachers is carefully noted. The first year in which the *dastar-i fazilat* is mentioned in family *roznamche* (daily diaries or date books) is 1267 Hijri (1859–60). The man honoured with the ceremonial turban in that year was Qazi Badr-ud Daula's fifth son, Muhammad Sa'id, about whom more information is available in Iqbal, *Tazkira-i Sa'id*.

75. Thus, for example, in an 1801 letter to his former tutor from Nawwab 'Azim-ud Daula, concerning the Muhammad Ghaus's intention to resign from his post because of the Nawwab's pecuniary extravagance, the writer says: 'I consider Mawlawi Sahab to be equivalent to my own father'. 'Umari, *Khanwada*, p. 160.

76. Nizami, 'Madrasahs, Scholars and Saints', p. 15.

77. 'Umari, *Khanwada*, pp. 134–8, 148–9.

78. Ibid., pp. 258–9, 334–6.

79. Muhammad Mahdi Wasif Madrasi, *Hadiqat-ul Maram: 'Ulama-i Madras*, tr. Sakhawat Mirza (Arabic to Urdu), Karachi: Anjuman-i Taraqqi-i Urdu, 1979–82 [1853–4]. This is also mentioned by the *qazi* in his unpublished *roznamcha*.

80. 'Umari, *Khanwada*, p. 498.

81. See, for example, Karen Leonard, *Social History of an Indian Caste: The Kayasths of Hyderabad*, Berkeley and Los Angeles: University of California Press, 1978.

82. Despite the ongoing administrative reforms, large sectors of Hyderabad's government bureaucracy continued to run along the existing lines. The jobs that young men of the *khandan* were able to obtain were within these older administrative structures. Leonard explains this two-tiered administrative system and its wider social and political implications in 'The Hyderabad Political System and its Participants', *The Journal of Asian Studies*, vol. 30, no. 3, May 1971, pp. 569–82, and in Leonard, *Social History*.
83. These figures are based on a *khandan* census that I engaged two young women of the *khandan* to conduct in Hyderabad and Madras in 1984. They surveyed 92 households in Madras and 49 in Hyderabad, with a combined total of 686 individuals. Through further inquiries I was able to add to the family's numbers another 500–600 *khandan* men and women living elsewhere in India or in Pakistan, the Middle East and Gulf States, England, Europe, and North America. This total corresponds quite closely to the number of living persons listed in a handwritten biographical register of the *khandan* that had been begun by a nineteenth-century ancestor and kept up-to-date at the time of my research by an elderly Hyderabadi woman, the late Amat-ul Majid.
84. For information about the history of this school, see Fazl Muhammad Khan, *Education under Asaf Jah VIII: A Retrospect*, Hyderabad: At the Government Central Press, 1937.
85. The mosque and its surrounding land and residential buildings had been left as a family *waqf* (endowment) by a childless female descendant of Madar-ul 'Umra, who had inherited the property upon her father's death. This period saw a marked efflorescence of Islamic institution-building all over southern India, as elsewhere in the subcontinent. 'Umari, in his *Arabic and Persian*, lists and describes a number of madrasas that were established in the region between 1885 and 1900.
86. In 1915, one of these school-educated men took the daring step of enrolling his daughter in an all-girls' school in Hyderabad. But he arranged her marriage soon afterwards, putting an end to her studies. It was another ten years before another girl could follow in her footsteps. This woman, now almost 90 years of age, continued on to college and became a school teacher, one of the first women of the *khandan* to be employed outside of the home. See Vatuk, 'Schooling for What?', pp. 141–3, for more details about the progress of formal schooling in this *khandan* during the twentieth century.
87. Haynes, *Rhetoric and Ritual in Colonial India*, p. 22.
88. Ibid.
89. Ibid., p. 21.

13

Charismatic Cubs

The Tiger as a Pet

JULIE E. HUGHES

> So far, so good; the cub is small,
> Let's wait awhile and see. . . .
>
> —E.W. FLANAGEN, 'Master Blang', stanza 6

THE BEST KNOWN Indian tiger in the British colonial period was none other than the ruler of Mysore, Tipu Sultan Fath Ali Khan (r.1782–99). Tipu Sultan followed precedents set by earlier rulers in adopting the tiger as his mascot. Tiger stripes adorned everything from his soldier's uniforms through his book bindings, while figural representations of the animal appeared on his royal throne and, most famously, took shape in the musical contraption known as Tipu's Tiger. The sort of tiger Tipu saw himself as was physically powerful, righteously associated with Hindu and Muslim religious figures, and innately legitimate as sovereign. The sultan was not alone in his ideas. Indian princes throughout the Deccan, Rajputana, and Bengal believed that tiger imagery and sovereignty went hand-in-hand.[1]

Tipu was a tiger, too, in the eyes of the British. Yet, particularly in the wake of their hard won conquest of Mysore at Srirangapatnam in 1799, British ideas of what a tiger was and what the moral consequences of being tiger-like were, were dramatically different from an Indian prince's. For most British people, Indian tigers were cruel, bloodthirsty, cowardly, and despotic animals—either man-eaters or potential man-eaters—that the Indian populace needed their protection from.[2]

British lions, in contrast, were noble, courageous, and Christian beasts. However, disciplined and educated, civilized, and reformed caged (and less frequently free-roaming) tigers and 'tame' princes suffered. They were subject to constant vigilance, and the slightest provocation could bring swift retribution. Any softening of attitudes towards tigers in British India, as well as any attempts by Indians in the princely territories to recast tigers, therefore, help illustrate the nineteenth- and twentieth-century struggles of Indian princes for self-determination and, indeed, for self-preservation.

Beginning in the 1850s and extending through the 1950s, pet cubs in British India and at least one well-documented cub from the Federated Malay States helped determine what tigers *were* for British colonialists, their subjects, and wider global audiences. Individual tigers—unbeknownst to themselves and through the mediation of their owners and other willing chroniclers—had the power to shape human understandings of the species and thereby to shift definitions of sportsmanship, scientific knowledge, and government policies about tigers. Warring perceptions of tigers as dangerous and powerful natural born killers of human beings, and yet as fragile animals capable of loving relationships, were proffered by various authors as they struggled to grasp what a tiger was, and increasingly from the 1930s, began championing an enhanced reputation for and humane treatment of these animals, particularly their young.[3]

It is possible to better explain how and why tigers changed their stripes between the early nineteenth and the mid- to late twentieth centuries—from savage and horrifying vermin requiring destruction to charismatic and endangered megafauna deserving protection—by learning how exotic pet-keeping practices interacted with, modified, and augmented trends associated with big game hunting, natural history, and conservationism. Natural historians, sportsmen-naturalists, and early conservationists all relied on first-hand observations of tigers in the wild and, more cautiously, on second-hand accounts related by fellow sportsmen, villagers, and huntsmen. Many augmented their observations on behaviour with physiological inquiries. Ongoing debates included whether or not the number of lobes in a tiger's liver correlated with its age, if their sense of smell was sharp or dull, if the hind foot's pugmark regularly overlapped or came in front of the forefoot's, and if all man-eaters were either old and in poor condition, or riddled with porcupine quills and shot. Some of these points were as arcane then as they are now, while others were of little interest to anyone besides sportsmen interested in predicting a tiger's next move during a hunt. Commentary on the nature of the tiger-as-species, in terms of its ferocity or cruelty as compared with other big cats, was also common and more accessible to general audiences. What these authors lacked was insight into the distinct personalities of individual tigers, based on intimate knowledge gained by keeping them as pets. A focus on the tiger as pet reintroduced this animal to a broad audience and reframed its identity as a species—approachable and even adorable in its youth, and understandably dangerous in adulthood—in ways conducive to an ethos of conservationism.

Accounts of pet tiger cubs existed at the intersections of science, old-fashioned natural history, and individual memoir. They were crafted to capture popular audiences and influence public opinion in India, Britain, and elsewhere, and in some cases sought to contribute to scientific knowledge or to shape government policy as well. My paper begins the process of identifying and analysing patterns within these narratives, which range from full length books about individual animals to classified advertisements offering cubs for sale. The degree to which pet tigers and the dissemination of their stories succeeded in moving governments, scientists, and the public will be addressed in future publications.

A few preliminary terminological and theoretical issues need to be raised here. First of all, what is a pet?[4] Does the category ever overlap with menagerie animals and circus acts, or does the blatant exercise of power and economic exploitation invalidate any existing bonds of affection? Yet, are pets not controlled, exploited, and made to 'work' in human interests, too, even as they are loved and, arguably, love in return?[5] If the distinction instead is one of genetics, such that a pet is by definition domesticated—the result of selective, controlled breeding—and not simply tamed, then very few of the animals considered here were pets.[6] Only one, Tara, was born in captivity and so in some sense selectively bred. Her status was further complicated by her owner's goal of introducing her to the wild, yet for almost two years she lived and played with a human companion who fed, pet, and caged her at night. Perhaps the captive bred white tigers of Rewa, all descendants of the wild-caught Mohan, were domestic animals, then. Yet the litters raised in Rewa in 1958 and the 1960s, along with Mohan himself, were not treated as pets: they were expected instead to become star attractions in zoos in India, Europe, and the United States.

Young, tamed cubs were welcomed as free-roaming pets and bedfellows for the first few months; by six months they were normally kept out-of-doors, chained, or caged; by twelve months or the onset of sexual maturity, and earlier if small children formed part of the household, tigers were transferred to zoos or private menageries. In some cases, 'euthanasia' was the final outcome.

I have tried to restrict my examples to animals that shared domestic spaces with humans or were kept nearby, on a verandah or in a courtyard perhaps. I have also taken evidence of people regularly walking, driving, or playing with, petting, or engaging in other activities typical of dog or cat keeping with their tigers, as indications that particular animals were in some sense pets. Finally, I have been quicker to identify a young cub under 9 months of age as a pet than an older one, but have thought of older cubs known to have been kept as pets in their youth as ex-pets rather than non-pets.

Owners and Numbers

Advertisements for cubs reveal Indians and Englishmen, as well as residents of British and princely India, engaged in owning and trading tigers. The names of the primary owners or sellers of 145 tigers are known. Taken together, ownership was just over 52 per cent Indian and just under 45 per cent British, with the remainder accounted for by two women, one Scandinavian and the other American. The princely states of Ajaigarh, Baroda, Bikaner, Jaipur, Kotah, and Rewa at one time or another all tried to sell a tiger or two. Return addresses and ages—ranging from 2 months to 'full grown'—hinted at the suitability of an animal for household or cage. With the exception of Kotah (offering a pair of 2-month-old cubs in 1920) and Rewa (an 11-month-old-cub in 1950), the princely states gave zoological parks or gardens as return addresses, not palaces or private residences, suggesting these were not pets.

Private sellers were occupationally diverse and predominantly from northern or central India. B.D. Ukidwe was a Divisional Forest Officer in Berar, for example, and Ladha Ram was the Manager of Lyallpur Bank in Lyallpur.[7] Among British sellers, there were likewise forest officers, deputy commissioners, engineers, a member of the Geological Survey of India, civil surgeons, and military men. Huntsmen and beaters hired by Indian and English sportsmen undoubtedly aided in capturing many cubs, but their efforts went unacknowledged in sales notices. Evidence from hunting memoirs, however, confirms they did assist. Tribal groups and villagers on their own initiative too would catch cubs and present them to local potentates in the forest department and other branches of government. For example, this is how Saroj Raj Choudhury obtained Khairi in 1974.

How many tigers were kept as pets in South Asia and who kept them? Research so far in various media and archives has turned up 180 or so tigers appearing for sale or being kept as pets for varying lengths of time from 1785 to 1976. About 30 of their names are known, showing a marked preference for common Indian and English personal names (Parbutti, Salim, Bhim; Jack, Sheila, Billy), descriptive titles (Tiny, Khairi, Blang), and monikers inspired by popular culture (Dopey, Grumpy, Happy).[8] Many more surely await discovery in the pages of hunting memoirs, sporting periodicals, natural history journals, and photograph albums, not to mention archival and private collections and the records of exotic pet dealers. It is impossible to say how many more than presently known—ten fold, a hundred fold, more?—never made it to the historical records at all.

Certainly the idea of the tiger cub as pet circulated far and wide in the colonies and the metropole, the old world and the new. Short stories ranging from the titillating—the tiger hero of 'The Captive' (1913) 'dreamt with fierce vividness that he fought with others of his kind for the favours of a young, slim tigress, who lay lashing her tail, watching the fray, licking herself . . . he conquered, and head erect approached her'—to the moralizing—'Haidee' (1890) featured an Englishman's Indian bride unable to break her passion for 'tigers and lions', i.e. her 'pagan' roots, with the predictable result of death-by-big-cat—through the humorous and nostalgic—Ruskin Bond's 'A Tiger in the House' (1963) is a prime example, and far too good to spoil with a synopsis.[9] The very fact of an established literary trope, of the adorable cub that is playful to begin with, then mischievous, then intimidating, and ultimately and inevitably dangerous—a tiger 'after all', destined to be Sher Khan to our Mowgli—dramatizes the lived experiences of those who came into contact with tame tigers.[10]

What is clear is that tiger keeping—or at the very least its visibility in the historical record—peaked from the mid-1870s through the mid-1890s, and then again in the 1940s and 1950s.[11] Just over two-thirds of all tigers owned or offered for sale as pets between 1785 and 1976 belong to these four decades. This finding is significant as the procurement of tiger cubs was intimately linked to hunting and forestry before the development of successful breeding programmes in captivity. The beginning of the former period coincides with the promulgation of the Indian Forest Act of 1878 and contemporaneous expansions of departmental control over and policing of Indian forests. This translated into more forest officers, predominantly English at first but increasingly Indian, more time spent in the forests by individuals likely to consider keeping a tiger—because they knew of and were inspired by precedents from India's royal courts, their ideas of sportsmanship enjoined caring for orphaned cubs, they fancied themselves amateur natural historians, or wished to appear fearless and powerful for local audiences—and more opportunities to obtain cubs in the first place. Indeed, so many advertisements carried return addresses from central India, the Central Provinces, and Berar because these were Forest Department strongholds and contained some of the subcontinent's best hunting grounds and tiger habitats. Other 'hot spots' were the Rajputana states and the United Provinces, with a few tigers advertised from Calcutta, Delhi, Peshawar, and Bombay, and a lone south Indian pair out of Kerala.

Tiger hunting also received official encouragement during much of this period in the form of bounties. To the extent that professional huntsmen and sportsmen took advantage of these offers, the bounty system presumably fed into the fad of cub-keeping by making cubs available. This was vital as captive breeding was not extensively practised and, at least in British India, captive-born tiger cubs were almost unknown as late as 1914.[12] Besides, the bounties offered for tigers were far below the market value of live cubs. In the 1870s, rewards between Rs.5 and Rs.30 were paid out for tigers in Bengal, regardless of age.[13] The reward in the 1880s for a cub in the Sundarbans was Rs.10 and for adults Rs.25, with both figures doubling by the 1890s.[14] In contrast, the average asking price between 1894 and 1873 (when a cub with two cages sold in Delhi for Rs.183) was about Rs.360.[15]

Between 1875 and 1894, over 29,000 tigers were killed for reward in British India and Burma.[16] Sex ratio at birth among tigers is approximately 1:1, but among adult populations in the wild, about 3.625:1, favouring the females. Assuming tigers were shot in proportion to sex, 22,730 females were killed. Assuming 38 per cent of these had a litter when killed, and that the average litter size was 2.8 cubs, we are left with 24,185 cubs.[17] Around a third of these would have been over 9 months, making them too large to be attractive pets and too old to thoroughly tame, and big enough to shoot on sight. Even if just a tenth of the remaining 16,123 cubs were caught, it would still yield a sizeable number. Furthermore, this estimate covers only two decades, does not factor in tigers killed for no reward, and entirely omits the princely states, which accounted for some 40 per cent of the subcontinental landmass and many of the best tiger grounds.

The second peak in tiger cub sales coincided with the interwar years, World War II, and the flurry of natural resource extraction extending from the 1940s through the first decades of India's independence. As in the 1870s, 1880s, and 1890s, these years saw heightened pressure on Indian forests, with increased human traffic in forests and forest produce including tiger cubs. Between 1919 and 1956, 55 tigers were advertised for sale or are known to have been kept as pets. Relatively few advertisers specified their prices, but from those who did it is clear that times had changed. The asking price for a 3-year-old tiger in 1953 was Rs.1,200. Another seller wanted at least Rs.3,500 for a 4-month-old cub. On average, between 1909 (when the price regime appears to have changed) and 1953, sellers listed their tigers for Rs.1,280 each. If the alleged asking price for the white tiger cub Mohan—around $28,000—or for the white cubs he and his offspring produced after 1958 were factored in, this number would be significantly higher.[18]

Blood

Advertisements indicated the ages of 78 cubs offered for sale between 1785 and 1963: the animals were quite young, with a median age of 5.5 months.[19] Even at just 6 months tiger cubs are large and still growing fast. Blang was nearly 5 ft. long and almost 70 lb. by the time he was 6 months old. Five months later, and despite a period of severe illness, he had packed on 30 lb. and gained 15 inches in length. A 'healthy and playful' 7-month-old female offered for sale in 1919 was nearly 4.5 ft. long. As for Khairi, she was only 6.2 kg. and 88 cm. long when first measured in October 1974, at two months. Her weight increased ten-fold and her length by 126 cm. over the following seven months, leaving her around the size of a Newfoundland dog. Nine months later her weight had doubled yet again. By maturity—around three years—the exceptionally well-fed Khairi topped 200 kg. and 273 cm.[20]

The significance of these rapid and dramatic changes in size were judged by owners with reference to the animals' behaviour, which itself was subject to change as sexual maturity loomed. One of the major characteristics that distinguishes domestic from wild animals is the former's retention of juvenile traits into adulthood, or neoteny, a characteristic that cat and dog owners regularly augment by spaying or neutering.[21] Wild animals are 'wild' in large part because they grow up and become sexual beings.

Popular opinion, however, anticipated a far worse fate than the behavioural realities that tiger ontogeny were likely to deliver. 'Blood lust', a taste for cruelty, and other savage desires allegedly came with maturity. Most authors and presumably their readers, too, assumed in the nineteenth century that adult tigers were innately cruel. Cruelty, in fact, was so accepted as their chief characteristic that less imaginative prose did little but repeat the point: 'Nabuco, after his cruel feline nature, was prolonging by anticipation the delight of his first full leap into liberty and carnage. There was exquisite and cruel revelry in every curve of him, and every line was as graceful as it was cruel.'[22] Given how dangerous tigresses with cubs were considered to be, the prospect of one's pet procreating could not have been welcome, either.

As part of the well documented shift from guns and vermin eradication in the nineteenth century to cameras and conservationism, British, Indians, and others were more likely by the early to mid-twentieth century to look beyond the 'repellent, ruthless, animal ferocity' and see the tiger as 'so much more than a killer'.[23] Kesri Singh by the 1960s insisted that while the tiger may have a 'savage instinct', it was not 'cruel at heart' and, in the words of Jim Corbett, 'behaves like a gentleman'. Tigers were drawn to killing because survival necessitated it. While this made them dangerous, they were nevertheless humane killers that accomplished their ends 'efficiently and instantaneously'. Moreover, he insisted, they took no particular pleasure in causing pain and only killed for food.[24]

With such advocacy, furthered by engaging stories of Blang, Happy, and their peers, tigers and not just tiger cubs were becoming 'playful, affectionate and mischievous' creatures by the 1930s. They were charismatic as well, fond of pranks, automobile rides, and 'sitting up to [the] neck in a bath-tub of water'.[25] Even if tigers were no longer cruel, most still trusted them only as helpless cubs not yet capable of killing. Choudhury, however, believed that his observations of Khairi 'prov[ed] abundantly that genuine love is the supreme influence that ultimately overrides other conflicting urges'. His tigress might be a killer, but she was no indiscriminate killer. When Khairi drew blood from her foster-mother Nihar Nalini, she developed no blood-lust and failed to become a man-eater. Instead she 'was immediately alerted, and profusely sorry', demonstrating her distress through vocalizations and attempts to re-enter the room to establish comforting physical contact with Nihar.[26]

Despite these interventions, the topic of sexuality remained awkward. No owners reported on signs of an older cub's incipient sexuality with the exception of Billy Arjan Singh and Choudhury, both of whom had scientific aspirations or training. Leaving aside zoo and circus animals as well as those in menageries, Khairi, Tara, and Selim were among the few known to have been kept through sexual maturity. Selim, a male, reportedly lived his entire lifespan of three years in the 1860s with his owner, but no information regarding his passage to sexual maturity has come to light. Khairi remained with Choudhury from 1974 through her death in 1981. Born in early August 1974, she experienced oestrus and mated for the first time when she was about 19 months old in May 1976. Her behaviour included 'brushing her cheek and ruff and rubbing her neck and shoulder on the legs of her human company' and rolling on a 'urine-soaked patch' left by a male tiger. Choudhury confirmed oestrus by examining a 'smear taken from her urino-genital opening . . . under the microscope', nicely demonstrating his scientific approach to her condition.[27] Tara was around the same age when she 'opted for freedom' and the company of a male tiger in January 1978. Before leaving, Tara would 'go off . . . and roll where the male tiger had rolled'. Less scientific and more circumspect than Choudhury, Billy Arjan Singh glossed this as the tigers' 'process of getting acquainted'.[28]

Although reticence surely was a factor, the main reason for silence among owners is that most cubs were sold off or transferred to zoos before sexual maturity. Tigers were short term pets to be disposed of after six to nine months. Almost 76 per cent of advertisements placed between 1785 and 1963 and specifying age were for cubs 9 months or younger, with 9 months or more of prepubescent youth left to recommend them. Only 9 spots, or 15 per cent of those placed, advertised tigers old enough to have been sexually mature. Notably, these animals were marketed almost exclusively on their health; only two advertisements mentioned temperament in addition to health.[29] If these tigers had been pets in their youth, they were now implicitly offered as additions to public zoos and menageries.

Young cubs, then, were preferred for their smaller size, the lesser dangers they posed, and their prepubescent innocence. Cubs were also more entertaining. The play of tiger cubs, however, is serious business during which they learn social cues and how to interact with others of their kind. Parbutti in the late 1870s often played with puppies and 'often would take one of their heads into her mouth'. Carefully heeding their vocal cues, she would let it go 'at the first squeak'.[30] This sort of behaviour appears to be learned and was not necessarily innate. When Billy Arjan Singh introduced Tara to his dog Eelie and the adult leopard Harriet, the cub 'had not yet started sheathing her claws' during play. As the animals became acquainted over the following days and weeks, 'Tara became increasingly aware of the extent of the liberties she could take with her two companions.'[31] Happy had learned this lesson, too, as he always took 'great care not to put out his claws or hurt [Kesri Singh] in any way' while playing.[32]

Besides teaching basic communication and etiquette for tigers, people, or dogs (along with striped hyenas, sloth bears, and four-horned antelope in Khairi's case), play helped develop skills, physical strength, coordination, and 'combat experience' necessary for survival in the wild. Besides this, Blang, Khairi, and other cubs enjoyed it immensely. Khairi would playfully attack the moment anyone 'feign[ed] inattention' and turned away and would 'rush in hot pursuit' of anyone running away. As for Blang, 'immediately any moving object in the distance caught his eye he would crouch, head held low, body sunk between his shoulders, and a stalk would be commenced'. His tactics once perfected would have served him well in the wild. As the cub approached his quarry, 'he took advantage of all cover and any drain or depression, creeping along with only the top of his head visible'.[33] Ladies, Tamil coolies, 'Malay dandies', visiting Englishmen, and domestic animals were all stalked in this way.

Playfulness was a minor selling point for tiger cubs, alongside attestations of tractability, beauty, and health. An unusually detailed advertisement dating to 1785 describes the cubs on offer as 'very tame and playful', besides being 'elegant' and 'very fat'.[34] Playfulness, however, seems to have been taken for granted and other assurances were far more common. Of advertisements that provided qualitative descriptions, 47 per cent referred (singly or in combination) to the cub's temperament, 57 per cent to its health, and 38 per cent to physical beauty, unusual size, or general quality. Just 8 per cent singled out the animal's playfulness. Assuming sellers correctly perceived buyers' desires, prospective owners were in the market for well-behaved, worry-free, and attractive pets. They wanted tame tigers, not wild animals.

The quality of tameness was signalled by glossing the animal as docile, domesticated, peaceful, quiet, good tempered, tractable, or a great pet. Some were so little trouble that they could 'take care of themselves'.

Others 'had never been tied up', were 'hand-reared', or 'trained very easily'. One had 'never tasted blood'. These tigers would respond to discipline and follow orders. They would cause no disturbances and behave themselves in mixed company. Ideally, they would sit quietly until their owners chose to engage with them.[35] Most importantly, they would never view people as potential food.

Conventional wisdom supposed that a cub with no exposure to blood, especially human blood, remained innocent. With the taste of blood, its inherent nature as a killer would awaken. Kesri Singh became wary of his old pet Happy after the tiger, by then an adult living in the Maharaja of Jaipur's zoo, tasted human blood. According to Kesri Singh, this was a 'dangerous' development.[36] Following his theories regarding the genesis of man-eaters, the presumed danger arose either because Happy might have learned to view human bodies as food, or because he had discovered how easily human skin could be punctured and thus how conveniently people might be taken as prey. Had Happy's mother been a man-eater, Kesri Singh might have mistrusted him even earlier. One of his other pets, Hero, was just such a cub. Despite coming under suspicion, Hero gave no 'signs of inheriting his mother's enmity towards mankind and became a most amiable pet'.[37] Operating on similar assumptions, 'J.O.' reportedly withheld 'raw flesh' from his cub Selim, feeding the animal instead on bread, milk, and the occasional stew of 'well-cooked meat and potatoes'. Yet, Selim remained a loyal pet even after mauling a would-be assassin come to kill his master and tasting the villain's blood. According to the tiger's gravestone, which Colonel F. T. Pollok came across some decades later in southern Maratha territory, Selim ultimately 'lost his life in the defence of his master'.[38]

Even if a cub never tasted blood, popular opinion asserted that sooner or later, a tiger's 'savage nature' would show itself.[39] Most owners viewed their growing cubs as 'potential killer[s]', especially around children. If a cub forgot its size and strength for a moment, or misjudged the hardiness of a playmate, the outcome could be catastrophic.[40] The line between wild and tame was both insurmountable and, so long as one remained alert, temporarily and conditionally negotiable.

Morality, Messes, Punishment

The morality of removing tiger cubs from the wild and keeping them as pets is dubious at best, but more complex than it first appears. For most of the period under consideration, tigers were far from endangered: an estimated 40,000 lived in the wild in India in 1900.[41] Many or perhaps even the majority of cubs were taken only after their mother, sometimes an animal accused of killing people or domestic cattle, had been shot. Orphaned cubs too young to fend for themselves die without intervention. As for Khairi, had she not been taken captive she might have died too due to a bad case of worms.[42] Unnatural conditions in captivity are also a problem. Leaving aside for the moment the related issue of inhumane conditions, is there only one natural way for a tiger to live? The success of *Panthera tigris tigris* in the watery Sundarbans, semi-arid Rajasthan, and Anglo-Indian bungalows is striking evidence of a significant evolutionary advantage: adaptability. This did not make British or Indian homes ideal tiger habitats; far from it. Yet, it was not these human environments in of themselves—although sufficient space and opportunities for intraspecies socialization were often lacking—but the consequences of acting like a tiger in them that caused trouble for these animals.

One of the issues most likely to have irritated human owners goes nearly unmentioned in the historical record: bathroom habits and other bodily secretions. This leaves us with very little insight into how elimination and marking were handled.[43] Were undesirable placements of urine, dung, and scent gland secretions tolerated or punished? Tigers are naturally inclined to mark their territories and in the wild derive clear benefits from doing so, perhaps even a feeling of satisfaction, so punishment would represent a clear conflict of interest between species. People are quick to abandon pets that soil their beds and spray their walls: 'inappropriate' elimination is a major reason companion animals end up in shelters, and for which elderly or ailing pets are euthanized today. There is little reason to suppose Englishmen and Indians let such behaviours pass without response.

Corporeal punishment surely was attempted by many owners, even most, as a corrective measure but few reported in detail on this darker side of pet-keeping. One exception was Choudhury in the 1970s, whose disciplinary philosophy towards all members of his 'multispecies family' rested on 'the good old saying, "spare the rod and spoil the child" [which] is nowhere so true as with cubs—not vindictive, but corrective [and] with such love as makes your heart bleed'. Not only his heart, but on occasion Khairi, too.[44] Fifty years earlier, V.W. Ryves 'dragged' Blang by the tail and he and his staff regularly threatened the cub with canes and big sticks. But Ryves reported beating Blang only for 'committ[ing] some really naughty act'.[45] Exactly what registered as really naughty goes unsaid, but Ryves once gave Blang a 'thrashing' over a 'very dead cock'. Yet he generally considered pullicide 'a quite natural amusement' perfectly in line with his expectations for more familiar domestic animals, including cats and dogs.[46] A tentative conclusion, then, is that Blang transgressed when he acted in ways Ryves considered unnatural, or when he violated expectations established by the behaviours of more familiar pets. These parameters could conflict: stalking is a natural behaviour for tigers and Ryves recognized it as instinctive, but unlike when pursued by a ten pound tabby or twenty pound terrier, owners felt uncomfortable when their pet tigers cast them in the role of quarry.

How did cubs respond to corporeal punishment? Blang would become 'a regular little fury—all teeth and claws, giving vent to growls and deep, coughing grunts'. Khairi would 'snarl and growl her resentment' and take evasive action by attempting to leave the scene, appealing to her 'foster-mother', Choudhury's cousin Nihar, or by assuming a submissive position interpreted by onlookers as 'begging' Choudhury 'not to beat her'. Thirty minutes or so after a beating both Blang and Khairi would initiate a return to the status quo of affectionate relations with purring, prusten, and other vocalizations, and tentative physical contact including licking and pawing.[47] In contrast to Choudhury, Billy Arjan Singh believed that only an adult tiger was qualified to 'judge the significance and appropriate context of a disciplinary act', and was therefore loathe to punish Tara for rough play, including stalking and ambushing, because her future 'survival [would] depend on trigger-sharp and uninhibited reflexes'. He would bang on a tin 'to induce her to toe the line', but otherwise accepted shredded pants, torn socks, multiple bite wounds, and deep scratches, putting Tara's needs, as he understood them, before his own physical comfort and material concerns.[48] His goal was to release Tara into the wilderness, in contrast with Choudhury who viewed Khairi as a permanent family member and Ryves who foresaw Blang's future in a zoo. This surely factored into Billy Arjan Singh's willingness to let Tara be rather than attempting to reform her more thoroughly.

Removing pet tigers from the household and chaining or caging them out-of-doors, unlike corporeal punishment, was frequently reported, as was isolation in a specific room during unsupervised hours, fortified and outfitted for the purpose. Kesri Singh habitually kept Happy and Grumpy chained outdoors in the 1940s, while Montague Gilbert Gerard in the late 1870s reported doing the same with Parbutti when she was a 'somewhat overgrown pet' only in deference to a lady who moved into the cantonment and complained.[49] Although accustomed to restraints from a young age, Happy would 'tug furiously at his chain so as to be allowed to come and play' whenever he saw his owner.[50] Parbutti, on the other hand, lived 'loose' for almost a year, freely opening peoples' doors and 'loung[ing] up . . . to have her head scratched', before being confined near the stables in the shade of a mango tree. The transition must have been difficult for her.[51]

Cages were most common in the context of princely zoos and private menageries, but were also used to contain pet cubs. This was especially so for older cubs, but even young ones like the small male Charles Armstrong transported from Itarsi to Lahore in the 1920s were sometimes caged. Cages could and did cause problems. Master Billy was caged in Cochin in the 1830s; this protected people from Master Billy, but left him vulnerable to the walking-sticks, bamboo, and Chinese crackers that people pushed in through the bars.[52] Jack was caged for his journey from India to England and, before his final transfer to the zoo in London, slept in his cage in his caretaker's kitchen. Such cages were extremely small by today's standards; some were even commissioned before the animal had reached its full size, as notoriously happened with the first tiger owned by the Bombay zoo. Rather than commissioning a new, larger cage, zoo authorities chose to 'euthanize' the animal when it outgrew its accommodation.[53]

More so than cages—where negative side-effects such as stereotyped behaviour and muscle atrophy developed over time—ad hoc containers like blankets, bags, and boxes inflicted acute injuries on delicate cubs.[54] One English gentleman inadvertently killed his young cub by putting it in a box 'to keep it quiet'; it suffocated and died. Armstrong 'smothered' his cub while catching it; this animal survived and reportedly suffered no adverse effects.[55] Worn teeth from chewing on bars and ingrown claws from a lack of proper scratching facilities, too, were problems associated with long-term caging rather than short-term containment.

Another problem most obvious with caging but also relevant to chaining and confinement in a room is loneliness. People tend to think of tigers as a solitary species, but this is far from true when it comes to cubs and their immediate families, or their human caretakers and playmates. On the basis of his observations Saroj Raj Choudhury speculated that even after cubs are able to fend for [themselves] in the forest, they must be forced by their mothers to leave, so content are they in their 'cocoon of love and fellowship'.[56] Jack, a pet cub in the 1880s, 'most distinctly objected to . . . solitude, and would howl most miserably if left for a moment'.[57] Ryves would 'shut [Blang] up for the night at half past six' in a bathroom. Like Jack, Blang objected to solitude. He 'howled and meowed in the most heart-breaking way' from behind the door, which Ryves eventually had to outfit with 'extra bolts'. With few distractions and no companionship, Blang threw himself into destructive behaviour. He chewed through his bedding of empty sacks and reduced a wooden plank to 'small chips'. He played 'football' with a tin dipper and soap dish. He played in, knocked over, and rolled about the Shanghai jar, a thirty-gallon jug of bathwater. He made a racket bashing at a tin bath. He learned to turn on the tap. He habitually resisted by making himself scarce at 6:30 p.m. It was evident 'he hated being shut up'.[58] Perhaps his distress at confinement, and later his sexual maturity, helps explain his alleged transformation from the universally friendly if mischievous and occasionally imposing cub that Ryves knew in 1933 and 1934, to the notoriously unfriendly animal known to zoo-keepers in London zoo by 1935.[59]

Containment options represented something of a compromise between an animal's desire to move about, socialize, play, and mark as it pleased and the interests of its keeper. Owners hoped to preserve bedsheets and cushions, as well as their own skins. Consciously or not, they also avoided destabilizing the self-affirming and socially acceptable aspects of pet-keeping by masking the uncomfortable truth that caring for an orphaned cub usually followed the killing of the mother, the forcible capture of the cub, and the use of restraints to break it to its owner's hand. Kesri Singh dragged five cubs out of a cave with rope nooses in 1943 and George Sanderson relied on 'the assistance of a bull-terrier' in 1870.[60] Khairi's captors delivered her in chains with 'many coils of thick rope wound over the entire length of her body'. Armstrong 'fell on top' of his cub with a blanket. Back at camp he tied a rope around its neck which he attached to a peg in front. He added another rope around its middle, anchored to a peg behind. This limited the cub's range of movement sufficiently to prevent it from reaching or dislodging either peg. It also allowed Armstrong, by pulling the ropes taut, to completely immobilize and safely 'stroke' it. Plied with peafowl, milk, and boiled rice, the cub quickly adapted and took to purring (or perhaps prusten) within two days, though Armstrong continued using his elaborate restraints for several more days and soon had a wooden 'pinjaree' or cage made by a local villager. Of course, it is unclear exactly how else, on short notice and with no specialized equipment, he might have trapped a wild tiger cub suddenly bereft of its mother and unable to care for itself, yet perfectly capable of 'spitting fury . . . and clawing'.[61]

In moments of real or perceived crisis, cubs were killed. This was the fate of Billy, whose attention was diverted from chasing a young boy by a tempting quarter of beef, causing him to 'spring over the banisters' and fall to the pavement below with his prize, apparently breaking his back in the process. He was shot immediately to end his suffering.[62] Another older cub began licking a fresh wound on his master's knee and, drawing blood, snarled his refusal to stop. He was killed with a shotgun, the muzzle held against his head.[63] Tom, also known as 'Shitan' or devil, playfully waylaid a carriage, startling the horses and causing them to overturn the vehicle. The occupants, 'a lady and a gentleman' as opposed to the 'native servants' who were Tom's usual quarry—landed in a ditch and 'poor Tom had to be shot to prevent further mischief'. He was over 6 months old at the time, but still well under a year and far from full grown.[64] Another cub, possibly Parbutti, was shot while swimming towards land at Pointe de Galle after a shipwreck, en route from India to a British zoo.[65] Most owners, it seems, would not kill their cubs over offences to 'natives', nor did most act when adult males were the recipients of playful attacks, although enclosure or chaining were prompted by such behaviour. While Master Billy's youthful quarry recalled 'officers and civilians' dismissing that cub's charge as a show of good-natured 'bounding and frolicking', transgressions against English women and children seem to have been taken most seriously.

Conclusion

> I note that as you stop to stare
>   You hold your children tighter;
> An insult that, upon my word,
>   You ignorant old blighter.
> For if they'd only let me out
>   I'd walk about like Fido;
> In fact, I'd do a little more,
>   I'd bathe in Hyde Park Lido.[66]

As E.W. Flanagan's poem 'Blang to the Visitors at the Zoo' reminds us, tigers still suffered a negative reputation early in the twentieth century. Only by looking past the lingering nineteenth century stereotypes— the 'cruel' and 'savage' beast as embodiment of 'ferocious courage, bloodthirstiness, untamability'—and getting to know the tiger more intimately, could a creature as civilized and faithful as a dog, and perhaps even more so in its own way, be seen.[67] Yet, by 1935, Blang was 'one of the most fierce tigers' in the London Zoo, accused of viciously attacking an old acquaintance from his Malayan days through the bars of his cage.[68] Residents of British India and Malaya and their audiences abroad may have begun recognizing traits that they could and did deem admirable in tigers, even as tigers themselves retained their wild genes and their own interests. It was now possible to view adult tigers with a measure of compassion and wonder. Accounts of pet tigers aimed to secure a bit of understanding for the species in the hope that 'human intelligence would be sober and considerate enough to spare the tiger', even when the actions of individual animals reminded everyone that the species was undomesticated and not, despite considerable beauty and charm, a suitable pet after all.[69]

It is ultimately unclear precisely what advantages tigers as a species may have earned from these developments. Anything that helped improve their reputation, such as the lessons of pet-keeping, may well have prepped the ground for the slowly growing groundswell of big cat conservationism in the twentieth century. By explaining these animals' violence away as, alternately, an accident of high spirits, the natural byproduct of their diet, or a manifestation of maternal instincts, tigers became more sympathetic and natural—behaving exactly as a top predator ought to behave—although no less dangerous. In contrast, the violence of princes—whether social, economic, or, in a few sensational cases, physical—could not be naturalized. Tigerish princes in colonial times were caught between being intractably cruel Sher Khans and affectionately obedient Fidos destined nevertheless to stray. In independent India, they were unnatural and potentially predatory ex-rulers, who refused against the interests of the state and the people to let go of their status. In a final fit of irony, Indian princes lost their last remaining privileges with the abolition of their Privy Purses by the 26th Amendment of the Constitution of India in 1971, just two years before the Government of India launched Project Tiger, guaranteeing funding and other supports for in situ conservation of the species in the subcontinent.

Acknowledgements

Under a separate heading, my bibliography includes archival materials that I have not found occasion to cite individually but which, along with newspapers and periodicals, contributed to a database that allowed me to calculate trends in sales prices, cub availability, typical ages, and desirable characteristics. I have had engaging and productive discussions about pet tiger cubs at Vassar College and would particularly like to thank my former colleagues Rebecca Edwards, Sophie Harvey, Michael Walsh, Maratha Kaplan, Lynn Christenson and Pinar Batur, and everyone else I have 'talked tigers' with. At the University of Texas, Syed Akbar Hyder supported my topic with enthusiasm and understanding, just when it was most needed. Further afield, Mahesh Rangarajan, Divyabhanusinh, Rohan D'Souza, Ian J. Miller, Shafqat Hussain, Aaron Skabelund, Thomas R. Metcalf, Barbara D. Metcalf, Rima Hooja, Nigel Rothfels, Michele Elliot, Matthew Watson, and Arash Khazeni all generously shared their wisdom and knowledge in conversation or email at one point or another. On the institutional front, the archival staff of the British Library in London kindly showed me loose snapshots and photograph albums featuring pet tiger cubs in 2013, while the Imperial War Museum, National Army Museum, and Nehru Memorial Museum and Library's digitized and freely available online collections proved invaluable. Last but certainly not least, I dedicate this to Gail Minault for graciously accepting and indefatigably supporting my unanticipated turn as a graduate student towards human-animal and environmental history. Any errors or omissions are entirely my own.

Notes

1. I have drawn throughout this paragraph from Kate Brittlebank, 'Shakti and Barakat: The Power of Tipu's Tiger, An Examination of the Tiger Emblem of Tipu Sultan of Mysore', *Modern Asian Studies*, vol. 29, no. 2, 1995, pp. 257–60.
2. Anand S. Pandian, 'Predatory Care: The Imperial Hunt in Mughal and British India', *Journal of Historical Sociology*, vol. 14, no. 1, 2001, pp. 83–4.
3. Kesri Singh, *Hints on Tiger Shooting: Tigers by Tiger*, New Delhi: Hindustan Times Ltd., 1965, p. 85.
4. More thorough discussions of the making of pets and their appropriate treatment in scholarship and beyond are available. In particular, see Yi-Fu Tuan, *Dominance and Affection: The Making of Pets*, New Haven: Yale University Press, 1984; Donna Haraway, *When Species Meet*, Minneapolis: University of Minnesota Press, 2008; James A. Serpell, 'People in Disguise: Anthropomorphism and the Human-Pet Relationship', in *Thinking with Animals: New Perspectives on Anthropomorphism*, ed. Lorraine Daston and Gregg Mitman, pp. 121–36, New York: Columbia University Press, 2005.

5. For a fairly conservative scientific perspective on emotions in dogs, see Alexandra Horowitz, *Inside of a Dog*, New York: Scribner, 2009, pp. 29–31; for cats, see John Bradshaw, *Cat Sense*, New York: Basic Books, 2013, pp. 190–2; for more species and less conservative views, see Marc Bekoff, *The Emotional Lives of Animals*, Novato, CA: New World Library, 2007.
6. The alarming number of white tigers bred, or rather inbred, for this recessive genetic trait in the United States today, on the other hand, might qualify.
7. 'Tiger Cub', Advertisement, *The Times of India*, 12 December 1919; 'Snow Leopards and Tiger', Advertisement, *The Tribune*, 29 October 1913.
8. Khairi was named for the river Khairi, where she was found. 'Blang' means 'striped or mottled'.
9. Oliver Sandys, 'The Captive', *English Review*, November 1913, p. 598; A.B. 'Haidee', *Bow Bells, A Magazine of General Literature and Art for Family Reading*, vol. 10, no. 130, 27 June 1890, p. 608; Ruskin Bond, 'A Tiger in the House', *The Times of India*, 10 March 1963.
10. H.J.B., 'The History of "Jack", a Young Tiger', *Leisure Hour*, November 1888, p. 764.
11. The number of tigers noted in newspapers does not correlate ($r^2 = 0.108$) with the number of newspapers in the databases consulted (Eighteenth Century Journals: A Portal to Newspapers and Periodicals, *c*.1685–1835; ProQuest Historical Newspapers: *The Times of India*, 1838–2006; World Newspaper Archive: South Asian Newspapers, 1865–1922), suggesting that these are actual increases in tigers or in the practice of advertising tigers, rather than some side-effect of more or less issues available for consultation in any given year.
12. 'Behind the Scenes at the Zoo, the Ape Who Smoked a Pipe', *Amrit Bazar Patrika*, 9 July 1914.
13. K. Sivaramakrishnan, *Modern Forests: Statemaking and Environmental Change in Colonial Eastern India*, Stanford, CA: Stanford University Press, 1999, p. 101.
14. 'Tiger Rewards', *Madras Mail*, 11 Decmber 1883; 'News in a Nutshell', *The Times of India*, 12 October 1891.
15. 'Proceedings of an Ordinary Meeting of the Delhi Municipality', *The Pioneer*, 23 May 1873.
16. *Statistical Abstract Relating to British India from 1876/7 to 1885/6*, no. 21, London: Her Majesty's Stationary Office, 1887, table 150; *Statistical Abstract Relating to British India from 1885–86 to 1894–95*, no. 30, London: Her Majesty's Stationary Office, 1896, table 151.
17. Evgeny N. Smirnov and Dale G. Miquelle, 'Population Dynamics of the Amur Tiger in Sikhote-Alin Zapovednik, Russia', in *Riding the Tiger: Tiger Conservation in Human Dominated Landscapes*, ed. John Seidensticker, Sarah Christie and Peter Jackson, Cambridge: Cambridge University Press, 1999, p. 68. I averaged the sex ratios for Kanha (5:1) and Royal Chitwan (2.25:1);

percentage of females with cubs is from Kanha; average litter size is from Royal Chitwan.

18. 'White Tiger: An Indian Maharaja is Trying to Sell His Rare Cub to a U.S. Zoo', *Life*, vol. 31, no. 69, 15 October 1951, pp. 69–72; John Kluge purchased Mohini, one of Mohan's white offspring, for $10,000 in 1960; she was delivered to the White House lawn and later presented to the Smithsonian Institution, 'Ike, Priceless White Tigress Meet on Lawn', *Chicago Daily Tribune*, 6 December 1960; in 1963, the Maharaja of Rewa agreed to sell a pair of Mohan's cubs to the Bristol Zoo for £6,500, 'White Tigers of Rewa for Bristol Zoo', *The Times*, 31 May 1963.

19. A few outliers well over a year old brought the average up to 7 months. Also a function of those outliers, the standard deviation was notably high at 5.17. Given that only 23 of the 78 cubs were over 7 months old, and only 9 a year old or more the median is a better, single statistical representative in this case than the average.

20. V.W. Ryves, *Blang, My Tiger: The Story of a Pet Malayan Tiger Cub*, London: Arrowsmith, 1935, p. 127; Tiger Cub, Advertisement, *The Times of India*, 12 December 1919; Saroj Raj Choudhury, *Khairi the Beloved Tigress*, Dehradun: Natraj Publishers, 1999, pp. 8, 16, 23.

21. Tuan, *Dominance and Affection*, pp. 88–9, 101.

22. 'The Tame Tiger', *Sheffield & Rotherham Independent*, 23 December 1876.

23. Anak Singapura, 'Notes of the Day', *Straits Times*, 10 June 1935.

24. K. Singh, *Hints on Tiger Shooting*, pp. 43–4, 50.

25. 'Notes of the Day'.

26. Choudhury, *Khairi*, pp. 126, 108.

27. Ibid., pp. 46–7.

28. Arjan Singh, *Tara a Tigress*, New York: Quartet Books, 1981, p. 55.

29. 'Tame Tigress', Advertisement, *Madras Mail*, 12 June 1886; 'A Real Royal Tiger', Advertisement, *Bombay Courier*, 18 June 1808.

30. Montague Gilbert Gerard, *Leaves from the Diaries of a Soldier and Sportsman During Twenty Years' Service in India, Afghanistan, Egypt and Other Countries, 1865–1885*, London: John Murray, 1903, p. 217.

31. A. Singh, *Tara a Tigress*, pp. 16, 18.

32. Kesri Singh, *One Man and a Thousand Tigers*, New York: Dodd, Mead & Company, 1959, p. 149; for Khairi's reaction after accidentally biting Nihar as a 9 month old, see Choudhury, *Khairi*, p. 108.

33. Ryves, *Blang*, pp. 56–7.

34. 'Royal Tigers', Advertisement, *Calcutta Gazette, or Oriental Advertiser*, 17 November 1785.

35. Tuan, *Dominance and Affection*, p. 107.

36. K. Singh, *Hints on Tiger Shooting*, p. 83.

37. K. Singh, *One Man and a Thousand Tigers*, p. 146.

38. F.T. Pollock, 'Faithful Unto Death, the Story of a Pet Tiger', *Wide World Magazine*, vol. 4, no. 21, December 1899, pp. 297–8. 'J.O.' was probably

Lieut. John William Willoughby Osborne, Political Agent at Bhopal, 1862–74, 1875–6, and 1878–9, and Gwalior, 1874–5 and 1880–1.
39. H.J.B., 'History of "Jack", a Young Tiger', p. 764.
40. Ryves, *Blang*, p. 95. Khairi accidentally killed Manika, a four-horned antelope, see Choudhury, *Khairi*, p. 25.
41. Charles McDougal, extract from *The Face of the Tiger* (1977), in *Saving Wild Tigers, 1900–2000: The Essential Writings*, ed. Valmik Thapar, New Delhi: Permanent Black, 2001, p. 189. The estimate is E.P. Gee's.
42. Choudhury, *Khairi*, preface. One might object that natural selection was thereby subverted.
43. Charles Douglas Armstrong, interview by Conrad Wood, 5 August 1977, cat. no. 959, Imperial War Museum Sound Archive, http://www.iwm.org.uk/collections/item/object/80000953, accessed 10 June 2015. Armstrong laid newspaper down for his month old cub's 'morning dump' while in transit from Itarsi to Lahore via train in the 1920s, and disposed of it out the window.
44. Choudhury, *Khairi*, pp. 14, 123.
45. Ryves, *Blang*, pp. 77, 94.
46. Ibid., pp. 43–4.
47. Choudhury, *Khairi*, pp. 27, 129; Ryves, *Blang*, pp. 89–90.
48. A. Singh, *Tara a Tigress*, pp. 23–4, 31.
49. Gerard, *Leaves from the Diaries of a Soldier and Sportsman*, p. 218.
50. K. Singh, *One Man and a Thousand Tigers*, p. 149.
51. Gerard, *Leaves from the Diaries of a Soldier and Sportsman*, p. 217.
52. 'Tigers in India', *Leisure Hour* 297, 3 September 1857, p. 567.
53. E.H.A, 'The Karachi Zoo: A Lesson for Bombay', *The Times of India*, 12 August 1903.
54. K. Singh, *One Man and a Thousand Tigers*, p. 148.
55. Armstrong, interview, 5 August 1977.
56. Choudhury, *Khairi*, p. 135.
57. H.J.B., 'The History of 'Jack', p. 764.
58. Ryves, *Blang*, pp. 41, 35–7.
59. 'Tame Tiger Goes Wild', *Canberra Times*, 11 July 1935.
60. Choudhury, *Khairi*, p. 4; K. Singh, *One Man and a Thousand Tigers*, pp. 146–7; George P. Sanderson, *Thirteen Years Among the Wild Beasts of India*, London: William H. Allen & Co., 1879, p. 259.
61. Armstrong, interview, 5 August 1977
62. 'Tigers in India', pp. 567–8.
63. K. Singh, *One Man and a Thousand Tigers*, p. 154.
64. O.W., 'A Pet Tiger', *Chatterbox* 47, 10 October 1885, p. 369.
65. Gerard, *Leaves from the Diaries of a Soldier and Sportsman*, p. 218. There were two cubs on board; one was shot in the water and one drowned.
66. E.W. Flanagen, 'Blang to the Visitors at the Zoo', pp. 125–6, in Ryves, *Blang*, p. 126.

67. W. Lauder Lindsay, *Mind in the Lower Animals*, New York: D. Appleton and Company, 1880, pp. 83, 85. Note that the Latin name 'Fido' as a root occurs in fidelity, confidence, and confide.
68. 'Tame Tiger Goes Wild', *Canberra Times*, 11 July 1935.
69. Choudhury, *Khairi*, p. 88.

References

ARCHIVAL MATERIAL

'Jawaharlal Nehru with Raja and Rani, 2–4 month old tiger cubs, presented to him by Algurai Shastri, U.P. Forest Minister, New Delhi, 17 May 1961'. Photograph, Nehru Memorial Museum and Library, New Delhi.
'"Plassey", the Pet Tiger of the Royal Madras Fusiliers, *c*.1870'. Carte de Visite Photograph, Acc. No. 1964-08-341-2. National Army Museum, London.
'Prime Minister, Jawaharlal Nehru, playing with tiger cubs at the PM's House on 12/8/55'. Photograph, Nehru Memorial Museum and Library, New Delhi.
'"Sheila" at Raipur, 1936'. Ramsden Collection, Photo 472/25 (132–3). British Library, London.
'Skull of "Plassey", the Pet Tiger of the 102nd Regiment of Foot (Royal Madras Fusiliers), *c*.1870'. Acc. No. 1958-02-34-1-1. National Army Museum, London.'Tiger Cub & Dog'. Hands & Son, Photographers, Jubbulpore, C.P., India, *c*.1900. Lechmere-Oertel Collection, Photo 261/(358), British Library, London.

WORKS CITED

Armstrong, Charles Douglas, Interview by Conrad Wood, 5 August 1977. Cat. No. 959. Imperial War Museum Sound Archive, London.
Bond, Ruskin, 'A Tiger in the House', *The Times of India*, 10 March 1963.
Choudhury, Saroj Raj, *Khairi the Beloved Tigress*, Dehradun: Natraj Publishers, 1999.
Flanagen, E.W., 'Blang to the Visitors at the Zoo', in *Blang, My Tiger*, ed. V.W. Ryves, London: Arrowsmith, 1935, pp. 125–6.
———, 'Master Blang', in *Blang, My Tiger*, ed. V.W. Ryves, London: Arrowsmith, 1935, pp. 103–4
Gerard, Montague Gilbert, *Leaves from the Diaries of a Soldier and Sportsman During Twenty Years' Service in India, Afghanistan, Egypt and Other Countries*, London: John Murray, 1903.
'Haidee', A.B., *Bow Bells, A Magazine of General Literature and Art for Family Reading*, 27 June 1890.
H.J.B., 'The History of "Jack", a Young Tiger', *Leisure Hour*, November 1888.
Lindsay, W. Lauder, *Mind in the Lower Animals*, New York: D. Appleton and Company, 1880.

McDougal, Charles, Extract from *The Face of the Tiger*, 1977, in *Saving Wild Tigers, 1900–2000: The Essential Writings*, ed. Valmik Thapar, pp. 181–96, New Delhi: Permanent Black, 2001.
O.W., 'A Pet Tiger', *Chatterbox*, 10 October 1885.
Pollock, F.T, 'Faithful Unto Death: The Story of a Pet Tiger', *Wide World Magazine*, December 1899.
Ryves, V.W., *Blang, My Tiger: The Story of a Pet Malayan Tiger Cub*, London: Arrowsmith, 1935.
Sanderson, George P., *Thirteen Years Among the Wild Beasts of India*, London: William H. Allen & Co., 1879.
Sandys, Oliver, 'The Captive', *English Review*, November 1913.
Singh, Arjan, *Tara a Tigress*, New York: Quartet Books, 1981.
Singh, Kesri, *Hints on Tiger Shooting: Tigers by Tiger*, New Delhi: Hindustan Times Limited, 1965.
———, *One Man and a Thousand Tigers*, New York: Dodd, Mead & Company, 1959.
Sivaramakrishnan, K., *Modern Forests: Statemaking and Environmental Change in Colonial Eastern India*, Stanford, CA: Stanford University Press, 1999.
Smirnov, Evgeny N., and Dale G. Miquelle, 'Population Dynamics of the Amur Tiger in Sikhote-Alin Zapovednik, Russia', in *Riding the Tiger: Tiger Conservation in Human Dominated Landscapes*, ed. John Seidensticker, Sarah Christie and Peter Jackson, Cambridge: Cambridge University Press, 1999, pp. 61–70.
Statistical Abstract Relating to British India from 1876/7 to 1885/6, London: Her Majesty's Stationery Office, 1887.
Statistical Abstract Relating to British India from 1885–86 to 1894–95, London: Her Majesty's Stationary Office, 1896.
'The Tame Tiger', *Sheffield & Rotherham Independent*, 23 December 1876.
'Tigers in India', *Leisure Hour*, 3 September 1857.
Tuan, Yi-Fu, *Dominance and Affection: The Making of Pets*, New Haven: Yale University Press, 1984.
'White Tiger: An Indian Maharaja is Trying to Sell His Rare Cub to a U.S. Zoo', *Life*, 15 October 1951.

A Tribute to Gail Minault

ISHRAT AFREEN
MAX BRUCE
IMRAN KHAN

Khirāj-e ʿaqīdat
(ISHRAT AFREEN)

tārīkh . . . jādū kī nagrī hai
jādū kī nagrī mēṅ dākhil to hotē haiṅ sab
vāpsī kā yahāṅ koī rastah nahīṅ

bām-o-dar is kē tum sē lipaṭ jāʾēṅgē
rāstē pāoṅ pakṛēṅgē
aur pēṛ hāthoṅ ko joṛē khaṛē
iltijāʾēṅ karēṅgē
to tum kiyā karogī
subukdosh ho kar bhī kēsē subukdosh hogī

karēṅgē ghanṭāhghar
(jis kī āvāz dīvānah kar dētī hai)
tum sē haṅs kar kahēgā
tumhārē sabhī rāz, sab rāt din
mērī muṭhī mēṅ haiṅ
maiṅ subukdosh honē nah dūṅgā tumhēṅ

tum jo guzrē zamānoṅ sē ātē zamānoṅ kē bīc
ēk pul roshnī kā
yah pul . . . jis kē qadmoṅ mēṅ behtā hai pānī
yah pānī . . . jo tārīkh hai . . . vaqt hai . . . zindagī hai
yah jab tak bahēgā
khirāj-e ʿaqīdat tumhēṅ pēsh kartā rahēgā
khirāj-e muḥabbat tumhēṅ pēsh kartā rahēgā

A Tribute
(TRANSLATION BY IMRAN KHAN)

History ... the valley of enchantment
All can step into the valley
Yet, it has no exits

Its columns and pavilions will embrace you
The roads leading to it will trap you
The trees lining it with folded hands
Will beseech you
Then what will you do?
Even after freeing yourself how will you gain freedom?

The mighty clock tower stands
The bells of which drive you insane
Laughingly it will tell you
All your secrets, your days and nights
Are captive in my grip
I will not let you ... let go of me

You, the bridge of light between the bygone days and the days to come
This bridge that stands tall above the flowing water
This water that is history, time, life
For as long as it flows
It will offer you tributes
Tributes of love are its offering to you

Malālā 'Ilm kī Sham'a
(ISHRAT AFREEN)

Malālā agar muskurātī
to un kā bhalā kyā bigaṛtā us mēṅ
keh jo ghāt mēṅ thē
voh hamjoliyoṅ mēṅ agar mil kē gātī
du'ā lab peh Iqbāl kī jo voh lātī
yah choṭī sī bastī kī bāsī
agar 'ilm kī shama' ghar ghar jalātī
Malālā agar apnī manzil ko pātī
to un kā bhalā kyā bigaṛtā thā us mēṅ
keh jo ghāt mēṅ thē
yah kamsin Sawātī

keh jis kā jahāṅ us kī choṭī sī bastī thī
yā ēk raṅgīn bastah...
voh iqrā' kā rastah...
keh jo us kē āqā-ē ummī-e laqab kī 'aṭā thā
Malālā ko lēkin kahāṅ yah patah thā
Keh iqrā' kē rastē mēṅ qazzāq bhī haiṅ
Malālā to bas apnī dhun mēṅ magan...
'ilm kē rāstē par caltī jā rahī thī...
usē kyā k͟habar thī
keh voh 'ilm dushman
kamīṅ gāh mēṅ chup kē baiṭhē hū'ē haiṅ
voh āṅkhēṅ...
jinhēṅ bacciyoṅ kā ko'ī rūp bhātā nahīṅ
jinhēṅ bacpanā hī naẓrāṅ mēṅ ātā nahīṅ
voh shahvat zadah żehen...
jo laṛkiyoṅ kī bulūġhat sē sehmē hū'ē haiṅ
kahīṅ tāk mēṅ haiṅ
to voh din bhī āyā
keh iqrā' kā rastah lahū ho gayā
voh aurāq jin par yah alfāẓ likhē hū'ē thē
'shurū' pāk Allah kē nām sē'
voh aurāq sab k͟hāk aur k͟hūṅ mēṅ lathṛē hū'ē thē
sabhī dhajyāṅ ban kē bikhrē hū'ē thē
keh vādī kē sab mehr-o-anjum mah-o lālah sehmē hū'ē thē
aur iqrā' kē dushman yahī cāhtē thē
keh bastī ko dehshat nishāṅ kar kē choṛēṅ
yahī un kā maḥbūbtar mashġhalah thā
Malālā ko'ī jo kahīṅ sar uṭhā'ē
... kabhī lab hilā'ē
usē darbadar
nīm jāṅ kar kē choṛēṅ
magar shāyad un ko k͟habar nahīṅ hai
Malālā to ab bhī vahīṅ hai!
unhī bastīyoṅ kē andhērē gharoṅ mēṅ...
voh ummīd kī roshnī ban kē ab jāgazīṅ hai
keh rātoṅ ko aksar
kahānī 'bahādur Malālā kī baccoṅ ko apnē sunātī haiṅ mā'ēṅ
usī nām kē gīt gātī haiṅ mā'ēṅ
keh ab loriyoṅ mēṅ usē gungunātī haiṅ mā'ēṅ

Malala the Light of Knowledge
(TRANSLATION BY IMRAN KHAN)

If Malala had reached her destination
How could it harm them?
Those who lie in ambush
When she sang with her playmates
When she brought Iqbal's dū'ā to her lips
This girl from a small town
Lighting the lamp of knowledge house after house
How could it harm them?
Those who lie in ambush
This young one from the valley of Swat
She, whose world is small
Perhaps a colorful backpack . . .
A way to the divine . . .
The world granted by the master who taught her
But how could Malala know
Waiting for her were bandits
Malala, content in conviction
Continued to walk
She did not know,
The foes of knowledge
Are hiding in ambush
Those eyes
Those not awed by the form of girls
Who cannot see the innocence of childhood
Those lecherous minds
Afraid that girls will come of age
They waited for her
That day did come
The path to the divine flowed with blood
Those pages, graced with words
'Begin in the name of Allah the pure'
Those pages, all of them smeared with blood, tainted with dust
Spread in shreds
To the shame of the sun, the stars, and the moon
The foes of knowledge wanted just this;
Reduce her turf to terror
This was their favorite hobby
Whenever any Malala raises her head

... moves her lips
She shall be exiled,
Half dead
Perhaps they did not realize;
Malala is still there
Still dwelling in the twilight of those houses
Turning into the light of hope she is set
Frequently during dark nights
Mothers sing songs, adorn their lullabies, and tell the story
Of 'Bahadur Malala', The Brave Malala

ummīd bharī āṅkheṅ (Ishrat Afreen)	**Hope-filled eyes** (Max Bruce)
voh dhūl bharā rastah	that dust-filled path
us dhūl sē rastē par	on that dust-like path
ik phūl sā baccah thā	was a flower-like child
pairoṅ meṅ sanī kīchaṛ	mud smeared on his feet
bāloṅ meṅ aṭī miṭṭī	clay caked in his hair
aur hāth meṅ kāsah thā	and a beggar's bowl in his hands
maiṅ nē jo usē dēkhā	when I saw him
pal bhar ko k͟hayāl āyā	for just a moment I thought
jān us sē churānā ab	to run for my life now
mushkil naẓar ātā hai	looks difficult
rah rah kē ṣadā dēgā	again and again he'll call out
do roz sē bhūkā hūṅ	I haven't eaten for two days
kuch ḍāl do jholī meṅ	put something in my pouch
yah dhyān meṅ ātē hī	as soon as I thought of this
raftār baṛhī mērī	my pace quickened
kuch dūr magar jā kar	but after going a ways
dēkhā jo palaṭ kar to	when I turned around and looked
hāthoṅ meṅ liyē kāsah	bowl in hand
k͟hāmosh nigāhoṅ sē	with silent eyes
vuh yūṅ mujhē taktā thā	he was staring at me
jaisē mirī ġhurbat par	as if laughing from afar
vuh dūr sē haṅstā ho	at my poverty
ghabrā kē maiṅ phir palṭī	worried, I turned around again

us dhūl sē rastē par	on that dust-like path
us phūl sē baccē ko	that flower-like child
lēkin usē kahīn nahīn pāyā	I didn't find anywhere
yah vāqi'ah guzrē bhī	though this incident happened
ik 'umr hu'ī lēkin	a lifetime ago
vuh phūl sā ik baccah	that single flower-like child
rahtā thā ta'āqub mēn	remained in pursuit
hāthon mēn liyē kāsah	bowl in hand
khāmosh nigāhon sē	with silent eyes
aksar mujhē taktā thā	he often stared at me
jī chāhtā thā baṛh kar	I wanted to go over
bāhon mēn usē bhar lūn	and scoop him into my arms
ānchal sē żarā ponchūn	and wipe with my shawl-hem
gālon pah ṭikē ānsū	the tears stuck to his cheeks
bālon mēn aṭī miṭṭī	the clay caked in his hair
aur pyār usē kar lūn	and show him love
ik bār to voh hans dē	that just once he might laugh
jab hāth baṛhātī thī	when I reached out my hand
kuch hāth nah ātā thā	I got hold of nothing
kal shām voh phir āyā	last evening he came back
main cīkh paṛī goyā	I cried out saying
tum kaun ho aē baccē?	who are you, o child?
aur kis liyē ātē ho?	and why do you come?
pahlē to voh kuch ṭhiṭkā	at first he stopped short
ummīd bharī ānkhēn	hope-filled eyes
phir mujh sē hu'īn goyā	then spoke to me again
tum nē nahīn pahcānā?	don't you recognize me?
yah dhūl bharā rastah	this dust-filled path
tārīkh ka dorāhā	crossroads of history
is dhūl sē rastē par	on this dust-like path
main phūl sā baccah hūn	I am a flower-like child
insān ka mustaqbil	the future of humanity
is phūl sē baccē kī	this flower-like child's
ummīd bharī ānkhēn	hope-filled eyes
ab bhī tumhēn taktī hain	still stare at you

tum māṅ ho, tumhārā dil	you are a mother, your heart
ummīd kā maskan hai	is hope's abode
hai ab bhī yaqīṅ mujh ko	I am still sure
tum lauṭ kē ā'ogī	you will come back
kāsah mirā toṛogī	you'll break my bowl
hāthoṅ mēṅ qalam dogī	you'll put a pen in my hands
tum mujh ko bacā logī!	you will save me!
tum mujh ko bacā logī!	you will save me!

A List of Gail Minault's Publications

BOOKS

(Edited), *The Extended Family: Women and Political Participation in India and Pakistan*, Columbia, Missouri: South Asia Books; Delhi: Chanakya Publications, 1981.

The Khilafat Movement: Religious Symbolism and Political Mobilization in India, New York: Columbia University Press; Delhi: Oxford University Press, 1982; paperback edn., 1999.

(Edited with Hanna Papanek), *Separate Worlds: Studies of Purdah in South Asia*, Columbia: South Asia Books; Delhi: Chanakya Publications, 1982.

Voices of Silence: Khwaja Altaf Husain Hali's Majalis un-Nissa (Assemblies of Women) and Chup ki Dad (Homage to the Silent), tr. into English with Introduction, Notes, Glossary, and Bibliography, Delhi: Chanakya Publications, 1986, http://www.columbia.edu/itc/mealac/pritchett/00urdu/hali/index.html, accessed 10 June 2017.

(Edited with Christian W. Troll), *Abul Kalam Azad: An Intellectual and Religious Biography, by the late Ian H. Douglas*, Delhi: Oxford University Press, 1988.

Secluded Scholars: Women's Education and Muslim Social Reform in Colonial India, Delhi: Oxford University Press, 1998; paperback edn., 1999.

Gender, Language, and Learning: Essays in Indo-Muslim Cultural History, Delhi: Permanent Black, 2009.

ARTICLES

'Akbar and Aurangzeb: Syncretism and Separatism in Mughal India—A Reexamination', *Muslim World*, vol. LIX, no. 2, April 1969, pp. 106–26.

'Islam and Mass Politics: The Indian Ulama and the Khilafat Movement', in *Religion and Political Modernization*, ed. Donald E. Smith, New Haven: Yale University Press, 1974, pp. 168–82.

(With David Lelyveld), 'The Campaign for a Muslim University', *Modern Asian Studies*, vol. VIII, no. 2, April 1974, pp. 145–89.

'Urdu Political Poetry during the Khilafat Movement', *Modern Asian Studies*, vol. VIII, no. 4, October 1974, pp. 459–71.

'Religious Symbolism and Political Mobilization: A Reinterpretation of the Khilafat Movement', in *Islam in Southern Asia*, ed. Dietmar Rothermund, Wiesbaden: Franz Steiner Verlag, 1975, pp. 37–9, 42–3.

'The Role of Indo-Muslim Women in the Freedom Movement', *South Asia Papers* (Lahore), vol. I, no. 3, March 1977, pp. 21–36.

'*Tehrik-e-Khilafat ke Daur ke Siyasi Sha'iri*', Urdu translation of: 'Urdu Political Poetry during the Khilafat Movement'), *Qaumi Zuban*, Karachi, June 1977, pp. 18–21.

'Urdu-Speaking Muslims of North India and Pakistan', in *Muslim Peoples: A World Ethnographic Survey*, ed. Richard V. Weekes, Westport, CT: Greenwood Press, 1978, pp. 454–60, 2nd revd. edn., 1984, pp. 823–30.

'Muslim Women in Conflict with Purdah: Their Role in the Indian Nationalist Movement', in *Asian Women in Transition*, ed. Sylvia Chipp and Justin J. Green, University Park, PA: Pennsylvania State University Press, 1980, pp. 194–203.

'Homage to the Silent: A Translation of Hali's *Chup ki Dad*', *Urdu Studies Annual*, vol. I, 1981, pp. 46–56.

'The Extended Family as Metaphor and the Expansion of Women's Realm', in *The Extended Family: Women and Political Participation in India and Pakistan*, ed. Gail Minault, Columbia, MO: South Asia Books; Delhi: Chanakya, 1981, pp. 3–18.

'Sisterhood or Separatism? The All-India Muslim Ladies' Conference and Indian Nationalism', in *The Extended Family: Women and Political Participation in India and Pakistan*, ed. Gail Minault, Columbia, MO: South Asia Books; Delhi: Chanakya, 1981, pp. 83–108.

'Purdah Politics: The Role of Muslim Women in the Indian Nationalist Movement, 1911-1924', in *Separate Worlds: Studies of Purdah in South Asia*, ed. Hanna Papanek and Gail Minault, Columbia: South Asia Books; Delhi: Chanakya, 1982, pp. 245–61.

'Purdah's Progress: The Beginnings of School Education for Indian Muslim Women', in *Individuals and Ideas in Modern India*, ed. J.P. Sharma, Calcutta: Firma KLM, 1982, pp. 76–97.

'Through a Glass Darkly: Naipaul's Post-Colonial Travel Accounts', *Osmania Journal of English Studies*, Hyderabad, Special Number, 1982, pp. 15–24.

'At Odds or In Tune with the Family? Some Reflections on Women's Activism in Indian and American History', *Indian Journal of American Studies*, vol. XIII, no. 2, July 1983, pp. 27–35. Reprinted in Amritjit Singh, Max Skidmore, and Isaac Sequeira, eds., *American Studies Today: An Introduction to Methods and Perspectives*, Delhi: Creative Books, 1995, pp. 394–403.

'Hali's *Majalis un-Nissa*: Purdah and Woman Power in Nineteenth-Century India', in *Islamic Society and Culture: Essays in Honour of Professor*, ed. Aziz Ahmad, M. Israel and N.K. Wagle, Delhi: Manohar Book Service, 1983, pp. 39–49.

'Shaikh Abdullah, Begam Abdullah, and *Sharif* Education for Girls at Aligarh', in *Modernization and Social Change among Muslims in India*, ed. Imtiaz Ahmad, Delhi: Manohar Book Service, 1983, pp. 207–36.

'Women and History: Some Theoretical Considerations', *Samya Shakti: A Journal of Women's Studies*, vol. I, no. 1, July 1983, pp. 59–62.

'*Begamati Zuban*: Women's Language and Culture in Nineteenth-Century Delhi', *India International Centre Quarterly*, vol. 11, no. 2, June 1984, pp. 155–70.

'Laila' (short story), *Choice India*, vol. I, no. 3, October 1984, pp. 29–31.

'Scholars and Activists: The Indian Association of Women's Studies Conference at Trivandrum', *Choice India*, vol. I, no. 1, August 1984, pp. 37–8.

'Some Reflections on Islamic Revivalism vs. Assimilation among Muslims in India', *Contributions to Indian Sociology*, vol. 18, no. 2, July–December 1984, pp. 301–5.

'Urdu Niswan Press: Samaji Tarikh ka Makhaz' (The Urdu Women's Press as a Source for Social History), tr. into Urdu by Sayyid Shahabuddin Desnavi, *Jamia*, vol. 81, no. 5, May 1984, pp. 7–16.

'Women's Education and Social Change among Indian Muslims in Historical Perspective', *Journal of Muslim Minority Affairs*, vol. VI, no. 1, Jiddah, January 1985, pp. 88–97.

'Making Invisible Women Visible: Studying the History of Muslim Women in South Asia', *South Asia*, vol. IX, no. 1, June 1986, pp. 1–13.

'Sayyid Ahmad Dehlavi and the Delhi Renaissance', in *Delhi Through the Ages: Essays in Urban History, Culture, and Society*, ed. Robert Eric Frykenberg, Delhi: Oxford University Press, 1986, pp. 287–98.

'Women in Contemporary India: The Quest for Equal Participation and Justice', in *India 2000: The Next Fifteen Years*, ed. James Roach, Riverdale MD: Riverdale Company, 1986, pp. 215–28.

'Urdu Women's Magazines in the Early Twentieth Century', *Manushi: Journal of Women and Society*, vol. 48, September–October 1988, pp. 2–9.

'Legal and Scholarly Activism: Recent Women's Studies in India: A Review Article', *Journal of Asian Studies*, vol. 47, no. 4, November 1988, pp. 814–20.

'*Ismat*: Rashid ul-Khairi's Novels and Urdu Literary Journalism for Women', in *Urdu and Muslim South Asia: Studies in Honour of Ralph Russell*, ed. Christopher Shackle, London: School of Oriental and African Studies, 1989, pp. 129–38.

'Sayyid Mumtaz Ali and *Huquq un-Niswan*: An Advocate of Women's Rights in Islam in the Late Nineteenth Century', *Modern Asian Studies*, vol. 24, no. 1, February 1990, pp. 147–72.

'Sayyid Mumtaz Ali and *Tahzib un-Niswan*: Women's Rights in Islam and Women's Journalism in Urdu', in *Religious Controversy in British India: Dialogues in South Asian Languages*, ed. Kenneth W. Jones Albany: State University of New York Press, 1992, pp. 179–99.

'The Elusive Maulana: Reflections on Writing Azad's Biography', in *Islam and*

Indian Nationalism: Reflections on Abul Kalam Azad, ed. Mushirul Hasan, Delhi: Manohar, 1992, pp. 17–27.

'The School for Wives: The Ideal Woman as Educated Muslim', Aziz Ahmad Memorial Lecture for 1993, Centre for South Asian Studies, University of Toronto, 1993.

'Indian Muslims' Reaction to the Abolition of the Caliphate in 1924: The Collapse of a Nationalist Political Alliance', *Annales de l'Autre Islam*, no. 2, Paris: INALCO, 1994, pp. 245–60.

'Other Voices, Other Rooms: The View from the *Zenana*', in *Women as Subjects*, ed. Nita Kumar, Calcutta: Stree; Charlottesville, VA: University Press of Virginia, 1994, pp. 108–24.

'Coming Out: Decisions to Leave Purdah', *Second Nature: Women and the Family: A Special Issue of India International Centre Quarterly*, vol. 23, ed. Geeti Sen and Susan Viswanathan, nos. 3–4, Winter 1996, pp. 93–105.

'L'ecole des femmes: meilleures femmes, meilleures musulmanes', in *Madrasa: La Transmission du Savoir dans le Monde Musulman*, ed. N. Grandin and M. Gaborieau, Paris: Editions Arguments, 1997, pp. 158–67.

'Sayyid Karamat Husain and Education for Women', in *Lucknow: Memories of a City*, ed. Violette Graff, Delhi: Oxford University Press, 1997, pp. 155–64.

'Women's Education Before Partition', *Dawn*, Karachi, Special Independence Day Supplement, 14 August 1997, pp. 18–19.

'Women, Legal Reform, and Muslim Identity', *Comparative Studies in South Asia, Africa, and the Middle East*, vol. 17, no. 2, 1998, pp. 1–10; repr. in Mushirul Hasan, ed., *Islam, Communities, and the Nation*, Delhi: Manohar, 1998, pp. 139–58.

'Women's Magazines in Urdu as Sources for Muslim Social History', *Indian Journal of Gender Studies*, vol. 5, no. 2, 1998, pp. 201–14.

'Delhi College and Urdu', *Annual of Urdu Studies*, vol. 14, 1999, pp. 119–34.

'*Qiran us-Sa'adain*: The Dialogue Between Eastern and Western Learning at Delhi College', in *Perspectives of Mutual Encounters in South Asian History, 1760–1860*, ed. Jamal Malik, Leiden: Brill, 2000, pp. 260–77.

'Bibiyon ke Madrase' (a translation into Urdu of 'Schools for Wives'), a chapter from *Secluded Scholars: Women's Education and Muslim Social Reform in Colonial India, Aligarh Magazine*: *Khawatin* Number (Special Issue on Women), 2001, pp. 36–105.

'Master Ramchandra of Delhi College: Teacher, Journalist, and Cultural Intermediary', *Annual of Urdu Studies*, vol. 18, 2003, pp. 95–104.

'The Emperor's Old Clothes: Robing and Sovereignty in Late Mughal and Early British India', in *Robes of Honour: Khil'at in Pre-colonial and Colonial India*, ed. Stewart Gordon, Delhi: Oxford University Press, 2003, pp. 125–39.

'Sources and Methods for Research on Women and Islamic Cultures in South Asia, from the Mid-Eighteenth to the Early Twentieth Century', in *Encyclopedia of Women in Islamic Cultures*, vol. I, ed. Suad Joseph, Leiden: Brill, 2004, pp. 176–85.

'Urdu Women's Magazines in the Early Twentieth Century', repr., in Eunice DeSouza, ed., *Purdah: An Anthology*, Delhi: Oxford University Press, 2004, pp. 144–55.

'Foreword' to Lubna Kazim, ed., *A Woman of Substance: The Memoirs of Begum Khurshid Mirza*, New Delhi: Zubaan, 2005, pp. ix–xxv.

'From *Akhbar* to News: The Development of the Urdu Press in Early Nineteenth Century Delhi', in *Wilderness of Possibilities: Urdu Studies in Transnational Perspective*, ed. Kathryn Hansen and David Lelyeld, Delhi: Oxford University Press, 2005, pp. 101–21.

'Growing up Bilingual and Other (Mis)adventures in Negotiating Cultures', in *Burnt Orange Britannia*, ed. W. Roger Louis, London: I.B. Taurus, 2005, pp. 318–29.

'A View of Indian Muslim Womanhood from Hali's *Majalis un-Nissa*, 1874', in *The Modern Middle East: A Sourcebook for History*, ed. Camron Amin, Benjamin Fortna and Elizabeth Frierson, New York: Oxford University Press, 2006, pp. 157–73.

'The Perils of Cultural Mediation: Master Ramchandra and Academic Journalism at Delhi College', in *The Delhi College: Traditional Elites, the Colonial State, and Education Before 1857*, ed. Margrit Pernau, Delhi: Oxford University Press, 2006, pp. 187–200.

'Other Voices, Other Rooms: The View from the *Zanana*', repr., in Manu Bhagavan and Anne Feldhaus, eds., *Speaking Truth to Power: Religion, Caste, and the Subaltern Question in India*, Delhi: Oxford University Press, 2008, pp. 121–36.

'Sayyid Mumtaz Ali and *Tahzib un-Niswan*: Women's Rights in Islam and Women's Journalism in Urdu', repr., in Sumit Sarkar and Tanika Sarkar, eds., *Women and Social Reform in Modern India*, vol. II, Delhi: Permanent Black, 2008, pp. 70–98.

'Zahida Khatun Sherwani (Zay Khay Sheen): Aligarh's *Pardah Nashin* Poet', *Crakow Indological Studies* (Crakow), vol. XI, 2009, pp. 87–96.

'Aloys Sprenger: German Orientalism's "Gift" to Delhi College', *South Asia Research*, vol. 31, no. 1, February 2011, London, pp. 7–23.

'Educated Muslim Women: Real and Ideal', in *Gendering Colonial India*, ed. Charu Gupta, New Delhi: Orient BlackSwan, 2012, pp. 109–35.

'Zay Khay Sheen: Aligarh's *Pardah Nashin* Poet', in *Muslim Voices: Community and the Self in South Asia*, ed. Usha Sanyal, David Gilmartin and Sandria Freitag, New Delhi: Yoda Press, 2013, pp. 193–204.

BIOGRAPHICAL DICTIONARY ARTICLES

'Abul Kalam Azad', in *Oxford Dictionary of National Biography*, Oxford: Oxford University Press, 2004, http://www.oxforddnb.com/view/article/30510, accessed 10 June 2017.

Syed Mumtaz Ali and Muhammadi Begam, *Oxford Dictionary of National Biography*, Oxford: Oxford University Press, 2012.

ENCYCLOPEDIA ARTICLES

'The Khilafat Movement', 'Hyderabad (Deccan)', 'Hydari, Akbar', and 'Ali Brothers' in *Encyclopedia of Asian History*, vol. I, New York: Charles Scribner's, 1988, pp. 44–5; vol. II, pp. 90–1, 296–7.

'Ameer Ali, Syed', 'Chiragh Ali', and 'Khilafat Movement', in *Encyclopedia of the Modern Islamic World*, ed. John L. Esposito, 4 vols., New York: Oxford University Press, 1994; vol. I, pp. 84–5, 278–9; vol. II, pp. 420–2.

'Abul Kalam Azad', in *Encyclopedia of Islam*, 3rd edn., Leiden: Brill, 2009, pt. 2, pp. 124–7.

'Khilafat Movement (1919–24)', in *Princeton Encyclopedia of Islamic Thought*, Princeton University Press, 2012.

'Syed Amir Ali', in *Oxford Encyclopedia of Islam and Law*, Oxford University Press (forthcoming).

Index

Abu-Lughod, Lila
   Do Muslim Women Need Saving? 135
ad hominem attacks 186, 188
Adib, Masud Hasan Rizvi 197–8
advice manuals 110, 117, 119
Ahmad, Khwaja Fariduddin 102
Ahmad, Nazir xiv, 92, 129, 141n27
   affiliations and competencies 53
   Ibnulvaqt 52–4
   personality 53–4
   Tawbat al-nusuh 67n30
Ahmed, Bashiruddin 112
Ahmed, Mirza 9
Ahmed, Nazir 109, 112–13
Ahmed, Rafiq 35–7, 45n34
Alam, Mahbub 13
Al-Huda International Welfare Foundation 69–70, 76
Ali, Muhammad 179
Ali, Shaukat 3
Ali, Syed Ameer 112
Ali, Syed Mumtaz 91, 103, 111
Aligarh Institute Gazette 97–8, 100
Aligarh Muslim University 29–30, 32–3, 35, 38
Amin, Qasim 92
Ancient Law (Maine) 97
Anwar, Bagh Maulana 2
apologetic modernity 96, 100

Arya Samaj 186
ashraf culture 32, 34, 42
ashvamedh (horse sacrifice ritual) 165
authoritarianism on Muslim women in South Asia 74–7, 83
authority 74
Azad, A.K. 10, 186
Azad, Maulana 15
Azeemabadi, Shah 119
Azimabadi, Yās 197

Bahr ul-Ulum, Maulana Abdul Ali 7–8
Bahr ul-Ulumi, Muhammad Kamil 8, 16
Bahr ul-Ulumis 7, 12
Bai, Mah Laqa 124
Balfour, Edward Green 228–30
Banaras Hindu University, myth related to 159–60, 162–5
   British role in establishment of 163, 166–7
   myth of a raja granting a brahman a boon of a gift of land 166–9
   narrative of acquisition of the land 163, 165, 169–71, 176n33
   Nizam myth 167
Banaras Regional Archives 169
Barabanki 4–5
Bari, Abdul 3, 186

Bari, Maulana Abdul 1
Baroda state 151
Battle of Karbala 192
Battle of Siffin 185, 187
Batutah, Ibn 84
Begum, Akbari 112
Begum, Azizunnissa 102
Begum, Muhammadi
  brief biography 109–10
  nature of articles and columns 110
  view of marriage 110–11
Begum, Nawab Shah Jahan 123–4
  basic reforms 124
  Bihishti Zewar 125
  childbearing and child rearing 127
  against conventional opinions 125–6
  density of Qur'anic verse and *hadith* citation 130–1
  empowerment of women 136, 143n53
  girl's age at marriage 130–2, 142n36
  girls' education 128–9, 140n22
  God concept 127
  health and health habits of women 128
  identity of 'Indian Muslim' 136
  interpretation of *hadith* 126, 131, 133
  interpretation of physical intimacy 128
  as 'Islamic feminist' 135
  Islamic reforms 126–7
  issues of reproductive health 127–8
  issues related to women 124
  man's duty 133
  marriage 129–30
  on matters of morality and behaviour 124–5
  model of Islamic reasoning 126, 134–5, 137
  objections to girls being married off young 132
  Pakistani edition of book 136–7

  in relation to mourning the dead 163n54
  remarriage of widowed and divorced women 132–3
  rights and entitlements of Muslim women 133–4
  status of women 134
  support of parda 124–5, 139n10
  Tahzibun niswan wa tarbiyatul insan 124, 138n5
  women's rights and entitlements 127
  world view 129
Begum, Parsa 102
Begum, Sikandar 130
Bengali Hindu nationalists 93
Bengali women 100
Bhagvatsinh, Raja 145
  as maker of modern Gondal 145
  reforms on social issues 146
  support to educational institutions 150
  women's education 146–51
Bhopal 123, 149
Bhutto, Zulfiqar Ali 79
Bijnauri, Abdul Rahman 196
Bilgrami, Saiyid Ali Asghar 109, 113
  concept of 'rights from nature' 115–16
  connection between heredity, health and marriageable age 118
  education and job 113–14
  literary works 113–14
bismillah ceremony 242
Bogra, Mohammad Ali 78
Bonjiba, Rani 147–9
Bulliet, Richard W.
  Islam: The View from the Edge 74

Carpenter, Mary 98
Changezi, Yās Yagānah 191–3, 196–7, 218
  critique of the Progressives 211
  critiques of Ghalib 203–5, 217
  Daryabadi's attack on 214–16

fight with Lucknow literary
   establishment 197–8
ghazals 198–201
on Islam 216–17
Nishtar-e Yās 198–9
in Pakistan 212–13
protection of Urdu 203
on verses of devotional poetry 211
Chatterjee, Partha 93
Chipko movement 162
Chishti Sufi order 2
Choudhury, Saroj Raj 263, 266–7, 270–2
Chundrigar, I.I. 5
Church Missionary Society 238
citizenship 19–21, 30
civilization 50
civilization (*tamaddun*) 60, 119
Cohn, Bernard 97
collective identity 29
collectivities 41–3
   boundaries and forms 42
   narrators' identification with 42
communal problem 35
conjugal love 117
conjugal relationships 115–17
Corbett, Kim 266
corporeal punishment 270
Coser, Lewis A. 41
Council for Scientific Research and Legal Opinions (CRLO) 80–1
cultural reform movement 37

Dakkhani language 242
Dalmia, Vasudha 169
Dars-i nizami madrasa curriculum 2
Daryabadi, Abdul Majid 185, 187–8
Daula, Qazi Badr-ud 244
Dehlavi, Nazir Ahmed 112
Dehlavi, Sayyid Ahmad xv
Desai, C.C. 19
Devji, Faisal 96
dharmashastra (Hindu law) text 165
divorce 99

Doniger, Wendy 162, 173
Draft Laws of Evidence Bill 80

Eck, Diana
   Banaras: City of Light 173
El Fadl, Khaled Abou 80–1
Eliade, Mircea 161
Elphinstone College 146
English-educated women 155
English education 163, 235
English-medium schools 223
environmental narratives 163
equality 72–3, 81
'ethical ideal' of Islam 35
ethnographic work among Muslim women 135
European civility 61–4, 66n10
Evacuee Property Act 20
Evacuee Property Act of 1950 14

Falsafa-e Izdivaj (Philosophy of Marriage) 109, 113
   'Eastern' thinking on marital relations 116–17
   issues of female sexual consent 116
   reciprocal conjugal relationships 115–16
   schema of conjugal traits 117
   sexual moderation and mutuality in marital relationships 114–15
   subject of the wife in 114–15, 117
   using force in post-marital sexual intercourse 116
   vs Stall's texts 115–16
Farangi Mahall family 1
Farangi Mahall madrasa 2, 4, 6–7, 11–12, 18
Farangi Mahall maulana 179
Faridi, Dr 5, 12
Faruque, Ghulam 14
father-daughter bond 113
fatherhood 113

Gandhi, Mohandas Karamchand 5

Gandhi, Feroze 15
Gangadhara image 168–9
Ghalib, Mirza Asadullah Khan 191–2, 195–6, 198–200, 203–5, 213–15, 217
Gondal state
　Bhagvatsinhji Orphanage 149
　education policy 145–6
　female education 147–51
　Nandkunvarba Zenana hospital for women 149
　philanthropic activities 149
　reforms 146–7

Hadiqat al-Salatin-i Qutb Shahi 114
Hali, Altaf Husain 123
　Assemblies of Women and *Homage to the Silent* 124
Hali, Khwaja Altaf Husain xiv, 109
Halīm Sharar, Abdul 92
Hamdam newspaper 6, 8, 11
Hamdard 179, 183–7
Haq of Hapur, Shaikh Zia'ul 183
Hardinge, Viceroy 167
Harris, Sybilla 238
Hasan, Mushirul
　Legacy of a Divided Nation 20
Hasan, Nafisul 11
Hasan, Sayyid Siddiq 130
Hashmi, Farhat 69, 80–2
　concept of 'equality' 72–3
　'feminist' discourse of 70
　Hassan's critique of 76
　lectures in 2003 and 2004 70
　primary audience of 70
　relation between husband and wife 73–4
　religious revivalism 75
　role of women in society 70–4
　'The Key to a Successful Family Life' (*azdavaji zindagi main kamyabi ka raz*) 70–4
Hassan, Riffat 74, 77

critique of Hashmi 76
epistemological crisis with regards to being a Muslim 77
higher education in India 163
Hindustani women 98
historical collectivity 42–3
History of Banaras Hindu University 172
history of the Pakistan Movement 29–30
history *vs* myth 171–4
honour killings of women 79
Hossain, Rokeya Sakhawat 93
Hudood (*hudud*) ordinances 79
Hujjatulislam 56, 60–2
human body 49–50
Hunter Commission Report 239
Hunter Education Commission 101
Hunter, W.W. 32, 224
　Indian Musalmans: Are they Bound in Conscience to Rebel against the Queen? 32
Huqūq-i Niswān 92
Hurayrah, Abu 81
Husain, Mirza Wajid 197
Husain, Moulvi Mohibb-i 139n9
Husain, Wajahat 32
Hussain Hali, Altaf 92

Ibnulvaqt (Nazir Ahmad) 52–4, 64, 66n20, 66n22
　central character 55
　characteristic of prose genres (*dastan* and *qissa*) 52, 57
　choice of personal names for characters 55–6
　description of the events of 1857 in 63
　Hujjatulislam 56, 60–1
　Ibnulvaqt's adoption of English lifestyle 57–8
　interjections in Persian, Arabic, and English of 54
　manner of eating 59–60

Noble's attitude towards Ibnulvaqt 55–6, 58–9
Noble's disguise in Indian habit 59–60
Noble's past, present and future 61
   relationship between the inner and the outer 60
   story 55–6
   view of Indian and British interaction 53–4
Idarah-i Adabayat-i Urdu 114
Ikramullah, Shaista 78
Imperial Order of the Crown of India 152
Inayatullah, Maulanas 3
Indian Forest Act of 1878 264
Indian Muslims 43n15. *See also* Muslims, educational and occupational disparity between Hindus and
   British attitudes towards 36
   convulsions of Partition and 6–12, 39
   cultural defensiveness 78
   and events of 1857 31–3, 36, 38
   'police action' of September 1948 7
   political resistance and 40
   political voice of 35
   solidarity among and Aligarh Muslim University 31–4
   vs Pakistani Muslims 13
Indian Muslim women 92
The Indian Policeman 180
Indian tiger 259
Indo-Muslim culture xiii, xv
Iqbal, Javid 43n15
Iqbal, Mohammad 35–7, 75
Islam 78
   arrival in India 36
   principle of equality 36
   rational reinterpretation by individual Muslims 75
   teaching 79
Islamic modernism 75–6
Islamist nationalism 137

Ispahani, Hassan 5, 12
Ispahani, Mirza Ahmed 3, 9, 12, 14–15
Ispahani, Sadri 11, 14

Jahan Begum, Nawab Shah 93
Jahangir, Asma 75, 77–8
Jahangirabads 2
Jamaat-i-Islami 80
Jamiat ul-Ulama-i Hind 2
Jashan, Maulvi Syed Hasan 113
Jauhar, Mohammad Ali 33
Jinnah, M.A. 3, 33, 37–8
   vision of unity 37
Joshi, Vidyagauri 155
Jung, Carl G. 161

Kashi: The City Luminous 173
Khairi, Rashid-ul 112
Khaliquzzaman, Chaudhuri 5–6, 10, 15
Khan, Durandesh 113
Khan, General Ayub 78–9
Khan, Iftikhar Alam 97
Khan, Liaquat Ali 5–6
Khan, Maulana Zafar Ali 183–6
Khan, Syed Ahmad (Sir Syed) 32, 35, 38, 53, 75, 91, 93–4, 112
   attraction to thinkers 97
   authority of a European woman 101
   condition of women 98–100, 103
   education of Muhammadans 101–2
   establishment of M.A.O. College at Aligarh 100
   intelligence and achievements of women 98
   polygamy 99
   recollections of his mother 102–3
   A Series of Essays on the Life of Mohammad: And Subjects Subsidiary Thereto 99
   social and economic conditions of Muhammadans 101
   time in England 98–9

women's rights 100
  on women's rights 100
Khan, Zafar Ali 186
Khandan of Muhammad Ghaus 230–2, 242–3
Khilafat Movement xiii, 33, 179
Khirāj-e'aqīdat (Ishrat Afreen) 283–4
Khurasani Muslims 74
Kitab al-Nikah (Book of Marriage) 72
Kudaisya, Gyanesh 29

Lahore Resolution 4, 38
Lakhnavi, Aziz 201
Lal, Ruby 126, 134
Lal, Vinay 160
Lari, Z.I. 10
Leblanc, Maurice
  The Hollow Needle 180
Lelyveld, David 225
Levi-Strauss, Claude 161
Life of Mohammed 99
Lucknow 197, 213–17

Ma'asir-i Deccan 114
Macaulay's *Minute on Education* 230
Madrasa-i 'Azam 233, 236–7
Mahabharata 165–6
Mahmud, Syed 7
Mahmudabads 2
Maine, Henry Sumner 97
Majaz 211
Malaviya, Pandit Madan Mohan 163, 166, 171
male reformers 147, 154
Malihabadi, Josh 210
Malālā 'Ilm kī Sham'a (Ishrat Afreen) 284–7
Mani, Lata 92
Manto, Sadat Hasan 191–3, 218
  birth centenary 192
  challenges as a writer 196
  discussion of annihilation of love 193–4
  memorable characters 193–6

Mirza Ghalib 196
  in Pakistan 212–13
Manusmriti 165
marital rape 116
marriage, relationship between men and women in
  Ahmed, Nazir 112–13
  Begum, Muhammadi 110–11
  conjugal relationships 115–17
  connection between heredity, health and marriageable age 118
  'Eastern' thinking on marital relations 116–17
  Shafiq, Maulvi Ahmed 110–12
  Stall, Sylvanus 113–14
memory/memories 28–30, 41
  redefined boundaries 28
  of survivors 29
Metcalf, T.R. 31
Mian, Jamal xv–xvi, 1
  becoming a Pakistani citizen 16–17, 20
  as a businessman in Dacca 13–14, 18–19
  in constitution-making process 15
  convulsions of Partition 6–12
  court case against Bahr ul-Ulumis 7–8
  death of sister, impact of 8
  decline of tea business 9
  devotional life of 2
  differences between Pakistani Muslims and Indian Muslims 13
  engagement with political elite of India and Pakistan 15
  entry into Muslim politics 3–6
  fighting for Muslim interests 2–4
  Indian citizenship 20
  in Lucknow 17
  poetry 9
  public speaking 3
  service for Sunni Waqf Board and Ajmer Dargah Committee 6
  stake in India 1–3

tour of West Pakistan 12–13
in UP Legislative Assembly 4
Mill, John Stuart 96–7
Mill, John Stuart
Political Economy 96
Milton, John
The Doctrine and Discipline of Divorce Restored to the Good of Both Sexes 99
Minault, Gail xiii, 78, 91, 93, 147
The Khilafat Movement: Religious Symbolism and Political Mobilization in India xiv
Secluded Scholars: Women's Education and Muslim Social Reform in Colonial India xv, 102, 123, 137n1, 145
Mirat ul-Arus (The Bride's Mirror) 112
reception of 113
story of 112–13
Mirza, Iskander 15, 18
Mirza, Sarfaraz Hussain 37–9
Mirza Ghalib 196
Mohani, Ali Husain 14
Mohani, Hasrat 3, 5–9, 11, 13
Mohyuddin, Ahmed 19
Monghiba, Rani 147–9, 152
Monghiba School for Girls 147, 150, 157n23
monotheism 36
Mountbatten, Louis 29
Movaheda agreement 16
Mu'allim-i Niswan 139n9
Muhammad 3
Muhammad Ali, Chaudhuri 18
Muhazzab Dākū 184, 186
Muhibb-e Husain 119
Muir, Sir William 98–9
Mulk, Nawab Mohsinul 180
Mulk, Zafarul 183–4, 187
Mullins, Hannah Catherine 100
Muradabadi, Jigar 210
Muslim aristocracy of the Madras Presidency 240

Muslim collectivity 42
Muslim Family Law Ordinance (MFLO) 78–9
Muslim identity
authority and 74–7
elite Pakistani women 76–7
of medieval Muslims 74
of middle and upper-class Pakistani women 70
social control and 78–82
Muslim League 78
Muslim nationalism 76
Muslim nationalist movement 28
Muslim-ness xv
Muslims, educational and occupational disparity between Hindus and 224–5
early concerns in Madras 226–8
Edward Balfour and 228–30, 233–6
enrolment in government institutions 239
Khandan of Muhammad Ghaus, role of 230–2, 242–3
Madrasa-i 'Azam 236–7
school for Muslim boys 233–6
study of Arabic 242
western education for Madras Muslims 238–41
Muslim unity, values of 40
Mutiny of 1857 31–4
myths 161
analysis and views of 161–2
creation of 162
distinction from history 171–4
functions of 166–9
Hindu myths of ancient origin 165–6
interpretation of a historical event in mythic terms 174
myth of descent of the Ganga 168–9
popularity of 173–4
South Asian mythic traditions 160–1

Nandkunvarba, Rani 146, 149, 151, 155–6
  definition of a good wife and mother 154
  description of a woman's domestic duties 154
  Gomandala Parikrama 152
  important differences between men and women 153–5
  merits of female education 152–3
  radical lifestyle 151–5
  Sita's image 154
Nasirean ethics 195
The Nationalization of Hindu Tradition 169
National Mohammadan Association 224
Nawwayats 231
Nazaria-i-Pakistan (Ideology of Pakistan) Trust 35–7
Nazimuddin, Khwaja 15, 18
Nehru, Jawaharlal 3, 7, 11, 13, 15, 19
Nehru, Rameshwari 138n8
Nizami, Khwaja Hasan 182–6, 188
  fall out with Shaikh Zia'ul Haq of Hapur 183–6
Nizam of Hyderabad 167

'Old Boys' of Aligarh, *see* Khan, Maulana Zafar Ali; Nizami, Khwaja Hasan; Omar, Zafar
Omar, Zafar 180, 187–8
  Bahrām kī Giriftārī ('The Arrest of Bahram') 180
  characterization 181–2
  Lāl Kathor ('The Red Hoard') 181
  Mirza Bilgirami of 181–2, 186
  modes of behaviour of a policeman 180
  Mustaqbil-e Islām ('The Future of Islam') 180
  Nīlī Chhatrī ('The Blue Parasol') 180
  Pulīsmain ('The Policeman') 180

oral narratives 29
Osmania University 209

Pakistan 36–7
  history 34–42, 82
  idea of a secular state in 37
  ideology and vision of 36–8, 41
  territorial definition of 40
Pakistan Movement 29–30, 37–40, 42
Pakistan Muslim League 6
Pandey, Gyanendra 27
Pant, G.B. 11
Panthera tigris tigris 270
Papanek, Hanna xiv
Parsi girls 98
partition martyrs 40
partition survivors 27–8
Pernau, Margrit 92
personal history 41
Phulmani and Karuna 100
polygamy 99
polytheism 36
Portelli, Alessandro 28
Powell, Avril 98
Praja Mandal Movement 167
Progressive Writers Association 211–12
Progressive Writers Movement 196, 209, 219n13
Punjabi politics 40

Qasim, Muhammad 10, 30
Qaumi Ishath Ghar 209
Qidwai, Rafi Ahmed 11, 15
Qidwai, Saidur Rahman 12–13
Qidwais 2
Qutbuddin, Mulla 2

Rab, Abdul 8
Rafiq, Dr 37
Rafiq-e Arus (The Bride's Companion) 109
  dilemmas of parenting children 112
  mention of self-respect 110

raja, duties of 165, 175n18
Raja of Mahmudabad 3, 5, 19
Rangan, Haripriya 162
Rao, Narayana 172
Rashid, Pyare Saheb 197–8
Rasul, Aizaz 10
Raza, Muhammad Ali Zainal 12
Razzaq, Abdul 2
rebellion of 1857
    fact and fiction 50–2
    and Indian Muslims 31–3, 36, 38
recognition 50
Remembering Partition 27
re-tribalization of society 78
Roy, Rammohun 92, 146
Ruswa, Mirza Mohammad Hadi 92
Ryves, V.W. 270–1

Saeed, Ahmad 39, 46n49
Sahajanand, Swami 149
Sajdi, Dana 139n14
Salamatullah 3
Sarkar, Sumit 92
Sarkar, Tanika 93
Saukhyana Srauta Sutra 165
Scientific Society 97
Scouting for Boys 180
secluded sovereign 123
A Series of Essays on the Life of Mohammad: And Subjects Subsidiary Thereto 99
service gentry 223
seva (service), acts of 149–50
sexual duties of a Muslim wife 81
Shafiq, Maulvi Ahmed 110
    advice about self and intimacy 110–11
    discourse around love, discretion and self-respect 110
    essentializing of women 111
    status of women in non-Muslim communities 111
Shah, Emperor Bahadur 31
Shahr-e Ashob 8
Sharif, Bansa 2
Sheen, Ze Khe xv
Shola, Dwarka Das 214
Shulman, David 172
Sibghatullah 3
Sibghatullah, Muhammad 244
Sidq-e Jadid 214
Singh, Billy Arjan 271
Singh, Bishan 192
Singh, Harpal 12
Singh, Prabhu Narayan (Maharaja of Banaras) 159–60, 163–6, 171, 173
slavery 99
Smith, Jonathan Z. 174
South Asian mythic traditions 160–1
South Asian studies xiii
Stall, Sylvanus
    What a Husband Ought to Know 113–14, 118
    'complementary' nature of emotions 115
    mutuality and reciprocity in conjugal relationships 115–16
    sections—'husband', 'wife', and 'children' 114, 116
Stephen, James Fitzjames 97
Strenski, Ivan 161
Subrahmanyam, Sanjay 172
Sufyan, Mu'aviya ibn 185
Sultan, Tipu 259
    conquest of Mysore 259
    Tiger of 259
Swaminarayan Hinduism 149

Tahzib-e Niswan (Culture of Women) 104, 110, 119
Tahzib-ul Akhlaq ('The Training of Etiquette' or 'The Social Reformer') 100, 104, 119
Tai Yong Tan 29
Talib, Ali ibn Abi 185, 218
Textures of Time 172
Thanavi, Maulana Ashraf 'Ali 126, 140n17

tiger
  attitudes towards by British India 260
  bounties offered for 264
  captive breeding 264
  cub sales 264–5
  Happy and Grumpy, case of 271–2
  hunting 264
  keeping an 263–4
  kept in zoo 272
  killing of 274
  morality of removing tiger cubs 269–70
  observations on behaviour 260–1
  orphaned cubs, case of 270–1
  owners and sellers of 262–3
  as pets in South Asia 263
  prices of 264–5
  problems of caging 272–4
  punishment for keeping 269–72
  sex ratio at birth among 264
  stories related to 263
  wild and tame 265–9
traditional educational system 241–4
Tripathi, A.P. 17
Tripathi, Govardhanram 146
Trouillot, Michel-Rolph 29
two nation theory 35–6

Udani, Manibai B. 150
ulama families 225–6, 237, 240, 243–4, 249
  reactions to British educational innovations 226
Umar, Major General (Retd) Ghulam 33–4, 43n19
ummīd bharī āṅkheṅ (Ishrat Afreen) 287–9
Urdu 192, 197–8, 201, 203, 205
  cultural zone 206
  poetry 199, 208
  pronunciation 206
Urdu mystery fiction 180–1
Urdu novel 52–3
Urdu political poetry xiii

Vamana avatar, story of 166
Varanasi 159
veiling (parda) practice 124–5, 139n10, 152

Wallace, Edgar 181
well-defined people 35
Western education 223, 225
  for Madras Muslims 238–41
  in the nineteenth century 225
women
  authoritarianism on Muslim women in South Asia 74–7, 83
  duty of wife 110–13
  education of 97–8
  honour killings of 79
  images and ideas about, before 1857 94–6
  norms of good mothering 112–13
  reformist writings, *see* Begum, Muhammadi; Begum, Nawab Shah Jahan; Bilgrami, Saiyid Ali Asghar; Khan, Syed Ahmad (Sir Syed); Shafiq, Maulvi Ahmed
  religious books for 81–2
  rights and entitlements 133–4
  role in reforms 146–7
  roles and rights of 93
  status of British women 97
  tahzīb ul-akhlāq for 98
women–men relation
  between husband and wife 73–4
  sexual duties of a Muslim wife 81
Women's Action Forum (WAF) 80
women's education xv
women's rights 78–80
The World's Eternal Religion 171

Zafar, Bahadur Shah 196
Zamindar, Wazira 1
Zia, General 79–80